Essays in Comparative History
Economy, Politics and Society in
Britain and America, 1850–1920

This reader is one part of an Open University integrated teaching system and the selection is therefore related to other material available to students. It is designed to evoke the critical understanding of students. Opinions expressed in it are not necessarily those of the course team or of the University.

Essays in Comparative History

Economy, Politics and Society in Britain and America, 1850–1920

Edited by Clive Emsley
at the Open University

Open University Press

Milton Keynes • *Philadelphia*

Open University Press
12 Cofferidge Close
Stony Stratford
Milton Keynes MK11 1BY, England.
and
242 Cherry Street, Philadelphia, PA 19106, U.S.A.

First published 1984

British Library Cataloguing in Publication Data

Essays in comparative history.
  1. Great Britain—Social conditions—19th
  century   2. Great Britain—Social conditions
  —20th century   3. United States—
  Social conditions—19th century
  4. United States—Social conditions—
  20th century
  I. Emsley, Clive
  941.081   HN385

ISBN 0-335-10592-0
Library of Congress Catalog Card No: 8416550

Text design by Clarke Williams

Typeset by Gilbert Composing Services, Leighton Buzzard.
Printed and bound in Great Britain by M. & A. Thomson Litho Limited,
East Kilbride, Scotland.

Contents

Acknowledgements

I. Early Party Politics

(a) Reprinted from Louis Hartz, *The Liberal Tradition in America*, Random House, 1955, by permission of Harcourt Brace Jovanovich Inc.

(b) Reprinted from J. H. Hanham, *Elections and Party Management: Politics in the Time of Disraeli and Gladstone*, Harvester Press, 1978 (2nd edition), by permission of Harvester Press Ltd.

(c) Reprinted from the *Journal of American History*, vol. 66 (Sept 1979), by permission of the Organization of American Historians.

II. Class and Class Conflict

(a) Reprinted from H. G. Gutman, *Essays in American Working-Class and Social History*, Basil Blackwell, 1977, by permission of Professor Herbert G. Gutman.

(b) Reprinted from T. Tholfsen, *Working Class Radicalism in Mid-Victorian England*, Croom Helm, 1976, by permission of Croom Helm Ltd.

(c) Reprinted from *Labor History*, vol. 18 (1979), by permission of *Labor History*.

III. Economic Development

(a) Reprinted from J. H. Habakkuk, *American and British Technology in the Nineteenth Century*, Cambridge University Press, 1962, by permission of the Cambridge University Press.

(b) Reprinted from *Business History*, vol. 3 (1967), by permission of Frank Cass & Co. Ltd.

IV. The City

(a) Reprinted from the *Western Pennsylvania Historical Magazine*, vol. 20 (1937), by permission.

(b) Reprinted from the *Journal of Social History*, Winter 1975, by permission of Peter N. Stearns.

(c) Reprinted from the *Journal of American History*, vol. 54 (1968), by permission of the Organization of American Historians.

V. Citizenship and Welfare

(a) Reprinted from H. C. Allen & R. Thompson (eds.) *Contrast and Connection: Bicentennial Essays in Anglo-American History*, Bell, 1976, by permission of Bell & Hyman Ltd.

(b) Reprinted from *Historical Studies*, 1969, by permission of the Irish Committee of Historical Sciences.

(c) Reprinted from G. V. Rimlinger, *Welfare Policy and Industrialization In Europe, America and Russia*, Wiley, 1971, by permission of Professor G. V. Rimlinger.

(d) Reprinted from the *Annals of the Association of American Geographers* by permission.

Introduction

> The process of Civilisation depends on transcending Nationality.
> Everything is tried by more courts, before a larger audience.
> Comparative methods are applied. Influences which are accidental
> yield to those which are rational.
>
> Lord Acton

All history is comparative history; for without recourse to the comparative
method the relationship between the unique and the general could never be
known and history, as a discipline, would be impossible. In short, the
comparative method is the application of the logic of experiment to the
study of man in the past. As such it assists in posing new questions,
defining historical problems, separating necessary and contingent factors,
isolating a single variable, identifying general patterns and testing
hypotheses.

The study of a single phenomenon in two or more societies, for example,
can raise some unexpected questions. Both the British and the Americans
speak of democracy and of the democratic process yet close analysis reveals
that American democracy is very different from British. Moreover, this
difference lies not only in the electoral process. Why is this? Why is the same
word used to describe similar but non-identical phenomena? A
comparative study indicates that the two democracies are not identical
twins but that they are, nonetheless, the twin offspring of the same parents.
These twins have inherited in differing combinations the genes of their
parents—they are easily recognizable as close relatives and yet boast very
distinctive features. The historian's task is that of identifying their
common heritage and indicating those prevalent conditions which led to
the development of particular features in each. This can be a daunting task
leading the historian to study traditions of political, social and religious
thought; contemporary socio-economic conditions; foreign influences; the
strength of rival political systems and so forth. Far from leading to
simplistic, unilinear analyses, the comparative method actually
complicates the historian's work, but it undoubtedly enriches its result.

The degree of historical awareness required by the historian using
comparative methods can be illustrated by the example of a study of divorce

rates in the various countries of Europe. The news media boldly announce that the divorce rate in Britain is now higher than anywhere else in Europe, with the exception of Denmark. The clear implication is that marriage is less successful as an institution here than elsewhere. Yet no mention is made of the comparability of the data on which this conclusion was based. Is, for instance, a lower divorce rate in France the result not of happier marriages in that country but of more rigid divorce laws? The legal system in a particular country might be a factor making for easy or difficult divorce but other influences are also important—the strength and nature of religious attitudes, for example, or the average age at marriage, or the number of married women who work. It would be a poor historian who took the statistics of divorce at their face value and neglected to look at the conditions which produced them.

The virtues of the comparative method have not always been apparent. Comparative history at one time was regarded as an exotic and somewhat suspect specialism. This misplaced scepticism was originally, no doubt, a reaction against the dangerous and erroneous belief of nineteenth-century theorists of social evolution that comparative studies could reveal universal laws, a science of society. Two features of evolutionary positivism were, rightly, considered disturbing. First, the assumption of a linear or cyclical pattern of human development, a route along which all must pass, meant that comparisons were not grounded in real historical experiences. Second, the tendency to abstract phenomena and consider them apart from their context meant that the relations between the various fragments, social or cultural, were also neglected. Comparison had become the servant of historicism.

Not all comparison is treacherous, however. Marx, who knew something of history and historians, put the case for the comparative method in a nutshell when he wrote in 1877 that:

> Events strikingly similar, but occurring in a different historical milieu, lead to completely different results. By studying each of these evolutions separately and then comparing them, it is easy to find the key to the understanding of this phenomenon; but it is never possible to arrive at this understanding by using the *passe-partout* of some historical-philosophical theory whose great virtue is to stand above history.[1]

Comparison, then, is an essential tool for the historian, a method designed to illuminate particular situations rather than to generate universal laws. It does not, however, constitute the whole of his craft. 'The comparative method', it has been written, 'is a method, a set of rules which can be methodically and systematically applied in gathering and using evidence to test explanatory hypotheses. It does not supply us with explanations to be subjected to test: this is the task for the historical imagination'.[2] Sympathy, insight, enthusiasm, a sensitivity to period and place, and, yes, a love of the past—all will still be required if we are to comprehend the chaos of human experience in the past.

The collection of essays presented here was assembled for a history course at the Open University called 'Themes in British and American History: A Comparative Approach *c.* 1750–1970'. Any history course, and any collection of essays must, of necessity, be selective. Our selection arose out of a belief that the comparative method, intelligently applied, could advance our understanding of the development of liberal capitalist society on both sides of the Atlantic. Limits of space and cost preclude the comparative treatment of the Anglo-American experience in its entirety, and we have therefore chosen to concentrate on the period from the early nineteenth century to the early twentieth century. The material is organized under five thematic headings: Early Party Politics; Class and Class Conflict; Economic Development; The City; and Citizenship and Welfare. Other groupings are, of course, possible but, in addition to their intrinsic interest, those adopted here provide some of the most fruitful areas in which comparisons can be made.

A word of caution: when using this Reader the distinction between a comparative essay and an essay in comparison needs to be borne in mind. Remember that it is the latter with which we are concerned. Most of the essays presented here demonstrate the usefulness of comparative history. None, however, was commissioned for this volume. In a few cases, moreover, a systematic comparative methodology is not adopted. Contributions from McCormick and Hanham and Gutman and Tholfsen nevertheless provide different insights into the development of party politics and class consciousness in America and Britain which enable us to make useful comparisons; for this reason we feel confident that *Essays in Comparative History* is not a misnomer.

The conditions in which the comparative method is most effective were described more than fifty years ago by the French historian, Marc Bloch, one of its greatest practitioners:

> This is to make a parallel study of societies that are at once neighbouring and contemporary, exercising a constant mutual influence, exposed throughout their development to the action of the same broad causes just because they are close and contemporaneous, and owing their existence in part at least to a common origin.[3]

Although distant, Britain and America were never remote. In every other respect Bloch's prescription fits them exactly.

Britain and America, or at least the thirteen colonies along the eastern seaboard of North America, were subject to the same monarch and were ultimately ruled from Westminster for most of the eighteenth century. In the 200 years following the War of Independence, they have both experienced massive industrialization and urbanization; their inhabitants have enjoyed increased enfranchisement and improved welfare. While today they are not united politically—tight economic bonds are another matter—they still enjoy a 'special relationship' whatever administrations are in power; and they share a common language. Yet, as must be clear to the most naive observer, their economic, political and social structures, and their perceptions of these, have evolved in vastly different ways. Herein is the crux of our interest in Britain and America: two societies with a measure of common heritage, continuing close ties, and the experience of similar phenomena such as industrialisation, which have emerged as very different entities.

Both modern Britain and the modern United States claim to be democracies and, in spite of attempts to 'break the mould' in Britain, both have political structures which for long have centred on two major political parties. The origins of these democratic systems can be traced back to the seventeenth century (or even earlier if we follow the Whig tradition of the inexorable rise of Parliament), but they emerged as something readily identifiable during the nineteenth century. The first three extracts explore different aspects of this topic, ranging from Louis Hartz's enthusiastic description of the early nineteenth-century American Democrat as a unique political animal who built a political system upon the basis of a fundamental consensus, to Richard McCormick's picture of American parties as channels for the distribution of 'spoils'. Placed side by side, these essays might be said to illustrate the notion that every age writes its own history. Hartz's concept of the liberal tradition in America was developed and published during the 1950s: a decade in which consensus, confidence and satisfaction appeared to dominate American life and which concluded with Daniel Bell's proclamation of the triumph of western consensus in *The End of Ideology*. McCormick's essay appeared in the very different context of post-Vietnam, post-Watergate America: yet McCormick's topic had been explored by generations of 'muckraker' journalists as much fired by the American dream as Hartz. The extract from H.J. Hanham which constitutes the third piece in this section is not so readily slotted into its contemporary framework. It stands firmly in the tradition of English empirical history. Hanham presents a survey of the practice and style of politics in nineteenth-century Britain which, he suggests, began more and more to resemble those of America as the franchise was extended and as bureaucratic party structures developed.

But what do parties actually represent within a democracy? Since the emergence of the Labour Party in Britain at the end of the nineteenth century it has been possible to perceive parties as representatives of class interests—although empirical evidence would not always support such an interpretation. Such a view is scarcely possible in the United States where the most unlikely alliances are found within parties; it was, for example, a broad coalition of big-city bosses, southern conservatives and liberals from northern and western states which helped secure the presidency for a succession of Democrats from Andrew Jackson to Harry Truman.

'Class' in political, economic and social terms, is seen as irrelevant to the course of their nation's development by many Americans. Yet 'class' is as clearly identifiable in American society as in British, where it has formed a key element in political debate for at least a century. Furthermore, class conflict in American society, as manifested in the shape of labour disputes, has generally been more brutal and bloody than its British counterpart. Questions of class and class conflict are explored in the second section of this volume. When taken together, the first two extracts underline the essential differences between the American and the British working class during the nineteenth century. In both countries the working class had to come to terms with changing economic and industrial practices: the transition was often a painful one. But, as Herbert Gutman points out, the American working class also had to cope with internal tensions as it absorbed not simply the native born but also massive numbers of immigrants imbued with different habits and values. The British working class remained much more homogeneous, reproducing itself from its native stock and developing its own ideology. The extract from Trygve Tholfsen's work discusses how working class activists developed ideology to counter that of the dominant Victorian middle classes. Neither Gutman nor Tholfsen is much concerned with trade unionism. But the third essay, by James Holt, confronts the key question directly: why were industrial and political organisations of manual workers so weak in the United States, in sharp contrast to Britain, at the end of the nineteenth and beginning of the twentieth centuries? While James Holt sets out to investigate this problem with reference to one industry—steel manufacture—it may well be that his conclusions are generally applicable.

In the early part of the nineteenth century Britain could justifiably boast of being the workshop of the world. In the last quarter of the century, however, her economic dominance was being undermined and one of her chief competitors was the United States. Economic historians have for long been interested in comparing British and American economic development. This is the subject of our third section which begins with the seminal work of H.J. Habakkuk. Habakkuk asks: what determined the nature of nineteenth-century technological change? Why did Britain and America adopt the new technology at differing rates? Why, in particular, did Britain respond so tardily to the new technological opportunities? His argument centres on the high cost of labour and the problems of labour supply in nineteenth-century America in contrast to Britain. His assumptions about the rewards and advantages of independent agriculture in America and the need for skilled labour have been challenged; other historians have drawn attention to the different expectations in the native market for protected American goods as opposed to the world-wide market for Britain goods: nevertheless, Habakkuk's work remains an essential basis for a study of the two economies during the nineteenth century.[4] The other essay in this section, by S.B. Saul, focuses on the American impact on British industry in the years before the First World War. British industry was, and has subsequently been, criticized for its performance compared to that of its competitors during this period. Saul's analysis calls for a reassessment, for he demonstrates that some British firms were quick to take up American methods and to make rapid strides both in producing American machine tools and in designing and improving their own. Decline there was, but there was no universal failure within British industry nor among British entrepreneurs.

The nineteenth century also witnessed massive urbanization in the two societies: again, this began earlier in Britain. Our fourth section explores aspects of cities and their growth and starts with a short comparative survey of the urbanization process by Leon S. Marshall. Social history has come a long way in the years since this essay was first published and many of its conclusions are now questionable but it still provides a valuable starting point for exploring the issue.[5] Wilbur Miller's essay investigates the development of professional police in London and New York, contrasting the impersonal authority of the former with the personal authority of the latter. The difference, Miller suggests, sprang from the understanding of legal power and of government in the two societies. It might fruitfully be asked how far these differences can be projected beyond London and New York, particularly as the London Metropolitan Police was the only English police force directly responsible to the central government. Local independence provided a rallying cry in Victorian Britain as well as in the United States, and some small English boroughs controlled their police with attitudes not entirely dissimilar from those of Mayor Fernando Wood. Mayor Wood was an archetypal big city boss; Zane Miller's essay is a balanced assessment of another such boss, George B. Cox of Cincinnati. Britain had its city bosses—men like Joseph Chamberlain of Birmingham—but they never achieved the notoriety of their American counterparts. Urban reform in Britain, as conducted by men like Chamberlain, meant improved sanitation, better housing, parks and so forth. Urban reform in the United States incorporated similar measures but it also meant the stamping out of corruption and the removal of 'bosses' like Cox who sat at its centre. Miller demonstrates that Cox himself undertook no small measure of municipal improvement and in so doing corrects the hitherto critical picture of Cox painted by historians. The

Cincinnati run by Cox was a city in flux: semi-skilled, skilled and white collar workers, liberated by a new rapid transport system, were moving into the periphery. David Ward's essay, the final piece in this section, takes up this transport theme by comparing the suburban development of Boston and Leeds. He explains the different conditions which determined the differing pattern and extent of such development in the two cities. The essay underlines, implicitly, the value of the skills of historical geography for the social historian.

In a series of lectures delivered in Cambridge in 1949 T.H. Marshall defined citizenship as consisting of three principal elements: civil rights (such as freedom of speech, equality before the law and the right to own property) which were largely achieved by the end of the eighteenth century; political rights, generally won during the nineteenth century; and social rights, namely welfare and education provided by the state, which have been, broadly speaking, a feature of the twentieth century.[6] Our final section treats citizenship with this definition in mind. We began here with David Morgan's comparative study of the achievement of political rights, in the form of the franchise, by women on both sides of the Atlantic early in the twentieth century. The second and third pieces explore the question of welfare. C.L. Mowat's article addresses itself to the question of why the climate of opinion in which social legislation was passed during the early twentieth century has been studied in such detail for America but not for Britain. He emphasizes the different relationship which American and British historians appear to have with their respective national pasts. This, he suggests, has tended to make American historians see history as progess effected by consensus and to locate social reform within a new climate of opinion, whereas British historians have stressed the role of individuals. Mowat provides a blue-print for the study of the British climate of opinion. In so doing, he makes some interesting comparisons between ideologies, constitution and party politics in the two countries. The final extract, taken from Gaston Rimlinger's ambitious analysis of welfare policy and industrialisation in Europe, America and Russia, brings us into the world of contemporary politics and public policy. The sections printed here principally concern the debate on welfare in early twentieth-century America; they emphasize the commitment to individualism in the United States in contrast to England, and the resulting hostility, even among American union leaders, to welfare provision.

Controversy is central to the study of history. None of the essays in this volume constitutes the last word on any of our themes but each should be seen as contributing to our understanding of them. Our attempt at comparative history will, we hope, liberate students from the narrow ethno-centrism which, alas, is still all too common in our universities. There are some historical questions which can be effectively answered only by means of comparison: we have raised some of them here. If our readers leave this volume with more questions than those with which they began about the deeper meaning of such concepts as 'democracy', 'citizenship', and 'economic development', then they will be in a position to begin a comparative study of the development of these two nations and to understand how and why they coped in different ways with similar ideas and problems.

It has been our policy to omit all original footnotes except where a note qualifies a reference in the text. These have been collected at the end of each article.

Clive Emsley
David Englander

NOTES

[1] Quotation from E. H. Carr, *What is History?*, 1964, p. 65, Penguin, Harmondsworth.

[2] William H. Sewell Jr. 'Marc Bloch and the logic of comparative history', *History and Theory*, Vol. VI, 1967, 217.

[3] Marc Bloch, 'A contribution towards a comparative history of European societies' in J. E. Andersen (trans.), *Land and Work in Medieval Europe: Selected Papers by Marc Bloch*, New York, 1969 p. 46.

[4] The debate on Habakkuk's work is taken up in S. B. Saul (ed.), *Technological Change: The United States and Britain in the Nineteenth Century*, London, 1970.

[5] For example, Marshall believed that crime and disorder increased with urbanization but for arguments that crime at least levelled out from the middle of the nineteenth century in both countries see V. A. C. Gatrell, 'The decline of theft and violence in Victorian and Edwardian England', in V. A. C. Gatrell, Bruce Lenman and Geoffrey Parker (eds), *Crime and Law: The Social History of Crime in Western Europe since 1500*, London, 1980, and Eric H. Monkkonen, *Police in Urban America*, Cambridge University Press, 1981. The comparative point might also be made that although Britain was an urbanized society well before the United States, she never appears to have been more violent, more disorderly or more crime-prone.

[6] T. H. Marshall, 'Citizenship and social class', in *Class, Citizenship and Social Development: Essays by T. H. Marshall*, 2nd edition, Cambridge University Press, 1964.

PART I

Early Party Politics

(a) Federalists, Whigs and the American Democrat

LOUIS HARTZ

In a society evolving along the American pattern of the Jeffersonian and Jacksonian eras, where the aristocracies, peasantries, and proletariats of Europe are missing, where virtually everyone, including the nascent industrial worker, has the mentality of an independent entrepreneur, two national impulses are bound to make themselves felt: the impulse toward democracy and the impulse toward capitalism. The mass of the people, in other words, are bound to be capitalistic, and capitalism, with its spirit disseminated widely, is bound to be democratic. This is one of the basic insights Tocqueville had about the actual behaviour of the American people. The irony of early American history, however, is that these impulses, instead of supplementing each other, seemed to fight a tremendous political battle. The capitalist Whiggery of Hamilton was frightened of democracy, and the democratic tradition of Jackson, which was therefore able to destroy it, formulated a philosophy which seemed to deny its faith in capitalism. The result was a massive confusion in political thought, comparable to the one that we find in the constitutional era, and a set of victories and defeats which the Americans who experienced them scarcely understood. One is reminded of two boxers, swinging wildly, knocking each other down with accidental punches.

Looked at from one point of view, it is strange that Federalism and Neo-Federalism should have been shattered so badly in the liberal setting of American politics. For in the old society of Europe, where these movements were surrounded by a whole series of aristocratic and proletarian enemies, they were reaping their greatest triumphs at precisely the moment they were defeated here. The blood relationship between the Federalist-Whig tradition in America and the tradition of upper middle class liberalism in

Louis Hartz, *The Liberal Tradition in America*, New York, Random House, 1955; pp 89–121, Abridged.

Europe, the tradition of the English Whigs and the French Liberals, has been as badly neglected in this case as in others. Parrington referred to it of course when he said that the Hamiltonian movement exemplified 'English Whiggery'. Henry Adams, in a characteristic flash of insight, once spoke of the 'instinctive cousinship' that bound the Boston of the 'upper class bourgeoisie' to the 'London of Robert Peel, Macaulay, and John Stuart Mill' and to the 'Paris of Louis Philippe, Guizot, and de Tocqueville'. But that is about as far as comparative analysis has gotten, even though the Federalists and the Whigs of America, in their love of capitalism and their fear of democracy, duplicate at virtually every point the European pattern of bourgeois thought.

And yet it is not, as I have said, this connection that in itself is really interesting. What is interesting is the fact that the Americans, unassailed by the manifold enemies their brethren have to face abroad, are defeated while their brethren are victorious. The eighteen thirties, which witness the Reform Act in England and the July Revolution in France, witness also the Jacksonian revolution in America. Just as the cry of 'enrichissez-vous' [make yourself rich] goes up in Paris and London, the grim cry of 'monopoly' goes up in the Boston that Adams compared them with. Just as Macaulay and Guizot are proclaiming that the day of universal suffrage will never come, Chancellor Kent and John Quincy Adams are bemoaning the disaster it has already brought. It would be hard to find a more vivid contrast than this, and what is curious is that Parrington and Adams, both imaginative minds, should have seen the basis for the contrast but should not have followed through to the contrast itself.

When we do, the peculiar mechanism of American politics begins to become apparent. We see that the American liberal community, if it did not confront its upper middle class with a set of European aristocracies, peasantries, and proletariats, was bound to confront it with something else which in certain ways was worse: a democratic movement of the lower middle class that it could not possibly master. The word 'petit-bourgeois' comes to mind as always in this connection, but now we see more vividly even than in the eighteenth century why it cannot effectively be used. Jackson was not another edition of Flocon, Jefferson another version of Ledru-Rollin. In the very process of expanding the European category of the 'petit-bourgeois' America shattered it, creating a movement so lusty and so powerful that it is more than a bit misleading to identify it with the continental shopkeepers on whom Marx and Engels poured their fine contempt in 1848. Of course small urban traders were enlisted in the American democratic movement, but they did not become its leaders. Two other groups, in Europe outside the 'petit-bourgeois', clearly over-shadowed them: the peasant who had been transformed into a capitalist farmer, and the laborer who had been transformed into an incipient entrepreneur. The result was a great new democratic hybrid unknown in any other land. America's unique contribution to the political culture of the West.

What America was doing here, one might say, was packing all of the traditional enemies of capitalist Whiggery into a single personality. From the angle of Whiggery nothing could have been worse. For the secret of its success in Europe, to put the matter a bit more bluntly than is justifiable, especially in the English case, lay in the fact that it could play its enemies off against one another. That was how it established a claim to national leadership. When the English Whigs and the French Liberals fought the aristocratic order of Europe, they became liberal heroes, rallying behind them the workers and small property owners both of England and France. When, on the other hand, they insisted on excluding their supporters from the suffrage—the workers from the Reform Act and both the workers and the petit-bourgeois from the July Charter—they became conservative heroes, rallying behind them the 'existing institutions', as Brougham put it, that they had before assailed. If on the continent the petit-bourgeois sought an independent destiny, there was always the image of a hungry proletariat that might be used to frighten it, as the career of the French Mountain so pathetically reveals in 1848. Thus out of the very diversity of its opponents European Whiggery forged a foothold on which to rest, and out of their diversity, too, it managed to give its political thought a series of glorious overtones. Macaulay when he faced the Duke of Wellington developed a high liberal optimism. Guizot when he faced Ledru-Rollin developed a rich empirical traditionalism. Granted that these were rather contradictory types of glory, and in the French case were pursued with a shocking allegiance to class interest, they nevertheless provided the basis for some sort of genuine political thought.

Now what America did when it created the American democrat is fairly obvious. It removed the European foothold and, doing so, removed all chance for philosophic glory. Here there are no aristocracies to fight, and the Federalists and the Whigs are denied the chance of dominating the people in a campaign against them. Here there are no aristocracies to ally with, and they cannot use their help to exclude the people from political power. Here there are no genuine proletarian outbursts to meet, and they cannot frighten people into fleeing from them. They are isolated, put at the mercy of a strange new democratic giant they cannot possibly control. Their political thought loses entirely its 'liberal' aspect, and its conservative denunciation of the people not only becomes suicidal, since it is precisely the people who are sure to shatter them, but loses most of its connection to reality. It is bad enough for Hamilton and Noah Webster to be denied the chance of developing Macaulay's liberalism, and thus to appear forever as conservatives only, but to be put in the position where their longing for a House of Lords, instead of being traditionalistic, is actually revolutionary, since none has ever existed, and where their denunciation of the 'mob' is peculiarly absurd since the 'mob' is as liberal as they are, is a horrible additional species of punishment. This knocks out all the props from under them, conservative as well as liberal.

And yet American Whiggery, had it not been strategically paralyzed over most of its early history, had it not had an impulse to duplicate European patterns which Henry Adams correctly described when he called it 'instinctive', could have avoided all of this. It could have transformed the very liability of the American liberal community into a tremendous asset. For if the American democrat was unconquerable, he was so only because he shared the liberal norm. And this meant two things: one, that he was not a real social threat to Whiggery; and two, that Whiggery had much to offer him in the way of feeding his capitalist impulse. Thus what Whiggery should have done, instead of opposing the American democrat, was to ally itself with him: to give up the idea of exploiting many enemies, as in Europe, and try to exploit the presence of many friends. It should have made a big issue out of the unity of American life, the fact that all Americans were bitten with the capitalist ethos which it was trying to foster. It should, in other words, have developed some sort of theory of democratic capitalism which fit the Tocquevillian facts of American life.

But this, as we know, is precisely what Whiggery failed to do until it saw the light in 1840, and indeed, in any large sense, until the post-Civil War days of Horatio Alger and Andrew Carnegie. Over most of its early history it pursued a thoroughly European policy, and instead of emphasizing what it had in common with the American democrat, it emphasized precisely what it did not have in common with him. Instead of wooing this giant, it chose, quite without any weapons, to fight him. This would be a high species of political heroism, were it not associated with such massive empirical blindness. One can admire a man who will not truckle to the mob, even though the mob is sure to beat him, provided there is actually a mob in the first place. But in America there was no mob: the American democrat was as liberal as the Whigs who denounced him. Consequently the suicidal grandeur of Fisher Ames is tinged with a type of stupidity which makes admiration difficult. At best one can find in the Whigs a kind of quixotic pathos. One can treat them as Europeans living in an alien world, unwilling and unable to understand it. They have great liberal energies but America has no use for them. They pursue the usual conservative strategies but are baffled and dumfounded at every turn. It is the sort of pathos one might expect to find in Macaulay had he suddenly been shipped to America—except for the fact, alas, that Macaulay saw more about America from London than Fisher Ames saw about it from Boston.

This analysis gives us, it seems to me, a clue to the solution of an ancient problem: the speedy triumph of democracy in America. Our efforts to explain the rise of American democracy have foundered largely on the fact that they have been unable to withstand any comparative test. Turner's frontier theory breaks down because frontiers are to be found in other lands. An emphasis on urban industrialism, which some of our newer historians are supplanting it with, breaks down even more, since industrialism was farther advanced in England and possibly even in France than it was in the United States in the eighteen twenties. But if we assert that the quick emergence of democracy was inherent in the American liberal community, we advance a proposition that comparative analysis cannot destroy. Indeed the inflexible European behaviour of American Whiggery gives this proposition the kind of support that one might almost expect to get from a laboratory experiment. Had the Whigs adapted themselves at once to the unique reality of America, had they donned something like the garb of Carnegie in the age of Fisher Ames, they would have confused the issue considerably. We would have had to work entirely with assumptions that could not be empirically verified. As it is, however, since Fisher Ames tried his best to operate like Guizot, we can clearly say that in a liberal society the only type of antagonism to democracy that can appear is the antagonism of the upper middle class and that in such a society the upper middle class is robbed of the capacity to implement it. In other words, if we could imagine England or France in the eighteen thirties with their feudalisms gone and their masses unified around the liberal norm, we could expect to find, on the basis of their own history, the same sort of pattern that appeared in America. We could expect to find all of the familiar techniques of Whiggery exploding in its face, a huge new democrat emerging, and the early triumph of manhood suffrage.

Given its early strategy, then, there were three parts to the problem American Whiggery faced: the absence of an aristocracy to fight, the absence of an aristocracy to ally with, and the absence of a mob to denounce [. . .]

The final dilemma of the Federalists and the Whigs, the fact that the people they denounced as lusting for Caesarism and the destruction of property were liberals like themselves, confronts us with a less intricate problem than the others. This was not a case of blows raining down from unknown sources, as with the absence of an aristocracy to fight, or of subtle adaptations to frustration, as with the absence of an aristocracy to ally with. It was a plain case of unjustly insulting a democracy that could not be controlled, and it reveals American Whiggery at its suicidal worst.

The truth is, the arguments of Whiggery against manhood suffrage were not even valid in Europe. The horror of Macaulay and Guizot at the thought of the universal vote overlooked the attachment of the European peasantry to the institution of property and exaggerated the hunger of the

European proletariat. A shrewd conservative like Bismarck saw this, and so did Berryer in France. What America did, when in the person of the American democrat it absorbed both of these groups into the liberal category, was to make the errors of Europe obvious. Indeed some of the European Whigs, unable to perceive these errors at home, actually perceived them here. Thomas Attwood, leader of the Birmingham Political Union in 1831, pointed out that America had 'at least nine men interested in property to one man interested in labor alone', which was 'exactly the reverse' of the situation in England, and Macaulay agreed that this condition actually justified the adoption of universal suffrage.[1] But their American brethren, orthodox to the end, behaving 'instinctively', advanced the European arguments nevertheless. Chancellor Kent, after concluding the familiar Platonic analysis of popular tyrannies and attacks on property in the New York Convention of 1821, asked: 'And dare we flatter ourselves that we are a peculiar people . . . ?' It did not occur to him that the answer might be yes.

Since it was such a patent distortion of the truth that even Macaulay and Attwood could see it, the argument of the Federalists and the Whigs was hardly designed to elicit a docile reaction from the American democrat. Of course the American democrat did not ordinarily defend himself by pleading that he was just as liberal as his opponents. He assailed them as 'aristocrats' and defined himself as a downtrodden 'laborer', thus shattering the Whigs with their own cosmology and in the end, alas, confusing himself almost as much as they were confused. But on occasion the plea of a common liberalism was stung out of him nevertheless. The American people, Leggett bitterly remarked, 'are just as well acquainted with the rights of person and property and have as just a regard for them as the most illustrious lordling of the scrip nobility'. In Virginia, John R. Cooke, replying to the charge that unpropertied men were potential 'levellers', put his finger on a basic mechanism of American life: men who did not own property dreamed of doing so and hence it could never be to their 'interest' to destroy it. And New York's General Root, infuriated by Chancellor Kent, declared: 'We are all of the same estate—all commoners. . . .'

All of the same estate: here was in five words the basic fact that ruined Whiggery in America. But that Whiggery should have beaten those words out of the American democrat, if only for an angry and enlightened second, shows how blind it was. For if they were the key to Whiggery's collapse in European terms, they were the only key to its survival in American terms: unable to control the American democrat by leading him in a liberal movement and blasting him in a conservative movement, it could only control him by uniting with him in a capitalist movement. Instead of making him say, 'we are all of the same estate', it should of course have said so itself—loudly and passionately and publicly. [. . .]

The clue to the American democrat lies in his hybrid character, and the clue to his hybrid character lies in the American liberal world. As we have seen, the Federalists and the Whigs are not a peculiar creation of American life. They are a familiar Western type, Whigs of the wealthy middle class, and what is remarkable about them is the fate that they experience: defeat in the age of Louis Philippe, success in the age of the Paris Commune. But the American democrat is the man who imposes this strange life on American Whiggery, and by doing so he displays in his own personality all of the nonliberal European elements that the American world has liberalized and inspirited with the ethos of Sydney and Locke. He is a liberal of the small propertied type, vastly expanded in size and character by a set of incongruous strains: the peasant who has become a capitalist farmer; the proletarian who has become an incipient entrepreneur; and in the time of Jefferson, even the Southern 'aristocrat' who emerges to lead them both. It is not hard to see why the term 'petit-bourgeois' loses its meaning in the case of a giant as rich, as complicated, and as various as this. When the European shopkeeper has absorbed practically the whole of a nation, what is to be gained by calling him a shopkeeper? Tocqueville, a man who came from the classic home of Europe's petit-bourgeois, from the Paris of Balzac and Marx, said that 'what astonishes me in the United States is not so much the marvelous grandeur of some undertakings as the innumerable multitude of small ones'.

The truth is, there is not a term in the Western political dictionary that can be used to describe the American democrat, and he is therefore, for one thing, immune to all types of political insult. If the Marxist calls him a 'humble and crouchingly submissive' small urban trader, he can point out at once that he is a man of the land, the factory, and the forge, a man who has all the proletarian virtues that Marx was forever contrasting with the pettiness of the petit-bourgeois. If the Marxist calls him a peasant, an agent of 'barbarism within civilization',[2] he can reply, with Tocqueville, that he is an aggressive entrepreneur, buying 'on speculation', combining 'some trade with agriculture', making 'agriculture itself a trade', indeed the leader of American progressivism. Nor do bourgeois epithets bother him any more than socialist ones. If in the time of Jefferson you call him a landed aristocrat, he can reply that he is a radical democrat. If in the time of Jackson you call him a dangerous proletarian, he can point to an undeviating attachment to liberalism and property rights.

There is, in other words, always something in the American democrat which redeems him from something else, so that the man who tries to attack him, or indeed even the man who tries to defend him, is confounded at every turn. At bottom, to lapse into Marxian language again, he has the 'mesquin' [mean, shabby] outlook of a Flocon or a Ledru-Rollin, a certain smallness of entrepreneurial preoccupation which has never been glamorous in Western thought. But overlaid on this story there are two

9

heroic dramas, the covered wagon drama of the American frontier and the strike-ridden drama of a rising labor movement, so that when we come to men like Jackson and Leggett we are never quite sure whether we are dealing with a petty hope or a glorious dream. But it is this very ethos of the small and independent liberal, this very shadow of the European 'petit-bourgeois', which saves the American land and American labor from the charge of reaction and revolution. What might be said about Jackson, he is not a Benjamin Disraeli; and whatever might be said about Leggett, he is something short of a Friedrich Lasalle. The American democrat, by compounding in his own small propertied liberal personality the ancient feudalism and the incipient socialism of Europe, is a man who may satisfy no one but he is also a man whom no one can thoroughly hate.

Here, of course, we have the reason the American democrat was able to demolish Whiggery during the time, prior to its conversion to the log-cabin faith, when it was pursuing the more genteel European strategies of Fisher Ames and J. Q. Adams. Swallowing up all of the social forces that in Europe Whiggery would have played off against each other in order to keep him down, above all the feudal aristocracy and the unpropertied proletariat, he took the props from under Whiggery and left it helpless in a liberal world. Thus another clue to his personality suggests itself at once. Had he suddenly gone to Western Europe, instead of finding the many 'instinctive cousins' that as Henry Adams noticed the American Whigs had there, he would not have found a man he could have called his brother. Imagine Daniel Webster and Andrew Jackson both in the England of the eighteen thirties or forties. It is not hard to conceive of Webster flourishing almost as much as Macaulay flourished, leading the masses against the aristocracy and joining with the aristocracy against the masses. But what would have happened to Jackson? Where would he have stood? Would he have stood with Disraeli and the land, or with Cobbett and the workers, or with the petty enterprisers who scarcely had an independent leadership? The fact is, he would not have known where to stand. He would have wandered homelessly over the face of Europe, a lost giant from another world, finding parts of his personality in various places but the whole of it nowhere. Victorious in the liberal society of America, he would have been, precisely for that reason, a massive misfit in the old society of Europe.

But the American democrat, for all of his giant size and his complex virtue, was a strangely pathetic figure even at home. First of all, there was a certain inherent logic to the Western European social divisions. It was not easy all at once to be a landed 'aristocrat', a farmer, a laborer. Psychic tensions appeared. Moreover, even if the American democrat was thus placed in a position where he could isolate an elitist Whiggery, the premium this placed on wild claims of social war was bound further to confuse his social thought. When you do not know precisely who you are yourself, the invitation to call your enemies the worst of names has a curious effect all around. But finally, and above all, the historic petit-bourgeois dilemmas of the Western world remained: individualist fear despite a faith in the majority, capitalist hunger despite talk of 'monopoly'. These drives, as we know, ultimately enchained the American democrat to the very Whigs he was able to shatter in 1800 and 1828. They were painful enough impulses for the Flocons of Europe, but when they appeared in the breast of a New World democrat with a love of hyperbole, they became the clue to endless bewilderment and self-betrayal. They completed a pattern of theoretical confusion which will require from us the steadiest analytic hand to unravel. [. . .]

As the American democrat struggled to reconcile the conglomerate elements of Western society out of which he was built, he produced a scheme of social thought that reminds one of a house of mirrors: the more rooms you enter the more bewildered you get. Consider, first of all, the way in which he absorbed the land and the factory into the ethos of democratic liberalism. Americans take this so completely for granted, especially the liberal agrarianism of Jefferson, that it rarely occurs to them how remarkable it actually is. The role of the land in the politics of modern Europe still needs much historical study, but one thing would seem to be fairly clear. When it was not without a philosophy, as was true in the case of the peasantry and the tenantry, save for sporadic anarchist dreams like those of Proudhon or frustrated yeomen dreams like those of Cobbett, its spokesmen were usually conservative thinkers: men like Disraeli and Bonald. Liberalism was associated with the towns. The Jeffersonian theory, making land the indispensable base of liberal democracy, is quite an American matter, which shows us, as Whitney Griswold has pointed out, how plastic the agrarian virtues of Aristotle are. Jefferson and Disraeli are agreed on many points. They agree that there is a peculiar goodness in the cultivation of the land, that industrial cities are dangerous things. But observe the way they differ: Disraeli sees the land as fostering an ancient feudal order and the towns as fostering democracy, while Jefferson sees the land as fostering democracy and the towns a quasi-feudal kind of social dependence. The only irony that is needed to round this situation out is that capitalist Whiggery is blasted either way: Bright is assailed from the right, Daniel Webster from the left.

But this is not the main point. The main point is that the democratic–liberal transformation of the land in America was not quite complete, for the great early Southern agrarians were large plantation magnates who cherished, as much as America permitted it, the aristocratic ethos. This is not true in the case of Jefferson, whose faith in 'small landholders' as the 'most precious part of the state' cannot be seriously questioned. John Taylor, however, is a case of another kind. It is not hard

11

to see that he is a radical democrat only because he cannot be an authentic aristocrat: because the land in America is predominantly in the hands of small entrepreneurs and if he wishes to defeat the Hamiltonian program he must join with a democracy that shares his debtor complex. He himself admitted as much as this when he said that a 'multitude of proprietors' had made the American land 'irretrievably republican', so that an 'aristocracy cannot exist', which meant that a gentleman had 'no alternative' but to move to the political left. Here was a strange frustration: living on the radical edge of the Enlightenment only because you could not live on the conservative edge of the Reaction, supporting the independent farmer only because the 'good discipline' of the English estate was impossible in a liberal world. What it meant, of course, was that the Mr. Hyde of an Edmund Burke was always struggling to explode beneath the Dr. Jekyll of a Thomas Paine. And eventually the explosion did in fact occur. When the tenants began to revolt in the Hudson Valley, James Fenimore Cooper, an 'aristocrat', moved from blasting Whiggery's stake-in-society argument to supporting the good Burkian notion that the 'column of society must have its capital as well as its base'. In the South, where slavery made the liberalism of the 'aristocrats' doubly dubious, the explosion was tremendous. When abolitionism got under way, John Taylor, transforming himself into George Fitzhugh, did his best to dream the dream of Scott and the European reaction. [. . .]

NOTES

[1] Macaulay's prediction as to the ultimate fate of American democracy was, of course, a gloomy one.
[2] The Marxian terms here are taken from F. Engels, *Germany: Revolution and Counter-Revolution* (New York, 1933), pp. 13, 104; K. Marx, *The Class Struggles in France* (New York, 1936), p. 71.

(b) Parties and Politics in Victorian Britain

H.J. HANHAM

Twenty years after the Reform Act of 1832, which set Britain on the road to American-style electoral democracy, Charles Dod published a 'Political Gazetteer' intended to show how the new system was working.[1] What must have struck contemporary readers of the book was not how much things had changed, but how much had remained the same. Here are a few examples. Chatham, which became a parliamentary borough for the first time in 1832, had easily slipped into the pattern of other dockyard towns which returned members of parliament.

> A committee of the House reported, March 8, 1853, that 'a large number of the electors are employed in the dockyard and other public departments', that they are 'under the influence of the government for the time being', and that 'there is no instance of a candidate being elected for this borough who has not had the support of the government'.

Chester, long a preserve of the Grosvenor family, continued to be under their influence, although money was now said to offer a significant source of competition.

> The Marquis of Westminster retains the greater part of the influence which he formerly enjoyed here; with trifling exceptions some member or other of his family has sat since the Restoration. Candidates with good pecuniary resources are said to have great weight in Chester.

Cricklade, once one of the most notoriously corrupt boroughs in the country, had passed through many phases, but its politics still belonged to the eighteenth century.

H. J. Hanham, *Elections and Party Management: Politics in the Time of Disraeli and Gladstone*, (2nd edition), Brighton, Harvester Press, 1978, pp. ix–xxxi. First published 1959. Abridged.

Formerly possessed by the second Earl of Carnarvon; next by Mr. Joseph Pitt, a banker at Cirencester; and next by Mr. Robert Gordon of Kemble Park, which last gentlemen now divides the influence with Lord Clarendon, Lord Radnor, Mr. Goddard, and Mr. Neeld.

The statesmen of the time had grown up in the world of such boroughs. Lord Palmerston represented one of them, Tiverton, for thirty years; William Ewart Gladstone, who first entered the House of Commons as one of the Duke of Newcastle's members for Newark immediately after the passage of the 1832 Reform Act, continued down into old age to lament the slow disappearance of nomination boroughs; while the third Earl Grey, son of the Lord Grey whose ministry had carried the Reform Act of 1832, was one of those who most vehemently defended the existence of little boroughs, with small populations, on the ground that they supplied the House of Commons with 'men of enlightened views and independent character, but unfitted for encountering the storms of popular election'.

Such men believed that the House of Commons was the only legitimate forum of the nation, where great issues could be expounded and resolved by men specially capable of coming to enlightened conclusions because of their long political training. Statesmen did not, while in office, make major public speeches to party audiences until Gladstone's path-breaking speeches to vast audiences in South Lancashire in 1865 and 1868. And for many years thereafter they were careful, whether in or out of office, to avoid the charge that they were 'stumping the country' for purposes of mere party advantage.

In short, as has been pointed out by William Nisbet Chambers, the style of British politics down to 1867 was about a generation behind that of American politics. In America the so-called second party system (1828–60) had already been in existence for many years before the British party system began to catch up.

The salient characteristic of the second party system was the mobilization of mass participation in elections and in politics generally. In a time when Great Britain, even after the widely-touted Reform Bill of 1832, could boast an electorate of only about 650,000 out of a population of some 16 million, presidential elections in the United States were drawing turnouts of 1,153,350 in 1828, and 2,409,474 in 1840, even though total population amounted to only about 12 million in 1830 and 17 million in 1840. A venerable piece of doggerel expresses the American enthusiasm for politics in the nineteenth century—

They marches in parades and they gets up hurrahs
And they tramps through the mud for the good old cause.

This sense of popular engagement came to maturity in the second party system. In an era when men often lived far from one another and even town dwellers were often starved for entertainment and excitement, the party battle took on the form of a game and a major source of entertainment . . .

Thousands *did* march, flaunt transparencies of party heroes, cheer at mass rallies in town squares or rural groves, and go to the polls to vote.

The outburst of popular participation was probably due in part to the ethos of Jacksonian, equalitarian democracy, but other factors were important too. Among these was the fact of nationwide party competition in an era of improved means of transportation and mass communication, including the emergence of a popular, partisan press. Voting turnout jumped from 26.9 per cent of white adult males in the multi-factional presidential election of 1824, in which six states still chose electors by legislature, to 57.6 and 57.8 per cent in 1828 and 1832, in the era of the restoration of parties. The election of 1840 brought voting participation to an unprecedented 80.2 per cent of white adult males . . . . The result was the democratization of parties and the party system, in popular participation and in the sources and kinds of leaders and cadres who came to the fore in both the Democratic and Whig parties.[2]

British politics began to catch up with American politics only after the Reform Act of 1867. Politics for more than twenty years after the 1867 Reform Act became the central preoccupation of the nation. The party system was remodelled to encourage popular participation on an unprecedented scale. The number of votes cast in general elections rose rapidly, each party gaining over a million votes for the first time in the general election of 1874. Political oratory became popular oratory, not just speeches to a small audience in the House of Commons. Disraeli and Gladstone became popular heroes featured on hundreds of thousands of plaques, horse brasses, salt cellars, and tiles. They also became villains, and the object of anonymous scurrilous verse like these four stanzas about Gladstone, printed on a plain sheet of paper and circulated in the north of England:

Gone from the sweets of office,
Gone from the head of affairs,
Gone in the head they tell us,
Gone, and no one cares.

Gone, not to join the angels,
Gone to reflect on the past,
Gone into opposition,
Gladstone's gone at last.

Gone, let us trust for ever,
Gone whither none can tell,
Gone, let us hope to heaven:
There are demons enough in hell.

Says Satan, 'The place is as full as can be.
But I'd like to make room if I can.'
So he let Ananias and Judas go free,
And he took in the G.O.M.[3]

The eighteen years that followed the Reform Act of 1867 were particularly important in British history, because they were the years in which the nation accustomed itself to the notion of democracy. The 1867 Act had enfranchised a large proportion of the householders in the boroughs, but had left most of those in the counties unenfranchised. It had created a considerable number of new parliamentary constituencies without abolishing any significant number of old ones, with the result that the size of electoral districts was grossly uneven. It had created mass working-class constituencies in the cities, but it had provided no simple and cheap way of electioneering in them, so that most of the biggest constituencies could only be contested by rich men or by those who had the support of such men. And it had done nothing to check bribery and treating, which reached massive levels in the general election of 1880, well after the introduction of the secret ballot in 1872. Such a system was so clearly provisional that further change was inevitable, and it came in a series of Acts passed between 1883 and 1885. These equalized the borough and county franchises, adopted single-member electoral districts of roughly equal size as the norm, limited the amounts candidates might spend on elections, and introduced new and more stringent prohibitions against corrupt practices.

As Walter Bagehot pointed out in 1872, the mere fact of passing the Reform Act of 1867 did not change very much. 'The people enfranchised under it', he commented, 'do not yet know their own power . . .' Its effects, he predicted, would be felt only in the future, when those brought up under the old system had ceased to play an active role in politics, and political leadership was in new hands. And the most notable changes which took place in the years immediately after 1867 were indeed those which flowed from a change in generations. With the death of Lord Palmerston in 1865 and the defeat of Lord Russell's government in the following year the last of the party leaders who had been active before 1820 passed from the forefront of political life. Those responsible for the disestablishment of the Irish Church in 1869, the Irish Land Act of 1870, the Education Act of 1870 and the reforms of the civil service, the army, and the courts of law which took place between 1870 and 1873 were seasoned politicians, but their careers had been made since the Reform Act of 1832. However, such men were not yet accustomed to think in terms of a largely working class electorate. Gladstone and Disraeli had grown up before 1832, and had reached maturity in the context of the quasi-aristocratic politics of the 1840s. Gladstone had first served as a cabinet minister in 1843, Disraeli in 1852. Those who served in their cabinets had for the most part entered political life in the 1840s or 1850s.

Like their predecessors after the earlier Reform Act of 1832, the political leaders of the generation of 1867 were forced to take an active interest in electoral management. For the new electorate created in 1867 had to be managed and led, elections had to be fought, party enthusiasm directed into suitable channels. It is not true, as is still commonly believed, that Robert Lowe, after the passage of the 1867 Reform Act, proclaimed, 'Now we must educate our masters'. But political education was after 1867 a practical necessity. Millions of new voters had to be absorbed into the political system, assimilated into the existing party structure and encouraged to vote. A new generation of provincial political leaders, akin to the party bosses of America, was required to make the system work. And such men speedily emerged. The first and best known of them was Joseph Chamberlain in Birmingham. But by the 1880s most large towns, at least in England and Ireland, had well-established local leaders, who formed the backbone of the first nationwide organizations of party workers, the National Union of Conservative Associations (1867), the National Liberal Federation (1877), and the Irish National League (1882).

Some of the provincial political leaders were also leaders of industry, like the Pullars of Perth, the Kitsons of Leeds, and the Crossleys of Halifax, or leaders of commerce, like the Forwoods of Liverpool. By establishing a close connection between economic leadership and political leadership, such men helped reinforce the central position of politics in British life. But everywhere the normal pattern was for the 'natural' leaders of the community to take their place as political leaders: Liberal and Conservative committees alike were largely composed in rural areas of: the gentry, the clergy, the estate agents, the bankers, the larger farmers, the manufacturers of agricultural implements, and the nonconformist ministers; in the towns of: lawyers, brewers, bankers, manufacturers, merchants, leading shopkeepers, Church of England and nonconformist ministers, and town councillors, plus a sprinkling of dentists, trade union leaders, master craftsmen, and school teachers.

In many parts of the country the political associations to which such men belonged almost imperceptibly became social organizations as well. Some wealthy central city clubs built club-houses, either in the palatial style of the Manchester Reform Club (1868) or the more modest style of the gentleman's clubs of watering places and county towns, to reinforce the social ties between members. Others were reluctant to tie up their resources in brick and stone and preferred the more spartan traditions of the little clubs that were established in modest houses and were often offshoots of nonconformist chapels. But almost everywhere politics came to occupy a central position in community life. Workingmen's clubs, co-operative societies, friendly societies, and other charitable organizations were often identified with one party or the other. The Conservative bank in a provincial town often glowered at a Liberal bank across the street. Conservative lawyers, active in working for their party, did not expect much business from Liberal clients: nor did Liberal lawyers expect much Conservative business. It was not that Liberal and Conservative did not mix. They often belonged to the same church, attended the same balls, engaged in the same sports, and had attended the same school. Their children were also likely to marry across party boundaries. But in the 1870s and 1880s everybody talked about politics, and worked hard at making the new politics a success, so that politics seemed to matter more than ever before. And when the great crises of the 1880s came—the death of Gordon and Gladstone's conversion to Home Rule for Ireland—politics quite often disrupted social life. Old friends would not speak and crossed the road to avoid one another. Dinner parties were disturbed by political wrangles. And nerves were so taut that it is not surprising that in the years that followed a reaction sets in. In the 1890s politics lost its undisputed primacy in the national consciousness, much as it had already done in America. Attention shifted to the suburban home, with its growing creature comforts, and to the revelations of social investigators who had begun to make it clear that great political issues like the extension of the franchise or Home Rule for Ireland had little bearing on the problem of how to diminish the worst evils of poverty and overcrowding. The trade unions began to assume a more central role in public life. Organized games began to replace politics as spectator sports. The newspapers gradually ceased to report speeches in full. Society, in short, began to forget its intense love affair with party politics.

In the meantime, however, a whole generation of new politicians had grown up who were attuned to the post-1867 political order. In 1874 the first two working men were returned to parliament. In 1886 a working-class M.P. for the first time became a minister of the Crown, when Henry Broadhurst became Under-Secretary at the Home Office. Trade unions, workingmen's clubs, and friendly societies were added to the list of the social organizations (headed by Eton) which provided a training for a political career.

By 1905, when the *Sheffield and District Who's Who* was published with the avowed purpose of 'giving an outline of the careers of the public men in the city and neighbourhood', the careers of working-class politicians were at last beginning to be regarded as significant enough to merit public attention, though their more aristocratic contemporaries still received disproportionate attention in the newspapers. The typical Sheffield politician was still in 1905 a professional man like Alderman Robert Styring, about whom it was reported:

> The 'Whip' of the Liberal Party in the Sheffield City Council is, professionally, a successful lawyer, partner in the firm of Webster and Styring, solicitors. Sprang from the sturdy middle class, which has for so long been the backbone of the country. He has been in public life for 20 years, entering the Council for St. Peter's ward as a Liberal in 1886, after an initial defeat in the early part of that year. He was successively re-elected for that ward until 1899, when he was appointed an alderman. Has for many years been prominently connected with the Cemetary Road Congregational Church and Sunday School, and in 1889–90 filled the office of Chairman of

the Sheffield Congregational Association. Since 1881 he has been hon. sec. of the Sheffield Athenaeum Club, and in 1896 a presentation was made to him by the members to mark their appreciation of his services during 15 years. As a member of the City Council it fell to Alderman Styring's lot to organise the Sheffield Electric Supply Department on the acquisition of the electric light by the Corporation in 1898, and he was Chairman of the Electric Light Committee down to November, 1904. To him mainly is due also the initiation of the Surplus Lands Committee, and the initiation of the Angel Street and other building schemes of the Corporation, some of which have been the subject of keen controversy. Was actively concerned in the arrangements under which the Corporation purchased the tramways and converted them to the electric system. Took a prominent part in the purchase and subsequent management of the water undertaking. Has been a member of the committee since the date of purchase. It was at his suggestion that the Corporation sought to obtain, and after a protracted Parliamentary struggle succeeded in establishing, Sheffield's claim to a large share of the Derwent Valley water. Since the formation of the Derwent Valley Water Board, has been one of Sheffield's three representatives on that body. Was for some time a member of the University College, and is now on the Court of Governors of the University of Sheffield. For many years has been one of the Corporation representative members of the Technical Department of the University. Is a member of the Education Committee, and a Governor of King Edward VII School at Sheffield.

On the Conservative side such professional men were commonly supplemented by publicans like Councillor Alfred Taylor:

Native of Sheffield, born in 1849: educated at Trinity Church Schools, Wicker. Served apprenticeship to edge tool and sheep shear trade, and though has now left that business, has maintained close association with his old trade, and remained member of his trade union. Has been a licence holder for 35 years, and is now landlord of the Corner Pin Hotel, and is much respected, not only in the 'trade' but in Sheffield generally. Has occupied position of President of Sheffield, Rotherham, and District Licensed Victuallers' Association; Vice-president Licensed Victuallers' National Defence League (No. 2 branch); trustee of Licensed Victuallers' Institution at Dore, Freemason and member of several Friendly Societies. Has always been prominently identified with Conservative Party in Sheffield, particularly in Brightside Division. Took leading part in elections in Brightside Old Ward when S. Q. L. candidates were 'hammered out'. First elected to City Council in 1894 for old Brightside Ward, afterwards St. Philip's Ward, and was afterwards allocated to Neepsend for which he now sits. Is a member of Health, Tramways, and General Purposes and Parks Committees. Takes great interest in provision of municipal music in the Parks in summer and in the courts and alleys in winter. Cemeteries and public burial grounds also take up a good deal of his time.

But the politics of the post-1867 period was best represented by trade unionists like Councillor A. J. Bailey:

Councillor Alfred J. Bailey is one of the soundest and least aggressive members of the Labour group in the City Council. Born July 15th, 1868, at Scredington, Lincolnshire, the son of an agricultural labourer. His education was received at a village National School, three miles from Scredington, and then at a new village Board School, the head of which was a schoolmistress. Mr. Bailey, who is a member of the Church of England, commenced work as a ploughboy at thirteen years of age, and stuck to farm work until he was 21. Then he came to Sheffield, and obtained employment as a drayman. On several occasions he lost situations, and found himself out of employment for long periods, owing to his advocacy of trade union principles. Worked at Treeton Colliery as a surfaceman, and was there affected by the miners' lockout of 1893. As a workman he assisted in organising the surfacemen, and in 1896 was appointed official organiser for the National Amalgamated Union of Labour, the membership of which has since increased by over 3,000. Was elected a member of the Sheffield Board of Guardians in April, 1902, and was re-elected in 1904, on both occasions without a contest. He had the unique experience of having to fight for his seat on the City Council twice in the same year. He was elected at a by-election in June, 1904 for Darnall Ward, the vacancy having been caused by the death of the late Councillor Castle. In November he had again to seek re-election, and was again opposed. The majority of 271 in June rose to 533 in November. [. . .]

That juxtaposition of old and new which gave the period between the Reform Acts of 1867 and 1884 its peculiar character, was occasioned by two factors: the Reform Act of 1867 itself and the long period of economic prosperity which lasted almost unbroken from about 1850 to 1879. The one deprived the Radicals of their most significant grievance against the existing social order, at the price of admitting them to a much greater share in the government of the country; the other confirmed both the popular belief in the inexorable march of progress and the economic supremacy of the aristocracy and the middle classes.

The 1867 Reform Act almost doubled the old electorate of close on a million, and gave the county vote to nearly all landowners, tenant farmers and middle-class householders, and to the better class of village tradesmen, and the borough vote to almost all settled householders. It withheld the franchise from working-class householders in the counties, and from all who in county or borough shared dwelling-houses or occupied them for short periods or as a condition of employment. In the counties the chief consequence was to give the rural districts much more weight than the small towns and mining villages. In the boroughs the effects were more varied. In the smallest boroughs like Dorchester and Hertford the 1867 franchise was little different from the old one, since the new voters were agricultural labourers and small tradesmen dependent on the local 'upper crust' for their livelihood and not sufficiently numerous to form effective political associations of their own. In many of them the new electorate was, indeed, only about fifty per cent bigger than the old. The medium-sized provincial centres like Cambridge and Ipswich were more affected, since their electorate was doubled or trebled. But as the new electors were mostly skilled tradesmen and shopkeepers of the poorer sort (bakers, butchers, carpenters and beer-shop proprietors were particularly numerous among them), who already played an important part in municipal elections, there was again nothing like a sweeping change in the political balance of forces. This took place only in the industrial towns, and in Scotland, where the electorate grew beyond all recognition. There were 1,165 electors in Gateshead in 1866, of whom 110 were working men; in 1872 there were 9,191 electors of whom the vast majority were working men: there were 6,630 electors in Newcastle-upon-Tyne in 1866, of whom 1,559 were working men; in 1872 there were 21,407 electors of whom the vast majority were working men: there were 768 electors in Warrington in 1866, of whom 149 were working men; in 1872 there were 4,848 electors, again mostly working men.

What the 1867 Reform Act signally failed to do was to carry out a much-needed redistribution of seats. On paper the fact that no fewer than fifty-three seats were redistributed was impressive, especially when coupled with the introduction of the so-called minority clause in thirteen big constituencies. But in practice it did very little to remedy existing inequalities. At one extreme there were still more than seventy boroughs with a population of less than 10,000, although many larger places were not enfranchised, while at the other there were over forty constituencies with a population of more than 200,000. Portarlington, with less than 3,000 people and 140 electors, was as much a parliamentary borough as Liverpool with 500,000 people and 60,000 electors; Tiverton, with a population of 10,000, had two members, like Marylebone with a population of 477,000; and Rutland, with a population of 22,000, had as many members as South-East Lancashire with a population of 403,000. And these discrepancies were growing every year because the popualtion of the smaller constituencies was either stationary or declining, while that of the larger was rapidly increasing. Moreover, the different classes of constituency by no means enjoyed equal representation. The boroughs had 281 members and the counties only 170, although the population of the counties was considerably larger (13,689,000 as against 12,286,000 in 1881): the boroughs and agricultural counties were over-represented in comparison with the industrial counties (notably Lancashire and Yorkshire); and most glaring of all, the south and west of England were over-represented in comparison with the rest of the country. Wiltshire and Dorset still had twenty-five members between them, eighteen for the boroughs and seven for the counties, although their population was no more than 450,000; yet the metropolis with three million people had only twenty-four members, and the West Riding with two million had only twenty-two.[4]

The greatest inequality or discrepancy in the system was not traditional at all. The reformers in 1867 deliberately went out of their way to give the boroughs a franchise entirely different from that of the counties, so increasing rather than playing down the traditional difference between them.[5] They came therefore to differ not only in size, in traditions, and in local government, but also in the whole way in which elections were fought. The counties became the strongholds of the old order; the boroughs, or rather the bigger boroughs, became the field for experiment in 'democratic' political organisation. The distinction was not however a rigid one. Neither 'borough' nor 'county' was a precise term, because of variations in size and character within the two categories, and because there existed, in addition to predominantly urban counties like South Essex,[6] a number of hybrid 'agricultural boroughs' which were a cross between county and borough. These were composed of a small town or village together with most of the neighbouring parishes or tithings, and in some cases included the whole of the hundred in which a town was situated. Some of them were quite small in area, but others meandered for miles— Great Marlow extended over some twenty-two square miles, Droitwich over forty-three, and Wallingford over twenty-eight—while the giants among them were really county divisions: Aylesbury with 108 square miles, New Shoreham with 175, Cricklade with 248, and East Retford with 325.[7] Thirty-seven of the most rural had, in fact, a population of less than one person to an acre, and Wareham actually had a lower ratio (0.196) than the very rural county of Dorset itself. Such boroughs inevitably produced queer effects on the electoral map. Buckinghamshire, for instance, was cut in two by the vast borough of Aylesbury, which stretched from Aylesbury itself to Missenden and from the outskirts of Thame to the outskirts of Tring, yet it also possessed three other large agricultural boroughs: Buckingham, Wycombe and Marlow. Similarly, in Sussex, the borough of New Shoreham stretched from the Surrey boundary to the sea, and completely surrounded the still extensive but smaller borough of Horsham. As the size of a borough bore no relation to its importance, the boroughs of Wiltshire, Dorset, Hampshire and Sussex present on the map a most extraordinary jumble: insignificant small boroughs like Bridport and Dorchester, whose parliamentary boundaries were the same as those of the municipal borough and included none of the surrounding parishes; sizeable towns like Brighton, Portsmouth and Southampton; and stretches of countryside like Midhurst, Wareham and Petersfield with scarcely a town in them.

Although the 1867 Reform Act, in spite of these deficiencies, was undoubtedly the first decisive event in what has been called the 'transition to democracy', the twenty years that followed it were far from democratic. As G. J. Holyoake told an audience of working men in 1868

Though Representation is open to us, we cannot understand too soon, that the House of Commons, like the London Tavern—is only open to those who can pay the tariff . . . All that the sons of labour have gained at present, is the advantage of being consulted. Whoever is member will have to take them into account. This is a great thing gained. But the electoral machinery of England is centuries old; and the people cannot expect to come into possession of it without conditions, nor to master its use all at once.

For the moment the preoccupations of parliament and the electorate were almost entirely middle class, and the Reform Act was less important because it gave some working men the vote than because it had touched off an era of reform.

The Reform Act of 1832 had called the new forces in English life into the parliamentary forum, but it had not decided what role they were to play. Indeed, after satisfying the most pressing demands of their supporters, the reformers had deliberately preserved for the old aristocracy much more power and influence than its experience of government and prestige alone would have won it. It still remained for the middle classes to seize effective power if they wanted it. For a few years it seemed that they would do so, but the burst of legislative enthusiasm associated with the disciples of Jeremy Bentham soon died away as a result of aristocratic inertia and the development of the great national conflicts over the Charter and the Corn Laws. Until the fierce antagonisms which gave rise to Chartism and the Anti-Corn-Law League had burned themselves out, or had been subdued by the long years of mid-Victorian prosperity, free trade was the only major issue with which parliament felt bound to deal. Indeed, for twenty years after the end of the 'hungry forties', men were too busy taking advantage of the good times which had come to them, and sampling the pleasures of their new-found power abroad, to care much for their abstract rights. There was, as a consequence, a general desire among all but convinced reformers to shelve questions of reform until Lord Palmerston should retire. Meanwhile, the reformers belonging to the disparate traditions of Peel, Bentham and Cobden drew closer together and joined forces with the Oxford reformers, the Radical working men, and the political dissenters in accepting Gladstone as their leader.

By 1865, with prosperity seemingly assured, only two things stood in the way of an era of reform designed to benefit the middle classes: Palmerston, who obstinately refused to retire, and the question of parliamentary reform, which had been so much agitated since 1859 that no other major reforms could well be given precedence over it. Death removed Lord Palmerston in October 1865, and in 1867, after two years of political confusion, the essentially Palmerstonian parliament which had refused reform at the hands of Lord Russell and Mr Gladstone accepted it at those of Lord Derby and Mr Disraeli. In the very next session Mr Gladstone brought forward a motion for the disestablishment of the Irish Church in very much the same terms as that which had first been carried by Lord John Russell in 1835. He was supported by Bright, and in the new Liberal cabinet formed at the end of 1868 Whigs, Peelites, and Radicals all found a place. In the course of the 1868 parliament the middle classes who had enjoyed nominal power since 1832 at last came into their own. The army, the universities, and indirectly the Civil Service, were opened to them; the first steps were taken in educational and temperance reforms; and the Irish Church was disestablished.

For the seventeen years after 1867 there was scarcely a break in the catalogue of reforms, even during the life of the Conservative parliament of 1874 to 1880. As Gladstone wrote prophetically in his *Chapter of Autobiography* (1868), the 'movement of the public mind has been of a nature entirely transcending former experience', and the public soon became prepared for changes which had seemed out of the question only a few years before. At the same time, a clear division between reformers and anti-reformers began to emerge, which gradually transformed both political parties, and which had the immediate effect of giving the electors a distinct choice of party programmes for the first time since 1847. Even more important, the reformers, by their own example and by their enactment of the Ballot Act, gave encouragement to the forces of nationalism in Ireland, which soon grew out of the party garments that English politicians would have had them wear.

The extraordinary number of reforms with which these years are associated should not, however, be allowed to obscure the essential continuity of political life before and after 1867. Gladstone and his associates belonged in outlook to the age of Peel and Cobden. The objectives they pursued in the seventies and eighties were almost without exception those which John Bright had been proclaiming twenty years before, just as their social attitudes had been shaped by the belief in the divine right of the middle classes to political leadership and by the ultra-individualism of the Manchester school. And the constituencies themselves continued to be dominated by the magnates of land and industry. The reason for this political continuity was undoubtedly the mid-Victorian period of economic prosperity. Its influence was two-fold: it created the atmosphere of optimism and confidence which made possible the great reforms of the late sixties and early seventies, and it sustained and invigorated the old hierarchical society which in the forties had seemed doomed to decay. It revived in particular that attitude of deference with which Bagehot made such play, and which was so alien to the mood of the Chartists and the world of *Sybil:* a deference which had the effect of prolonging the privileges of the aristocracy and the landed gentry. What Radical writer of the thirties could have written, as Leslie Stephen wrote in 1867, of the aristocracy as an integral and even essential part of society whose privileges no Reform Act would seriously diminish?

> The main influence . . . of the upper classes undoubtedly depends upon what may be called the occult and unacknowledged forces which are not dependent upon any legislative machinery. England is still an aristocratic country; not because the nobility have certain privileges, or possess influence in certain boroughs. A power resting upon such a basis would be very fragile and would go to pieces at the first strain upon the Constitution. The country is aristocratic, because the whole upper and middle, and a great part of the lower, classes have still an instinctive liking for the established order of things; because innumerable social ties bind us together spontaneously, so as to give to the aristocracy a position tolerably corresponding to their political privileges.

Radicals still carped at the petty tyranny of landlords and resented their wealth, but they could not ignore the fact that landlords were the wealthiest men in the country, that they dominated Society with a capital S, and that they sent more members to parliament than any other class.[8] Moreoever, where seats like Nostell Priory, Knowsley Hall, and Chatsworth House were as much party offices as those in Westminster.

Prosperity also affected the towns. In the oldest ones new industries sprang up: bicycle-making at Coventry, cocoa and tobacco processing at Bristol, agricultural machinery works at Bedford and Lincoln, and Colman's mustard works at Norwich. In those whose prosperity had come with the industrial revolution there was also a change of tempo as new industries, mainly concerned with engineering, moved in alongside textiles. There were also new towns like Birkenhead, Middlesbrough, Crewe, and Swindon.

These developments directly affected the position of the skilled workmen, whose value in an industrial society was only just coming to be recognised, and whose material position had been steadily improving. Their new houses were better than ever before, and although many of them are today slum property, they made possible a new order and cleanliness which was quite alien to the chaos and filth of Engels' Manchester of 1844. Wages had risen, and by 1871 prices had begun to fall without (except for a short time in 1879—80) any serious rise in unemployment. Trade unionism enjoyed a boom, and for a while spread even to the agricultural labourers. Nor was there any lack of incentives. A skilled man could earn as much as five times the income of an agricultural labourer, and enjoyed all the social advantages which society linked with the successful application of the doctrine of self-help. For the time being, at least, there was no serious call for a movement to redress working-class grievances.

But by 1880 the long period of prosperity which had lasted since the fifties was at an end, although few were yet aware of it. The working classes were not greatly affected at first, but the bulwarks of Victorian society, the landlord, the capitalist, and the church, soon found themselves in difficulties. Now at last, the Protectionists of the forties were vindicated as free trade put an end to the unexampled prosperity of English agriculture, and increased competition reduced the return from industrial investments. And the break in English political life, in so far as there was one, came not in 1867 but in the years between 1880 and 1886.

The general election of 1874 was the last to take place in the old conditions. By 1880 the Home Rule movement had grown from small and very respectable beginnings to become a real menace to the English supremacy in Ireland. Through the medium of parliamentary obstruction the Home Rulers had also put an end to many of the comforts which had made parliamentary life agreeable to English country gentlemen. Already sorely troubled by the demands which their constituents were making upon their time, these now began to relinquish parliamentary ambitions altogether. Much of the remaining flavour of mid-Victorian politics also disappeared with the death of Disraeli in 1881—as the nostalgic success of the Primrose League was to show—and was never recaptured. The Conservative party which he had done so much to create took on a new role only five years after his death, when the Liberal party finally collapsed as a result of its many internal conflicts.

The machinery of politics changed along with the parties. The Corrupt Practices Act of 1883 which limited election expenditure made it easier and cheaper to get into parliament and gave a new importance to party organisation. The voluntary worker in the constituency, organised by a body like the Primrose League, and the party headquarters, with their large financial resources and supply of posters and leaflets, became for the first time the key to electioneering. The old constituencies inherited from the middle ages were swept away in 1884—5, and the gross inequalities in their size and the difference between the borough and the county franchise went with them. The single-member constituency became the rule, even though it meant breaking up the big towns and creating entirely working-class constituencies without middle-class leaders. As the big towns, the metropolis, and the industrial districts for the first time received their fair share of the seats there was also a great influx of members of a new type, and for the first time the number of commercial men and manufacturers in the House of Commons was greater than the number of landowners. The chapter of political history that opened with the general election of 1885 was, in short, a completely new one.

NOTES

[1]Charles R. Dod, *Electoral Facts from 1832 to 1853, Impartially Stated, Constituting a Complete Political Gazetteer*, ed. by H. J. Hanham, Brighton 1972.

[2] William Nisbet Chambers and Walter Dean Burnham, eds. *The American Party Systems: Stages of Political Development*, New York 1967.

[3] From a fly-sheet in the possession of the author. The G. O. M. [Grand Old Man] was W. E. Gladstone.

[4] The extent of this over-representation was recognized in 1885 when the southern and western counties were deprived of thirty-eight seats. Cornwall lost 6 members, Devon 4, Dorset 6, Wiltshire 9, Hampshire 4, Berkshire 3 and Sussex 6. For comments on the change see *Spectator*, 27 December 1884.

[5] The electorate of the boroughs of England and Wales was increased by about 134% in 1867, that of the counties by only 45%.

[6] The centre of South Essex was West Ham with a population of 129,000 in 1881. Middlesex, West Kent, South West and South East Lancashire and parts of the West Riding had a similar character.

[7] These boroughs were classed by statute with the counties for electioneering purposes, and under the 1868 Act candidates in them were permitted to hire cabs to take voters to the poll.

[8] The number of members who came from families with more than 2,000 acres of land (according to John Bateman's *The Great Landowners of Great Britain and Ireland*, 4 edn, London 1883, and 'The New Domesday') was as follows:

	Number of Members	
	1868	*1880*
2,000–5,000 acres	*c.* 86	85
5,000–10,000 acres	104	86
10,000–20,000 acres	88	62
20,000–50,000 acres	70	49
Over 50,000 acres	59	40
	407	322

(c) The Party Period and Public Policy: An Exploratory Hypothesis

RICHARD L. McCORMICK

When historians in any field simultaneously become uncertain about the relationships among the most important classes of events they study and have fundamental disagreements about periodization, their field may be said to be experiencing a crisis. Such is the condition of American political history. Voting and elections, on the one hand, and government policies, on the other, provide the substance of political history, yet today scholars are wondering how, if at all, these bedrock phenomena affected one another in the American past. Their uncertainty contributes to the second problem, the lack of consensus on a periodizing framework. While the presidential synthesis no longer commands wide support among political historians, they are divided on the leading alternative that has been proposed—the concept of successive party systems separated by periodic critical elections. The two problems are related because without a theory that connects voting and policy, a periodizing scheme based on successive electoral alignments covers, at best, only half the subject matter of political history.

Until twenty years ago, something like a responsible-party-government model implicitly guided most historical study of elections and policy-making. Party leaders were depicted as voicing support for government programs and receiving votes on that basis. Once in office, it was assumed, they tried to enact the promised policies. The presidential synthesis lent support to such an approach by suggesting the correspondence between a president's election and the programs of his administration.

Thomas C. Cochran challenged the presidential synthesis in 1948,[1] but not until the 1960s did scholars question the assumption that party programs linked voters and policies or offer an alternative periodizing formulation. Taking numerous different approaches, researchers within the past two decades have cast doubt on whether policy divisions led to party formation, questioned whether partisan rhetoric on policy matters

The Journal of American History, Vol. 66, No. 2, September 1979, pp. 279-98.

should be taken at face value, shown that parties were often weak instruments of government decision-making, and suggested that ethno-religious values shaped voting choices far more than did policy demands. None of this research has proved voting and governance to be unrelated, but all of it makes plain that whatever relations existed were more complex than historians traditionally assumed them to be.

While historians were reexamining the connections between voting and policy-making, a political scientist, Walter Dean Burnham, offered a new formulation for periodizing American political history. He delineated five successive party systems, covering the 1790s to the 1960s, each with its own policy patterns as well as distinctive voting characteristics. While Burnham's formulation plainly rested more heavily on electoral behaviour than on policy-making, his work suggested, just as did studies by historians, that the relations between voting and policy were far from simple.[2]

Researchers are currently following two lines of inquiry into the complex connections between elections and policy formation in American history. One approach, based on quantitative studies of electoral and legislative behavior, suggests that political parties appealed to different cultural groups in the electorate and employed distinct governmental means to promote the public welfare. A second tack, being taken by scholars testing Burnham's contention that electoral changes from one party system to the next were accompanied by corresponding policy transformations, has produced studies associating critical elections with new patterns of congressional recruitment, sharper party conflict in Congress, and innovations in national legislative policy.

While these two approaches have yielded useful results, and will continue to do so, it seems important to find a broader way of dealing with the historic connections between voting and policy-making. Several large and growing bodies of scholarship facilitate such a perspective. First are the recent voting studies—quantitative, theoretical, and, even to their critics, immensely exciting. Second is an older, but still vital, literature on economic policy-making that has yet to be integrated with the new accounts of electoral behavior. Finally, there are the burgeoning community studies by social historians with much to say about the perceptions of Americans, including their expectations for politics and government. Taken together with certain key concepts from political science, these works suggest that for most of the nineteenth century there was a complementary relationship between voting and one major category of government decisions, economic policies.

Indeed, the decades from the 1830s to the early 1900s form a distinctive era in American political history, with patterns of party politics, electoral behavior, and economic policy that set it apart from the eras that came before and after. Covering the second and third party systems, in addition to some of the fourth, this was the period when parties dominated political participation and channeled the flow of government policies. Even as the nation grew in size and numbers, fought the Civil War, and industrialized, parties continued to perform these functions and retained their dominance. They did so because they admirably filled two roles: as objects of vital attachments grounded in the people's cultural backgrounds and as vehicles for managing the limited sort of economic policies that nineteenth-century conditions called forth. From the age of Andrew Jackson to that of Theodore Roosevelt, the parties' fulfillment of these roles gave American politics its distinctive character. An understanding of how the parties performed and why there efforts broke down after 1900 provides a new perspective on the voting-policy connection and the related problem of periodization.

From the 1830s until the early 1900s parties shaped campaigns and elections into popular spectacles featuring widespread participation and celebration. Three-quarters of the nation's adult male citizens voted in presidential elections and nearly two-thirds also participated in off-year contests. Most of them cast straight tickets conveniently supplied by the party organizations. While illicit voting may have swelled the electoral totals and fraudulent counting likely reduced the recorded levels of split ballots, it is probable that the great majority of adult males voted honestly, enthusiastically, and partisanly.

In an age when sources of information and diversion were limited, parties and elections provided crucial forms of education and entertainment. Newspapers were almost uniformly partisan and heavily political in their content. Party speakers were often centers of attraction at community gatherings such as fairs and market days. At least once a year, election campaigns offered drama and aroused emotions. Attending primaries and conventions, joining in parades and rallies, hearing speeches, waiting for the returns, and celebrating victories—all provided enjoyment and social satisfaction as well as a feeling of political participation.

Recent studies show that voting alignments commonly followed ethno-religious lines and suggest that citizens found parties effective vehicles for the values they learned in their homes and churches. Though they did not always abide by their ideologies, the parties voiced distinctive beliefs and exhibited characteristic styles which citizens recognized and with which they identified. Casting a ballot expressed group solidarity and affirmed the shared values of one's community. Partisan loyalties typically passed from father to son, just as religion did. Partly as a result, towns, counties, and states displayed considerable electoral stability from year to year and decade to decade.[3]

For two-thirds of a century, through political cataclysms of the first magnitude, electoral behavior followed these patterns far more often than not, in far more places than not. When voter turnout dropped, it usually rose again before long; when party loyalties faded, they soon were restored or replaced by new ones; when politicians failed to voice values the people cared for, leaders who did soon replace them. The persistence of these patterns suggests the validity of designating the era as the 'party period' of American political history, when voting was more partisan and more widespread than ever before or since.

Electoral alignments were, however, far from static during the party period. Twice during the era—in the 1850s and 1890s—a combination of new electors, abstainers, and voters shifting from the party to another, created fresh coalitional patterns. As a result of the upheaval of the 1850s, the major parties became more sectionally polarized and, in the North, more strongly divided along religious lines than they had been in the Jackson period. In the lower South, interparty politics broke down for a period of time. But it would be misleading to exaggerate the disruption in the party period's electoral style caused by either the realignment of the 1850s or the Civil War. Several recent studies, especially Joel Silbey's volume on the Democratic party, have stressed the electoral continuity of the Civil War era and the war's effect in strengthening preexisting voting patterns. The issues and appeals, the structure of the vote, and the meaning and importance of political participation were surprisingly unaltered by war and continued into the Gilded Age. Even when fewer places had close interparty competition, electoral turnout remained as high as it had been in the 1840s. The basic structure of party organizations persisted, as did their techniques for mobilizing the voters. In the 1890s, coalitional lines were once again redrawn, and the parties' sectional polarization was further enhanced. In time, that polarity would help diminish electoral turnout. But for almost a decade after the realignment of the 1890s, except in the South, the fundamental behavior of a highly mobilized, partisan electorate persisted.

Throughout the party period, while these characteristic forms of voting continued, economic policy-making manifested distinctive patterns of its own. The government's most pervasive role was that of promoting development by distributing resources and privileges to individuals and groups. An understanding of distributive policies and their centrality in nineteenth century politics helps establish the complementary relationship between electoral behaviour and government decision-making.

The riches that governments bestowed were various indeed. Land formed one such resource, and for almost the whole of the century federal and state officials allocated and sold it. Charters and franchises for banking, transportation, and manufacturing likewise were given away, especially by the states. Special privileges and immunities also came from government: for example, tax exemptions, the right of eminent domain, the privilege of charging tolls on roads and bridges, and the right to dam or channel streams and rivers. Public bounties occasionally encouraged privileged private enterprises, just as government investments sometimes funded mixed corporations. The federal government's tariff also represented a kind of public gift to the individuals and corporations whose products received protection. Public authorities at every level distributed aid by constructing or subsidizing highways, canals, railways, bridges, and harbors.

Forever giving things away, governments were laggard in regulating the economic activities they subsidized. At the federal level the Congress bestowed vast land grants on the transcontinental railroad companies but virtually ignored the rules it established for them. In the states, where regulation was considered a basic function of government, the forms it took often bespoke developmental purposes rather than restrictive ones. Corporation charters commonly specified operating procedures, the quality of service, and maximum rates. General laws, too, frequently regulated banks, insurance companies, transportation corporations, and other public utilities. But through weak laws and weaker enforcement, the results of regulation usually proved meager.

Administration, too, was difficult to accomplish for nineteenth-century governments. According to Leonard White, federal administrative practices remained as rudimentary at the end of the century as in the 1830s. Historians of state politics have similarly observed the limits of administration, including the states' unwillingness to rely on independent commissions for policy formation, fact finding, and day-to-day regulation.

A paucity of planning also characterized government in the party period. According to Willard Hurst, 'We often made policy piecemeal and in disconnected efforts and areas, where a more rational practicality would have told us to link our efforts, fill in gaps, and move on a broad front'. Even states that experimented with economic planning, as some did, particularly in the area of transportation, saw their efforts ultimately fall victim to interest-group conflicts and localistic rivalries. 'Policy' was little more than the accumulation of isolated, individual choices, usually of a distributive nature.[4]

It seems pointless and present-minded to blame nineteenth-century authorities for these 'failures'. From everything we know, the American people got roughly the economic policies they wanted. Given a choice between governmental promotion and restraint, they clearly preferred the former. Except for the abolition of slavery, the distribution of economic benefits probably represents the outstanding achievement of nineteenth-century American government. Certainly it formed the most characteristic achievement.

Distributive decisions may have been roughly what the American people wanted, but the details of such policies perpetually fueled conflict. For one thing, there were never enough of the choicest resources and privileges to go around. Competition for the best land, the most lucrative charters, and the finest transportation facilities inspired battles at every level of government. Inevitably, those who lost called into question the legitimacy of bestowing special privileges on some and depriving others. From the 1830s forward, politics reverberated with the Jacksonian complaint that virtually everything the government did helped only the few. That accusation in turn aroused the historic American distrust of public power and brought forth recurring efforts to preserve liberty by scaling down governmental authority.

For most of the century, however, countervailing circumstances dampened conflict and distrust sufficiently to permit the continuance of a policy structure based on distribution. Land and natural resources remained abundant, while new communities offering charters and privileges to entrepreneurs continually opened up. These favorable circumstances, deriving from the extent and richness of the national domain and from the ongoing spread of population, mitigated scarcity or at least disguised it.

A second set of encouraging circumstances lay in the policy process itself and in the inherent qualities of distributive goods. At every governmental level, the dominant legislative branch threw open its doors to special, local interests demanding assistance and decrying restraints. The very nature of the benefits they sought facilitated legislative acquiescence. While public revenues were limited, heavily taxed citizens sometimes insisted on the reduction of spending, some distributive policies conveniently generated the revenue to support others. Land sales did this at every level of government, just as tariff protection did at the federal level. Of equal importance, distributive policies were highly divisible. Voting tariff protection for one commodity did not preclude protecting others; aiding one canal company was no bar to helping a second and a third. As Harry N. Scheiber puts it, 'repeated trips to the public trough are possible, both for those who come away empty-handed and for those already well fed. If interests X and Y have already been well served—say, by grants of land to aid railroad projects, or by grants of a franchise to build a long boom or a millrace dam—similar gifts can be devolved upon Z the next year'.[5]

A crucial transformation in the form of distributive policies provided a third force for sustaining a policy structure based on such outputs. Occurring from the 1830s through the 1860s, the shift involved making benefits available to everyone who met certain requirements rather than to favored recipients only. At the state level, free banking and general incorporation laws embodied the new approach, as did the related shift from special to general legislation in other fields. At the federal level, the Homestead Act and National Banking Act similarly embraced the principle of allowing all who qualified to avail themselves of benefits.

Finally, distribution was facilitated by an ideological counterweight to the dread of government authority. As a general principle, nineteenth-century citizens accepted public assistance to industry; they possessed only an imprecise conception of the distinction between what was public and what was private. Robert Lively remarks how regularly 'official vision and public resources' were 'associated . . . with private skill and individual desire'. That association was possible, according to Carter Goodrich, because 'Americans did not feel themselves bound by any permanent and unalterable demarcation of the spheres of state action and private enterprise'. Thus an ideolgoy permitting the spread of government aid, in combination with other favorable circumstances, encouraged distributive policies to thrive, despite the conflicts they continually inspired.[6]

The same party organizations that mobilized citizens on election day also structured their receipt of government goods. The divisibility and abundance of distributive benefits, the general acceptance of their legitimacy, and the diversity of forms in which distributive matters could be debated and decided all made them excellent grist for partisan mills. The policy equivalent of patronage, distribution strengthened the parties and helped build bridges between their voters leaders, and representatives in office.

Party leaders took various approaches to managing distribution. Especially in the Jackson period, public promotion of economic development ideologically divided the two major parties. Acting on a vision of social harmony, Whig leaders claimed that subsidies for some meant economic growth for all. Perceiving divisions instead of harmony, Democratic leaders denied the assumption about shared benefits and frequently opposed distributive policies. Through such appeals, often voiced together with ethno-religious keywords, the leaders of both parties transformed the debate over distribution into an ideological conflict that aroused their members and mobilized them to vote.

While the evidence is not yet all in, the ideological debate over promoting private enterprise, which marked one phase of the second party system, seems to have formed a special case in the parties' management of distributive issues. By the late 1840s and early 1850s, the Democrats were succumbing to the lure of public promotional ventures, particularly railroads, and thereafter distribution ceased to divide the parties so starkly. Especially at the state and local levels, Democrats as well as Whigs and Republicans granted charters, aided transportation companies, and sought tariff protection for local industries. To have abjured would have been as remarkable as to have declined to appoint men to office. While both parties thus took up the 'Whig' approach to economic policy, both voiced the 'Democratic' complaint against special privilege. Just as neither party could resist constituent demands for public benefits, neither could ignore the long-standing distrust of active government. Undeniably, there remained a tendency for those with the most expansive conceptions of public policy to group in opposition to the Democrats, and for those with the most limited notions of government to support the party of Jackson. Especially at the national level, and particularly in connection with the tariff and currency issues, ideology remained a feature of nineteenth-century politics. Nonetheless, the key to party management of distribution usually lay not in its ideological potential but in its infinite variety and divisibility.

With policy recipients organized geographically like the parties themselves, log-rolling legislators fashioned awesome combinations of benefits that won widespread support. From the 1830s on, such schemes were common. In Illinois in 1837, the Whig majority crafted a package of internal improvements that satisfied a large constituency. In North Carolina in 1855, the Democratic legislature assisted the residents of a majority of the state's counties by voting money for three large railroads, smaller lines, plank roads, and river improvements. In New York in the 1890s, the Republican legislature combined improvements on the Eire Canal with state aid for macadam roads in noncanal counties. While such projects often received bipartisan support and rarely drew strict party lines, the party organizations usually provided the means of channeling demands and deciding on the successful policies. With so much similarity between managing a party coalition and devising a socially acceptable package of benefits, parties and distributive policies fit one another well.

Divisible as they were, distributive benefits were not unlimited. Tremendous tensions sometimes built up within the parties, as well as between them, over who would get what. But because the claimants were usually small, geographically based groups, rather than broad occupational, sectional, or cultural classes, distributive measures did not delineate irrevocable social divisions. Almost everyone basically wanted the same thing: his own share (or more) at the least possible cost to himself. In this respect, distributive issues were relatively safe ones for party leaders to take up. Unlike regulatory questions, sectional issues, or cultural matters, distributive decisions seldom threatened consensus or risked unmanageable divisions. in the party coalitions.

Although distributive policies predated the 1830s and continued beyond the early 1900s, the manner in which they came to be decided and the dominance they achieved in that period mark it as a distinctive era in public policy-making, just as it formed an identifiable era of electoral behavior. Before the 1830s, distribution was based on the Federalist conception of government aid to an economic elite. The events of that decade, including the bank war and depression, effectively killed the old approach and replaced it with a more democratic one. As Lee Benson has shown in his study of New York, both parties broke 'irrevocably' with Federalist policies and 'adopted programs whose *stated objectives* were to democratize American enterprise'.[7] Even when Jacksonian rhetoric wore thin, the essential character of economic policy discussions begun in the 1830s persisted. The attack on special privilege and the inauguration of the movement toward the more general form of distribution began an era of economic policy-making that lasted until the first years of the twentieth century.

While distributive policies were characteristic of the party period, that long era was far from monolithic in its economic policies. In both the states and the nation, the amounts and types of government aid changed over time. Sometimes the passage of power from one party to the other precipitated policy transformations. At the beginning of the era, Jackson's administration cut back numerous federal ventures which the Republicans revived a generation later. Economic conditions also caused changes in the level of distribution. In general, prosperity encouraged contentment with distributive policies and brought on demands for more, while hard times led to dissatisfaction and cries for retrenchment. At the state and local levels, the effects of the economic cycle may be observed most clearly. There, throughout the century, authorities alternately extended and withdrew aid to private enterprises.

Over the long run, governmental undertakings significantly expanded. The growth and diversification of the population alone assured higher levels and new forms of aid. The Civil War also brought about an enlargement of governmental activity. While, as Morton Keller has shown, localism, cultural diversity, and economic conflicts later forced retreats from the most advanced wartime projects, public activity and expenditures never returned to their prewar levels. The postwar decades saw a continuing debate about the scope of public duties and a steady rise of pressures to assume new ones.

Amidst these cyclical and long-term changes in policy, distribution continued to form the government's basic economic activity. Not until early in the twentieth century did social and economic developments permanently enlarge governmental responsibilities by strengthening both regulation and administration. The new policies, when they came, coincided with the decline of partisan voting. Together the two developments marked the end of an era when parties shaped the political participation of the great majority of male citizens and managed economic policies of the single type they universally expected.

The chronological correspondence of massive, partisan voting and distributive policy-making suggests a significant relationship between electoral behaviour and governance in the nineteenth century. The parties' central role in managing both strengthens the suggestion. It remains to be worked out, however, just what the connection was and what shaped it. Admittedly, such an analysis must be somewhat speculative, for the question has not previously received the attention it merits from historians. Moreover, because the relationship between voting and policy-making was less direct than might be anticipated, it must be defined with appropriate qualifications.

Some, but not all, of the evidence points to responsible party government. Especially at the state and local levels, and particularly in the short run, policy-makers were extremely responsive to the voters. Legislators, as we have seen, readily acquiesced in constituent demands for government assistance or, when times were hard, for retrenchment. Out of a desire to be reelected to office, public authorities in both parties behaved in this manner. Such a responsive policy process was not confined to the economic matters treated here. When sectional or cultural questions were at stake, leaders championed their constituents' values and sought to preserve them through government action. On all these subjects, voters evidently paid attention to what the authorities did and were capable of casting their ballots accordingly.

Because they molded both voting and policy-making, the political parties formed the linkage between the two processes. In ways already suggested, the management of distributive policies strengthened the parties as electoral machines and enhanced participation. Distribution, by affording relatively safe issues at every level of government, enabled parties to satisfy disparate constituencies through the allocation of aid. It is not necessary to believe that material benefits formed the people's highest political priority or that economic issues shaped partisan alignments in order to conclude that the parties' management of the particular sort of economic policies citizens expected helps explain the devotion and participation the parties inspired.

Correspondingly, the parties' virtuosity as electoral organizations strengthened their policy roles and influenced government decision-making. In close contact with the people, the party leaders who got out the vote also learned what the citizens wanted. Successful in electing candidates to office, the party organizations placed men in positions to procure the desired benefits. Party voters were confident in the men elected and gave officials relative freedom to determine the details of policy outcomes. It is not necessary to assume a complete identity of interests between party voters, party organizers, and party legislators to see that these connections—all deriving from the parties' electoral strength—helped shape the final form of public policy.

The parties' two roles interacted in other ways. To attract and maintain a broad constituency, party leaders encouraged distribution, which was widely accepted, and forestalled regulation and administration, which were far more divisive. Electoral politics thus influenced the details of economic policy, through the agency of party. The reverse was also true A party's role in managing distributive outputs affected its electoral performance by setting limits on how it fashioned its appeals and to whom they were directed. If a party's congressmen voted against tariff protection on a certain product or party legislators approved aid for one of several competing railroad lines, the local party organization could not very well make fresh inroads among producers of the unlucky commodity or in towns bypassed by the chosen railroad. Policy-making thus made its mark on the details of electoral behavior.

What all this suggests is that at the level of party politics, the interactions between voting and policy-making were numerous and complex. Because the parties structured both processes, the different needs of party voters, party organizers, and party officeholders caused elections and policy to influence one another in ways that may always defy complete historical analysis.

While they intensely affected one another, however, voting and policy-making were sufficiently independent to cast doubt on the responsible-party-government model. Nineteenth-century voting choices reflected long-term commitments, grounded in cultural, communal, and geographic factors. Although they sometimes fluctuated in accord with policy demands, those loyalties were largely determined by factors outside the process of governance. By the same token, policy patterns transcended elections. While a new administration might reverse some of its predecessor's decisions, the fundamental continuities in nineteenth-century economic policy-making suggest that more was at work in shaping government action than elections alone.

The responsible-party-government model is also flawed by its basis in the assumption that people voted because they wanted the government to do things. Actually, nineteenth-century citizens were profoundly ambivalent about public authority. Expecting the government's assistance for their enterprises, they also distrusted its actions and continually sought to assure its subservience to the electorate. In the Jackson period, the same state constitutional conventions that reduced legislative authority also extended popular control over the choice of government officials. Far from a means to secure expansive policy programs, the spread of electoral participation thus helped assure the extension of restrictions on government action. Far from contradictory, both developments bespoke the long-standing aim of securing liberty against authority.

The relationship between curtailing public power to act and enlarging popular participation is difficult to understand only if we assume that people vote chiefly to get tangible goods from government. But their participation may have other purposes entirely, and it may be more intimately related to confidence in weak government than to gratification by strong and active public authorities.

Indeed, for voters who distrusted power, specific benefits from govrnment often proved less important than general satisfaction with the process of governance. Some policies had symbolic meanings that provided psychic benefits when the actual results were inconsequential, impossible to trace, or contrary to the policy's declared purpose. The bank veto, the Homestead Act, and the Sherman Anti-Trust Act all had such symbolic value. Many nineteenth-century citizens presumably found satisfaction in the basic methods of government as well as in the general patterns of public policy. Taken together, such satisfactions produced what David Easton calls 'diffuse support' for the political system. Independent of particular policies, such support encouraged political participation by citizens no matter what specific programs the officials enacted.[8]

These considerations all imply that, however much voting and policy-making interacted in the short run, neither was fundamentally determined by the other. This is precisely the conclusion suggested by recent political science studies showing that socio-economic factors are better than purely political factors in explaining contemporary policy outcomes. Using expenditure levels as policy indicators, comparative state analyses have demonstrated that such variables as wealth, education, industrialization, and urbanization statistically account for more policy variance than do such political variables as participation, competitiveness, and election type. Limited in some respects, these studies nonetheless offer a suggestive insight for analyzing nineteenth-century electoral behavior and policy formation: both processes were fundamentally shaped not by one another but jointly by factors beyond politics.

According to such a hypothesis, voting and policy interacted only within limits set by the socioeconomic environment. Empirical evidence for this theory lies beyond the scope of the present essay, but crucial support is provided by studies—especially those of individual communities—exploring the conditions and perceptions of nineteenth-century Americans. These works suggest how social circumstances led to widespread political participation and to an economic policy structure based on distribution. Political factors, operating through the parties, helped shape the precise forms these processes took, but the fundamentals of voting and policy were products of a common environment, not of one another.

Historians have already done much to explain how the people's social and cultural conditions led to high degrees of party loyalty and electoral participation. Varied and fragmented as a nation, urban as well as rural Americans lived in 'island communities' each closely knit by bonds of culture and history. Through a diversity of organizations and activities, they discovered their group's identity and expressed its distinctive beliefs. Political parties filled these purposes well, while campaigns and elections offered the means to show commitment to the community and its values. These forms of behavior are understandable without assuming they were mainly directed to determining government action.

Correspondingly, policy formation originated independently of electoral behavior, in the conditions and aspirations of the American people. The economic circumstances underlying distribution are well known. A developing economy, where entrepreneurial opportunity primarily befell individuals and small groups, called for governmental assistance without excessive restraints. With land and capital heavily in the control of public authorities, and with no abstract theory holding Americans back from demanding aid, government policies spreading the resources naturally found support.

Community studies disclose how often mercantile elites succeeded in persuading their towns to pave streets, subsidize railroads, and build public docks. These studies also suggest why such policies proved so widely acceptable. Part of the answer lies in the capacity of promoters to convince others that the desired benefits would advance the town's general prosperity. Pointing to the fundamental harmony of the producing classes, entrepreneurs argued that what helped one group helped all. With upward (and downward) social mobility sufficient to suggest that class lines were neither impassable nor permanent, the promise of such prosperity must have been believable to many. Often false, but often plausible, the harmony argument fed the people's hopes for advancement and helped make distributive benefits popular.

But studies of local communities also show that the nineteenth-century United States was not a harmonious society; Americans were neither unconscious of inequality nor oblivious to the clash of interests. Nor, finally, were they in agreement on industrial values. As Herbert Gutman and others have shown, many Americans clung to traditional perceptions and continued to reject the habits and beliefs of a business civilization. Often they spurned the political leadership of businessmen. These factors increase the difficulty of understanding how entrepreneurial elites obtained community support for their economic programs.

Actually, however, the nature of distributive goods helps explain how promoters fastened them on a mobile society of unequals who disagreed on economic ends. Dependent on fluidity and plenty, rather than on consensus or an identity of interests, distribution seemed to encourage flexibility in using resources and in interpreting economic development. Unlike regulation, it left large economic classes undefined and unidentified. On the face of things, distributive benefits opened up possibilities rather than foreclosed them and permitted differences of opinion about economy and society. Under nineteenth-century conditions, such policies had the appearance of benefiting a diversity of interests. The conditions, not the election returns, explain the policies.

This interpretation squares with much that we know about the nineteenth-century American people. Impatient for material progress, they welcomed the government's assistance to their profit-making enterprises but felt little need to weigh up all the costs against the benefits. Individualistic and upwardly mobile, they readily identified with their community and its beliefs but resisted thinking in the class terms that might have led to sterner demands for calculation in government policy-making. Distrustful of power and jealous of their liberties, the people restricted the authority of public officials. But citizens relished joining and participating and expressing group values, and they bestowed on parties a measure of loyalty they never would have given to government itself.

The party period's practices suited a nation that had put aside the recognized political elite of the colonial and early national periods and had not yet succumbed to the interest-group politics of the twentieth century. Addressing a fragmented electorate in litanies that reinforced cultural and social diversity, seldom in broad ideological terms, and granting particularistic distributive benefits rather than comprehensive policy demands, the parties flourished in a society more fluid than it had ever been before or would be again. But as the growing nation modernized, new loyalties and new demands on government threatened the existing patterns of politics. Functional economic organizations began to make stronger policy demands than individuals or ethnoreligious groups ever had. Fresh needs arose that required supplementing distributive decisions with regulatory and redistributive ones. Parties handled these changes with difficulty, and by the early 1900s the party period's practices no longer matched the country's social circumstances.

Changes in politics and governance at the beginning of the twentieth century marked the start of a new political era, distinct in its patterns of participation and policy-making from the party period before it. Early in the 1900s, electoral turnout fell and party loyalties became weaker, while new avenues of political participation opened up. In the same years, distributive policies came under sustained assault, while the government's regulatory and administrative functions were strengthened. Brief consideration of what destroyed the party period's characteristic practices may bring the epoch itself into fuller perspective and distinguish it from the political era that followed.

In the presidential election of 1904, voter turnout fell below 70 percent for the first time since 1836; eight years later turnout again dropped sharply, to below 60 percent. While they were highest in the South, the participation losses affected virtually every part of the country. Voter turnout has never returned to its nineteenth-century levels. Beginning in the same year, 1904, high rates of ticket-splitting marked another dimension of the decline in partisan voting. Commentators observed the apathy that seemed to overcome the voters and remarked on the loss of the old excitement that had traditionally accompanied campaigns and elections.

Three things caused the changes in voting behavior. First, the realignment of the 1890s had brought one-party dominance to more places than at any time since before the Jackson period. Athough the effects on turnout were not felt immediately, over the course of a decade the loss of competition slowly discouraged participation. A second cause lay in efforts to disfranchise allegedly discordant social elements. Southern blacks and poor whites, by participating in the Populist movement, and new immigrants, by supporting the most corrupt city machines and flirting with socialism, convinced elites everywhere that unlimited suffrage fueled disorder. Under the banner of 'reform', they enacted registration requirements, ballot laws, and other measures to restrict suffrage and reduce the discipline of party machines.

The third challenge to traditional party voting emanated from the rise of interest-group identities and activities that competed with partisan ones. As urban and industrial growth caused people to become more conscious of their distinct economic interests, they joined together to fulfill the needs of their separate groups. Unable to speak with what Samuel P. Hays calls 'a clear-cut, single-interest voice', parties—with their broad coalitions—lost the full loyalty of those who now formed functional economic organizations to represent them.[9]

The same broad forces that changed electoral behaviour also contributed to the transformation of policy patterns. Where nineteenth-century conditions had suggested the plausibility of 'the harmony of interests', or at least permitted divergent groups to utilize and interpret government benefits according to their own lights, the scarcities and complexities of an urban-industrial society now made it too plain to deny that government actions helping one group often hurt another. The main casualty was a policy structure based on distributive goods.

All the conditions that had encouraged unrestrained distribution succumbed to new circumstances. The frontier's disappearance only symbolized the scarcity. Rights and immunities bestowed by government clashed inevitably with the rights of others and brought on legal battles or worse. At the same time, the belief in public aid to private enterprise waned. Uncovered by muckrakers, scandals disclosing the extent to which favor-seeking businessmen corrupted government suggested regulation as a more fitting approach to business than promotion. Finally, the growth of large, organized interests, each seeking help from government at the expense of others, reduced the divisibility of distributive goods and heightened the conflict over their allocation. The government scarcely stopped giving things away, but distribution no longer enjoyed the confidence it once had or formed the government's main means of relating to private enterprise.

Into the policy process came what Hurst calls 'a new disposition of calculation . . . a new inclination to think in matter-of-fact terms about cause and effect in social relations and to cast up balance sheets of profit and loss in matters of community-wide effect'. Such calculation required new and expanded methods of governance. This meant regulation with effective enforcement provisions. It also meant administration to collect information and to perform the calculations that a more rational approach to government required. Emerging at almost exactly the same time as the electoral changes of the early 1900s, the new policy structure flowered during 'the creative decade from about 1905 to 1915'. These were the years when, at the federal level, the Interstate Commerce Commission finally acquired significant strength and, in the states, newly enlarged and empowered public service commissions began their work. At both levels of government, independent administrative boards invigorated old public functions and assumed new ones.[10]

The transition from distribution to regulation and administration often proved to be complex and subtle, rather than clear-cut. Sometimes the change involved strengthening the regulatory aspects of ongoing policies and curtailing the distributive features. Utility franchises, given away so freely by city governments in the 1870s and 1880s, now came with many more strings attached. Sometimes existing policy areas, such as taxation or utility regulation, were transferred from the legislature, where particularistic forces held sway, to independent agencies, where calculation and planning supposedly prevailed. The changes by no means always hurt the regulated interests, and the promotion of economic development did not cease to be a governmental purpose. Cooperation between public and private interests certainly did not stop. But now government explicitly took account of the clash of interests and fashioned definite means to adjust, regulate, and mitigate the consequences of social disharmony.

The new patterns of voting behavior and policy-making effectively strengthened one another. In several ways the policy changes almost certainly helped to reduce electoral participation. So long as distribution formed the government's main approach to economic matters, individuals and groups routinely became aware only of government actions they favored. But with the adoption of divisive economic policies that assisted some groups at the expense of others, almost everyone found the government doing some things he disliked. Although there are no opinion polls to document the change, it is probable that fewer people now found satisfaction in the process of governance or in its general policy patterns. In Easton's terms, 'diffuse support' for the political system probably declined, and voter turnout fell with it.

The rise of agencies and bureaucracies to perform the burgeoning tasks of regulation and administration encouraged forms of political participation that reduced the importance of voting. Ranging from formal hearings before regulatory agencies to routine communications with administrative officials, these new kinds of contact with government required money and special skills to carry on, just as electioneering did.

Inevitably they reduced the resources and manpower available in the electoral arena.

Correspondingly, the decline of loyal, partisan voting strengthened the new policy patterns by weakening the party leaders' old ability to promote distribution and forestall regulation and administration. The removal of discordant social groups from the electorate helped make the government mainly responsive to well-organized economic interests, each served by specialized agencies. These processes of change proved to be cumulative, and, with the progressive decay of the old patterns, voting and policy-making ceased to have so complementary a relationship as they did during the nineteenth century when parties structured both.

It would be misleading to exaggerate the extent of political change at the beginning of the twentieth century. Despite election laws designed to weaken party machines, the structure of party organizations remained traditional, and in the year-in-and-year-out choice of men for public office the parties yielded to no one. Distributive decision-making continued to be an element of legislation, and parties retained a strong voice in shaping such allocation. Even the new administrative agencies, with their client interest groups, sometimes performed their functions in ways that called to mind the old policy patterns.

Yet the political changes of the early twentieth century marked the end of an era when party voting provided the main means of political participation and the distribution of resources and privileges formed the government's most characteristic activity. Basically determined by the conditions and expectations of nineteenth-century Americans, voting and economic policy had met and interacted through the parties that managed them both. When industrialism brought new social conditions, politics mirrored the changes. Participation and policy-making assumed new forms, while the parties only weakly carried on their old function of bringing the two together.

NOTES

[1] Thomas C. Cochran, 'The "Presidential synthesis" in American history", *American Historical Review*, LIII (July 1948), 748–59.

[2] Walter Dean Burnham, 'Party systems and the political process', in *American Party Systems*, ed. Chambers and Burnham, 277–307; Burnham, *Critical Elections and the Mainsprings of American Politics* (New York, 1970).

[3] To date, historians have found the ethnoreligious interpretation mainly applicable outside the South. Even the South, however, shared the other electoral characteristics noted here, including high participation, long-term stability, and voting choices grounded in community values.

[4] James Willard Hurst, 'Legal elements in United States history', *Perspectives in American History*, V (1971), 63; James Willard Hurst, *Law and Social*

Process in United States History (Ann Arbor, 1960), 28, 63–69, 104, 120–25;
Hurst, *Law and the Conditions of Freedom in the Nineteenth Century United
States* (Madison, 1956).

[5] Harry N. Schreiber, 'Federalism and the American economy 1789–1910', *Law and
Society Review*, 10 (Fall, 1975), 89.

[6] Robert A. Lively, 'The American system: a review', *Business History Review*,
xxix, 1955; 94; Carter Goodrich, 'The revulsion against internal improvement',
Journal of Economic History, X (Nov. 1950), 169.

[7] Lee Benson, *The Concept of Jacksonian Democracy; New York as a Test Case*
(Princeton, 1961), 105.

[8] David Easton, *A Systems Analysis of Political Life* (New York, 1965).

[9] Samuël P. Hays, *The Response to Industrialism, 1885–1914* (Chicago, 1957);
Hays, 'Political parties and the community-society continuum', in *The
American Party Systems: Stages of Political Development*, ed. W. Chambers and
W.D. Burnham (New York, 1967), 167.

[10] Hurst, *Law and the Conditions of Freedom*, 73, 71–108; Hurst, *Law and Social
Order in the United States* (Ithaca, 1977), 33, 36.

PART II

Class and Class Conflict

(a) Work, Culture and Society in Industrializing America

HERBERT G. GUTMAN

I

The work ethic remains a central theme in the American experience, and to study this subject afresh means to re-examine much that has been assumed as given in the writing of American working-class and social history. Such study, moreover, casts new light on yet other aspects of the larger American experience that are usually not associated with the study of ordinary working men and women. Until quite recently, few historians questioned as fact the ease with which most past Americans affirmed the 'Protestant' work ethic. Persons much more prestigious and influential than mere historians have regularly praised the powerful historical presence of such an ethic in the national culture. A single recent example suffices. In celebrating Labor Day in 1971, the nation's president saluted 'the dignity of work, the value of achievement, [and] the morality of self-reliance. None of these', he affirmed, 'is going out of style.' And yet he worried somewhat. 'Let us also recognize', he admitted, 'that the work ethic in America is undergoing some changes'. The tone of his concern strongly suggested that it had never changed before and even that men like Henry Ford and F. W. Taylor had been among the signers of the Mayflower Compact or, better still, the Declaration of Independence.

It was never that simple. At all times in American history—when the country was still a preindustrial society, while it industrialized, and after it had become the world's leading industrial nation—quite diverse Americans, some of them more prominent and powerful than others, made it clear in their thought and behavior that the Protestant work ethic was not deeply ingrained in the nation's social fabric. Some merely noticed its

H. G. Gutman, *Essays in American Working-class and Social History*, Oxford, Basil Blackwell, 1977; pp. 3–78. Abridged. First published in *The American Historical Review*, 1973.

absence, others advocated its imposition, and still others represented an entirely different work ethic. [. . .] Even in the land of Benjamin Franklin, Andrew Carnegie, and Henry Ford, nonindustrial cultures and work habits regularly thrived and were nourished by new workers alien to the 'Protestant' work ethic. It was John Adams, not Max Weber, who claimed that 'manufactures cannot live, much less thrive, without honor, fidelity, punctuality, and private faith, a sacred respect for property, and the moral obligations of promises and contracts'. Only a 'decisive, as well as an intelligent and honest, government', Adams believed, could develop such 'virtues' and 'habits'. Others among the Founding Fathers worried about the absence of such virtues within the laboring classes. When Alexander Hamilton proposed his grand scheme to industrialize the young republic, an intimate commented, 'Unless God should send us saints for workmen and angels to conduct them, there is the greatest reason to fear for the success of the plan'. Benjamin Franklin shared such fears. He condemned poor relief in 1768 and lamented the absence among English workers of regular work habits. 'Saint *Monday*,' he said, 'is as duly kept by our working people as *Sunday*; the only difference is that instead of employing their time cheaply at church they are wasting it expensively at the ale house'. Franklin believed that if poorhouses shut down 'Saint Monday and Saint Tuesday' would 'soon cease to be holidays'.

Franklin's worries should not surprise us. The Founding Fathers, after all, lived in a preindustrial, not simply an 'agrarian' society, and the prevalence of premodern work habits among their contemporaries was natural. What matters here, however, is that Benjamin Franklin's ghost haunted later generations of Americans. Just before the first World War the International Harvester Corporation, converted to 'scientific management' and 'welfare capitalism', prepared a brochure to teach its Polish common laborers the English language. 'Lesson One', entitled 'General', read:

I hear the whistle. I must hurry.
I hear the five minute whistle.
It is time to go into the shop.
I take my check from the gate board and hang it on the department board.
I change my clothes and get ready to work.
The starting whistle blows.
I eat my lunch.
It is forbidden to eat until then.
The whistle blows at five minutes of starting time.
I get ready to go to work.
I work until the whistle blows to quit.
I leave my place nice and clean.
I put all my clothes in the locker.
I must go home.

This document illustrates a great deal. That it shows the debasement of the

English language, a process closely related to the changing ethnic composition of the American working population and the social need for simplified English commands, is a subject for another study. Our immediate interest is in the relationship it implies between Americanization, factory work habits, and improved labor efficiency.[1]

Nearly a century and a half separated the International Harvester Corporation from Benjamin Franklin, but both wanted to reshape the work habits of others about them. Machines required that men and women adapt older work routines to new necessities and strained those wedded to premodern patterns of labor. Half a century separated similar popular laments about the impact of the machine on traditional patterns of labor. In 1873 the Chicago *Workingman's Advocate* published 'The Sewing Machine', a poem in which the author scorned Elias Howe's invention by comparing it to his wife:

> Mine is not one of those stupid affairs
> That stands in the corner with what-nots and chairs . . .
> Mine is one of the kind to love,
> And wears a shawl and a soft kid glove . . .
> None of your patent machines for me,
> Unless Dame Nature's the patentee!
> I like the sort that can laugh and talk,
> And take my arm for an evening walk;
> And will do whatever the owner may choose,
> With the slightest perceptible turn of the screws.
> One that can dance—and possibly flirt—
> And make a pudding as well as a shirt;
> One that can sing without dropping a stitch,
> And play the housewife, lady, and witch . . .
> What do you think of my machine,
> Ain't it the best that ever was seen?
> 'Tisn't a clumsy, mechanical toy,
> But flesh and blood! Hear that my boy.

Fifty years later, when significant numbers of Mexicans lived in Chicago and its industrial suburbs and labored in its railroad yards, packing houses, and steel mills (in 1926, 35 percent of Chicago Inland Steel's labor force had come from Mexico), 'El Enganchado' (The Hooked One'), a popular Spanish tune, celebrated the disappointments of immigrant factory workers:

> I came under contract from Lorelia.
> To earn dollars was my dream,
> I bought shoes and I bought a hat
> And even put on trousers.
> For they told me that here the dollars
> Were scattered about in heaps
> That there were girls and theatres
> And that here everything was fun.

And now I'm overwhelmed—
I am a shoemaker by trade
But here they say I'm a camel
And good only for pick and shovel.
What good is it to know my trade
If there are manufacturers by the score
And while I make two little shoes
They turn out more than a million?
Many Mexicans don't care to speak
The language their mother taught them
And go about saying they are Spanish
And denying their country's flag . . .
My kids speak perfect English
And have no use for Spanish,
They call me 'fadder' and don't work
And are crazy about the Charleston.
I am tired of all this nonsense
I'm going back to Michogan.

American society differed greatly in each of the periods when these documents were written. Franklin personified the successful preindustrial American artisan. The 'sewing girl' lived through the decades that witnessed the transformation of preindustrial into industrial America. Harvester proved the nation's world-wide industrial supremacy before the First World War. The Mexican song served as an ethnic Jazz Age pop tune. A significant strand, however, tied these four documents together. And in unraveling that strand at particular moments in the nation's history between 1815 and 1920, a good deal is learned about recurrent tensions over work habits that shaped the national experience.

The traditional imperial boundaries (a function, perhaps, of the professional subdivision of labor) that have fixed the territory open to American labor historians for exploration have closed off to them the study of such important subjects as changing work habits and the culture of work. Neither the questions American labor historians usually ask nor the methods they use encourage such inquiry. With a few significant exceptions, for more than half a century American labor history has continued to reflect both the strengths and the weaknesses of the conceptual scheme sketched by its founding fathers, John R. Commons and others of the so-called Wisconsin school of labor history. Even their most severe critics, including the orthodox 'Marxist' labour historians of the 1930s, 1940s, and 1950s and the few New Left historians who have devoted attention to American labor history, rarely questioned that conceptual framework. Commons and his colleagues asked large questions, gathered important source materials, and put forth impressive ideas. Together with able disciples, they studied the development of the trade union as an institution and explained its place in a changing labor market. But they gave attention primarily to those few workers who belonged to trade unions and neglected much else of importance about the American working population. Two flaws especially marred this older labor history. Because so few workers belonged to permanent trade unions before 1940, its overall conceptualization excluded most working people from detailed and serious study. More than this, its methods encouraged labor historians to spin a cocoon around American workers, isolating them from their own particular subcultures and from the larger national culture. An increasingly narrow 'economic' analysis caused the study of American working-class history to grow more constricted and become more detached from larger developments in American social and cultural history and from the writing of American social and cultural history itself. After 1945 American working-class history remained imprisoned by self-imposed limitations and therefore fell far behind the more imaginative and innovative British and Continental European work in the field. [. . .]

The pages that follow give little attention to the subject matter usually considered the proper sphere of labor history (trade-union development and behavior, strikes and lockouts, and radical movements) and instead emphasize the frequent tension between different groups of men and women new to the machine and a changing American society. [. . .]

The focus in these pages is on free white labor in quite different time periods: 1815–1843, 1843–1893, 1893–1919. The precise years serve only as guideposts to mark the fact that American society differed greatly in each period. Between 1815 and 1843, the United States remained a predominantly preindustrial society and most workers drawn to its few factories were the products of rural and village preindustrial culture. Preindustrial American society was not premodern in the same way that European peasant societies were, but it was, nevertheless, premodern. In the half-century after 1843 industrial development radically transformed the earlier American social structure, and during this Middle Period (an era not framed around the coming and the aftermath of the Civil War) a profound tension existed between the older American preindustrial social structure and the modernizing institutions that accompanied the development of industrial capitalism. After 1893 the United States ranked as a mature industrial society. In each of these distinctive stages of change in American society, a recurrent tension also existed between native and immigrant men and women fresh to the factory and the demands imposed upon them by the regularities and disciplines of factory labor. That state of tension was regularly revitalized by the migration of diverse premodern native and foreign peoples into an industrializing or a fully industrialized society. The British economic historian Sidney Pollard has described well this process whereby 'a society of peasants, craftsmen, and versatile labourers became a society of modern industrial workers.' 'There was more to overcome', Pollard writes of industrializing England, than the change of employment or the new rhythm of work: there was a whole new culture to be absorbed and an old one to be traduced and spurned, there were new surroundings, often in a different part of the country, new relations with employers, and new uncertainties of livelihood, new friends and neighbors, new marriage patterns and behavior patterns of children within the family and without.[2]

That same process occurred in the United States. Just as in all modernizing countries, the United States faced the difficult task of industrializing whole cultures, but in this country the process was regularly repeated, each stage of American economic growth and development involving different first-generation factory workers. The social transformation Pollard described occurred in England between 1770 and 1850, and in those decades premodern British cultures and the modernizing institutions associated primarily with factory and machine labor collided and interacted. A painful transition occurred, dominated the ethos of an entire era, and then faded in relative importance. After 1850 and until quite recently, the British working class reproduced itself and retained a relative national homogeneity. New tensions emerged but not those of a society continually busy (and worried about) industrializing persons born out of that society and often alien in birth and color and in work habits, customary values, and behavior. 'Traditional social habits and customs,' J. F. C. Harrison reminds us, 'seldom fitted into the patterns of industrial life, and they had ... to be discredited as hindrances to progress'. That happened regularly in the United States after 1815 as the nation absorbed and worked to transform new groups of preindustrial peoples, native whites among them. The result, however, was neither a static tension nor the mere recurrence of similar cycles, because American society itself changed as did the composition of its laboring population. But the source of the tension remained the same, and conflict often resulted. It was neither the conflict emphasized by the older Progressive historians (agrarianism versus capitalism, or sectional disagreement) nor that emphasized by recent critics of that early twentieth-century synthesis (conflict between competing elites). It resulted instead from the fact that the American working class was continually altered in its composition by infusions, from within and without the nation, of peasants, farmers, skilled artisans, and casual day laborers who brought into industrial society ways of work and other habits and values not associated with industrial necessities and the industrial ethos. Some shed these older ways to conform to new imperatives. Others fell victim or fled, moving from place to place. Some sought to extend and adapt older patterns of work and life to a new society. Others challenged the social system through varieties of collective associations. But for all—at different historical moments—the transition to industrial society, as E. P. Thompson has written, 'entailed a severe restructuring of working habits—new disciplines, new incentives, and a new human nature upon which these incentives could bite effectively'.[3] [. . .]

Men and women who sell their labor to an employer bring more to a new or changing work situation than their physical presence. What they bring to a factory depends, in good part, on their culture of origin, and how they behave is shaped by the interaction between that culture and the particular society into which they enter. Because so little is yet known about preindustrial American culture and subcultures, some caution is necessary in moving from the level of generalization to historical actuality. What follows compares and contrasts working people new to industrial society but living in quite different time periods. First, the expectations and work habits of first-generation predominantly native American factory workers before 1843 are compared with first-generation immigrant factory workers between 1893 and 1920. Similarities in the work habits and expectations of men and women who experienced quite different premodern cultures are indicated. Second, the work habits and culture of artisans in the industrializing decades (1843–1893) are examined to indicate the persistence of powerful cultural continuities in that era of radical economic change. Third, evidence of premodern working-class behavior that parallels European patterns of premodern working-class behavior in the early phases of industrialization is briefly described to suggest that throughout the entire period (1815–1920) the changing composition of the American working class caused the recurrence of 'premodern' patterns of collective behavior usually only associated with the early phases of industrialization. And, finally, attention is given to some of the larger implications resulting from this recurrent tension between work, culture, and society.

II

The work habits and the aspirations and expectations of men and women new to factory life and labor are examined first. Common work habits rooted in diverse premodern cultures (different in many ways but nevertheless all ill fitted to the regular routines demanded by machine-centered factory processes) existed among distinctive first-generation factory workers all through American history. We focus on two quite different time periods: the years before 1843 when the factory and machine were still new to America and the years between 1893 and 1917 when the country had become the world's industrial colossus. In both periods workers new to factory production brought strange and seemingly useless work habits to the factory gate. The irregular and undisciplined work patterns of factory hands before 1843 frustrated cost-conscious manufacturers and caused frequent complaint among them. Textile factory work rules often were designed to tame such rude customs. A New Hampshire cotton factory that hired mostly women and children forbade 'spirituous liquor, smoking, nor any kind of amusement . . . in the workshops, yards, or factories' and promised the 'immediate and disgraceful dismissal' of employees found gambling, drinking, or committing 'any other debaucheries'. A Massachusetts firm nearby insisted that young workers unwilling to attend church stay 'within doors and improve their time in reading, writing, and in other valuable and harmless employment'. Tardy and absent Philadelphia workers paid fines and could not 'carry into the factory nuts, fruits, etc.; books or paper'. A Connecticut textile mill owner justified the twelve-hour day and the six-day week because it kept 'workmen and children' from 'vicious amusements'. He forbade 'gaming . . . in any private house'. Manufacturers elsewhere worried about the example 'idle' men set for women and children. Massachusetts family heads who rented 'a piece of land on shares' to grow corn and potatoes while their wives and children labored in factories worried one manufacturer. 'I would prefer giving constant employment at some sacrifice,' he said, 'to having a man of the village seen in the streets on a rainy day at leisure.' Men who worked in Massachussetts woollen mills upset expected work routines in other ways. 'The wool business requires more man labour,' said a manufacturer, 'and this we study to avoid. Women are much more ready to follow good regulations, are not captious, and do not clan as the men do against the overseers.' Male factory workers posed other difficulties, too. In 1817 a shipbuilder in Medford, Massachusetts, refused his men grog privileges. They quit work, but he managed to finish a ship without using further spirits, 'a remarkable achievement'. An English visitor in 1832 heard an American complain that British workers in the Paterson cotton and machine shops drank excessively and figured as 'the most beastly people I have ever seen'. Four years later a New Jersey manufacturer of hats and caps boasted in a public card that he finally had '4 and 20 good, permanent workmen', not one infected with 'the brutal leprosy of blue Monday habits and the moral gangrene of 'trades union' principles'. Other manufacturers had less good fortune. Absenteeism occurred frequently among the Pennsylvania ironworkers at the rural Hopewell Village forge; hunting, harvesting, wedding parties, frequent 'frolicking' that sometimes lasted for days, and uproarious Election and Independence Day celebrations plagued the mill operators. In the early nineteenth century, a New Jersey iron manufacturer filled his diary with notations about irregular work habits: 'all hands drunk'; 'Jacob Ventling hunting'; 'molders all agree to quit work and went to the beach'; 'Peter Cox very drunk and gone to bed. Mr. Evans made a solemn resolution any person or persons bringing liquor to the work enough to make drunk shall be liable to a fine'; 'Edward Rutter off a-drinking. It was reported he got drunk on cheese.'

Employers responded differently to such behavior by first-generation factory hands. 'Moral reform' as well as what Sidney Pollard calls carrot-

and-stick policies meant to tame or to transform such work habits. Fining was common. Hopewell Furnace managers deducted on dollar from Samuel York's wages 'for getting intoxesitated [sic] with liquer [sic] and neglecting hauling 4 loads wash Dird at Joneses'. Special material rewards encouraged steady work. A Hopewell Village blacksmith contracted for nineteen dollars a month, and 'if he does his work well we are to give him a pair of coarse boots'. In these and later years manufacturers in Fall River and Paterson institutionalized traditional customs and arranged for festivals and parades to celebrate with their workers a new mill, a retiring superintendent, or a finished locomotive. Some rewarded disciplined workers in special ways. When Paterson locomotive workers pressed for higher wages, their employer instructed an underling: 'Book keeper, make up a roll of the men . . . making *fulltime;* if they can't support their families on the wages they are now getting, they must have more. But the other men, who are drunk every Monday morning, I don't want them around the shop under any circumstances.' Where factory work could be learned easily, new hands replaced irregular old ones. A factory worker in New England remembered that years before the Civil War her employer had hired 'all American girls' but later shifted to immigrant laborers because 'not coming from country homes, but living as the Irish do, in the town, they take no vacations, and can be relied on at the mill all year round'. Not all such devices worked to the satisfaction of the workers or their employers. Sometime in the late 1830s merchant capitalists sent a skilled British silk weaver to manage a new mill in Nantucket that would employ the wives and children of local whalers and fishermen. Machinery was installed, and in the first days women and children besieged the mill for work. After a month had passed, they started dropping off in small groups. Soon nearly all had returned 'to their shore gazing and to their seats by the sea'. The Nantucket mill shut down, its hollow frame an empty monument to the unwillingness of resident women and children to conform to the regularities demanded by rising manufacturers.

First-generation factory workers were not unique to premodern America. And the work habits common to such workers plagued American manufacturers in later generations when manufacturers and most native urban whites scarcely remembered that native Americans had once been hesitant first-generation factory workers. To shift forward in time to East and South European immigrants new to steam, machinery, and electricity and new to the United States itself is to find much that seems the same. American society, of course, had changed greatly, but in some ways it is as if a film—run at a much faster speed—is being viewed for the second time: primitive work rules for unskilled labor, fines, gang labor, and subcontracting were commonplace. In 1910 two-thirds of the workers in twenty-one major manufacturing and mining industries came from Eastern and Southern Europe or were native American blacks, and studies of these 'new immigrants' record much evidence of preindustrial work habits among the men and women new to American industry. According to Moses Rischin, skilled immigrant Jews carried to New York City town and village employment patterns, such as the *landsmannschaft* economy and a preference for small shops as opposed to larger factories, that sparked frequent disorders but hindered stable trade unions until 1910. Specialization spurred anxiety: in Chicago Jewish glovemakers resisted the subdivision of labor even though it promised better wages. 'You shrink from doing either kind of work itself, nine hours a day,' said two observers of these immigrant women. 'You cling to the variety . . . , the mental luxury of first, finger-sides, and then, five separate leather pieces, for relaxation, to play with! *Here* is a luxury worth fighting for!' American work rules also conflicted with religious imperatives. On the eighth day after the birth of a son, Orthodox Jews in Eastern Europe held a festival, 'an occasion of much rejoicing'. But the American work week had a different logic, and if the day fell during the week the celebration occurred the following Sunday. 'The host . . . and his guests,' David Blaustein remarked, 'know it is not the right day,' and 'they fall to mourning over the conditions that will not permit them to observe the old custom.' The occasion became 'one for secret sadness rather than rejoicing'. Radical Yiddish poets, like Morris Rosenfeld, the presser of men's clothing, measured in verse the psychic and social costs exacted by American industrial work rules:

> The clock in the workshop,—it rests not a moment;
> It points on, and ticks on: eternity—time;
> Once someone told me the clock had a meaning,—
> In pointing and ticking had reason and rhyme. . . .
> At times, when I listen, I hear the clock plainly:—
> The reason of old—the old meaning—is gone!
> The maddening pendulum urges me forward
> To labor and still labor on.
> The tick of the clock is the boss in his anger.
> The face of the clock has the eyes of the foe.
> The clock—I shudder—Dost hear how it draws me?
> It calls me 'Machine' and it cries [to] me 'Sew'!

Slavic and Italian immigrants carried with them to industrial America subcultures quite different from that of village Jews, but their work habits were just as alien to the modern factory. Rudolph Vecoli has reconstructed Chicago's South Italian community to show that adult male seasonal construction gangs as constrasted to factory labor were one of many traditional customs adapted to the new environment, and in her study of South Italian peasant immigrants Phyllis H. Williams found among them men who never adjusted to factory labor. After 'years' of 'excellent' factory work, some 'began . . . to have minor accidents' and others 'suddenly give up and are found in their homes complaining of a vague indisposition with no apparent physical basis'. Such labor worried early twentieth-century efficiency experts, and so did Slavic festivals, church holidays, and 'prolonged merriment'. 'Man,' Adam Smith observed, 'is, of all sorts of luggage, the most difficult to be transported.' That was just as true for these Slavic immigrants as for the early nineteenth-century native American factory workers. A Polish wedding in a Pennsylvania mining or mill town lasted between three and five days. Greek and Roman Catholics shared the same jobs but had different holy days, 'an annoyance to many employers'. The Greek Church had 'more than eighty festivals in the year', and 'the Slav religiously observes the days on which the saints are commemorated and invariably takes a holiday'. A celebration of the American Day of Independence in Mahanoy City, Pennsylvania, caught the eye of a hostile observer. Men parading the streets drew a handcart with a barrel of lager in it. Over the barrel 'stood a comrade, goblet in hand and crowned with a garland of laurel, singing some jargon'. Another sat and played an accordion. At intervals, the men stopped to 'drink the good beverage they celebrated in song'. The witness called the entertainment 'an imitation of the honor paid Bacchus which was one of the most joyous festivals of ancient Rome' and felt it proof of 'a lower type of civilization'. Great Lakes dock workers 'believed that a vessel could not be unloaded unless they had from four to five kegs of beer'. (And in the early irregular strikes among male Jewish garment workers, employers negotiated with them out of doors and after each settlement 'would roll out a keg of beer for their entertainment of the workers'.) Contemporary betters could not comprehend such behavior. Worried over a three-day Slavic wedding frolic, a woman concluded: 'You don't think they have souls, do you? No, they are beasts, and in their lust they'll perish.' Another disturbed observer called drink 'un-American, . . . a curse worse than the white plague'. About that time, a young Italian boy lay ill in a hospital. The only English words he knew were 'boots' and 'hurry up'.

More than irregular work habits bound together the behavior of first-generation factory workers separated from one another by time and by the larger structure of the society they first encountered. Few distinctive American working-class populations differed in so many essentials (their sex, their religions, their nativity, and their prior rural and village cultures) as the Lowell mill girls and women of the Era of Good Feelings and the South and East European steelworkers of the Progressive Era. To describe similarities in their expectations of factory labor is not to blur these important differences but to suggest that otherwise quite distinctive men and women interpreted such work in similar ways. The Boston Associates, pioneer American industrialists, had built up Lowell and other towns like it to overcome early nineteenth-century rural and village prejudices and fears about factory work and life and in their regulation of lower-class social habits hoped to assure a steady flow of young rural women ('girls') to and from the looms. 'The sagacity of self-interest as well as more disinterested considerations,' explained a Lowell clergyman in 1845, 'had led to the adoption of a strict system of moral police.' Without 'sober, orderly, and moral' workers, profits would be 'absorbed by cases of irregularity, carelessness, and neglect'. The Lowell capitalists thrived by hiring rural women who supplemented a distant family's income, keeping them a few years, and then renewing the process. Such steady labor turnover kept the country from developing a permanent proletariat and so was thought to assure stability. Lowell's busy cotton mills, well-ordered boarding-houses, temples of religion and culture, factory girls, and moral police so impressed Anthony Trollope that he called the entire enterprise a 'philanthropic manufacturing college'. John Quincy Adams thought the New England cotton mills 'palaces of the Poor', and Henry Clay marveled over places like the Lowell mills. 'Who has not been delighted with the clock-work movements of a large cotton factory?' asked the father of the American System. The French traveler Michel Chevalier had a less sanguine reaction. He found Lowell 'neat and decent, peaceable and sage', but worried, 'Will this become like Lancashire? Does this brilliant glare hide the misery and suffering of the working girls?'

Historians of the Lowell mill girls find little evidence before 1840 of organized protest among them and attribute their collective passivity to corporation policing policies, the frequent turnover in the labor force, the irregular pace of work (after it was rationalized in the 1840s, it provoked collective protest), the freedom the mill girls enjoyed away from rural family dominance, and their relatively decent earnings. The women managed the transition to mill life because they did not expect to remain factory workers too long. Nevertheless frequent inner tension revealed itself among the mobile mill women. In an early year, a single mill discharged twenty-eight women for such reasons as 'misconduct', 'captiousness', 'disobedience', 'impudence', 'levity', and even 'mutiny'. The difficult transition from rural life to factory work also caused tensions outside the mills. Rural girls and women, Harriet Robinson later recalled, came to Lowell in 'outlandish fashions' and with 'queer names,' 'Samantha, Triphena, Plumy, Kezia, Aseneth, Elgardy, Leafy, Ruhamah, Almaretta, Sarpeta, and Florilla . . . among them'. They spoke a 'very peculiar' dialect ('a language almost unintelligible'). 'On the broken English and Scotch of their ancestors,' said Robinson, 'was engrafted the nasal Yankee twang.' Some soon learned the 'city way of speaking'; others changed their names to 'Susan' or 'Jane'; and for still others new clothing, especially straw hats, became important. But the machines they worked still left them depressed and with feelings of anxiety. 'I never cared much for machinery', Lucy Larcom said of her early Lowell years. 'I could not see into their complications or feel interested in them. . . . In sweet June weather I would lean far out of the window, and try not to hear the unceasing clash of sound inside.' She kept a plant beside her and recollected an overseer who confiscated newspaper clippings and even the pages of a 'torn Testament' some women had slipped into the factory. Years after she had left the textile mills, Lucy Larcom ridiculed her mill-girl poems: 'I continued to dismalize myself at times quite unnecessarily.' Their titles included 'The Early Doomed' and 'The Complaint of a Nobody' (in which she compared herself to 'a weed growing up in a garden'). When she finally quit the mill, the paymaster asked, 'Going where you can earn more money?' 'No', she remembered answering, 'I am going where I can have more time.' 'Ah, yes!' he responded, 'time is money.'

Even the *Lowell Offering* testified to the tensions between mill routines and rural rhythms and feelings. Historians have dismissed it too handily because the company sponsored it and refused to publish prose openly critical of mill policies. But the fiction and poetry of its contributors, derivative in style and frequently escapist, also often revealed dissatisfactions with the pace of work. Susan, explaining her first day in the mill to Ann, said the girls awoke early and one sang, 'Morning bells, I hate to hear,/Ringing dolefully, loud and clear.'. Susan went on:

> You cannot think how odd everything seemed to me. I wanted to laugh at everything, but did not know what to make sport of first. They set me to threading shuttles, and tying weaver's knots and such things, and now I have improved so that I can take care of one loom. I could take care of two if I only had eyes in the back of my head. . . . When I went out at night, the sound of the mill was in my ears, as of crickets, frogs, and Jew-harps, all mingled together in strange discord. After, it seemed as though cotton-wool was in my ears. But now I do not mind it at all. You know that people learn to sleep with the thunder of Niagara in their ears, and the cotton mill is no worse.

Ellen Collins quit the mill complaining about her 'obedience to the ding-dong of the bell—just as though we were so many living machines'. In 'A Weaver's Reverie,' Ella explained why the mill women wrote 'so much about the beauties of nature':

> Why is it that the delirious deams of the famine-stricken are of tables loaded with the richest viands? . . . Oh, tell me why this is, and I will tell you why the factory girl sits in the hours of meditation and thinks, not of the crowded, clattering mill, nor of the noisy tenement which is her home.

Contemporary labor critics who scorned the *Lowell Offering* as little more than the work of 'poor, caged birds', who 'while singing of the roses . . . forget the bars of their prison', had not read it carefully. Their attachment to nature was the concern of persons working machines in a society still predominantly 'a garden', and it was not unique to these Lowell women. In New Hampshire five hundred men and women petitioned the Amoskeag Manufacturing Company's proprietors in 1853 not to cut down an elm tree to allow room for an additional mill: 'It was a beautiful and goodly tree' and belonged to a time 'when the yell of the red man and the scream of the eagle were alone heard on the banks of the Merrimack, instead of two giant edifices filled with the buzz of busy and well-remunerated industry.' Each day, the workers said, they viewed that tree as 'a connecting link between the past and the present,' and 'each autumn [it] remind[s] us of our own mortality.'

Aspirations and expectations interpret experience and thereby help shape behavior. Some Lowell mill girls revealed dissatisfactions, and others made a difficult transition from rural New England to that model factory town, but that so few planned to remain mill workers eased that transition and hampered collective protest. Men as well as women who expect to spend only a few years as factory workers have little incentive to join unions. That was just as true of the immigrant male common laborers in the steel mills of the late nineteenth and early twentieth centuries (when multiplant oligopoly characterized the nation's most important manufacturing industry) as in the Lowell cotton mills nearly a century earlier. David Brody has explained much about the common laborers. In those years, the steel companies successfully divorced wages from productivity to allow the market to shape them. Between 1890 and 1910, efficiencies in plant organization cut labor costs by about a third. The great Carnegie Pittsburgh plants employed 14,359 common laborers, 11,694 of them South and East Europeans. Most, peasant in origin, earned less than $12.50 a week (a family needed fifteen dollars for subsistence). A staggering accident rate damaged these and other men: nearly 25 percent of the recent immigrants employed at the Carnegie South Works were injured or killed each year between 1907 and 1910, 3,723 in all. But like the Lowell mill women, these men rarely protested in collective ways, and for good reason. They did not plan to stay in the steel mills long. Most had come to the United States as single men (or married men who had left their families behind) to work briefly in the mills, save some money, return home, and purchase farmland. Their private letters to European relatives indicated a realistic awareness of their working life that paralleled some of the Lowell fiction: 'if I don't earn $1.50 a day, it would not be worth thinking about America'; 'a golden land so long as there is work'; 'here in America one must work for three horses'; 'let him not risk coming, for he is too young'; 'too weak for America'. Men who wrote such letters and avoided injury often saved small amounts of money, and a significant number fulfilled their expectations and quit the factory and even the country. Forty-four South and East Europeans left the United States for every one hundred that arrived between 1908 and 1910. Not a steelworker, a young Italian boy living in Rochester, New York, summed up the expectations of many such immigrant men in a poem he wrote after studying English just three months:

Nothing job, nothing job,
I come back to Italy;
Nothing job, nothing job,
Adieu, land northerly. . . .

Nothing job, nothing job,
O! sweet sky of my Italy;
Nothing job, nothing job,
How cold in this country. . . .

Nothing job, nothing job,
I return to Italy;
Comrades, laborers, good-bye;
Adieu, land of 'Fourth of July'.

Immigrant expectations coincided for a time with the fiscal needs of industrial manufacturers. The Pittsburgh steel magnates had as much good fortune as the Boston Associates. But the stability and passivity they counted on among their unskilled workers depended upon steady work and the opportunity to escape the mills. When frequent recessions caused recurrent unemployment, immigrant expectations and behavior changed. What Brody calls peasant 'group consciousness' and 'communal loyalty' sustained bitter wildcat strikes after employment picked up. The tenacity of these immigrant strikers for higher wages amazed contemporaries, and brutal suppression often accompanied them (Cleveland, 1899; East Chicago, 1905; McKees Rock, 1909; Bethlehem, 1910; and Youngstown in 1915 where, after a policeman shot into a peaceful parade, a riot caused an estimated one million dollars in damages). The First World War and its aftermath blocked the traditional route of overseas outward mobility, and the consciousness of immigrant steelworkers changed. They sparked the 1919 steel strike. The steel mill had become a way of life for them and was no longer the means by which to reaffirm and even strengthen older peasant and village life-styles.[4]

III

Let us sharply shift the time perspective from the years before 1843 and those between 1893 and 1919 to the decades between 1843 and 1893 and also shift our attention to the artisans and skilled workers who differed so greatly in the culture and work-styles they brought to the factory from men and women bred in rural and village cultures. The focus, however, remains the same—the relationship between settled work habits and culture. This half-century saw the United States (not small pockets within it) industrialize as steam and machinery radically transformed the premodern American economic structure. That so much attention has been given to the Civil War as a crucial divide in the nation's history (and it was, of course, for certain purposes) too frequently has meant neglect by historians of common patterns of behavior that give coherence to this period. Few contemporaries described these large structural changes more effectively if indirectly than the Boston labor reformer Jennie Collins in 1871:

> If you should enter a factory and find the water-wheels in the garret, the heaviest machinery in the seventh story, and the dressing and weaving in the basement, you would find the machinery and system less out of joint than at present it seems to be in this strange country of ours. The structure of our society is like a building for which the stones were carefully designed and carved, but in the construction of which the masons seized upon whatever block came handiest, without regard to design or fitness, using window-sills for partition walls, capstones for the foundation, and chink-pieces for the corner-stone.

The magnitude of the changes noticed by Collins cannot be understated. In 1869 half of the country's manufacturing enterprises still managed on water power. The nation in 1860 counted more slaves than factory workers. In his unpublished study of six upstate New York counties Richard L. Ehrlich has found that in five counties during that same year employment in manufacturing plants having at least fifty workers accounted for 37 percent or less of their respective labor forces. In the six counties (Albany, Erie, Monroe, Oneida, Onondaga, and Rensselaer) the average number of persons employed by firms engaging fewer than fifty employees was less than nine. In the year of Abraham Lincoln's election as president, the United States ranked behind England, France, and Germany in the value of its manufactured product. In 1894 the United States led the field: its manufactured product nearly equalled in value that of Great Britain, France, and Germany together. But such profound economic changes did not entirely shatter the older American social structure and the settled cultures of premodern native and immigrant American artisans. 'There is no such thing as economic growth which is not, at the same time, growth or change of a culture,' E. P. Thompson has written. Yet he also warns that 'we should not assume any automatic, or over-direct, correspondence between the dynamic of economic growth and the dynamic of social or cultural life'. That significant stricture applies as much to the United States as to England during its industrial revolution and especially to its native and immigrant artisans between 1843 and 1893.[5]

It is not surprising to find tenacious artisan work habits before the Civil War, what Thompson calls 'alternate bouts of intense labour and of idleness wherever men were in control of their working lives.'[6] An English cabinetmaker shared a New York City workplace with seven others (two native Americans, two Germans, and one man each from Ireland, England, and France), and the readers of *Knight's Penny Magazine* learned from him that 'frequently . . . after several weeks of real hard work . . . a simultaneous cessation from work took place'. 'As if . . . by tacit agreement, every hand' contributed 'loose change', and an apprentice left the place and 'speedily returned laden with wine, brandy, biscuits, and cheese'. Songs came forth 'from those who felt musical', and the same near-ritual repeated itself two more times that day. Similar relaxations, apparently self-imposed, also broke up the artisans' work day in the New York City shipyards, and a ship carpenter described them as 'an indulgence that custom had made as much of a necessity in a New York shipyard as a grind-stone':

> In our yard, at half-past eight a.m., Aunt Arlie McVane, a clever kind-hearted but awfully uncouth, rough sample of the 'Ould Sod', would make her welcome appearance in the yard with her two great baskets, stowed and checked off with crullers, doughnuts, ginger-bread, turnovers, pieces, and a variety of sweet cookies and cakes; and from the time Aunt Arlie's baskets came in sight until every man and boy, bosses and all, in the yard, had been supplied, always at one cent a piece for any article on the cargo, the pie, cake and cookie trade was a brisk one. Aunt Arlie would usually make the rounds of the yard and supply all hands in about an hour, bringing the forenoon up to half-past nine, and giving us from ten to fifteen minutes 'breathing spell' during lunch; no one ever hurried during 'cake-time'.

Nor was this all:

> After this was over we would fall to again, until interrupted by Johnnie Gogean, the English candyman, who came in always at half-past ten, with his great board, the size of a medium extension dining table, slung before him, covered with all sort of 'stick', and several of sticky candy, in one-cent lots. Bosses, boys and men—all hand, everybody—invested one to three cents in Johnnie's sweet wares, and another ten to fifteen minutes is spent in consuming it. Johnnie usually sailed out with a bare board until 11 o'clock at which time there was a general sailing out of the yard and into convenient grog-shops after whiskey; only we had four or five men among us, and one apprentice—not quite a year my senior—who used to sail out pretty regularly ten times a day on the average; two that went for whiskey only when some one invited them to drink, being too mean to treat themselves; and two more who never went at all.
>
> In the afternoon, about half-past three, we had a cake-lunch, supplied by Uncle Jack Gridder, an old, crippled, superannuated ship carpenter. No one else was ever allowed to come in competition with our caterers. Let a foreign candyboard or cake basket make their appearance inside the gates of the yard, and they would get shipped out of that directly.
>
> At about five o'clock p.m., always, Johnnie used to put in his second appearance; and then, having expended money in another stick or two of candy, and ten minutes in its consumption, we were ready to drive away again until sundown; then home to supper.

Less well-ordered in their daily pleasures, the shoemakers in Lynn, Massachusetts, nevertheless surrounded their way of work with a way of life. The former cobbler David Johnson recorded in minute detail in *Sketches of Old Lynn* how fishermen and farmers retained settled ways first as part-time shoemakers in small shops behind their homes. The language of the sea was adapted to the new craft:

> There were a good many sea phrases, or 'salt notes' as they were called, used in the shops. In the morning one would hear, 'Come Jake, hoist the sails', which simply was a call to roll up the curtains . . . .If debate ran high upon some exciting topic, some veteran would quietly remark, 'Squally, squally, today. Come better *luff* and bear away'.

At times a shoemaker read from a newspaper to other men at work. Festivals, fairs, games ('trolling the tog'), and excursions were common rituals among the Lynn cobblers. So was heavy drinking with the bill often incurred by 'the one who made the most or the fewest shoes, the best or the poorest'. The man 'paid "the scot" '. 'These were the days', Johnson reminded later and more repressed New England readers, 'when temperance organizations were hardly known.'

Despite the profound economic changes that followed the American Civil War, Gilded Age artisans did not easily shed stubborn and time-honored work habits. Such work habits and the life-styles and subcultures related to them retained a vitality long into these industrializing decades. Not all artisans worked in factories, but some that did retained traditional craft skills. Mechanization came in different ways and at different times to diverse industries. Samuel Gompers recollected that New York City cigarmakers paid a fellow craftsman to read a newspaper to them while they worked, and Milwaukee cigarmakers struck in 1882 to retain such privileges as keeping (and then selling) damaged cigars and leaving the shop without a foreman's permission. 'The difficulty with many cigarmakers', complained a New York City manufacturer in 1877, 'is this. They come down to the shop in the morning; roll a few cigars and then go to a beer saloon and play pinnocio or some other game. . . . working probably only two or three hours a day.' Coopers felt new machinery 'hard and insensate', not a blessing but an evil that 'took a great deal of joy out of life' because machine-made barrels undercut a subculture of work and leisure. Skilled coopers 'lounged about' on Saturday (the regular payday), a 'lost day' to their employers. A historian of American cooper-age explained:

> Early on Saturday morning, the big brewery wagon would drive up to the shop. Several of the coopers would club together, each paying his proper share, and one of them would call out the window to the driver, 'Bring me a Goose Egg', meaning a half-barrel of beer. Then others would buy 'Goose Eggs', and there would be a merry time all around. . . . Little groups of jolly fellows would often sit around upturned barrels playing poker, using rivets for chips, until they had received their pay and the 'Goose Egg' was dry.
>
> Saturday night was a big night for the old-time cooper. It meant going out, strolling around the town, meeting friends, usually at a favorite saloon, and having a good time generally, after a week of hard work. Usually the good

time continued over into Sunday, so that on the following day he usually was not in the best of condition to settle down to the regular day's work.

Many coopers used to spend this day [Monday] sharpening up their tools, carrying in stock, discussing current events, and in getting things in shape for the big day of work on the morrow. Thus, 'Blue Monday' was something of a tradition with the coopers, and the day was also more or less lost as far as production was concerned.

'Can't do much today, but I'll give her hell tomorrow', seemed to be the Monday slogan. But bright and early Tuesday morning, 'Give her hell' they would, banging away lustily for the rest of the week until Saturday which was pay day again, and its thoughts of the 'Goose Eggs'.[7]

Such traditions of work and leisure—in this case, a four-day work week and a three-day weekend—angered manufacturers anxious to ship goods as much as it worried Sabbatarians and temperance reformers. Conflicts over life- and work-styles occurred frequently and often involved control over the work process and over time. The immigrant Staffordshire potters in Trenton, New Jersey, worked in 'bursts of great activity' and then quit for 'several days at a time'. 'Monday,' said a manufacturer, 'was given up to debauchery.' After the potters lost a bitter lockout in 1877 that included torchlight parades and effigy burnings, the *Crockery and Glass Journal* mockingly advised:

Run your factories to please the crowd. . . . Don't expect work to begin before 9 a.m. or to continue after 3 p.m. Every employee should be served hot coffee and a bouquet at 7 a.m. and allowed the two hours to take a free perfumed bath. . . . During the summer, ice cream and fruit should be served at 12 p.m. to the accompaniment of witching music.

Hand coopers (and potters and cigarmakers, among others) worked hard but in distinctly preindustrial styles. Machine-made barrels pitted modernizing technology and modern habits against traditional ways. To the owners of competitive firms struggling to improve efficiency and cut labor costs, the Goose Egg and Blue Monday proved the laziness and obstinacy of craftsmen as well as the tyranny of craft unions that upheld venerable traditions. To the skilled cooper, the long weekend symbolized a way of work and life filled with almost ritualistic meanings. Between 1843 and 1893, compromise between such conflicting interests was hardly possible.

Settled premodern work habits existed among others than those employed in nonfactory crafts. Owners of already partially mechanized industries complained of them, too. 'Saturday night debauches and Sunday carousels though they be few and far between,' lamented the *Age of Steel* in 1882, 'are destructive of modest hoardings, and he who indulges in them will in time become a striker for higher wages.' In 1880 a British steelworker boasted that native Americans never would match immigrants in their skills: "adn't the 'ops, you know.' Manufacturers, when able, did not hesitate to act decisively to end such troubles. In Fall river new technology allowed a print cloth manufacturer to settle a long-standing grievance against his stubborn mule spinners. 'On Saturday afternoon after they had gone home,' a boastful mill superintendent later recollected, 'we started right in and smashed a room full of mules with sledge hammers. . . . On Monday morning, they were astonished to find that there was not work for them. That room is now full of ring frames run by girls.' Woollen manufacturers also displaced handjack spinners with improved machinery and did so because of 'the disorderly habits of English workmen. Often on a Monday morning, half of them would be absent from the mill in consequence of the Sunday's dissipation.' Blue Monday, however, did not entirely disappear. Paterson artisans and factory hands held a May festival on a Monday each year ('Labor Monday') and that popular holiday soon became state law, the American Labor Day. It had its roots in earlier premodern work habits.

The persistence of such traditional artisan work habits well into the nineteenth century deserves notice from others besides labor historians, because those work habits did not exist in a cultural or social vacuum. If modernizing technology threatened and even displaced such work patterns, diverse nineteenth-century subcultures sustained and nourished them. 'The old nations of the earth creep on at a snail's pace,' boasted Andrew Carnegie in *Triumphant Democracy* (1886), 'the Republic thunders past with the rush of an express.' The articulate steelmaster, however, had missed the point. The very rapidity of the economic changes occurring in Carnegie's lifetime meant that many, unlike him, lacked the time, historically, culturally, and psychologically, to be separated or alienated from settled ways of work and life and from relatively fixed beliefs. Continuity not consensus counted for much in explaining working-class and especially artisan behavior in those decades that witnessed the coming of the factory and the radical transformation of American society. Persistent work habits were one example of that significant continuity. But these elements of continuity were often revealed among nineteenth-century American workers cut off by birth from direct contact with the preindustrial American past, a fact that has been ignored or blurred by the artificial separation between labor history and immigration history. In Gilded Age America (and afterward in the Progressive Era despite the radical change in patterns of immigration), working-class and immigration history regularly intersected, and that intermingling made for powerful continuities. In 1880, for example, 63 of every 100 Londoners were native to that city, 94 coming from England and Wales, and 98 from Great Britain and Ireland. Foreign countries together contributed only 1.6 percent to London's massive population. At the same moment, more than 70 of every 100 persons in San Francisco (78), St. Louis (78), Cleveland (80), New York (80), Detroit (84), Milwaukee (84), and

Chicago (87) were immigrants or the children of immigrants, and the percentage was just as high in many smaller American industrial towns and cities. 'Not every foreigner is a workingman,' noticed the clergyman Samuel Lane Loomis in 1887, 'but in the cities, at least, it may almost be said that every workingman is a foreigner.' And until the 1890s most immigrants came from Northern and Western Europe, French- and English-speaking Canada, and China. In 1890, only 3 percent of the nation's foreign-born residents—290,000 of 9,200,000 immigrants—had been born in Eastern or Southern Europe. (It is a little recognized fact that most North and West European immigrants migrated to the United States after, not before, the American Civil War.) When so much else changed in the industrializing decades, tenacious traditions flourished among immigrants in ethnic subcultures that varied greatly among particular groups and according to the size, age, and location of different cities and industries. ('The Irish,' Henry George insisted, 'burn like chips, the English like logs.') Class and occupational distinctions within a particular ethnic group also made for different patterns of cultural adaptation, but powerful subcultures thrived among them all.

Suffering and plain poverty cut deeply into these ethnic working-class worlds. In reconstructing their everyday texture there is no reason to neglect or idealize such suffering, but it is time to discard the notion that the large-scale uprooting and exploitative processes that accompanied industrialization caused little more than cultural breakdown and social anomie. Family, class, and ethnic ties did not dissolve easily. 'Almost as a matter of definition,' the sociologist Neil Smelzer has written, 'we associate the factory system with the decline of the family and the onset of anonymity.'[8] Smelzer criticized such a view of early industrializing England, and it has just as little validity for nineteenth-century industrializing America. Family roles changed in important ways, and strain was widespread, but the immigrant working-class family held together. Examination of household composition in sixteen census enumeration districts in Paterson in 1880 makes that clear for this predominantly working-class immigrant city, and while research on other ethnic working-class communities will reveal significant variations, the overall patterns should not differ greatly. The Paterson immigrant (and native white) communities were predominantly working class, and most families among them were intact in their composition. For this population, at least (and without accounting for age and sex ratio differences between the ethnic groups), a greater percentage of immigrant than native white households included two parents. Ethnic and predominantly working-class communities in industrial towns like Paterson and in larger cities, too, built on these strained but hardly broken familial and kin ties. [. . .] Tough familial and kin ties made possible the transmission and adaptation of European working-class cultural patterns

Table 1   Male occupational structure and household composition by ethnic group, Paterson, New Jersey, 1880, enumeration districts 150-53, 161-72[1]

	British	German	Irish	Native White
Total Males 20 and Older	2090	927	2841	1461
Total Females 20 and Older	1941	804	3466	1689
Male Occupational Structure				
Unskilled Laborer	8.2%	9.8%	43.6%	20.8%
Skilled Worker	75.5%	64.3%	44.8%	62.5%
Nonlaborer	16.3%	25.9%	11.6%	16.7%
Household Composition				
Number of Kin-related Households	1402	686	2142	905
Number of Subfamilies[2]	117	41	158	125
Nuclear Households	73.9%	78.1%	73.1%	65.7%
Extended Households	13.5%	10.3%	13.6%	18.7%
Augmented Households[3]	14.6%	13.1%	15.3%	19.0%
Percent of Households and Subfamilies with a Husband and/or Father Present	87.2%	91.6%	81.1%	78.9%

[1] I am indebted to Carol Waserloos for gathering the raw Paterson data from the 1880 federal manuscript census schedules.

[2] A subfamily is defined as a complete or incomplete nuclear family residing with another nuclear family.

[3] Augmented households include lodgers. The sum of nuclear, augmented, and extended households is greater than 100 percent because some households included both relatives and lodgers and have been counted twice.

and beliefs to industrializing America. As late as 1888, residents in some Rhode Island mill villages figured their wages in British currency. Common rituals and festivals bound together such communities. Paterson silk weavers had their Macclesfield wakes, and Fall River cotton mill workers their Ashton wakes. British immigrants 'banded together to uphold the popular culture of the homeland' and celebrated saints' days: St. George's Day, St. Andrew's Day, and St. David's Day. Even funerals retained an archaic flavor. Samuel Sigley, a Chartist house painter, had fled Ashton-under-Lyne in 1848, and built American trade unions. When his wife died in the late 1890s a significant ritual occurred during the funeral: some friends placed a chaff of wheat on her grave. Mythic beliefs also cemented ethnic and class solidarities. The Irish-American press, for example, gave Martin O'Brennan much space to argue that Celtic had been spoken in the Garden of Eden, and in Paterson Irish-born silk, cotton, and iron workers believed in the magical powers of that town's 'Dublin Spring'. An old resident remembered:

> There is a legend that an Irish fairy brought over the water in her apron from the Lakes of Killarney and planted it in the humble part of that town. . . . There were dozens of legends connected with the Dublin Spring and if a man drank from its precious depository . . . he could never leave Paterson [but] only under the fairy influence, and the wand of the nymph would be sure to bring him back again some time or other.

When a 'fairy' appeared in Paterson in human form, some believed she walked the streets 'as a tottering old woman begging with a cane'. Here was a way to assure concern for the elderly and the disabled.

Much remains to be studied about these cross-class but predominantly working-class ethnic subcultures common to industrializing America. Relations within them between skilled and unskilled workers, for example, remain unclear. But the larger shape of these diverse immigrant communities can be sketched. More than mythic beliefs and common work habits sustained them. Such worlds had in them what Thompson has called 'working-class intellectual traditions, working-class community patterns, and a working-class structure of feeling', and men with artisan skill powerfully affected the everyday texture of such communities.[9] A model subculture included friendly and benevolent societies as well as friendly local politicians, community-wide holiday celebrations, an occasional library (the Baltimore Journeymen Bricklayer's Union taxed members one dollar a year in the 1880s to sustain a library that included the collected works of William Shakespeare and Sir Walter Scott's Waverley novels), participant sports, churches sometimes headed by a sympathetic clergy, saloons, beer gardens, and concert halls or music halls and, depending upon circumstances, trade unionists, labor reformers, and radicals. The Massachusetts cleric Jonathan Baxter Harrison published in 1880 an unusually detailed description of one such ethnic, working-class institution, a Fall River music hall and saloon. About fifty persons were there when he visited it, nearly one-fourth of them young women. 'Most of those present,' he noticed, were 'persons whom I had met before, in the mills and on the streets. They were nearly all operatives, or had at some time belonged to that class.' An Englishman sang first, and then a black whose songs 'were of many kinds, comic, sentimental, pathetic, and silly. . . . When he sang "I got a mammy in the promised land", with a strange, wailing refrain, the English waiter-girl, who was sitting at my table, wiped her eyes with her apron, and everybody was very quiet.' Harrison said of such places in Fall River:

> All the attendants . . . had worked in the mills. The young man who plays the piano is usually paid four or five dollars per week, besides his board. The young men who sing receive one dollar per night, but most of them board themselves. . . . The most usual course for a man who for any reason falls out of the ranks of mill workers (if he loses his place by sickness or is discharged) is the opening of a liquor saloon or drinking place.

Ethnic ties with particlar class dimensions sometimes stretched far beyond local boundaries and even revealed themselves in the behavior of the most successful practitioners of Gilded Age popular culture. In 1884, for example, the pugilist John L. Sullivan and the music-hall entertainers Harrigan and Hart promised support to striking Irish coal miners in the Ohio Hocking Valley. Local ties, however, counted for much more and had their roots inside and outside of the factory and workshop. Soon after Cyrus H. McCormick, then twenty-one, took over the management of his father's great Chicago iron machinery factory (which in the early 1880s employed twelve hundred men and boys), a petition signed by 'Many Employees' reached his hands:

> It only pains us to relate to you . . . that a good many of our old hands is not here this season and if Mr. Evarts is kept another season a good many more will leave . . . . We pray for you . . . to remove this man. . . . We are treated as though we were dogs. . . . He has cut wages down so low they are living on nothing but bread. . . . We can't talk to him about wages if we do he will tell us to go out side the gate. . . . He discharged old John the other day he has been here seventeen years. . . . There is Mr. Church who left us last Saturday he went about and shook hands with every old hand in the shop . . . this brought tears to many mens eyes. He has been here nineteen years and has got along well with them all until he came to Mr. Evarts the present superintendent.

Artisans, themselves among those later displaced by new technology, signed this petition, and self-educated artisans (or professionals and petty enterprisers who had themselves usually risen from the artisan class) often emerged as civic and community leaders, 'Intellectually', Jennie Collins noticed in Boston in the early 1870s, 'the journeymen tailors . . . are ever discussing among themselves questions of local and national politics, points of law, philosophy, physics, and religion.'

Such life-styles and subcultures adapted and changed over time. In the Gilded Age piece-rates in nearly all manufacturing industries helped reshape traditional work habits. 'Two generations ago,' said the Connecticut Bureau of Labor Statistics in 1885, 'time-work was the universal rule.' 'Piece-work had all but replaced it, and the Connecticut Bureau called it 'a moral force which corresponds to machinery as a physical force'. Additional pressures came in traditional industries such as shoe, cigar, furniture, barrel, and clothing manufacture, which significantly mechanized in these years. Strain also resulted where factories employed large numbers of children and young women (in the 1880 manuscript census 49.3 percent of all Paterson boys and 52.1 percent of all girls aged eleven to fourteen had occupations listed by their names) and was especially common among the as yet little-studied pools of casual male laborers found everywhere. More than this, mobility patterns significantly affected the structure and the behavior of these predominantly working-class communities. A good deal of geographic mobility, property mobility (home ownership), and occupational mobility (skilled status in new industries or in the expanding building trades, petty retail enterprise, the professions, and public employment counted as the most important ways to advance occupationally) reshaped these ethnic communities [. . .] But so little is yet known about the society in which such men and women lived and about the cultures which had produced them that it is entirely premature to infer 'consciousness' (beliefs and values) only from mobility rates. Such patterns and rates of mobility, for example, did not entirely shatter working-class capacities for self-protection. The fifty-year period between 1843 and 1893 was not conducive to permanent, stable trade unions, but these decades were a time of frequent strikes and lockouts and other forms of sustained conflict.

Not all strikes and lockouts resulted in the defeat of poorly organized workers. For the years 1881 to 1887, for example, the New Jersey Bureau of Labor statistics collected information on 890 New Jersey industrial disputes involving mostly workers in the textile, glass, metal, transportation, and building trades: 6 percent ended in compromise settlements; employers gained the advantage in 40 percent; strikers won the rest (54 percent). In four or five disputes concerning higher wages and shorter hours, New Jersey workers, not their employers, were victorious. Large numbers of such workers there and elsewhere were foreign-born or the children of immigrants. More than this, immigrant workers in the mid-1880s joined trade unions in numbers far out of proportion to their place in

Table 2 Organized workers, male whites in nonagricultural pursuits, Illinois (1886) and New Jersey (1887)

	Illinois 1886		New Jersey 1887	
Nativity	Bread-winners	Organized	Bread-winners	Organized
Number				
Native-born	423,290	25,985	243,093	24,463
Foreign-born	308,595	57,163	137,385	26,704
Percent				
Native-born	57.8%	31.3%	63.9%	47.8%
Foreign-born	42.2%	68.7%	36.1%	52.2%

the labor force. Statistical inquiries by the Bureau of Labor Statistics in Illinois in 1886 and in New Jersey in 1887 make this clear. Even these data may not have fully reflected the proclivity of immigrants to seek self-protection. (Such a distortion would occur if, for example, the children of immigrants apparently counted by the bureaus as native-born had remained a part of the ethnic subcultures into which they had been born and joined trade unions as regularly as the foreign-born.) Such information from Illinois and New Jersey suggests the need to treat the meaning of social mobility with some care. So does the sketchy outline of Hugh O'Donnell's career. By 1892, when he was twenty-nine years old, he had already improved his social status a great deal. Before the dispute with Andrew Carnegie and Henry Clay Frick culminated in the bitter Homestead lockout that year. O'Donnell had voted Republican, owned a home, and had in it a Brussels carpet and even a piano. Nevertheless this Irish-American skilled worker led the Homestead workers and was even indicted under a Civil War treason statute never before used. The material improvements O'Donnell had experienced mattered greatly to him and suggested significant mobility, but culture and tradition together with the way in which men like O'Donnell interpreted the transformation of Old America defined the value of those material improvements and their meaning to him.

Other continuities between 1843 and 1893 besides those rooted in artisan work habits and diverse ethnic working-class subcultures deserve brief attention as important considerations in understanding the behavior of artisans and other workers in these decades. I have suggested in other writings that significant patterns of opposition to the ways in which industrial capitalism developed will remain baffling until historians re-examine the relationship between the premodern American political system and the coming of the factory along with the strains in premodern popular American ideology shared by workers and large numbers of successful self-made Americans (policemen, clergymen, politicians, small businessmen, and even some 'traditional' manufacturers) that rejected the legitimacy of the modern factory system and its owners. One strain of thought common to the rhetoric of nineteenth-century immigrant and native-born artisans is considered here. It helps explain their recurrent enthusiasm for land and currency reform, cooperatives, and trade unions. It was the fear of dependence, 'proletarianization', and centralization, and the worry that industrial capitalism threatened to transform 'the Great Republic of the West' into a 'European' country. In 1869, the same year that saw the completion of the transcontinental railroad, the chartering of the Standard Oil Company, the founding of the Knights of Labor, and the dedication of a New York City statue to Cornelius Vanderbilt, some London workers from Westbourne Park and Notting Hill petitioned the American ambassador for help to emigrate. 'Dependence,' they said of

Great Britain, 'not independence, is inculcated. Hon. Sir, this state of things we wish to fly from . . . to become citizens of that great Republican country, which has no parallels in the world's history.' Such men had a vision of Old America, but it was not a new vision. Industrial transformation between 1840 and 1890 tested and redefined that vision. Seven years after their visit, the New York *Labor Standard,* then edited by an Irish socialist, bemoaned what had come over the country: 'There was a time when the United States was the workingman's country, . . . the land of promise for the workingman. . . . We are now in an *old country.'* This theme recurred frequently as disaffected workers, usually self-educated artisans, described the transformation of premodern America. 'America,' said the Detroit *Labour Leaf,* 'used to be the land of promise to the poor. . . . The Golden Age is indeed over—the Age of Iron has taken its place. The iron of necessity has taken the place of golden rule.' We need not join in mythicizing preindustrial American society in order to suggest that this tension between the old and the new helps give a coherence to the decades between 1843 and 1893 that even the trauma of the Civil War does not disturb.

As early as the 1830s, the theme that industrialism promised to make over the United States into a 'European' country had its artisan and working-class advocates. Seth Luther then made this clear in his complaint about 'gentlemen' who 'exultingly call LOWELL the Manchester of America' and in his plea that the Bunker Hill monument 'stand *unfinished,* until the time passes away when aristocrats talk about mercy to mechanics and laborers, . . . until our rights are acknowledged'. The tensions revealed in labor rhetoric between the promises of the Republic and the practices of those who combined capital and technology to build factories continued into the 1890s. In 1844 New England shoemakers rewrote the Declaration of Independence to protest that the employers 'have robbed us of certain rights', and two years later New England textile workers planned without success a general strike to start July 4, 1846, calling it 'a second Independence Day'. The great 1860 shoemakers' strike in Lynn started on George Washington's birthday, a celebration strikers called 'sacred to the memory of one of the greatest men the world has ever produced'. Fear for the Republic did not end with the Civil War. The use of state militia to help put down a strike of Northeastern Pennsylvania workers in 1874 caused *Equality,* a Boston labor weekly, to condemn the Erie Railroad as 'the George III of the working-man's movement' and 'the Government of Pennsylvania' as 'but its parliament'. ('Regiments,' it added, 'to protect dead things.')

Such beliefs, not the status anxieties of Progressive muckrakers and New Deal historians, gave rise to the pejorative phrase 'robber baron'. Discontented Gilded Age workers found in the phrase a way to summarize their worries about dependence and centralization. 'In America,' exploded the *National Labor Tribune* in 1874, 'we have realized the ideal of republican government at least in form.' 'America,' it went on, 'was the star of the political Bethlehem which shone radiantly out in the dark night of political misrule in Europe. The masses of the old world gazed upon her as their escape.' Men in America could be 'their own rulers'; 'no one could or should become their masters.' But industrialization had created instead a nightmare. 'These dreams have not been realized . . . The working people of this country . . . suddenly find capital as rigid as an absolute monarchy.' Two years later, the same Pittsburgh labor weekly asked, 'Shall we let the gold barons of the nineteenth century put iron collars of ownership around our necks as did the feudal barons with their serfs in the fourteenth century?' The rhetoric surrounding the little-understood 1877 railroad strikes and riots summed up these fears. Critics of the strikers urged repressive measures such as the building of armories in large cities and the restriction of the ballot, and a few, including Elihu Burritt, even favored importing 'British' institutions to the New World. But the disorders also had their defenders, and a strain in their rhetoric deserves notice. A radical Massachusetts clergyman called the strikers 'the lineal descendants of Samuel Adams, John Hancock, and the Massachusetts yeomen who began so great a disturbance a hundred years ago . . . only now the kings are money kings and then they were political kings.' George McNeill, a major figure in the nineteenth-century labor movement and later a founder of the American Federation of Labor, denied that the Paris Commune had come to America: 'The system which the pilgrims planted here has yet a residue of followers. No cry of 'commune' can frighten the descendants of the New England commune. This is the COMMONWEALTH, not the *Class* wealth, of Massachusetts.' A discharged Pittsburgh brakeman put it differently in blaming the violence on a general manager who treated the railroad workers 'no better than the serfs of Great Britain, sir, . . . introduced into this country a lot of English ideas and customs, [and] made our men wear uniforms and traveling bags,' 'A uniform,' he worried, 'constantly reminds them of their serfdom, and I for one would rather remain out of work than wear one.' An amazed reporter wondered how this man could 'assert his right as a free born American, even if in so doing himself and family starved.'

This Pittsburgh brakeman revealed values that persisted throughout the decades of industrialization, that expressed themselves most commonly in the rhetoric and behavior of artisans and skilled workers, and that worried other influential Americans besides railroad magnates and industrial manufacturers. In 1896 an army officer won a prize for writing the best essay submitted to the *Journal of the Military Service Institutions of the United States.* Theodore Roosevelt helped to judge the contest. The officer insisted that 'discipline' needed to be more rigorous in an American as opposed to a European army. Even though he knew little about European societies, his insistence that 'means of discipline are entirely artificial productions of law' in the United States counted as a profound insight into a social condition that plagued industrialists and sparked frequent discontent among skilled and other workers in industrializing America:

> Discipline should be as a rod of iron. It may seem hopelessly illogical to claim that the army of a free people needs to be kept in stricter discipline than any other army, with wider space between the officers and the enlisted men, yet there are natural reasons why it should be so. The armies of Europe are drawn from people who for countless generations have lived under monarchical institutions and class government, where every man is born and bred to pay homage to some other man, and the habit of subordination to the will of another is a matter of heredity. It is natural that when such a man finds himself in the army he is not only amenable to discipline, but any relaxation on the part of the officer would be accepted as a matter of grace.
>
> With us these conditions are reversed. Every man is born and bred in the idea of equality, and means of discipline are entirely artificial productions of law, not only without support from traditional habit, but they have that habit to overcome, and familiarity on the part of the officer would breed contempt of authority.

Two decades earlier, the London editor of the *Industrial Review* and increasingly conservative British trade-union leader, George Potter, posed the same problem somewhat differently. The disorders incident to the 1877 railroad strikes convinced him that Americans then lived through an earlier stage of English history, before 'habit' had 'begotten' men to 'use their combinations peacably and wisely'. The state of things that existed then in England', Potter insisted, 'exists now in the United States. It was at one time believed that this was impossible within the borders of the great Republic, but it has proved itself wrong'. Potter believed that the widespread violence in 1877 had been caused by men 'suddenly or newly brought together to defend an interest' and therefore lacking 'that wisdom of method that time and experience develop'. But Potter was wrong. The men who quit work in 1877 (and before and after that) included many deeply rooted in traditional crafts and worried that the transformation of the American social and economic structure threatened settled ways of work and life and particular visions of a just society. Their behavior—in particular the little-understood violence that accompanied the strikes (including the burning and destruction of the Pennsylvania Railroad's Pittsburgh yards and equipment)—makes this clear. It had specific purposes and was the product of long-standing grievances that accompanied the transformation of Old America to New America.

IV

Quite diverse patterns of collective lower-class behavior (some of them disorderly and even violent) accompanied the industrialization of the United States, and certain of them (especially those related to artisan culture and to peasant and village cultures still fresh to factory labor and to the machine) deserve brief attention. Characteristic European forms of 'premodern' artisan and lower-class protest in the United States occurred before (prior to 1843), during (1843–1893), and after (1893–1919) the years when the country 'modernized'. The continuing existence of such behavior followed from the changing composition of the working-class population. Asa Briggs's insistence that 'to understand how people respond to industrial change it is important to examine what kind of people they were at the beginning of the process' and 'to take account of continuities as well as new ways of thinking', poses in different words the subtle interplay between culture and society that is an essential factor in explaining lower-class behavior. Although their frequency remains the subject for much further detailed study, examples of premodern lower-class behavior abound for the entire period from 1815 to 1919, and their presence suggests how much damage has been done to the past American working-class experiences by historians busy, as R. H. Tawney complained more than half a century ago, 'dragging into prominence forces which have triumphed and thrusting into the background those which have been swallowed up.'[10] Attention is briefly given to three types of American artisan and lower-class behavior explored in depth and with much illumination by European social historians ('church-and-king' crowds, machine-breaking, and food riots) and to the presence in quite different working-class protests of powerful secular and religious rituals. These occurred over the entire period under examination, not just in the early phases of industrial development.

Not much is yet known about premodern American artisan and urban lower-class cultures, but scattered evidence suggests a possible American variant of the European church-and-king phenomenon. Although artisan and lower-class urban cultures before 1843 await their historians, popular street disorders (sometimes sanctioned by the established authorities) happened frequently and increasingly caused concern to the premodern elite classes. Street gangs, about which little is yet known except the suggestion that some had as members artisans (not just casual or day laborers) and were often organized along ethnic lines, grew more important in the coastal and river towns after 1830. New York City, among other towns, had its Fly Boys, Chichesters, Plug Uglies, Buckaroos, and Slaughterhouse Gangs, and their violence against recent immigrants provoked disorderly counterthrusts. Political disorders on election days, moreover, were apparently well-organized and may have involved such gangs. The recurrence of such disorders through the pre-Civil War decades (including the nativist outbursts in nearly all major Northern and Southern cities in the 1850s) may have meant that local political parties, in their infancy, served as the American substitute for the king and the church, a third party 'protecting' artisans and even day laborers from real and imagined adversaries and winning clanlike loyalty. Although the testimony of Mike Walsh, a Tammany leader and later the publisher of the *Police Gazette,* must be read with care, he suggested an interesting relationship between the decline of premodern lower-class entertainments and the rise of modern political 'machines'. Election politics, Walsh noted in the *Subterranean,* saw 'the Goth-and-Vandal-like eruption of the shirtless and unwashed democracy' which Walsh connected to the disappearance of popular lower-class entertainments. A 'gloomy, churlish, money-worshipping . . . spirit' had 'swept nearly all the poetry out of the poor man's sphere,' said the editor-politician. 'Ballad-singing, street dancing, tumbling, public games, all are either prohibited or discountenanced, so that Fourth of July and election sports alone remain.' Workers flocked to political clubs and labored hard for a party to 'get a taste of the equality which they hear so much preached, but never, save there, see even partially practiced.' If Walsh's insight has merit, political parties quite possibly competed with early craft unions in adapting older forms of popular entertainment and ritual to changing needs. That process, once started, had a life beyond the early years of the premodern political party and continued as the composition of the working class changed. The ethnic political 'boss' created a new dependence that exploited well-understood class feelings and resentments but blunted class consciousness. The relationship, however, was not simple, and in the 1880s the socialist Joseph P. McDonnell exploited that same relationship to convince local New Jersey politicians to respond to pressures from predominantly immigrant workers and thereby to pioneer in the passage of humane social legislation, a process that began well before the stirring of the middle- and upper-class conscience in Progressive America.

Available evidence does not yet indicate that machine-breaking of the 'Luddite' variety was widespread in the United States. There are suggestive hints in reports that Ohio farm laborers burnt and destroyed farm machinery in 1878 and that twenty years later in Buffalo a crowd of Polish common day laborers and their wives rioted to break a street-paving machine, but the only clear evidence found of classic machine-breaking occurred early in the Civil War among rural blacks in the South Carolina Sea Islands, who resisted Yankee missionary and military efforts to make them plant cotton instead of corn and therefore broke up cotton gins and hid the iron work. 'They do not see the use of cotton,' said a Northern woman school-teacher, and a Yankee entrepreneur among them added that 'nothing was more remote from their shallow pates than the idea of planting cotton for "white-folks" again'. (Some time later, this same man ordered a steam-run cotton gin. 'This engine,' he confided, ' serves as a moral stimulus to keep the people at work at their hand-gins, for they want to gin all the cotton by hand, and I tell them if they don't by the middle of January I shall get it by steam.') If white workers rarely broke machines to protest their introduction, they sometimes destroyed the product of new technology. In the early 1830s Brooklyn ropemakers paraded a 'hated machine' through town and then 'committed to the flames' its product. Theirs was not an irrational act. They paid for the destroyed hemp, spun 'a like quantity' to allow the machine's owner to 'fulfill his engagement for its delivery', and advertised their product in a newspaper, boasting that its quality far surpassed machine-made rope 'as is well known to any practical ropemaker and seaman'. Silk weavers in the Hudson River towns of new Jersey broke looms in 1877 but only to prevent production during a strike. A more common practice saw the destruction of the product of labor or damage to factory and mining properties to punish employers and owners. Paterson silk weavers regularly left unfinished warps to spoil in the looms. Crowds often stoned factories, burned mine tipples, and did other damage to industrial properties (as in the bitter Western Pennsylvania coke strikes between 1884 and 1894) but mostly to protest the hiring of new hands or violence against themselves by 'police'. Construction gangs especially in railroad work also frequently destroyed property. In 1831, between two and three hundred construction workers, mostly Irish, punished an absconding contractor by 'wantonly' tearing up track they built. Similar penalties were meted out by Italian construction gangs between 1880 and 1910 and by unorganized railroad workers, mostly native-born repairmen and trainmen, between 1850 and 1880, who tore up track, spiked switches, stole coupling links and pins, and did other damage to protest changing work rules or to collect back wages.

'Luddism' may have been rare, but classic 'European' food riots occurred in the United States, and two in New York City—the first in 1837 and the second in 1902—that involved quite different groups of workers are briefly examined to illustrate the ways in which traditional cultural forms and expectations helped shape lower-class behavior. (Other evidence of similar disorders, including the Confederate food riots led by white women in Mobile, Savannah, and Richmond, await careful study.) In February 1837, thousands gathered in City Hall Park to protest against 'monopolies' and rising food prices. Some months before, that park had witnessed yet another demonstration against the conspiracy trial of twenty-five striking journeymen tailors. In their rhetoric the protesters identified the trial with the betrayal of the premodern 'Republic'. 'Aristocrats' had robbed the people of 'that liberty bequeathed to them, as a sacred inheritance by their revolutionary sires' and 'so mystified' the laws that 'men of common understanding cannot unravel them'. 'What the people thought was liberty, bore not a semblance to its name.' Resolutions compared the tailors to that 'holy combination of that immortal band of Mechanics who . . . did throw into Boston Harbor the Tea'. In 1837 a crowd dumped flour, not tea, and in its behavior revealed a commonplace form of premodern protest. [...] The crowd in City Hall Park heard protests about the high price of rent, food, and especially flour and denunciations of 'engrossers', and the New York *Herald* called the gathering 'a flour meeting—a fuel meeting—a rent meeting—a food meeting—a bread meeting—every kind of a meeting except a political meeting'. But a New York newspaper had printed advice from Portland, Maine, that 'speculating' flour dealers be punished with 'some mark of public infamy', and after the meeting adjourned a crowd (estimates range from two hundred to several thousand) paraded to Eli Hart's wholesale flour depot. A speaker advised it to 'go to the flour stores and offer a fair price, and if refused take 'the flour'. Crowd members dumped two hundred barrels of flour and one thousand bushels of wheat in the streets, broke windows, did other minor damage, and chased the city's mayor with stones and 'balls of flour'. At first, little looting occurred, and when wagons finally appeared to carry home sacks of flour 'a tall athletic fellow in a carman's frock' shouted: 'No plunder, no plunder; destroy as much as you please. Teach these monopolists that we know our rights and will have them, but d--n it don't rob them.' The crowd moved on to other flour wholesalers and continued its work. It smashed the windows of B. S. Herrick and Son, dumped more flour, and finally stopped when 'a person of respectable appearance' came from inside the building to promise that what remained untouched would be distributed gratis the next day to the 'poor'. The crowd cheered and melted away. More than twenty-eight persons were arrested (among them 'mere boys', a few 'black and ignorant laborers', a woman, and as yet unidentified white men), but the *Herald* found 'mere humbug . . . the unholy cry of "It's the foreigners who have done all this mischief." ' The daily press, including the *Herald*, denounced the crowd as 'the very canaille of the city', but the *Herald* also pleaded for the reimposition of the assize of bread. 'Let the Mayor have the regulation of it,' said the *Herald*. 'Let the public authorities regulate the price of such an essential of life.' (In 1857, incidentally, New Yorkers again filled the city Hall Park to again demand the restoration of the assize of bread and to ask for public works.)

More than half a century later different New York City workers re-enacted the 1837 food 'riot'. Unlike the rioters of 1837 in origins and rhetoric, the later rioters nevertheless displayed strikingly similar behavior. In 1902, and a few years before Upton Sinclair published *The Jungle*, orthodox New York City Jews, mostly women and led by a woman butcher, protested the rising price of kosher meat and the betrayal of a promised boycott of the Meat Trust by retail butchers. The complaint started on the Lower East Side and then spontaneously spread among Jews further uptown and even among Jews in Brooklyn, Newark, and Boston. The Lower East Side Jews demanded lower prices. Some called for a rabbi to fix for the entire New York Jewish community the price of meat, as in the East

European *shtetl*. Others formed a cooperative retail outlet. But it is their behavior that reveals the most. The nation's financial metropolis saw angry immigrant women engage in seemingly archaic traditional protest. Outsiders could not understand its internal logic and order. These women did not loot. Like the 1837 demonstrators, they punished. Custom and tradition that reached far back in historical time gave a coherence to their rage. The disorders started on a Wednesday, stopped on Friday at sundown, and resumed the following evening. The women battered butcher shops but did not steal meat. Some carried pieces of meat 'aloft on pointed sticks . . . like flags'. Most poured kerosene on it in the street or in other ways spoiled it. 'Eat no meat while the Trust is taking meat from the bones of your women and children,' said a Yiddish circular apparently decorated with a skull and crossbones. The New York police and *The New Times* came down quite hard on these Jewish women. A 'dangerous class . . . very ignorant,' said *The Times*, explaining:

> They mostly speak a foreign language. They do not understand the duties or the rights of Americans. They have no inbred or acquired respect for law and order as the basis of the life of the society into which they have come. . . . The instant they take the law into their own hands . . . they should be handled in a way that they can understand and cannot forget. . . . Let the blows fall instantly and effectively.

Two days later, *The Times* reflected on a British Royal Commission then examining the effects of Jewish immigration on British society. 'Stepney,' *The Times* of New York noted, also was 'becoming a foreign town . . . Perhaps when the Royal Commission reports on what England should do about its un-English Londoners we shall learn what to do about these not yet Americanized New Yorkers whose meat riots were stranger than any nightmare.' *The Times* found comfort in what it felt to be a 'fact'. Immigrant Jews had sparked the 1902 troubles. 'The attempted incendiarism,' it believed, 'could not happen in an American crowd at all.' *The New York Times* had done more than idealize a world that had never been lost in suggesting that premodern Americans had been little more than ordered and expectant entrepreneurs. In comparing its response in 1902 to that of the New York *Herald* in 1837, we measure some of the distance that proper Americans had traveled from their own, premodern American roots.

Even though American society itself underwent radical structural changes between 1815 and the First World War, the shifting composition of its wage-earning population meant that traditional customs, rituals, and beliefs repeatedly helped shape the behavior of its diverse working-class groups. The street battle in 1843 that followed Irish efforts to prevent New York City authorities from stopping pigs from running loose in the streets is but one example of the force of old styles of behavior. Both the form and the content of much expressive working-class behavior, including labor disputes, often revealed the powerful role of secular and religious rituals. In 1857 the New York City unemployed kidnapped a musical band to give legitimacy to its parade for public works. After the Civil War, a Fall River cotton manufacturer boasted that the arrival of fresh Lancashire operatives meant the coming of 'a lot of greenhorns here', but an overseer advised him, 'Yes, but you'll find they have brought their horns with them.' A few years later, the Pittsburgh courts prevented three women married to coal miners from 'tinhorning' nonstrikers. The women, however, purchased mouth organs. ('Tinhorning', of course, was not merely an imported institution. In Franklin, Virginia, in 1867, for example, a Northern white clergyman who started a school for former slave children had two nighttime 'tin horn serenade[s]' from hostile whites.) Recurrent street demonstrations in Paterson accompanying frequent strikes and lockouts nearly always involved horns, whistles, and even Irish 'banshee' calls. These had a deep symbolic meaning, and, rooted in a shared culture, they sustained disputes. A Paterson manufacturer said of nonstrikers; 'They cannot go anywhere without being molested or insulted, and no matter what they do they are met and blackguarded and taunted in a way that no one can stand . . . which is a great deal worse than actual assaults'. Another manufacturer agreed:

> All the police in the world could not reach the annoyances that the weavers have at home and on the street that are not offenses—taunts and flings, insults and remarks. A weaver would rather have his head punched in than be called a 'knobstick', and this is the class of injury they hate worst, and that keeps them out more than direct assault.

But the manufacturers could not convince the town's mayor (himself a British immigrant and an artisan who had become a small manufacturer) to ban street demonstrations. The manufacturers even financed their own private militia to manage further disorders, but the street demonstrations continued with varying effectiveness until 1901 when a court injunction essentially defined the streets as private space by banning talking and singing banshee (or death) wails in them during industrial disputes. In part, the frequent recourse to the courts and to the state militia after the Civil War during industrial disputes was the consequence of working-class rituals that helped sustain long and protracted conflicts.

Symbolic secular and, especially, religious rituals and beliefs differed among Catholic and Jewish workers fresh to industrial America between 1894 and the First World War, but their function remained the same. Striking Jewish vestmakers finished a formal complaint by quoting the Law of Moses to prove that 'our bosses who rob us and don't pay us regularly commit a sin and that the cause of our union is a just one'. ('What do we come to America for?' these same men asked. 'To bathe in tears and to see our wives and children rot in poverty?') An old Jewish ritual oath helped spark the shirtwaist strike of women workers in 1909 that laid the basis for the International Ladies Garment Workers Union. A strike vote resulted in the plea, 'Do you mean faith? Will you take the old Jewish oath?' The audience responded in Yiddish: 'If I turn traitor to the cause, I now pledge, may this hand wither and drop off at the wrist from the arm I now raise.' (Incidentally, during the same strike a magistrate who advised troublesome Jewish women that 'you are on strike against God' provoked Bernard Shaw's classic quip, 'Delightful, medieval America always in the most intimate personal confidence of the Almighty.') Immigrant Catholic workers shared similar experiences with these immigrant Jews. A reporter noticed in 1910 at a meeting of striking Slavic steelworkers in Hammond, Indiana: 'The lights of the hall were extinguished. A candle stuck into a bottle was placed on a platform. One by one the men came and kissed the ivory image on the cross, kneeling before it. They swore not to scab.' Not all rituals were that pacific. That same year, Slavic miners in Avelia, Pennsylvania, a tiny patch on the West Virginia border, crucified George Rabish, a mine boss and an alleged labor spy. An amazed journalist felt their behaviour 'in the twentieth century . . . almost beyond belief':

> Rabish was dragged from his bed and driven out into the street amid the jeers of the merciless throng. . . . Several men set about fashioning a huge cross out of mine timbers. They even pressed a crown of thorns upon his temples. After they had nailed him to the cross, the final blasphemy was to dance and sing about the still living man.

That event was certainly unusual, but it was commonplace for time-honored religious symbols as well as American flags to be carried in the frequent parades of American workers. Western Pennsylvania Slavic and Italian coal miners in a bitter strike just east of Pittsburgh (eighteen of twenty thousand miners quit work for seventeen months when denied the right to join the United Mine Workers of America) in 1910 and 1911 carried such symbols. 'These rural marches,' said Paul Kellogg, 'were in a way reminiscent of the old time agrarian uprisings which have marked English history.' But theirs was the behaviour of peasant and village Slavs and Italians fresh to modern industrial America, and it was just such tenacious peasant-worker protests that caused the head of the Pennsylvania State Police to say that he modelled his force on the Royal Irish Constabulary, not, he insisted, 'as an anti-labor measure' but because 'conditions in Pennsylvania resembled those in strife-torn Ireland'. Peasant parades and rituals, religious oaths and food riots, and much else in the culture and behaviour of early twentieth-century immigrant American factory workers were cultural anachronisms to this man and to others, including Theodore Roosevelt, William Jennings Bryan, Elbert Gary, and even Samuel Gompers, but participants found them natural and effective forms of self-assertion and self-protection.

HERBERT G. GUTMAN

V

The perspective emphasized in these pages tells about more than the behaviour of diverse groups of American working men and women. It also suggests how larger, well-studied aspects of American society have been affected by a historical process that has 'industrialized' different peoples over protracted periods of time. [. . .] Contact and conflict between diverse preindustrial cultures and a changing and increasingly bureaucratized industrial society also affected the larger society in ways that await systematic examination. Contemporaries realized this fact. Concerned in 1886 about the South's 'dead'—that is, unproductive—population, the Richmond *Whig* felt the 'true remedy' to be 'educating the industrial morale of the people'. The *Whig* emphasized socializing institutions primarily outside of the working class itself. 'In the work of inculcating industrial ideas and impulses,' said the *Whig*, 'all proper agencies should be enlisted–family discipline, public school education, pulpit instruction, business standards and requirements, and the power and influence of the workingmen's associations.' What the *Whig* worried over in 1886 concerned other Americans before and after that time. And the resultant tension shaped society in important ways. Some are briefly suggested here. In a *New York Times* symposium ('Is America by Nature a Violent Society?') soon after the murder of Martin Luther King, the anthropologist Clifford Geertz warned: 'Vague references to the frontier tradition, to the unsettledness of American life, to our exploitative attitude toward nature or to our "youthfulness" as a nation, provide us with prefabricated "explanations" for events we, in fact, not only do not understand, but do not want to understand.'[11] More needs to be said than that Americans are 'the spiritual descendants of Billy the Kid, John Brown, and Bonnie and Clyde'. It has been suggested here that certain recurrent disorders and conflicts relate directly to the process that has continually 'adjusted' men and women to regular work habits and to the discipline of factory labor. [. . .].

The same process has even greater implications for the larger national American culture. Hannah Arendt has brilliantly suggested that the continual absorption of distinctive native and foreign 'alien' peoples has meant that 'each time the law had to be confirmed anew against the lawlessness inherent in an uprooted people', and that the severity of that process helps explain to her why the United States has 'never been a nation-state'.[12] The same process also affected the shaping and reshaping of American police and domestic military institutions. We need only realize that the burning of a Boston convent in 1834 by a crowd of Charlestown truckmen and New Hampshire Scotch-Irish brickmakers caused the first revision of the Massachusetts Riot Act since Shays' Rebellion, and that three years later interference by native firemen in a Sunday Irish funeral procession led to a two-hour riot involving upward of fifteen thousand persons (more than a sixth of Boston's population), brought militia to that city for the first time, and caused the first of many reorganizations of the Boston police force. The regular contact between alien work cultures and a larger industrializing or industrial society had other consequences. It often worried industrialists, causing C.E. Perkins, the president of the Chicago, Burlington, and Quincy Railroad to confide in a friend in the late nineteenth century. 'If I were able, I would found a school for the study of political economy in order to harden men's hearts'. It affected the popular culture. A guidebook for immigrant Jews in the 1890s advised how to make it in the New World. 'Hold fast, this is most necessary in America. Forget your past, your customs, and your ideals. . . . A bit of advise to you: do not take a moment's rest. Run, do, work, and keep your own good in mind.' Cultures and customs, however, are not that easily discarded. So it may be that America's extraordinary technological supremacy—its talent before the Second World War for developing labor-saving machinery and simplifying complex mechanical processes—depended less on 'Yankee know-how' than on the continued infusion of prefactory peoples into an increasingly industrialized society. The same process, moreover, may also explain why movements to legislate morality and to alter habits have lasted much longer in the United States than in most other industrial countries, extending from the temperance crusades of the 1820s and the 1830s to the violent opposition among Germans to such rules in the 1850s and the 1860s and finally to formal prohibition earlier in this century. Important relationships also exist between this process and the elite and popular nativist and racist social movements that have ebbed and flowed regularly from the 1840s until our own time, as well as between this process and elite political 'reform' movements between 1850 and the First World War.

The sweeping social process had yet another important consequence: it reinforced the biases that otherwise distort the ways in which elite observers perceive the world below them. When in 1902 *The New York Times* cast scorn upon and urged that force be used against the Jewish women food rioters, it conformed to a fairly settled elite tradition. Immigrant groups and the working population had changed in composition over time, but the rhetoric of influential nineteenth- and early twentieth-century elite observers remained constant. Disorders among the Jersey City Irish seeking wages due them from the Erie Railroad in 1859 led the Jersey City *American Standard* to call them 'imported *beggars*' and '*animals*', 'a mongrel mass of ignorance and crime and superstition, as utterly unfit for its duties, as they are for the common courtesies and decencies of civilized life'. [. . .] Although the Civil War ended slavery, it did not abolish these distorted perceptions and fears of new American workers. In 1869 *Scientific American* welcomed the 'ruder' laborers of Europe but urged them to 'assimilate' quickly or face 'a quiet but sure extermination'. Those who retained their alien ways, it insisted, 'will share the fate of the native Indian'. Elite nativism neither died out during the Civil War nor awaited a rebirth under the auspices of the American Protective Association and the Immigration Restriction League. In the mid-1870s, for example, the Chicago *Tribune* called striking immigrant brickmakers men but 'not reasoning creatures', and the Chicago *Post-Mail* described that city's Bohemian residents as 'depraved beasts, harpies, decayed physically and spiritually, mentally and morally, thievish and licentious'. The Democratic Chicago *Times* cast an even wider net in complaining that the country had become 'the cess-pool of Europe under the pretense that it is the asylum of the poor'. Most Chicago inhabitants in the Gilded Age were foreign-born or the children of the foreign-born, and most English-language Chicago newspapers scorned them. The Chicago *Times* told readers that Slavic Chicagoans were descended from 'the Scythians', 'eaters of raw animal food, fond of drinking the blood of their enemies whom they slew in battle, and [men] who preserved as trophies the scalps and skins of enemies whom they overthrew'. 'The old taste for the blood of an enemy has never been obliterated,' said this proper Chicago newspaper. And the Slavs had now 'invaded the peaceful republic'. In words echoed differently in *The New York Times* fifteen years later, the Chicago *Times* advised: 'Let us whip these slavic wolves back to the European dens from which they issue, or in some way exterminate them.' Here, as in the Jersey City *American Standard* (1859) and *The New York Times* (1902), much more was involved than mere ethnic distaste or 'nativism'. In quite a different connection and in a relatively homogenous country, the Italian Antonio Gramsci concluded of such evidence that 'for a social elite the features of subordinate groups always display something barbaric and pathological'. The changing composition of the American working class may make so severe a dictum more pertinent to the United States than to Italy. Class and ethnic fears and biases combined together to worry elite observers about the diverse worlds below them and to distort gravely their perceptions of these worlds. Few revealed these perceptual difficulties and genuine fears more clearly than John L. Hart in 1879:

> About one half of our poor can neither read nor write, have never been in any school, and know little, positively nothing, of the doctrines of the Christian religion, or of moral duties, or of any higher pleasures than beer-drinking and spirit-drinking, and the grossest sensual indulgence. . . . They have unclear, indefinable ideas of all around them: they eat, drink, breed, work, and die; and while they pass through their brute-like existence here, the rich and more intelligent classes are obliged to guard them with police and standing armies, and to cover the land with prisons, cages, and all kinds of receptacles for the perpetrators of crime.

Hart was not an uneducated 'nativst'. He had been professor of rhetoric, the English language, and literature at the College of New Jersey and also the principal of the New Jersey State Normal School. These words appeared in his book entitled *In The School-Room* (1879) where he argued that 'schoolhouses are cheaper than jails' and that 'teachers and books are better security than handcuffs and policemen'. We have returned to Lesson One.

VI

[. . .] The changing composition of the working population, the continued entry into the United States of nonindustrial people with distinctive cultures, and the changing structure of American society have combined together to produce common modes of thought and patterns of behaviour. But these have been experiences disconnected in time and shared by quite distinctive first-generation native and immigrant industrial Americans. It was not possible for the grandchildren of the Lowell mill girls to understand that their Massachusetts literary ancestors shared a great deal with their contemporaries, the peasant Slavs in the Pennsylvania steel mills and coal fields. And the grandchildren of New York City Jewish garment workers see little connection between black ghetto unrest in the 1960s and kosher meat riots seventy years ago. A half-century has passed since Robert Park and Herbert Miller published W. I. Thomas's *Old World Traits Transplanted*, a study which worried that the function of Americanization was the 'destruction of memories'.

Not all fled such a past. Born of Croatian parents in McKeesport, Pennsylvania, in 1912 (his father and brother later killed in industrial accidents), Gabro Karabin published a prize-winning short story in *Scribner's Magazine* (1947) that reflected on the experiences replayed in different ways by diverse Americans and near-Americans:

> Around Pittsburgh, a Croat is commonplace and at no time distinctive. As people think of us, we are cultureless, creedless, and colorless in life, though in reality we possess a positive and almost excessive amount of those qualities. Among ourselves, it is known that we keep our culture to ourselves because of the heterogeneous and unwholesome grain of that about us. . . . We are, in the light of general impression, just another type of laboring foreigner . . . fit only as industrial fuel.

The native-born American poet William Carlos Williams made a similar point. He lived near the city of Paterson and grasped its tragic but rich and deeply human interior textures far more incisively that temporary visitors such as Alexander Hamilton and William D. Haywood and illustrious native sons such as William Graham Sumner and Nicholas Murray Butler. The poet celebrated what gave life to a city in which men, women, and children made iron bars and locomotives and cotton and silk cloth:

> It's the anarchy of poverty
> delights me, the old
> yellow wooden house indented
> among the new brick tenements

Or a cast iron balcony
with panels showing oak branches
in full leaf. It fits
the dress of the children

reflecting every stage and
custom of necessity—
chimneys, roofs, fences of
wood and metal in an unfenced
age and enclosing next to
nothing at all: the old man
in a sweater and soft black
hat who sweeps the sidewalk—

his own ten feet of it—
in a wind that fitfully
turning his corner had
overwhelmed the entire city.

Karabin and Carlos Williams interpreted life and labor differently from the Chicago *Times* editor who in the centennial year (1876) boasted that Americans did not enquire 'when looking at a piece of lace whether the woman who wove it is a saint or a courtesan'.

APPENDIX

Table 3 Male occupational structure and household composition, selected Jews and Italians, New York City, 1905

	Jews	Italians
Total Males 20 and Older	6250	4518
Total Females 20 and Older	4875	3433
Male Occupational Structure		
Unskilled Labour	7.7%	39.1%
Clothing Worker	44.7%	18.0%
Skilled Worker (Nonclothing)	21.5%	29.2%
Nonlaborer	26.1%	13.7%
Household Composition		
Percentage of All Households with a Nuclear Kin-related Core	96.6%	94.5%
Number of Kin-related Households	3584	2945
Number of Subfamilies	159	262
Nuclear Households	48.6%	59.9%
Extended Households	11.8%	23.2%
Augmented Households	43.1%	21.1%
Percentage of Households and Subfamilies with a Husband and/or Father Present	93.2%	92.9%

Note: As in 1880 the percentages again total more than 100 percent because a small number of households that included both lodgers and relatives are counted twice.

The data are drawn from the New York State 1905 manuscript census schedules, and I am indebted to Mark Sosower, Leslie Neustadt, and Richard Mendales for gathering this material. As with the 1880 Paterson data, they cast grave doubts on the widely held belief that working-class family disruption commonly occurred as the byproduct of immigration, urbanization, and factory work. The 1905 Jews studied lived on the Lower East Side (Rutgers, Cherry, Pelham, Monroe, Water, Pike, Jefferson, Clinton, Madison, Livingston, Henry, Division, Montgomery, Delancey, Rivington, Norfolk, Suffolk, and East Third Streets, East Broadway, and Avenue B). The Italians resided on Hancock, Thompson, Mulberry, Bayard, Mott, Canal, Baxter, Elizabeth, Spring, Prince, Grand, Hester, MacDougal, Sullivan, West Houston, Bleecker, Bedford, Downing, and Carmine Streets, and the Bowery. The table above deserves another brief comment. Clothing workers are listed as a separate occupational category because census job descriptions make it impossible to determine their skill levels. A large percentage of those listed as nonlaborers engaged in petty enterprise (including peddling): 10.9 percent of all the Jewish males and 8.3 percent of all the Italian males. [. . .]

NOTES

[1] These instructions should be compared to those issued in February 1971 by LaGrange, Illinois, General Motors officials to engine division supervisory personnel:

BELL TO BELL POLICY: It is the policy of the [electromotive] division that all employe[e]s be given work assignments such that all will be working effectively and efficiently during their scheduled working hours except for the time required for allowable personal considerations. EACH EMPLOYEE WILL BE INSTRUCTED ON THE FOLLOWING POINTS: 1. Be at their work assignment at the start of the shift. 2. Be at their work assignment at the conclusion of their lunch period. 3. All employe[e]s will be working effectively and efficiently until the bell of their scheduled lunch period and at the end of their scheduled shift. 4. Employe[e]s are to work uninterrupted to the end of the scheduled shift. In most instances, machines and area clean-up can be accomplished during periods of interrupted production prior to the last full hour of the shift'.

The instructions came to my attention after I read an earlier version of this paper to students and faculty at Northern Illinois University. Edward Jennings, a student and a member of Local 719, United Automobile Workers, delivered the document to me the following day. See also the copy of the work rules posted in 1888 in the Abbot-Downing Factory in Concord, New Hampshire, and deposited in the New Hampshire Historical Society. Headed 'NOTICE! TIME IS MONEY!' the rules included the following factory edict: 'There are conveniences for washing, but it must be done outside of working hours, and not at our expense'. I am indebted to Harry Scheiber for bringing this document to my attention.

[2] Sidney Pollard, 'The adaptation of the labour force', in *Genesis of Modern Management* (Cambridge, 1965), 160–208.

[3] J. F. C. Harrison, *Learning and Living* (London, 1961), 268: E. P. Thompson. 'Time, work-discipline, and industrial capitalism', *Past and Present*, 50 (1971), 57.

[4] David Brody, *Steelworkers in America: The Non-Union Era* (Cambridge, Mass., 1960) *passim;* David Brody, *Labour in Crisis* (Philadelphia, 1965) 15–45.

[5] Richard L. Ehrlich, 'The Development of Manufacturing in Selected Counties in the Erie Canal Corridor, 1815-1860', (Ph.D. dissertation. State University of New York, Buffalo, 1972); E. P. Thompson, *The Making of the English Working Class*, (London, 1963) 97, 192.

[6] Thompson, *ibid.*, p. 73.

[7] Franklin E. Coyne, *The Development of the Cooperage Industry in the United States* (Chicago, 1940), 7–26, especially 21–22.

[8] Neil Smelzer, *Social Change in the Industrial Revolution* (Chicago, 1959), 193.

[9] Thompson, *Making of the English Working Class, op. cit.*, 194.

[10] Asa Briggs, review of Thompson, *Making of the English Working Class*, in *Labor History*, 6 (1965), 84–91, R. H. Tawney, *Agrarian Problem in the Sixteenth Century* (London, 1912), 177.

[11] Clifford Geertz, 'We can claim no special gift for violence', *New York Times Magazine*, April 28, 1968, 24–25.

[12] Hannah Arendt, 'Lawlessness is inherent in the Uprooted', *New York Times Magazine*, April 28, 1968, 24–25.

(b) Middle Class Hegemony: Working Class Sub-Culture

TRYGVE THOLFSEN

The middle classes dominated the Victorian city and left their mark on every aspect of its common life. They confront us with two faces, each reflecting their unrivalled ascendancy. On the one hand, they were earnest and articulate spokesmen for the highest values of the community, especially the ideal of improvement for all. As such they were exemplars of a culture that esteemed the public pursuit of moral ideals. They preached the gospel of improvement and prized good works done in that cause. On the other hand, merchants, manufacturers, and professional men also constituted a ruling class, exercising dominion over the wage earners below them. Their social values and their behaviour reflected the imperatives inherent in their position in the class structure. Implicit in their articulation of formally universal consensus values were social presuppositions that bent them into the shape required by an inegalitarian society; differential social roles assumed middle-class pre-eminence. They also engaged in overtly ideological activity—explicitly directed to the defence of their privileged position against the working-class challenge.

In this social and cultural setting the middle classes established a moral and intellectual hegemony. They secured a substantial degree of popular acquiescence in their conception of consensus values and class relations, not by imposing an ideology through propaganda, but by putting to good use the various advantages accruing to the dominant class in this culture. A number of interlocking elements legitimised middle-class pre-eminence and eroded working-class radical ideology. First of all, merely by playing the idealised social role of leaders in the common enterprise of improvement, merchants and manufacturers were justifying their implicit claim to continued superiority. Secondly, as community spokesmen

T. Tholfsen, *Working Class Radicalism in Mid-Victorian England*, London, Croom Helm, 1976; pp. 197–257. Abridged.

acclaiming the progress that was being made towards shared goals, they were confirming the legitimacy of underlying social and economic arrangements. They most effectively consolidated their hegemony when they were not engaged in defensive propaganda directed against working-class radicalism. Third, the structure of power and status ensured that the middle-class version of consensus values would be embedded in the cultural pattern of the mid-Victorian cities. The end product of the moral and intellectual improvement of the working classes would be the 'respectable working man': educated well enough to understand the reasoned arguments of his social superiors, to respect their aacomplishments, and to strive to get on in the world within the limits set from above. While the habitual deference that the villager accorded to the squire was officially banished from the manufacturing towns, new forms of subordination emerged, ostensibly based on the reasoned acceptance of demonstrably valid ideas and policies. Finally, middle-class hegemony was sustained by intertwined social and institutional forms that moulded working-class behaviour to the contours of the class structure. [. . .]

The pursuit of profit was the primary concern of mid-Victorian businessmen and they did not permit ancillary interests to interfere. It could be said of most of them, as it was of Richard Smith, a Nottingham manufacturer, that 'his ruling passion through life was a desire to gain wealth'. The pious Methodist who was confiding to his journal a description of his recently deceased friend and employer hastened to qualify this judgement somewhat: 'Or more properly it was the passion which would have ruled on every occasion and with absolute power had not religion kept a check upon it and moderated its operation.' But religion had no easy task of it: 'He was really fond of making money, and this led him sometimes to deviate slightly from what I considered the path of perfect honour.' Smith made plain to his employee just where he stood on the matter of money. ' "Money is not my object", I said to him one day when he increased my salary, and I shall never forget how emphatically he replied, "Then it ought to be, George—it *ought* to be." ' When he parted with his money Smith expected something in exchange: 'As a Methodist, he was useful in various offices, and always liberal in his givings. His liberality was surprising to anyone who knew his fondness for money. But he invariably tried to keep a leading position in the Church, and as he could not accomplish it otherwise, he did it by giving his cash.' Smith's life was centred on his business: 'He was exceedingly industrious, and never seemed contented unless hard at work.' Six working men served as pallbearers at his funeral.

Like Smith the Victorian middle classes conducted their affairs with mixed motives and values, combined in varying proportions. Without neglecting their profits or reducing their privileges, they also responded, however sporadically and fitfully, to the imperatives of their culture. The disparate claims of class and culture introduced a deep ambivalence into their relations with the working classes. While paying their employees the lowest wages and exercising the maximum authority, they hoped for harmony, cordiality and even affection. They made the most of the hegemonic possibilities inherent in the social and cultural patterns of the mid-Victorian cities.

1 THE GOSPEL OF IMPROVEMENT

As the high priests of mid-Victorian culture middle-class leaders preached the gospel of improvement. In countless secular sermons they affirmed the overriding ideal of the community—the pursuit of progress and advancement for all. They presided over the ritual and litany of the established forms of public worship. In this milieu the middle-class defined its social role in terms of the shared ideals of a culture that prized high aspiration. Members of the middle-class proudly assumed leadership in the enterprise of improvement, extending a helping hand to those less fortunate, who had further to go in the quest for the highest qualities of mind and spirit. In this spirit they took on the mission of elevating the working classes, not to keep them in their place, but to fulfil the highest aims of mid-Victorian society. Their hegemony rested on the pride they could take in thus acting in behalf of high principle.

Edward Baines, Jr. was second to none as a preacher of the gospel of improvement. As editor of the *Leeds Mercury* and as the head of the Yorkshire Union of Mechanics' Institutes, he was an eloquent spokesman for nonconformist liberalism in the West Riding. One of the talks that Baines was in the habit of giving on his visit to mechanics' institutes was entitled 'On the Advantages and Pleasure of Institutions for the Promotion of Mental Improvement, and on the Spirit of the Student'. In the text of this secular sermon, written out and revised in his own hand, Baines touched on the main themes of the culture. He opened his remarks with a standard reference to the presence of men from all classes in the institutes: 'There are few spectacles more interesting and delightful than an assembly, composed of persons of various ranks, occupations, and ages, drawn together by the desire of mutually promoting their intellectual and moral improvement.' From this commonplace beginning, he moved on to a lyrical passage celebrating

> The man upon whose soul Knowledge has beamed with its sweet and salutary influences. He walks erect with his face towards heaven, pursuing truth, seeing clearly the path of duty, enjoying the beauties and wonders of nature, distinguishing the evil from the good, and the false from true, appreciating justly the faculties bestowed upon him, and employing them for wise and noble purposes.

By contrast, Baines shuddered with revulsion at the 'criminality of the man whom his maker has endowed with the lofty powers of reason, and who ungratefully and shamefully neglects to cultivate them. . . . To neglect those talents is to despise them, and to despise them is to mock their Author'. The mechanics' institute was a great deal more than an agency of adult education: it was the incarnation of the sacred values of a Christian and liberal community.

Like Baines, official spokesmen for the ideals of the community on public occasions came from the upper middle class of the great towns, the new urban patriciate that had established itself by the 1850s. But the same sensibility of exalted aspiration also found insistent expression at a lower social level, among the middling and lower middle classes. For the social historian the *Surrey Street Circuit Reporter*, with its platitudes and heavy-handed prose, provides even more vivid evidence of the texture of the dominant ethos. Especially noteworthy is the extent to which these Sheffield Methodists were preoccupied with secular values and interests. The mid-Victorian tendency to moralise and spiritualise material reality is conspicuously present. The *Reporter* for November 1868 opens with a paean to the 'hives of industry in Sheffield', which are acclaimed as illustrations of 'colossal power, the superiority of mind over material things'. The city is itself evidence of the fact that 'happily we have passed away from the old barbaric notion that power lived in bone and brawn, thews, and sinews'. In the present day the 'true type of personal power' does not reside in high birth or even in wealth. 'The hard-hearted and close-handed money lender cannot reach the vital interests of being: he only touches the outer rim. Hence men turn to a cultured intellect, and say that "intellectual stature is the true stature of a man".' To be sure, the reader is warned that 'the tree of knowledge is not the tree of life. He who lives for intellect alone, lives beneath a cold sky.' But the theme so central to classic Methodism has been translated into a sentimental mid-Victorian idiom:

> There is something higher than mere mental culture, and this is moral power: its seat is in the heart, its companion is an enlightened and peaceful conscience, its central law is love; and its pulses act in a thousand ways—it denounces wrong, asserts right, places the standard of moral principle high and yields to it allegiance; it is the law of heaven for earth and all time and all being.

The main message, however, is the triumph, power and omnipresence of mind in the economic and political life of the day:

> The impulses of thought are far-felt and permanent. What stately and strong monuments of mind power are around us. A word—a thought passes from you: it lives in ages, becomes a seedling and germ to give birth to the unknown and untold. Thoughts live as watchwords in temptation and stimulants in struggle; they are not the mausoleums of the thinker, but his immortal incarnation, [. . .]; this it is that sways its wand over popular

assemblies, decrees judicial judgements, directs statesmen, rules cabinets, charms our evenings, guides our history, and beguiles the student till his lamp pales before the light of day.

The middle-class defined its social role in terms of the ideal of moral and intellectual improvement for all. The obligation of men who had already reached a high level of personal development was 'to ameliorate the condition of the people, and to promote the physical, intellectual, or moral well-being of the masses'. By the 1850s talk about elevating the working classes was so common that it could be suggested that 'reading and writing articles on the "elevation of the working classes" are good, but *work* is infinitely better'. It was usual to take note of the good works already being achieved in this area, while recognising that more needed to be done: 'One of the most hopeful signs in English society is the active interest which is now shown in the welfare of the humbler classes. It is, we think, widely felt that some more serious effort must be employed in their behalf. Their condition presses on the nation's conscience.' Other spokesmen were even more optimistic about the extent of benevolent activity under way in behalf of the well-being of the working classes. 'The well-informed and the benevolent of all classes seem moved by a noble desire to instruct the ignorant, and to reclaim the vicious.' The Manchester area was praised for the institutions that had been established by the inhabitants and dedicated to 'religion, to science, to education, to the improvement of the tastes and habits of the people'.

Inevitably, middle-class improvers took an ostentatiously high-minded and even 'spiritual' approach to the task of elevating and instructing the working classes. An article on 'Our Working Classes', for example, reflects the outlook of Baines and of Surrey Street Methodism. If the author was overdoing it a bit even for the 1850s, his excesses do no more than overstate recurring cultural themes. The article was addressed to a large question grandly stated: 'How then are the masses to be educated to a living consciousness of the dignity and purposes of human nature?' The answer was to be found in

> education of the spiritual nature, the invigorating of the moral forces of the soul [. . .] and the enlightenment of the understanding [. . .] In a word, we want the workmanship [. . .] to stand out in visible *bas relief* from the mass, and to realise the perfection of his being in the culture of his every mental and moral faculty in the service of his fellow-men.

The common mind 'must be made to feel the vitalising influence of living earnestness in the persons of those who have grasped the true idea of progress for themselves, and are striving to reduce it to conscious reality'. Similar tone prevails in leading articles in the newspapers of the manufacturing districts: 'We have faith in truth—in its vitality, and in the power of honest manly action; and we have confidence in nothing else as means of improving and elevating our fellow-men.' A few weeks later another leader explained the value of poetry for 'educating our masses'. Poetry would 'do much to elevate their thoughts, refine their tastes, and improve their habits'. [. . .]

The middle-class role in improving the working classes was acted out ceremonially on those frequent occasions that marked the founding of a new institution or the completion of a year's work. In January 1864, for example, a group of progressive businessmen of Leeds asembled to lend their support to a newly-established working men's hall. A building had been purchased and this meeting was intended to raise money to furnish and operate it. From the platform the sponsors of the meeting described to the assembled working men what they proposed to do. 'Their object was to provide a place in which the working men could assemble and feel themselves at home', read newspapers, books and periodicals, listen to songs and concerts, and 'have friendly intercourse without being surrounded by any of the attractions of vice'. It was also intended to give working men 'an opportunity, if they were so disposed, of elevating themselves by educating their minds in such education classes as they proposed to have, and by listening to lectures and readings'. The sponsors flattered working-class independence in the new mode that had replaced the hostility of 1834:

> They desired that the working men should feel that that was their institution, and not an institution of any class above them. (Hear, hear.) If employers of labour and others united with them in that movement, it was not to take the management out of their hands, but to give them that friendly help which they might perhaps need, and which would enable them to carry out the better their own wishes and purposes.

Just three months later the mayor presided over a soirée celebrating the successful operation of the working men's hall. In his speech he reminded the members that 'their thanks were due to the gentlemen who had used their influence in establishing this institution in Leeds, that "union is strength", and that the success or failure solely depended upon themselves'. At the soirée, a representative of the Leeds Working Men's Institute reported on the activity of that organisation in the first three months of the year. He announced that 'with certain of the members there had been altered homes, refurnished dwellings, children better clad, and families frequenting places of worship, where before there had been nothing but raggedness, wretchedness, and misery'. He expressed the belief that working men's institutions 'would effect, if generally adopted, a complete renovation in our social system; and he was happy to think that where they had one common object in view—raising the working classes to a higher level—there would be no rivalry in establishing them'. It was a familiar pattern; modest activity and utopian rhetoric; middle-class pre-eminence and working-class gratitude.

These ceremonial transactions between the classes also reflected the middle-class desire for a community characterised by genuinely harmonious and friendly relations. In itself this was not surprising, since the harmony of interests among those classes had been a basic tenet of political economy and liberal ideology from the beginning. What is noteworthy, however, was the mid-Victorian obsession with the achievement of 'cordial' relations between the classes. Looking back anxiously on the disorders of the early-Victorian decades, the middle classes were not content merely with tranquillity, but hoped for something grander. They wanted something more than mere submission or rational acquiescence from the working classes: they wished for a pure and noble relationship between those of different station. A Norwich minister expressed this social ideal in the form of a familiar comparison between the mid-1860s and the generation that preceded it. He took satisfaction in the fact that there had come into being 'a far better spirit between classes, and a sounder feeling of trust in the men, both as between themselves and as regards employers and the richer orders. As elsewhere there has been far greater personal intercourse between the labouring and higher classes of late years than formerly, which has tended to a more human feeling on both sides'. It was commonplace to call for more intimate and friendly communication between masters and men'. 'It is high time', wrote a factory owner, 'that these struggles of physical strength and brute force should give way to reason and more kindly feeling'.

Samuel Smiles shared this mid-Victorian aspiration to the achievement of class harmony, through a universal commitment to the enterprise of improvement. His *Self-Help*, published in 1859, was the best known of all the books of advice and counsel for the working classes. Even in his own day Smiles was the most celebrated expositor of the mid-Victorian social gospel. In the conventional wisdom of later generations, Smiles was to become the archetype of bourgeois ideology, self-serving, smug and hypocritical. While Smiles certainly deserves his reputation as an exemplar of mid-Victorianism, he was by no means the cardboard figure of popular mythology. Historical scholarship [. . .] has underlined the complexity of Smiles' thought. His early radicalism has been demonstrated, and we have been reminded that he was capable not only of rejecting laissez-faire dogmatism but deriding it. In sum, Smiles exemplifies a complex culture that resists generalisation.

The first point to be made about *Self-Help* is that it did not preach a narrowly economic creed, urging workmen to work hard in order to get on in the world, and providing helpful advice to that end. In fact, as a representative expression of mid-Victorian culture, its primary emphasis was on the moral and intellectual development of the individual; and the end product of self-help was depicted as an individual of unsurpassed nobility of mind and character. Smiles celebrated self-culture for its own sake and rebuked those who saw it 'too exclusively as a means of "getting on" '. He had little sympathy for those who 'have perhaps looked upon knowledge in the light of a marketable commodity, and are consequently mortified because it does not sell as they expected it would do'. He warned them against becoming disappointed in the work of self-culture when 'they do not "get on" in the world so fast as they think they deserve to do'. To be sure, Smiles noted that from the point of view of advancing in the world 'education is one of the best investments of time and labour'. Nevertheless, he pointed out that 'the great majority of men, in all times, however, enlightened', must necessarily remain working men. Smiles, of course, took a very high line on the matter of the intrinsic value of self-culture for such men: 'We can elevate the condition of labour by allying it to noble thoughts, which confer a grace upon the lowliest as well as highest rank ... Even though self-culture may not bring wealth, it will at all events give one the companionship of elevated thoughts'.

There was a great deal in Smiles to which even radical working men might subscribe. For that matter, there was a great deal that would be acceptable to many moralists. His observations on respectability, for example, were unexceptionable. On the one hand, he denounced 'average worldly respectability' and tried to develop an acceptable version. 'The respectable man is one worthy of regard, literally worth turning to look at. But the respectability that consists in merely keeping up appearances is not worth looking at in any sense. Far better and more respectable is the good poor man than the bad rich one—better the humble silent man than the agreeable well-appointed rogue who keeps his gig'. In this connection he reiterated a theme that recurs in his writings and in mid-Victorian social idealism as a whole: what really matters is not material success but the development of mind and character. 'The highest object of life we take to be to form a manly character, and to work out the best development possible, of body and spirit—of mind, conscience, heart, and soul. This is the end: all else ought to be regarded but as the means'. He did his best to redefine 'success' in these terms: 'That is not the most successful life in which a man gets the most pleasure, the most money, the most power or place, honour or fame; but that in which a man gets the most manhood, and performs the greatest amount of useful work and of human duty'. He also tried to keep money in its proper place, subordinate to nobler things: 'Money is power after its sort, it is true; but intelligence, public spirit, and moral virtue, are powers too, and far nobler ones.' Smiles' vestigial radicalism emerged in his indignation at those whose only concern was the acquisition of wealth. 'The manner in which many allow themselves to be sacrificed to their love of wealth reminds one of the cupidity of the monkey—that caricature of our species'. Smiles conceded that 'worldly success, measured by the accumulation of money is no doubt a very dazzling thing; and all men are naturally more or less the admirers of worldly success'. But he emphasised that wealth must not be mistaken for virtue.

> Though men of persevering, sharp, dexterous and unscrupulous habits, ever
> on the watch to push opportunities, may and do 'get on' in the world, yet it is
> quite possible that they may not possess the slightest elevation of character,
> nor a particle of real goodness. He who recognises no higher logic than that of
> the shilling may become a very rich man, and yet remain all the while an
> exceedingly poor creature. For riches are no proof whatever of moral worth;
> and their glitter often serves only to draw attention to the worthlessness of
> their possessor, as the light of the glow-worm reveals the grub.

[. . .] Smiles did not single out the vices of the working classes, but
subjected all ranks to his stern moralism. Thus on the subject of those who
failed to recognise the value of self-culture for its own sake, he did not limit
himself to strictures about working men who were too eager to 'get on' but
took the propertied classes to task as well:

> The same low idea of self-culture is but too prevalent in other classes, and is
> encouraged by the false views of life which are always more or less current in
> society. But to regard self-culture either as a means of getting past others in
> the world or of intellectual dissipation and amusement, rather than as a
> power to elevate the character and expand the spiritual nature, is to place it on
> a very low level.

If anything, Smiles' Puritanism found an even handier target among the
classes that had enough time and money for the pursuit of pleasure.

Smiles tried to treat class differences as irrelevant to the common
humanity of men. His advice applied equally to all men, regardless of class.
He drew examples from all society levels. He singled out instances of noble
behaviour among the common people, but only to underline the uni-
versality of his message. Hence it is fitting that *Self-Help* should end with a
chapter inviting all men to aspire to be true gentlemen:

> Riches and rank have no necessary connexion with genuine gentlemanly
> qualities. The poor man may be a true gentleman—in spirit and in daily life.
> He may be honest, truthful, upright, polite, temperate, courageous, self-
> respecting, and self-helping—that is, be a true gentleman. The poor man with
> a rich spirit is in all ways superior to the rich man with a poor spirit.

Smiles probably differed from most of his middle-class contemporaries in
believing all that he said; there was no unspoken qualifications. He spoke
from a background of radicalism and populism. Smiles meant every word
of it when he wrote that the qualities of the true gentleman depend 'not
upon fashion or manners, but upon moral worth—not on personal
possessions, but on personal qualities'. In fact, of course, gentility was
primarily a social category, with a gloss of moral qualities. Smiles,
however, was not writing as an observer but as a moralist, and was treating
the 'gentleman' as a moral ideal.

Smiles and Edward Baines, Jr., both eloquent exponents of the middle-class version of consensus values, arrived at a similar ideological destination by rather different routes. In the 1830s and 1840s Baines and his father, writing from the platform of the *Leeds Mercury,* took a hard line towards the working classes. They acclaimed the new poor law and resisted factory legislation in the name of political economy, while Smiles in the *Leeds Times* denounced the new poor law and rebuked Baines for his hostility to the working classes. By 1859, however, both men were expressing substantially the same type of benevolent middle-class liberalism. [. . .]

2 'NOBLER FORMS OF AUTHORITY'

In preaching the gospel of improvement and pursuing good works the middle classes were strengthening their hegemony without necessarily seeking to defend their privileges against the threat from below. In fact, the moral strength of their position rested to a large extent on the fact that they embodied so well the shared ideals of the community. At the same time, of course, the middle classes pursued the grand aims of the culture within a social framework that conditioned every aspect of their outlook and behaviour. Their social values presupposed middle-class pre-eminence and working-class subordination. Implicit in the middle-class version of consensus values was a justification of its privileged position and a rejection of egalitarian alternatives. Their formulation of mid-Victorian ideals reflected a perspective that presupposed the continuing dominance of the middle classes.

In addition to these indirect effects of the class structure, the middle-class also actively sought to impose its own stamp on mid-Victorian cultural patterns. They used the resources of their society and culture to construct new forms of working-class subordination. They imparted a middle-class slant to the ruling ideals of the community as a whole; improvement, self-respect, rationality, and independence were defined in a way that undermined the working-class radical attempt to define them in universal terms. Much of their preaching was animated by the consciously ideological determination to convince working men of Chartist errors and sins. This meant persuading working men to accept the cult of respectability and the myth of success.

In the very act of preaching improvement and elevating the masses, the middle classes were also constructing new forms of working-class subordination. Characteristically, they did so while explicitly rejecting the sort of habitual deference that had characterised the social order of rural England:

The notion that men would more readily obey legitimate authority because they were utterly ignorant of its claims and their obligations, or that they would better discharge the duties and fulfil the responsibilities Providence had assigned them because they were kept in total darkness as to the reciprocities of social life, will now be universally rejected as the most preposterous of fallacies . . .

Such spokesmen for the new order made it clear, however, that they expected working men to accept leadership from above voluntarily and on the basis of rational choice. In fact, one of the chief signs of 'improvement', not to say 'respectability', was the ability to understand the world as perceived by the educated and progressive middle classes. Fortified by a self-image of rectitude, rationality, and liberality, they took it for granted that they deserved enthusiastic support from below. There was a corollary to every stock liberal denunciation of Tory-style deference: once working men were enlightened about the duties and responsibilities of each social class, they would understand that legitimate authority was entitled to obedience and would act accordingly. Working men who had been given the opportunity to develop their rational powers would recognise the merits of their superiors and gladly follow their lead.

In keeping with the mid-Victorian ethos, the middle classes sought 'nobler forms of authority'. This phrase occurs in a pamphlet published in 1856 that brings together a number of liberal ideas and attitudes usually found only in fragmentary form.[1] The author expresses a central doctrine of middle-class liberalism in the framework of a progressive view of history: 'The power of sheer naked *will* over dependent classes always gives place to nobler forms of authority as those classes become less rude and ignorant, and more intelligent and moral'. As in the speeches of John Bright, the 'iron despotism of the feudal system' is depicted as giving way to the liberal and rational regime of the present. The 'slow growth of civilisation' involves the replacement of the raw power of the aristocracy by a regime characterised by rationality, morality, and responsiveness to public opinion. The liberal view of history traces the sentimentalised origins of an idealised present:

> As the intellectual, and still more the moral, faculties of the people (and of their rulers) were developed, the government found itself obliged, and at length even disposed, to appeal to reason and the sense of right in its subjects until, at last, authority came to rest entirely upon an enlightened public opinion.

Moving easily from the realm of government to 'factory rule', the author of the pamphlet suggests that these new forms of authority have a much broader application. He sounds a theme that recurs in mid-Victorian ideology—upright and independent working men freely assenting to the views of benevolent employers. Characteristically, he notes that the more rational and benign forms of authority will also be a good deal more effective:

> Precisely in proportion as working men and women shall stand erect before
> their employers, in the unassuming dignity of conscious intelligence and
> uprightness, so will the bearing of the latter become respectful, losing the
> tone and manner of command, yet consciously acquiring more and more of
> the reality of power.

In the spirit of even-handedness required by the mid-Victorian consensus,
he points out that employers were to blame for much of the 'perverseness' of
working-class behaviour, which originated in 'a natural resentment
against a still lingering though greatly mitigated peremptoriness, hauteur,
harshness and selfishness among employers'. He attributes the
considerable improvement that has since taken place, such as the end of
machine breaking, to 'increased intelligence, with a kindlier demeanour on
the part of capitalists'. While denouncing working-class combinations, he
recommends that employers deal with them by a 'conciliatory and healing
line of conduct'. Employers ought to 'attract to themselves the better and
higher feelings of the Employed, by an unvarying manifestation of respect,
of courtesy, and of a benevolent interest in their well-being'. The author's
premise was a commonplace of enlightened and progressive middle-class
thought: 'We are persuaded that the existing antagonism between these
mutually dependent classes, arises chiefly from their isolation, and would
soon give place to better sentiments, if a closer union could be effected between them'; and the 'closer union' was to take place on middle-class terms.
Cordiality and friendliness would pay off in more effective social control.

In developing new forms of hegemony the middle-class bent consensus
values into a shape that conformed to the imperatives of the social
structure. Seemingly universal principles were emptied of their uni-
versality and re-defined in class terms. This ideological pattern can be
seen, for example, in a series of letters written in 1854 by Samuel Robinson,
a progressive Manchester manufacturer. In one of the letters, addressed to
the workers in his factory, Robinson took as his text a statement made by a
judge at the Stafford assizes 'lamenting the separation between class and
class as being one great cause of many of our social evils, and
insisting on the necessity of closer intercourse as one of the
remedies'. In putting out his version of one of the standard social pieties of
the day the judge had said, 'If I were asked what is the great want of English
society, I would say, in one word, the want is THE WANT OF
SYMPATHY'. When trade union leaders seized on this dictum and posted
it on the walls of the town, Robinson was moved to comment. While
earnestly expressing his most 'cordial' agreement with the judge's remarks,
he gave it a distinctly middle-class slant. Reversing the trade union's
interpretation, Robinson warned working men not to make the mistake of
assuming that what was needed was more sympathy by masters towards
men. On the contrary, he explained why the men must develop a more
sympathetic understanding of their employers. In the course of his homily

Robinson took another consensus principle—the independence of the individual—and gave it a middle-class coloration: 'It is not true benevolence to the working classes to do for them anything which tends to foster in them a spirit of dependence upon the acts of others instead of a manly reliance upon their own; to be constantly doing in their behalf what they have the means and the power to do for themselves'. In fact, 'real benevolence will show itself rather in ready sympathy with every plan formed by yourselves for your own advancement and improvement and by active endeavours to promote it'. Thus, independence was re-defined to mean avoiding reliance on trade unions and concentrating instead on self-improvement.

Behind the middle-class version of consensus ideals lay the assumption that working men occupied a particular position in society, at the base of the social order, and ought to conduct themselves accordingly. From this perspective, the surest sign of moral and intellectual improvement in a working man was his readiness to recognise the merits of middle-class arguments and to accept enlightened leadership from above. If he proved resistant to such arguments or refractory in his relations with his superiors, this was an indication that something had gone awry. A working man who sent off a rather moderate and well-written letter to the *Bradford Observer* found himself none the less the object of editorial rebuke. While the editor conceded that the letter writer was 'a man above the average of his class in point of intelligence', he pointed out that he 'has not yet learnt to govern himself'. The working man had 'evinced a proud and turbulent spirit', Such an offence could not be tolerated. It seems that the man who wrote the letter had not behaved in the proper manner when applying for poor relief: 'His conduct both towards the Relieving Officer and the Relief Committee was frequently unbecoming a man in his position.' What the middle-classes expected of the improving working man was not pride or turbulence, but humility and moderation. They had in mind the traits described in a *Manchester Guardian* editorial in 1858, congratulating the working-class on having stopped demanding the vote as a cure for all its ills:

It is not because education has made the lower classes more intelligent, more self-reliant, more energetic, has taught them to think more justly of their fellow countrymen, to feel ashamed of their former prejudices, and to acknowledge that it rests with them and not with any Government to ameliorate their social condition?

Even in strikes 'moderation and order are generally manifested in their proceedings, and there is a better appreciation of the laws that govern the rise and fall of wages'. This was what the majority of the middle classes meant by working-class rationality and moderation.

One of the more pervasive social assumptions underlying middle-class improving activity was the notion that working men would derive great benefits merely from associating with their social superiors. There was a great deal of talk about the importance of bringing the classes together and overcoming social isolation, all of which tended to confirm and reinforce middle-class claims to superiority. The annual report of the mechanics' institute in Ripon for 1856, describing the establishment of a girls' school to teach domestic economy, is an interesting example of the fusion of the newer attitudes of liberalism with older traditions of Christian charity in a context that underlines the persistence of the social attitudes of a stratified society. Three evening classes per week were provided for the benefit of the 'Daughters of the poor'. The teaching was done by middle-class women, who took 'a real and truly Christian interest' in the welfare of their pupils. The report that described their activity in glowing terms also included a blunt statement of class relations and the social function of charitable activity: 'An intercourse has been established between two Classes; the educated and the uneducated. It must not cease here. Kindness, and Christian charity, or love, are levers of unexpressed power. With these much may be done.' The writer is referring, of course, to the power to do good, but it is also clear from the context that the maintenance of social discipline and the exercise of social power are perceived as essential aspects of the charitable activity. The levers of power 'give admission where doors would otherwise be closed against us; and once in, God working with us, great help may be given to the advancement of that true social reformation, which, in our day, so many efforts are being made to accomplish'. That 'true social reformation' envisaged an extension of the cult of respectability. Such social presuppositions underlay the high-minded intentions of the teachers, who were doing their best to 'inculcate right principles', to open the minds of their pupils 'for the reception of better nourishment than they have been wont to feed upon', and to create a taste for 'what is good, and pure and holy'. It was also taken for granted that their pupils would benefit from 'the refinement introduced by the intercourse with persons of a superior social rank'.

Implicit in middle-class efforts to elevate the working classes and in their ideological accompaniment was a determination to emancipate working men from any vestiges of Chartism or other forms of radicalism. The propertied classes looked back on the Chartist era with dismay and a lingering anxiety. Mid-Victorian panegyrics to class harmony reflected a feeling of relief that the radical threat had been turned aside. The middle classes hoped that they had won the sort of lasting victory over Chartism that an editorial writer had called for in 1848: 'Our governing classes must address themselves to the task of *conquering the will of the Chartists*. This is the only way of putting them down and *keeping them down*. They may be put down by physical force, but they can be kept down only by moral force.'

Although such plain talk soon gave way to a softer mid-Victorian idiom, the basic attitudes persisted. The frequent contrasts that were drawn between the tranquil 1850s and 1860s and the disorders of the previous generation reflect a continuing concern with the working-class Left. Typically, however, spokesman for the middle-class put the most most positive construction on the changes that had taken place. In mid-Victorian liberal ideology the abandonment of Chartist militancy was extolled as evidence of the progress that had been made since those dark days. The following account of the transformation of Longton, in the Potteries, is typical:

> On political questions the people were excitable and violent. The creed of the lower classes was rabid Chartism; and during elections a most malignant spirit manifested itself. I am proud, however, to say, that Chartism is only known as a thing that was. Improved circumstances and better information have wiped out that stain from the character of the town for ever.

There had been a great change for the better, as public improvement had a beneficial influence on the people: 'Their tastes have been elevated, their ambitions excited, and a desire for progress has been turned into a proper channel. An onward march has been started in good earnest.'

Implicit in the ideology of improvement was a rebuke to working men who, not so long before, had been receptive to Chartist demagoguery. The ideological implications of the improvement ethic could also be made quite explicit: 'The most effectual remedy for all grievances which afflict the working classes is to be found in the increase of their intelligence', and 'the most powerful assertions of the fraternity and equality of men lies in the universal demonstration of moral and intellectual culture'. Similarly, an M.P. addressing a mechanics' institute produced a new and democratic version of the old be-content-with-your-lot theme. While regaling his audience with the prospect of great moral and intellectual benefits, he added that in most cases they would not be accompanied by worldly advancement:

> High positions were not open to all, but those who educated themselves would find the benefit in a moral and religious point of view, in love of their fellows, in the peace in their bosoms, and in their increased usefulness in discharging the duties of this life and in carrying to their homes an amount of honest affection, and intellectual light which did not exist there before.

Usually, however, the gospel of improvement was preached in more positive terms, promising social and economic benefits. [. . .]

3 THE CULT OF RESPECTABILITY

The mid-Victorian cult of respectability was an extreme expression of the ideological tendencies inherent in the social situation of the dominant middle-class. It had not been contrived by ideologues but had grown organically out of the interplay between the structure of power and status and the distinctive traits of mid-Victorian culture. Although the gospel of respectability was not preached at full strength by every member of the middle-class, it was invariably present in some form. [. . .]

In a society dominated by the middle classes it was natural for working men to look up to them, since they enjoyed higher status, more money, better education and manifold forms of authority. Working men were conditioned to defer to their superiors, emulate their behaviour and manners, and look to them for approval. There was no mistaking the role assigned to them: to work hard, please their boss, accept gratefully the wages offered, and perhaps to strive for slightly better jobs for themselves and their children. There was no place here for genuine working-class independence. On the contrary, totally different attitudes and behaviour patterns—subordination, deference, materialism—were pervasive and inescapable, for they were inherent in the underlying social and economic structure. Even without middle-class propaganda such structural forces would have operated effectively to inhibit working-class efforts to achieve genuine independence. It was very much in the spirit of mid-Victorian urban culture, however, that the middle classes often elevated these norms into a creed that they preached to working men.

The cult of respectability represented a class version of consensus values, cut to the prevailing pattern of power and status. The 'respectable working man' had been created in the middle-class image of what a decent and respectful working man ought to be. The cult of respectability, therefore, offered a sort of mirror image of the values of the working-class subculture. Each of the character traits which the independent working man esteemed was here refracted through a middle-class prism and emerged in a very different form. His proud demand for respect for the worth and dignity of his class was transmuted into a respectability conferred by the middle classes on working men who behaved themselves 'properly'. What the working-class sub-culture perceived as intrinsic virtues, valuable for their own sake—rationality, morality, civility—became merely the signs of a social status bestowed by the middle classes. In the version handed down from above, 'rationality' came to be identified with an ability to 'understand' the middle-class view of the world. Civility meant toadying to superiors. The aspiration to genuine independence—conceived as an all-embracing moral, intellectual and social ideal—became, in the self-help creed of middle-class propagandists, merely a striving to stay out of the work house and to be 'deserving' of aid in the event of misfortune. Thus the impulse to independence was reversed, for the essence of the cult of respectability was an acceptance of the superiority of the middle classes. Finally, the aspiration to improvement was reduced to a desire to get on in the world on terms acceptable to the middle classes.

On the surface, the middle-class invitation to working men to come within the pale of respectability seemed innocent enough. In fact, the offer was made as if it represented the ultimate in generosity: working men were now to be encouraged to aspire to what had long been considered the quintessence of middle-classness. Yet the offer was ambiguous at best and hypocritical at worst. The whole point of the notion of respectability to begin with was to separate the middle classes from the masses by asserting a claim to moral superiority. In theory, to be sure, respectability was a moral ideal unconnected with class: the respectable man was one worthy of respect, because he possessed traits of character which entitled him to admiration and esteem. In reality, respectability was a social category posing as a moral category. Its function was purely ideological: to enable the middle-class to justify its status by asserting a moral superiority and laying claim to virtues which were denied to inferiors. The point of respectability was the automatic attribution of certain moral traits to a particular socio-economic group. To be sure, a member of the middle-class might lose the badge of respectability as a result of improper behaviour; in the absence of evidence to the contrary, however, a member of the middle-class was presumed to possess a character worthy of respect. Implicit in the notion of respectability at the outset was the presumption that the lower orders lacked the virtues inherent in their social superiors. That fundamental assumption remained in full force when the Victorian middle classes extended the cult of respectability to the upper strata of the working classes. The middle classes, in effect, were born respectable, whereas working men had to achieve it through their own efforts. Working men had to prove their respectability. And the middle classes would decide on the success of their efforts. Working men were to receive the Order of Respectability, Second Class. In theory, however, respectability united men of all classes in a common moral status.

The cult of respectability then, undercut the values of the working-class subculture while professing to advance them. In converting character traits into mere badges of status, it confirmed the basic claims of the class system. In making the middle classes the arbiter of moral character, it confirmed the inherent inferiority of the working classes. By converting social traits such as deference and docility into moral virtues it demeaned morality itself.

The best expression of the cult of respectability in its working-class form is to be found, not in secular sermons of middle-class propagandists, but in the writings of working men who had succumbed and who preached the gospel with the zeal of true believers. A case in point is a volume of prize essays by working men, published in 1861.[2] The author of an essay on 'Courtesy', for example, not only takes it for granted that working men wish to 'obtain the respect of those above them', but suggests that this will enable them to 'lessen the distance which is supposed to separate the two classes'. He follows this with the ingenious notion that the rich have already contributed all that can be expected of them to the lessening of this 'distance', and that it is time for working men to do their part:

> It would be well if there were more sympathy shown by the rich towards the poor, and it would be better still if the class distinctions were so far abolished as to enable both parties to associate together in society, and mutually to co-operate with each other, but are we to expect that all the sacrifice is to be made by the higher to the lower?

This appeal to working men to be fair and recognise the extent of the sacrifice made by their betters sets the tone for what follows, as the author urges working men to take the initiative in eliminating class distinctions by earning the respect of their superiors.

> Are they [the rich] to accommodate themselves to rudeness of speech, to uncivil behaviour, or disgusting habits, when these things can be easily avoided by the exercise of thoughtfulness and the practice of courtesy? Rather should we strive to raise ourselves in the social scale, to dignify our nature, to educate and cultivate our mental and moral being. We may be real, though not refined; wise, though not wealthy.

This was a precise statement of just what the middle classes wanted of 'respectable working men'. [. . .]

Another essayist makes quite transparent the class character of his exhortation to working men to be courteous. Lack of cordiality in class relations, as he sees it, is primarily the result of working-class prejudice and rudeness. He complains that working men are all too often unresponsive to the good advice that is coming to them from above.

> When some noble or gentle lecturer comes forward and proposes to cultivate more cordial intercourse between the different ranks of society, the ice may seem to be melted for a time by the heat of temporary enthusiasm; but soon old Prejudice returns with his churlish host, and builds up again the chilly barriers.

Speaking 'for my class', he explains why working men are so reluctant to 'second the endeavours of philanthropic individuals, of rank or wealth to establish more amicable relations between their respective classes'. He attributes this stubbornness to 'old grudges and old prejudices'. To be sure, he raps knuckles on both sides: employers are faulted for 'ruthlessly' reducing wages, thus contributing to 'the want of interchange of courtesy and belief in common interests'. But in the same breath he rebukes working men for 'obstinately' attempting to keep up wages. Such seeming even-handedness, of course, like the application of seemingly universal standards of courtesy, had the effect of playing into the hands of employers who would benefit most from working men who 'courteously' refrained from demanding higher wages.

The essay on Self-Education by William Glazier, a carpenter, is noteworthy for the expression of impossibly exalted aspirations in the context of a classically 'ideological' justification of the class structure and its norms. He preaches a sentimentalised and romanticised version of the creed of respectability, in which the contented working man cultivates his mind and spirit, untouched by the squalid world around him. Even the gospel of success is dismissed as too worldly. Education is not to be prized as a means of social advancement, but for its ennobling influence on the soul. The important question, he writes, is

> how shall education be made subservient towards enabling man, whilst abiding in that station of life to which it has pleased God to call him, to become more respected, more influential, more useful and more happy—a fountain of greater blessings to himself, his family, his country, and the world . . .

At first glance, it seems that we are back with Sarah Trimmer and Hannah More, especially when Glazier refers, in his climax, to 'the great end of being which, in every station of life, is to glorify God and enjoy Him, and with Him all other things here and hereafter'. But Glazier is interesting precisely because these highly traditional conservative doctrines are clothed in the new ideological forms of the mid-nineteenth century. Whereas the eighteenth-century ideologist was urging the poor to eschew sin and escape poverty, Glazier asks working men to aspire to the ennobling works of the mind and spirit. Now the conquest of sin is merely a first step towards positive achievements:

> He who has accomplished this—who has rendered passions, appetite, and habits subordinate to the will—stands at a vantage ground for all future battlings. Henceforth, all things are easy to him, and he can go on from conquering to conquer. Such a man, however lowly his station, acquires a nobility of character that entitles him to the admiration of the world.

He does not really have to wait for the next world. He has achieved the highest religious-cultural goal in this world, and respectability to boot.

Glazier exemplifies—not as a paradigm, but as a caricature—the ideological implications of sentimental utopianism in mid-Victorian urban culture. He takes the platitudes of aspiration and treats them as self-evident truths. Thus he blandly denies that materialistic motives will have any effect on 'the vast bulk of workers', whom he describes in Pelagian terms remote from the Calvinism of Hannah More:

> We believe that all men are susceptible to some particular influence, or influences, of a pure and elevating character, [. . .]. To seek out, multiply, extend, and bring into operation amongst the mass of the people, these elevating and ennobling influences, unmixed with sordid considerations is, in our opinion, worthy the profound study of the most exalted intelligence.

He takes the working-class ideal of independence and self-help and dissolves it in a syrupy sentimentality:

> No man, or class of men, will ever rise to the true dignity of our common humanity who hangs on the skirts of others. There will be no real nobility of character, no real and lasting progress—mentally, morally and socially—without the vigorous exercise of our own capacities and powers.

Carried away by his utopian vision, Glazier even expresses doubts about mechanics' institutes, because they may lead to the 'neglect of home and family duties'. 'Highly as we esteem intellectual improvement, we should deem it dearly bought if its accomplishment weakened the influence of home'. And in the best tradition of preachers advocating what no one would dare to oppose, but which no reasonable man expects to be actualised this side of the after-life, Glazier presents his own programme:

> We would rather see home institutes multiplied a thousandfold than the extension of elaborate organisations for educating the people. The latter have done and are still doing good: but let us rather see fathers, the high priests of knowledge within the temple of Home, and wives and children, the eager and expectant auditors. [. . .]

4 WORKING-CLASS SUBCULTURE: INDEPENDENCE AND SELF-RESPECT

[. . .] Although there was, of course, no 'typical' Victorian working man, certain ideas and attitudes tend to recur in various contexts. Occasionally a number of familiar themes are compactly expressed in a few sentences, as in a passage from the autobiography of Robert Lowery, a Chartist who later became active in the temperance movement. Lowery's statement can serve as a point of departure for a consideration of the values of the working-class subculture:

> It is in the very nature of the intelligent and virtuous to feel self-respect, and the claims of manhood as man. They can bear poverty and exclusion from the ranks of the wealthy. They know they are not equals in wealth, but they cannot bear insult, and to be told that because they are not their equals in wealth they are not capable of being equal in intelligence, integrity, and manhood.

This passage makes explicit a number of attitudes which are clearly present, although often only implicitly, in working-class documents of the period. First there is the egalitarian assertion of equal moral and intellectual potential among all men, regardless of class. The tone of the passage is not at all deferential, but populist. The 'claims of manhood' are made in the face of a middle-class denial of such claims, whether explicitly in the form of 'insult', or implicitly in attitude, gesture and tone of voice.

Lowery demands respect, on the basis of demonstrated virtue and intelligence. It is a demand for respect for moral and intellectual qualities, regardless of class status. All this is remote from the cult of respectability.

Ordinary working men were quite aware of the operation of the class system and the working-class subculture embodied a continuing effort to resist the imposition of a narrowly middle-class version of shared ideals. Two letters written by an ironworker's wife during a strike in 1866 illustrate the way in which working men combined a commitment to consensus values with an assertion of working-class independence and a critique of the shortcomings of the middle classes. In their exposure of middle-class hypocrisy, the letters provide a vivid picture of a social system which took pride in the profession of the highest moral ideals only to have them abandoned in practice when they conflicted with class interest.

In a scathing indictment of employers' bad faith, the ironworkers' wife contrasted their platform rhetoric with their actual behaviour: 'We are told that we ought to live in good houses, clothe and educate our children properly; and yet at every opportunity the masters have, they come down upon us for a reduction. Well, the Lord forgive them for their cruelty this time'. She recalled the patronising attitude of the middle-class improvers towards working men:

> We are told of the extravagance, wickedness and immorality of the working classes, and how we have kept ourselves 'quiet and peaceable during these trying times', just as if we were some species of wild beast, whom it was the special province of these platform reformers to keep right.

She pointed out that their tune would change as soon as they decided that they needed working-class support in a political movement: 'But wait, Sir, until this reform agitation takes place; then we shall hear of all the good qualities possessed by the workmen. All our virtues will be discovered then.' She found the same sort of hypocrisy among the ministers and elders of the chapels and churches and concluded that the poor could expect sympathy only from each other:

> We know by this time how many of our pastors, deacons, and elders have visited us in our troubles; we know how many of them have studied 'Mrs Grundy' more than the teachings of Christ; [. . .] I know many of you have worked hard at your sewing meetings, bazaars, and in many other ways, to free your little Bethels from debt. Which of them, and how many of your ministers and leaders have come to you in your affliction and asked if you had bread in your cupboards? Have they not rather given you the cold shoulder, and all their sympathies have gone to the oppressor?

She was appalled by the fact that when the strike was broken the steadiest and most respected working men were fired. 'And who are the men who are singled out? Not the men who can leave their work to drink during hours and waste the property of their employers, but steady, intelligent, and upright men who try to do justly towards master and man'. Because they had served as delegates to other towns in an attempt to win support for the strike, their high moral character was not enough to get them their jobs back. 'Does it not appear a mockery and a sham to talk to the working man of "mechanics' institutes", "reading rooms", and "clubs", when we know from bitter experience that whenever a working man takes advantage of the same he becomes the target for all to shoot at'. She had just about lost all faith in the employing class:

> There was far more meant in the words of that Staffordshire employer 'than met the ear' when he asked the question, 'what do the working classes want with reading rooms and mechanics' institutes; all they require is the gin palace and the beer house'. Does it not seem that there was a premium held out to the man to keep himself as low as possible in morality; no inducement to advance himself. It appears so paltry and mean to take revenge in such a way upon their best workmen.

The ironworker's wife, like many mid-Victorian working men, had no illusions about masters who 'so often break the faith'. She was especially contemptuous of their pious talk of improvement for the working classes. Here commitment to the familiar cultural values, so similar to the official line, was not the result of middle-class propaganda, but in spite of it. She was expressing an aspiration to independence and emancipation, in the best tradition of working-class radicalism.

Beneath the often abstract and formal language of the 'intelligent working man' lay a clearsighted awareness of social realities, especially the actual attitudes of the middle classes. Working men were quite capable of recognising the cult of respectability for what it was, despite its superficial resemblance to many of their own values. Although for the most part one finds only scattered and indirect indications of this sort of thing, occasionally one runs across a document which discloses more fully this realistic and hard-headed component of the working-class subculture. A case in point is a letter written by an apprentice to his master after seven years of service in a Sheffield warehouse. The apprentice made it plain, on the one hand, that his master's conduct had always been 'gentlemanly', and that he had provided the best food and excellent lodgings. What bothered him, however, was that the master had the cheek to reproach his apprentice for 'loving money'. This was too much, and he proceeded to explain to his former master exactly what social values were actually dominant in the warehouse:

> The one lesson taught everyone, by every arrangement in your establishment, was to preach up the importance of money [. . .] morning, noon, and night, the staple topic of admiration was wealth. He that had obtained it no matter how, was 'the fortunate', the 'respectable man', the 'honourable and high minded person'; while he that was poor, was the constant object of sneer, or pity, or lampoon.

As for the complaint that he loved money, the apprentice asked: 'How was it possible for a young man that ate with you, and worked at your elbow, to escape being mammonised?' In fact, all masters taught the same lesson: 'That one lesson every day and everywhere, on every occasion, and to every man, woman, and child, is the paramount value of money, respectability, station and pleasure'.

This sort of realism reinforced by resentment at middle-class pretensions to superiority, led to widespread working-class resistance to the preaching of middle-class improvers. Here also much of the evidence is necessarily indirect, since prudence required the appearance of acquiescence in the line handed down from above. But there would seem to be good reason to take at face value the complaint of a prize essayist, who had himself succumbed to the blandishments of the middle classes, that many working men were hostile to high-minded pleas for more cordial relations between classes. There were thousands of 'malcontents', he said, who were given to comments of this sort to philanthropists who wanted to improve the working classes:

> You make laws in your own favour; you lay burdens on our shoulders that you will not touch with your fingers; you overtask us; you underpay us; and when we receive our miserable pittance of wages, you would have us make our obeisance and say, 'Thank you, sir'. Go to; enjoy your rank and wealth, and if you do us no good in the way of bettering our circumstances, never mind mending our manners: let us alone.

Although the essayist attributed these views primarily to the worst paid operatives, they were undoubtedly widespread also among the more affluent, who were tired of sweet talk from above about elevating the masses.

Far from being confined to occasional carping by failures and malcontents, criticism of middle-class propaganda and pretensions was an established pattern of the working-class subculture. It represented a continuing effort to assert an egalitarian version of the consensus values in the face of constant middle-class pressure to give them a narrow class form. William Aitken illustrates the readiness of working men to reject the myths and propaganda with which they were being deluged by the middle classes. A provincial grand master of the Oddfellows, Aitken exemplifies the responsible and 'respectable' leader of a working-class institution that was deeply committed to the official values of the culture. Throughout his life, however, he remained faithful to his class and to the values underlying his youthful radicalism. In 1825, at the age of eleven, Aitken worked as a piecer in a cotton mill. When he became active in the short time movement, he was fired. He then turned to school teaching, and continued his participation in the factory movement and in Chartism. The *Northern Star* described him as a man who 'has suffered considerably from the rampant enemies of man's rights'. Although in occupational and economic terms, he may be said to have moved out of the working-class, he displayed few signs of *'embourgeoisement'*. When he rose to a position of leadership in the Oddfellows, he remained an eloquent spokesman for radical values. In that spirit he denounced Benjamin Franklin's platitudes.

Aitken attacked both political economy and the gospel of success in his article on Franklin. Dismissing as 'absurdity' the maxim. 'Early to bed and early to rise, makes a man healthy, wealthy, and wise', Aitken pointed out that 'the great bulk of mankind are hard workers, go to bed "early", and rise "early", but the work that millions endure destroys their "health", the small earnings they receive do not find them the necessaries of life, to say nothing of "wealth", and they have not time by study and an exhausted daily frame to make themselves "wise".' Thousands of men and women, 'labouring hard from year end to year end, are under-fed, under-clothed and badly housed', and 'the small amount of money earned by the multitude of workers prevents them paying any great sum of money for the teaching of their children'. As for the maxim, 'There are no gains without pains', Aitken reversed it: 'There are many pains with few gains, and plenty gains with few pains'. That is, 'The multitude of hard workers have the "pains" minus the "gains", while the usurer . . . the speculators in consols, money dealers generally, and a shoal of others of the same kith and kin, have the "gains", minus the "pains".'

A similar example of the ability of working men to see through the ideological mystification practised by middle-class propagandists turns up in the minute book of a mutual improvement society in Manchester in the 1860s, composed of Sunday school teachers and students over the age of sixteen. Their acceptance of the dominant value system was accompanied by a criticism of the social order and a rejection of attempts to explain away its deficiencies. In August 1868, following the usual practice of the group, a member read an essay that served as the basis for discussion. He took the negative on the question, 'Are the working men of England treated as men and do they get a fair day's wage for a fair day's work?' In the essay he denounced the evil effects arising from the working man not being paid sufficient for his labour to enable him to keep his wife at home to nurse and train up his children in the way they ought to go'. Not only spinners but also 'too many mechanics, both fitters and turners are working for little over 20/- per week'. 'The self-acting minders . . . are a class much to be pitied for the long tedious hours which they work and the miserable wages they receive'. The minutes summarise his remarks: 'He requests us, if we would believe, to go and see for ourselves the men and women who work in our cotton mills, for then we would see them pale, worn and withered. Men who if they had not been worked harder than the slave would have been robust, healthy looking men'. The essayist was equally blunt in dealing with the second part of the topic:

Let those [. . .] who think that the men are treated as they ought, ask themselves whether it is right after a man has served his master faithfully and given him the best of his days to turn him off when he sees the frost of years begin to whiten his hair or when his sight begins to fail him? And yet, there are plenty of firms who claim respectability who do such things. As a result, because their wages have been so low, and through no fault of their own, men have to end their days in our workhouses.

He cited another example, based on personal knowledge, in which a cotton spinner was sacked immediately when he took the trouble to give his employer advance notice that he was going to take a better job with another firm.

The essayist also explained the disastrous effect of low wages on family life. If young working men decided to wait until they were able to support a wife before getting married, 'they must wait until the end of their days'. When a man did marry, his wife would have to go out to work. According to the minutes, the essayist 'pictured in piteous words—where married women who have for the better support of their families to work in our cotton mills and leave their young children out to nurse and the nurses in many cases drug them to sleep—thus ensuring to us in years to come a sickly and weakly generation'. He concluded by advising working men to 'combine into Unions and promising them if they do not that the days of Feudalism or worse than that will come when we shall lose the proud name of Free-born English Men'.

In the debate that ensued, not much opposition developed. An attempt at rebuttal, citing the laws of supply and demand, evoked a spirited rejoinder from another member of the group, who argued that the essayist had merely stated the facts: 'His arguments were chiefly brought from the cotton operatives. The men of England undoubtedly are slaves and every cotton lord, he can prove, wastes a generation in ten years'. When the adjourned debate resumed two weeks later, the same speaker disposed of the rags to riches myth: 'We point out to him one or two rich men who have risen from humble ranks, but we forget to tell him of the many hundreds who though they have been persevering, hard working men have not risen'. These young men had not been taken in by the myth of success. On the contrary, they took pride in rejecting its grandiose claims.

Even working-class rhetoric which at first glance seems indistinguishable from the preachments of middle-class improvers on closer inspection turns out to be rather different. A case in point is a letter supporting a proposal for the creation of a system of secular education, written by a working man who was also a Wesleyan local preacher. Although the writer perceived himself in terms of that thoroughly mid-Victorian category. 'the intelligent working man', he did not speak the language of deference. On the contrary, the burden of his letter was that the Wesleyan ministers who opposed secular education were merely expressing the views of the rich and had failed to consult the poorer members of the congregation. 'As a member and local preacher in the body, I move and have continual intercourse with my own order—operatives and artisans of intelligence—who complain to be so misrepresented. The fact is, our opinions are unascertained; we are never consulted'. He contrasted the views of 'the Wesleyan artisan and the Wesleyan poor' with those of 'the Plutocracy' who dominated the congregation. In this populist vein he delivered a paean to education which combined official pieties with an anti-Establishment bias:

> The tendency is to imbue the mind with a power which enables the possessor to estimate true excellence, and begets the aspiration which is necessary to a personal attainment of it. It tends to check that fulsome cant and fanaticism which degrades the Christian Church—to induce that self-respect so salutary in social life, in restraining from excess of all kinds.

Underlying the demand for respect so pervasive in the working-class subculture was resentment at the casual assumption of superiority on the part of the middle classes. Quite often, therefore, what appear to be the clichés of respectability actually functioned as a defence of working men against the strictures being levelled at them by their 'betters'. An official of the Oddfellows praising members for 'their independence, their moral manhood, and their general probity' was engaged in the unending enterprise of refuting middle-class critics. Increasingly in the course of the 1850s working men had to contend with more subtle forms of condescension, in addition to the 'insults' that concerned Lowery. The patronage that was oten extended so aggressively to 'deserving' working men carried with it such a presumption of class superiority that even the studiously respectful author of one of Cassell's prize essays was moved to write rather plaintively that although some members of the middle classes

> may have amassed considerable wealth, and thereby have attained a better position in society, it does not follow that they are necessarily more intelligent, or better workers in the cause [of mechanics' institutes] than many of the working men, who take such a lively and active interest in the progress of such institutions.

In these circumstances the class consciousness and class pride so prominent in the radical movements of the first half of the nineteenth century persisted into the mid-Victorian decades. Among the more militant such sentiments took the form of scornful criticism of working men who had defected to the cult of respectability. Those who pursued the sort of 'respect' bestowed by the middle classes as a reward for docility and conformity found themselves under attack in Harney's *Friend of the People*:

> We have known such—men of some ability, and more self-conceit, who, having made some little progress from misery and obscurity, have forthwith aped 'the respectables', offered themselves for purchase to those who had occasion for needy and unscrupulous instruments, and turned their backs

upon the class from whom they sprang. Gerald Massey is not one of this rotten tribe.

This passage occurs in a review of a volume of Massey's poetry. In the sentimental mid-Victorian idiom the reviewer praised Massey for not having deserted his class: 'Entertaining a high opinion of Gerald Massey's poetry, there is that about him which we esteem of much greater value than the noblest gifts ever bestowed by Genius on her favourite sons; we allude to his chivalrous devotion to his order—the long-suffering children of Labour'.

Although the demand for a transformation of the social and political system had been abandoned, the co-operative societies provided an institutional vehicle for continuing the old critique of a competitive and acquisitive society. For many working men the co-operative shops were not only a means of buying necessities at a lower price but also a way of preserving a vision of a social order emancipated from the vices of competition. In the face of the overwhelming power of Victorian capitalism, the co-operative movement sought to maintain the working-class values of mutuality and fellowship and to proclaim the possibility of an alternative social order. The co-operators' criticism of the competitive system had a real bite to it. Taking a properly Victorian moral stance, they announced that competition was 'not only a defective but an evil principle, and not calculated to produce that justice between man and man, and th.it social happiness in society, that human nature requires'. Their view of Victorian society was free of the soothing platitudes of platform rhetoric: 'We see that the fruits of competition are selfishness, discord, contention, and strife; ignorance, vice, and crime in all the forms that misdirected and prostituted human ingenuity can devise'. Where the official line was class harmony, the co-operatives pointed to distrust and conflict: 'It were hopeless to expect man ever to be extricated from the ice-bound grasp of selfishness, so long as competition regulates either social or commercial affairs. Every glance at the results traceable to competitive strife, confirms our opinion that it is unworthy of an honest people'. In principle, the co-operative movement remained committed to the eventual achievement of a total change of system: nothing less than the replacement of competition by co-operation. It was sometimes suggested that shopkeeping was only the first phase in the co-operative movement. The second phase in the movement would bring much more fundamental changes: then the working-class will 'begin to see that the evils and anomalies by which we are surrounded are in the *system*, and not in the *men* who are engaged in it', and that 'we are individually rather the victims than the agents in this system of cursed competition and strife'.

James Hole, an Owenite who took the lead in establishing a co-operative society in Leeds in the mid-1840s, illustrates the two aspects of the working-class subculture with which this chapter is concerned: a continuing commitment to the traditions of radicalism that combined shrewd realism and utopian optimism. His *Lectures on Social Science and the Organisation of Labour* provides a systematic statement of ideas and values usually expressed only in fragmentary form. To be sure, Hole himself was not a working man, but a *petit bourgeois*. Nevertheless, as an advocate of radical social transformation he was very much a man of the Left. In 1845 he was a founding member of the Leeds Redemption Society, one of a number of Owenite societies formed in the late 1840s to enable the Working Classes to work out their own Redemption by Union amongst themselves'. The Leeds society consisted of both Owenites and Radicals. In 1848 Hole became secretary of the Yorkshire Union of Mechanics' Institutes and thereafter devoted himself primarily to the adult education movement. Despite his affiliation with an institution that was the incarnation of middle-class liberalism, however, Hole did not abandon his radicalism. The *Lectures* reaffirmed the principles and aspirations of Owenism along with its critique of the social and economic system. Like other early-Victorian spokesman of the working-class Left, however, Hole gave up the hope of the transformation of society and concentrated on improvement and reform within the existing order. His *Lectures* illustrate the tension between radicalism and mid-Victorianism that underlay the working-class subculture.

Like many mid-Victorian working men Hole combined a soft and sentimental diction with a shrewd assessment of social reality: and a *de facto* acceptance of the social order with a continuing commitment to egalitarian values. Although his eyes were fixed on distant spiritual horizons, Hole never lost sight of the underlying structure of power and status or failed to perceive it as an obstacle to the achievement of his social ideals. He was under no illusions about the situation in which working men found themselves: 'Their weakness invites oppression; irresponsible power and the abuse of it being inseparably linked. From this realistic vantage point Hole denounced the 'tremendous degradation of rendering one man dependent for his bread, and that of those near and dear to him, on the whim and caprice of his fellow creature'. His mid-Victorian rhetoric was accompanied by an acute perception of class relationships and a total rejection of the pretensions of the bourgeoisie. 'It cannot be', Hole wrote, 'that a child of God in his true estate of being should enter the presence of his fellows, as tho' he were an interloper, a mere grub or worm on whom it were a condescension for the great man to tread'. The 'serf-like' relation between employer and employed had 'repressed the sentiments of self-respect and moral responsibility'. He also made it plain that social inequality was not conducive to the virtues of which the Victorians were so fond:

> Consider how little of true nobleness and independence can lodge in the breast of the worker, entering his employer's presence as a socially inferior being, not daring to express his thoughts if conscious that they differed from his Master's, and who must take note of his slightest word, lest he smile at an inopportune moment.

Hole never let his reader forget that it was power that counted: 'The relation between master and servant approaches slavery in the degree in which the servant is deficient in counteractive force'.

Hole was just as realistic in his assessment of the middle-class and its ideology. He dismissed the arguments of political economy as impudent rationalisations. 'The right of the capitalist to grasp all he can, and give his workmen as little as he can, is only surpassed in injustice by the impudence with which it is avowed and defended'. Hole was willing to make no concessions to ruling economic doctrine: 'The master who makes the most he can out of his labourers, differs but in degree from the slave driver, and the principle of political economy justifies the slavery of Greece and Rome as much as it does the system of modern labour'. While giving the mill owners credit for good intentions in their contributions to schools, chapels and soup kitchens, Hole considered their philanthropic efforts misplaced. Such 'mistaken philanthropy . . . often saps the spirit of independence in the labourer, and ultimately increases the evil. The labourer *wants* work, the means of earning his own comforts'. Hole also made short shrift of the success myth. He pointed out that the system was still fundamentally defective even though it permitted an occasional workman to escape from the ranks: such an isolated event 'is no compensation of the system—the one prize cannot atone for the nine hundred and ninety-nine blanks'. He called instead for the 'interaction of just and fraternal arrangements' which 'might possibly turn all into prizes'. He denounced a system in which the way a man is treated 'depends not on what he *is,* but on what he *has*'.

Yet Hole hoped that the social system whose evils he described so well would be transformed gradually but inexorably by the improving institutions of the mid-Victorian cities. He illustrates, in somewhat extreme form, the inner logic that led radical working men to transfer their utopian idealism to the celebration of minuscule increments of improvement. Seeking to maintain a socialist position in the *Lectures*, he deplored the inferior education provided to the mass of the people under the existing system and called for the creation of a regime of genuine social and cultural equality:

> Socialism proclaims that the life of the masses ought not to be one dull blank, unhallowed by noble thought or lofty sentiments, its course purely animal, swallowed up in the drudgery of labour, or buried in the mire of sensuality [. . .] it announces that both man's inner and outer life may be raised and beautified—that the abuses of property may be remedied, and more humane relations established among men.

The young Marx had projected a similar vision of the socialist utopia in his Paris writings a few years before. Hole, however, took a rather different view of how these socialist principles might be realised. Having concentrated on the adverse moral and intellectual consequences of capitalism, and having emphasised the fact that socialism would raise the cultural level of all men, and having rejected any hint of revolutionary action to transform the existing social and economic order, Hole moved easily into a position where he became convinced that any number of working-class activities might contribute substantially to the achievement of the utopia that he envisaged. Thus he found 'true exemplifications of Socialism' in the various movements whose object was 'to elevate the masses of Society'.

Hole had in mind 'Working Associations, Mechanics' Institutes, Co-operative stores, Flour-mills, Freehold-land societies, and the like'. Even if they did not accomplish much, such organisations were nevertheless of great value, because they demonstrated 'the vast latent power of association'. In model lodging houses, baths and wash-houses, and mechanics' institutes, he found 'the germ of those magnificent organisations which the world will one day witness'. In the name of practicality and common sense, he argued that 'it is not the part of wise men to *wait* for the realisation of large schemes, but to seize present opportunities and make the most of them'. What linked such diverse activities to socialism was 'the principle of Association, or co-operation'. They were part of a grand design: 'Each of these various movements is (often unconscious of its promoters) working out the parts of a grand problem the solution of which can only be arrived at experimentally'. One could move slowly, in confidence that intellectual improvement was an all-powerful engine of progress. 'The degrees of association of which men are capable, depends on the height of moral and intellectual cultivation to which they may have attained'. Having put his faith in the principle of association, Hole gave free rein to his utopian optimism. Here was an 'instrument in the hands of the working classes' which 'requires only their own active participation'; they have the 'means of emancipation in their hands'. He defined the idea so broadly that just about any aspect of working-class activity could be interpreted as an important aspect of the overall movement towards socialism.

Thus the realism that distinguished Hole's analysis of the existing social system was blunted by a number of optimistic assumptions that encouraged the expectation that 'socialism' might be achieved through the day-to-day co-operation of men of good will associated on behalf of improving activity. His trenchant analysis of the human consequences of excessive social dependence was considerably softened by his assumption that the majority of working men 'are dependent because they are ignorant' and that 'no employer can despise or oppress a man with as much soul as himself'. This sort of wishful thinking was part of the legacy that Hole had inherited from early-Victorian radicalism. His rationalist faith led him to the conclusion that 'even in their present state, the diffusion of intelligence ameliorates the servile conditions of labour'. In the best tradition of Enlightenment rationalism he concluded that 'the only effectual mode of arriving at social organisation is by the dissemination of Ideas'.

Starting from an exceedingly radical perspective, Hole ended up advising the working classes to continue the sort of improving activity which they were also being urged to carry on by spokesmen for the middle classes. To be sure, he hoped for a totally different result in the long run, and he took a highly unfavourable view of the capitalist society in which this activity was taking place. Nevertheless, he ended up praising the basic institutions of mid-Victorian culture in the name of socialism and co operation.

NOTES

[1] Arbitrator, *Employers and Employed*, Manchester, 1856.
[2] *Social Science; Being Selections from John Cassell's Prize Essays by Working Men and Women*, London, 1861.

(c) Trade Unionism in the British and US Steel Industries, 1880–1914: A Comparative Study

JAMES HOLT

From the 1880s to the First World War, trade unions grew and flourished among British steelworkers. In the U.S. steel industry, on the other hand, trade unionism lost ground rapidly after 1892 and all but disappeared. By 1914 the British steel industry was heavily unionized and the initial steps had been taken towards the creation of a single national organization embracing most of the major trade unions in the field. Meanwhile, in America, the open shop had become the rule in steelmaking. It would be an exageration to suggest that these contrasting patterns typified trade union development in the two countries, since it was in this period that the national unions and the American Federation of Labor became firmly established in the United States. Nevertheless the fate of the trade unions in the U.S. steel industry may reasonably be seen as an example of a general trend. Compared with Britain and most other industrialized capitalist countries, the unionized proportion of the non-agricultural labor force remained low in the United States before the 1930s, and until that time trade unionism was peculiarly weak in America's mass production industries.

The relatively slow growth of trade unionism in the United States is an important subject in itself, but it takes on added significance when considered in the light of political developments. In Britain, Australia, New Zealand, and Scandinavia, trade unions launched political labor movements which ultimately achieved national power. Elsewhere trade unions were created by or closely associated with strong socialist parties. The absence of a nationally powerful socialist or political labor movement in the United States may be explained in part by factors quite independent of trade union development, such as the peculiar nature of American

Labor History, Vol. 18, 1977, pp. 5–35.

political institutions, but it seems probable that the comparative weakness of American socialism is associated in some way with the slow and painful growth of the trade unions in the United States. This study deals with industrial organizations only, and focuses on a single industry, but the aim is to throw some light on a more general question, *viz.:* why, in broad comparative terms were industrial and political organizations of manual workers so weak in the United States during the late 19th and early 20th centuries?

There are many aspects of trade union organization that might usefully be considered in a comparative study, depending on the ultimate purpose of the inquiry. Here the focus is on contrasting patterns of growth and decline, and subjects such as the structure of union government, dues, benefits, and rules of membership are dealt with only as they appear to bear on the major question. A full narrative history of the various unions involved has not been attempted either, but a brief outline of the major institutions and developments under study is necessary and will serve as an introduction to the discussion that follows.

In Britain steelworkers were organized by several trade unions with overlapping jurisdictions, a pattern typical of British industry. First of the important unions in the field was the Amalgamated Malleable Ironworkers of Great Britain which was founded in 1862 and reorganized in 1867 as the Associated Iron and Steelworkers of Great Britain. The Ironworkers' Union, as it was generally known, began its life as an organization of puddlers and skilled rolling mill hands in the wrought iron industry, but as steel supplanted wrought iron, the Ironworkers began taking in steelworkers. At least some Bessemer converter men were represented by the Ironworkers as early as the 1860s, and skilled rolling mill hands in the steel industry, especially those in Northeast England, gradually assumed a prominent place in the union's affairs. Yet though it was flexible enough to survive the transition from wrought iron to steel, the Ironworkers' union remained throughout its existence a complacent and conservative organization. It largely ignored the interests of the unskilled, made no effort to establish itself in Scotland or Wales, and showed no interest in the rapidly growing number of open hearth furnace workers. Early in its existence, the Ironworkers' leaders committed the union to formal conciliation and arbitration procedures as a wage fixing device and to a sliding scale of wages based on the selling price of iron and steel products. By accepting this system, the Ironworkers acquiesced in automatic wage cuts whenever prices fell, and although this may have been a necessary condition for the union's survival in its early years, 'its intrinsic advantages', in the words of Clegg, Fox, and Thompson, 'were obvious only to employers.'[1] Membership of this undynamic organization fluctuated between 5,000 and 8,000 during the 1890s and the first decade of the 20th century.[2]

More important in the long run was the British Steel Smelters'

Amalgamated Association which was founded by Scottish open hearth furnace workers in 1886, and which soon spread its activities to England and Wales. In its early years the Smelters' union concentrated on the skilled men working open hearth furnaces. For these men it succeeded in winning the abolition of the contract system of wages and in negotiating tonnage (piece) rates which covered most of the open hearth industry by 1890. Lesser skilled men working around the open hearth furnaces were excluded from the union altogether by some branches in the early years and throughout the 1890s the Smelters had difficulty retaining the loyalty of the 'gas producer men'. These workers were paid like laborers by daily rather than tonnage rates and frequently complained that their interests were being ignored by the Smelters.

However the Smelters' redoubtable secretary, John Hodge, later a Labour M.P. and cabinet minister, worked consistently to broaden the basis of the union. In 1894 Hodge negotiated a scheme for amalgamation with the Scottish Millmen, but it was rejected overwhelmingly by the membership. When negotiations with the Ironworkers for amalgamation also led to nothing, the Smelters began recruiting rolling mill hands. By 1900 the Smelters were also welcoming the unskilled into their ranks. In 1899 a new class of membership was established for these men whose dues were fixed at one quarter of those of first class members.

Though ably led and highly successful in one branch of the industry, the Smelters' union grew only slowly until the late 1890s. Then, in 1899, the collapse of the South Wales, Monmouthshire, and Gloucestershire Tinplate Workers' Union enabled the Smelters (among others) to move in and recruit a large number of Welsh tinplate workers. Membership more than doubled (from 4,605 to 9,976) in that year. An organizing drive in Sheffield in 1907 reaped another rich harvest of new members. By then the Smelters represented over 15,000 workers, its capital assets stood at 76,000 pounds, and two of its paid officials, John Hodge and John McPherson, sat in Parliament.

In Scotland rolling mill hands formed their own union in 1888, known as the Associated Society of Millmen and after 1895 the Amalgamated Society of Steel and Iron Workers. In the early 1890s, the Millmen attempted to establish branches in England but failed to make significant progress there or to persuade the stronger Smelters to amalgamate with them. An arbitration agreement entered into with employers covered only four out of seven Scottish mills in 1892 and the Millmen compensated for their relatively weak position in the rolling mills by taking in wrought iron and foundry workers. By 1900, membership had risen to over 9,000 but it declined in subsequent years.

Two societies of blastfurnacemen amalgamated in 1887 to form a national organization which became the National Federation of Blastfurnacemen in 1892. Its membership grew from 4,544 in 1895 to nearly

9,000 in 1904. In Wales, the Amalgamated Association of Iron and Steel Workers and Mechanics of South Wales and Monmouthshire [. . .] had 3–5000 members throughout the period 1892 to 1904. Several unions of enginemen, cranemen, and firemen organized these specialized trades in the steelworks and the general laborers' unions organized some of the unskilled workers in the industry. In addition to all of these there were a number of smaller local unions in the industry.

Clearly the pattern of trade union organization in the British steel industry down to 1910 was complicated and confused in the extreme. Rolling mill hands for example were organized by the Ironworkers, the Smelters, and the Millmen, and unskilled laborers in the steel industry were divided among even more organizations. In 1911, however, serious negotiations aimed at the amalgamation or federation of all of the major unions in the steel industry were opened. Eventually there emerged in 1917 the Iron and Steel Trade Confederation which embraced all of the important unions except the Blastfurnacemen.

Between 1897 and 1913 total membership in British iron and steel trade unions rose from about 30,000 to approximately 80,000. It is impossible to calculate precisely what 'density' (i.e., proportion of workers in the industry) this figure represented, since census reports lumped together workers engaged in the manufacture of iron and steel with some who worked *with* the metals, including foundrymen. It is also impossible to work out how many steelworkers belonged to the several trade unions which organized other groups of workers as well. Nevertheless it can safely be concluded that trade unionism was very strong in the British steel industry by the outbreak of the First World War and was still growing stronger.

In the American steel industry, only two labor organizations were of any great significance in the late 19th and early 20th centuries. These were the Amalgamated Association of Iron, Steel and Tin Workers (The A.A.), and the Knights of Labour. The A.A. was formed in 1876 when the United Sons of Vulcan, composed of iron puddlers and boilers, joined forces with several smaller unions of rolling mill hands and other skilled iron workers. Membership of the A.A. rose from 3,755 in 1877 to 16,003 in 1882, declined to 5,702 in 1885 and climbed again to a peak of 24,068 in 1891. After its crushing defeat in the Homestead strike of 1892, the A.A. lost ground steadily and never regained its former strength.

Throughout the period in which it was a large and powerful organization, the A.A. was dominated by iron workers, and especially by puddlers and boilers. Each year, delegates to the union's annual convention drew up elaborate scales of prices for the boiling, puddling, heating, and rolling of wrought iron, and when endorsed by the convention these scales were presented to the ironmasters. As in Britain, the ironworkers based their scales on the selling price of the products they made (i.e., they were sliding scales) but unlike the British Ironworkers' Union, the A.A. rejected arbitration as a method of settling disputes. Differences between the A.A. and the employers sometimes led to strikes or lockouts, and the union was not always victorious in these struggles. In general, however, the A.A. established a powerful position in the iron industry and claimed to control three quarters of the iron mills in the United States by 1891.

The A.A. began as an 'exclusive' organization, confining membership to the skilled men in the iron and steel industries. Yet as early as 1877 the union's president was deploring the tendency of boilers to exclude their 'helpers' from A.A. lodges, despite their eligibility for membership, and unions leaders were constantly warning members that it would be dangerous to exclude lesser skilled men. New categories of workers were added to those eligible for membership at almost every convention after 1876 until by 1882 it took almost an entire page of the constitution to list them all. By 1890 the membership provisions had been simplified to include simply 'all men working in and around rolling mills, steel works, nail, tack, spike, bolt and nut factories, pipe mills, and all works run in connection with the same, except laborers, the latter to be admitted at the discretion of the subordinate lodges to which application is made for membership'. As with the British Steel Smelters then, the trend was towards a more broadly based membership including more and more of the lesser skilled men.

The ironworkers of the A.A. viewed the rise of steel production in the United States with apprehension. In 1885, the national officers suggested reducing scales with the exception of those covering mills making steel nails, the object being 'to deal a blow at steel nails that will kill them and enforce [the] return to iron nails, thereby employing our boilers again . . . [and stopping] the introduction of steel in general to supercede iron'. Unfortunately for the A.A., the main effect of this policy seems to have been to drive the nailers out of the union rather than steel out of the nail industry, and obstructionist tactics of this sort were not attempted again; at least not on any systematic basis. Instead, the A.A. encouraged steelworkers to join the union and formulate their own scales. In December 1887 a meeting of delegates from all the steel lodges in the A.A. was held to draw up scales for steel, and at the 1888 convention a steel workers' committee was established to consider the proposals. Yet in 1891 steel delegates at the annual convention complained that few of the delegates understood their industry, and that the four lodges representing Bessemer converting departments at the meeting were all working on different scales.

Coverage of the skilled steel workers by the A.A. was never more than patchy. Several major steel producing firms, such as the Cambria and Bethlehem companies never recognized the union at any stage. Nevertheless the A.A. made significant progress in the steel industry until its disastrous defeat at Homestead in 1892 as a brief survey of the union's history in the nation's two major steelmaking districts, Pittsburgh and Chicago, shows. The major mills concerned in the Chicago area were the North Chicago mills, the South Chicago mills, and the Joliet mill, which were all operated after 1889 by the Illinois Steel Company. In the Pittsburgh area the major mills concerned were the Edgar Thompson, Homestead, and Duquesne, all ultimately owned by the Carnegie company. During the 1890s the Carnegie and Illinois Steel companies were the largest steelmaking firms in the United States.

In the early 1880s, the A.A. had reason to feel reasonably satisfied with its progress in the steel mills of both Chicago and Pittsburgh. Although an A.A. lodge at the Edgar Thompson had been suspended in 1877 when its members had signed an ironclad oath, two lodges were successfully established there in 1882–83. Two lodges were also established at Homestead soon after that plant opened in 1881 and won recognition after a bitter and violent strike in 1882. An A.A. lodge was formed in North Chicago in 1881, two were organized at South Chicago in 1883–84, and Joliet boasted five A.A. lodges in the early 1880s.

Most of this ground was lost in 1884 and 1885 when the industry was depressed and the union weakened by internal dissension. At North Chicago the A.A.'s one lodge folded up when the mill lay idle for six months. At South Chicago, the men left the A.A. and joined the Knights of Labor when the A.A. refused to admit a lodge of blastfurnacemen. All the A.A. lodges at Joliet collapsed at least for a time during 1885. At Carnegie's Edgar Thompson mill, the A.A. lodges lost both recognition and their (unusual) eight hour shifts when the company closed the mill for an extended period, announced the introduction of labor-saving machinery that would supposedly cost many jobs, and began to recruit non-union labor. Only at Homestead, of the mills under discussion, did the A.A. retain lodges in good standing in August 1885, and there the number of lodges had fallen from three to two during the previous year.

This vacuum was filled to some extent by the Knights of Labor in the mid-1880s. At the Edgar Thompson, assemblies of Knights had co-existed and co-operated with A.A. lodges until 1884, and survived there till 1888 when they too were driven out by the Carnegie company. Whether the Knights represented any of the skilled men formerly belonging to the A.A. at the Edgar Thompson after 1884 is not clear, but at both North and South Chicago and elsewhere the Knights certainly took in dropouts from the A.A. In other cases assemblies of Knights represented lesser skilled workers who were excluded from the A.A. Unfortunately it is not possible to tell from the surviving records which form of recruitment was more important to the growth of the Knights in the iron and steel industries in the 1880s. In any case it is clear that the Knights were for a short period a force to be reckoned with in iron and steel. In Allegheny county alone there were 17 local assemblies of iron and steel workers recorded in 1886, most of them recently formed. Until 1886, relationships between the A.A. and the Knights at the national level were at least cordial. Grand Master Powderly was invited to the A.A.'s annual convention that year when he invited the union to affiliate with the Knights. The proposal was overwhelmingly rejected by the A.A. lodges in December however and the following two years brought a flood of complaints by A.A. men about encroachments by the Knights and several bitter jurisdictional disputes.

In 1887 a National District Assembly of iron and steel workers (D.A. 217) was formed by the Knights but this time the organization was in decline in the industry as it was in the country as a whole. D.A. 217 never became firmly established and by 1890 the Knights no longer posed any serious threat to the A.A. which had regained much of the ground lost since 1885. At Joliet two lodges were reorganized in 1885–86 and four had been established by 1890. The men who had been organized by the Knights at North Chicago in the mid-1880s came back to the A.A. in a body in 1888 and the new lodges remained in existence well into the 1890s. In 1891, two A.A. lodges were re-established at South Chicago and the local Vice President declared that the mammoth Illinois Steel Company was now 'pretty well organized'. At Homestead, where the A.A. had hung on during the lean years of the 1880s the number of lodges increased from two in 1885 to four in 1887 to seven in 1891. On the other hand the A.A. never recaptured the Edgar Thomspon after its defeat there in 1885 and several attempts to organize the Duquesne mill, which opened in 1889, were defeated.

On the eve of the Homestead strike, the strength of trade unionism in the U.S. iron and steel industry overall was in some respects greater than it was in Britain. The 24,000 members of the A.A. in 1892 must have represented a greater proportion of the total workforce than the 21,000 who belonged to the various British unions at this date. Moreover the British unionists were divided among several unions, the largest with 7,800 members, whereas the Americans were combined in one apparently powerful organization. On the other hand the A.A.'s strength lay chiefly in the declining iron trade and no branch of the U.S. steel industry was covered by the kind of industry-wide agreement that John Hodge had negotiated for the open hearth furnace workers at least for Scotland and North-east England.

The defeat of the A.A. in the infamous Homestead strike, a familiar story which will not be repeated here, was a staggering blow to the union. It meant that the A.A. had lost control of all three of the Carnegie Company's great steel mills in the Pittsburgh area. Without some say in Pittsburgh there could be no prospect of a nationwide scale agreement for steel. Furthermore Homestead was one of the best organized steel mills in the United States in 1892 and the workers there had fought long and hard after the company had provoked them into a contest. Nevertheless they were overwhelmingly defeated and lost everything. Union morale plummeted as a result. Most important of all, the Homestead struggle demonstrated that a great corporation could refuse to negotiate with a strong trade union, use the most oppressive strike-breaking tactics available, and ignore the flood of adverse publicity which resulted. Despite heavy criticism from politicians and the press, the Carnegie company refused to budge an inch at Homestead and followed up its victory by instituting a system of blacklists and industrial spying to ensure that unionism never raised its head in the company's mills again.

The A.A. retained its lodges in the Chicago mills after 1892 and was recognised in a number of finishing mills around the country throughout the 1890s, but it was clearly on a downhill path after Homestead. Defeat by the newly organized U.S. Steel Corporation in 1901 was merely the *coup de grace*. After 1892 the U.S. steel industry was run largely on open shop lines, a state of affairs which persisted until the 1930s.

Why did the A.A. fail where the British steelworkers' unions succeeded? According to Selig Perlman, 'the fragility so characteristic of American labor organizations had arisen in the main. . . from the lack of class consciousness in American labor'.[3] A weak sense of class solidarity has in turn been attributed by different historians to various aspects of the economic and social order in America, each of which will be considered as it applies to the workingmen on the steel industry.

Most historians of American labor have emphasized the impact of mass migration from Europe of the wage-earning class in the United States. It has often been argued that particular nationality groups, especially the 'new' immigrants from Southern and Eastern Europe were 'poor union material' because they were accustomed to low living standards and hence developed modest material aspirations, or because they were used to paternalistic patterns of authority, or because they saw themselves as transient residents of the United States who would shortly return to their homes in Europe, or simply because they were cowed into submissiveness by the sheer novelty of the environment. A different, though related argument is that mass migration created such an ethno-cultural mixture among American wage-earners that co-operation and even communication between the various groups was rendered difficult if not impossible. What mattered, according to this view, was not so much the cultural characteristics of particular immigrant groups but the rivalries and tensions that emerged from the mixing together of several different ethno-cultural groups. How do these themes fit the case of the steelworkers in the United States?

In 1890 the 142,588 men who labored in the U.S. iron and steel industry included 79,053 native born Americans, 5,778 colored Americans, and 57,574 foreign born whites. Of the latter the overwhelming majority

(43,816) came from the British Isles and Germany. There is at least one piece of evidence which suggests that American employers saw the ethnocultural diversity of their employees as a blessing and deliberately fostered it in order to build up a compliant workforce. 'My experience has shown', wrote Captain William Jones, famous superintendent of Carnegie's Edgar Thompson plant, to E. V. McCadness in a much quoted letter of February 1875, 'that Germans and Irish, Swedes, and what I denominate 'Buckwheats'—young American country boys, judiciously mixed, make the most effective and tractable force you can find.' Englishmen, 'great sticklers for high wages and strikes', were above all to be avoided. It would be interesting to know whether other American employers shared Captain Jones's view and attempted this 'judicious mixture' of their workforce, but if so, the policy cannot be adjudged a success. Unionism, as we have seen, spread through the American iron and steel industry during Captain Jones's lifetime about as fast as it was spreading in Britain during the 1880s, and Captain Jones's own Edgar Thompson plant spawned both A.A. lodges and Knights of Labor Assemblies while he was in charge there. Perhaps rivalries and distrust between Germans, Swedes, Irish and American-born workers inhibited the growth of unionism in the steel industry but other than Captain Jones's letter, I have found no evidence to support the contention.[4]

During the 1890s there was a massive influx of immigrants from Southern and Eastern Europe into the labor force of the U.S. steel industry, especially Slavs (chiefly Poles, Slovaks, and Croations) and Hungarians. In his study of Slavic workers in the anthracite coalfields of Pennsylvania, Victor Greene has argued persuasively that these new immigrants did not prove to be 'poor union material' but on the contrary became solid and militant supporters of the United Mineworkers of America (UMW). By the time the Slavic workers entered the American steel mills in large numbers there was not much of a union left to be loyal to, but there is scattered evidence suggesting that when industrial disputes did occur in the steel industry the Slavic workers were 'more tenacious in their hold upon their right to organize even than the Americans.....'[5]

On the other hand there can be no doubt that the impact of the Slavic-Hungarian immigration on the workforce in steel as a whole was profoundly divisive. Greene's account of the anthracite coalfields makes it clear that the Slavic workers there encountered strong nativistic hostility, and labor leaders were among those who lobbied for legislation restricting the employment of immigrants in the mines. In the steel mills there is ample evidence that 'Hunkies', 'Polaks', etc., were despised and discriminated against by older-established groups and that ethno-cultural divisions and tensions were pervasive features of milltown life from the 1890s onwards.

Nevertheless nativism did not prevent the U.M.W. from recruiting the new immigrants in the Pennsylvania coalfields and the A.A. might well have done the same, had it had the opportunity, for by 1890 it was moving away from the craft exclusiveness of its early years. The critical point is that the A.A. was drawn into battle by the Carnegie company at Homestead in 1892 and delivered a knockout blow at a time when the influx of 'new' immigrants had scarcely begun. The most that can be said about the impact of the Slavic-Hungarian migration on the fortunes of the A.A. therefore, is that it may conceivably have made a very bad situation even worse.

In this context it is important to recognize too that the labor force in the British steel industry was not without its internal divisions, including ethno-cultural ones. In Wales, John Hodge had to struggle against Welsh hostility towards all outsiders and with workers who spoke only the Welsh language. In Lancashire, another steel-making region, P. F. Clarke has described the rift between the English and Irish communities as 'the most basic and persistent feature of social and hence political life in the region'. Much the same could be said of Scotch/Irish divisions in the west of Scotland where Hodge attributed the loss of at least one strike to Protestant/Catholic rivalries.[6]

Another divisive force among wage-earners, the rift between highly-paid skilled 'labor aristocrats' and poorer lesser skilled workers, was almost certainly more intense in Britain than in the United States at least until the arrival of the new immigrants in America. In both countries the steel unions were launched and built up by the skilled men, initially on an exclusive basis. In Britain, however, the wage differentials between skilled and unskilled were greater than they were in America where common labor was scarcer and consequently more expensive. The wages of first hand melters, who dominated the Smelters, 'stood out like skyscrapers in a town of two-storey buildings' and these men were often arrogant in their dealings with the less favored men who worked with them.[7] Discontent among the lesser skilled steelworkers in Britain led to internal disputes within the Smelters and occasional secessions. It was also a source of inter-union rivalry. The bitter and drawn-out struggle between the Ironworkers and the Steel Smelters at the Hawarden Bridge Works in 1909–1910, for example, arose from a dispute between the day wage men who belonged to the smelters and the skilled tonnage rate men who were members of the Ironworkers.

Jurisdictional disputes were not unknown in the U.S. steel industry of course. The A.A. faced formidable competition from the Knights in the late 1880s and had to cope with rival organizations of nailers in the 1880s and finishers in the 1890s. At the time the A.A. received its knockout blow in 1892, however, it faced little serious competition from organizations within the world of unionism. By contrast, several organizations competed for the same classes of steelworkers in Britain, and the records of the Smelters show that they were constantly at odds with the other unions on both minor and major issues. All things considered, it is difficult to make much of the proposition that internal disunity was a primary cause of the relative weakness of the A.A. as against its British counterparts.

A lack of class consciousness among American workers also 'owes a great deal,' according to Henry Pelling, 'to the factor of high wages, which has enabled American workers to exhibit many of the same consumption and behaviour patterns as those of other social groups'. In a somewhat similar vein, Perlman has argued that 'the American employer has, in general, been able to keep his employees contented with the conditions, determined by himself, on which they individually accepted employment', and this, according to Perlman, was a primary cause of 'the want of inner cohesiveness' in American labor organizations. Whatever the impact of high wages and good working and living conditions on class consciousness in general, however, the idea that they inhibit trade union growth is not especially persuasive. All over the capitalist world, trade unions emerged first among better paid workers and usually developed most rapidly in periods of economic boom. If trade unions were comparatively weak in the United States, where real wages were high, they were unusually strong in the late 19th century Australia, another high wage country.[8]

In the case of British and American steelworkers, it is not easy to determine with any degree of precision just how real wages compared in the late 19th century. The skilled men in both countries were paid by piece rates and it is difficult to find out how these translated into actual earnings. Furthermore estimates of comparative real wages rest on the construction of comparable cost-of-living indices, and this is a very complex task. Contemporary observers, however, were united in the opinion that the unskilled men in America were better paid, both in monetary and real terms, than those in Britain, and most thought that skilled American steelworkers were better paid also.

Though their earnings were high, both by U.S. and world standards, the American steel workers were forced to accept long periods of unemployment and frequent wage cuts as a matter of course. Round the clock shift work, the twelve hour day, and the seven day week were normal practices. Industrial accidents, often fatal, were frequent in the steel industry and working conditions were extremely unpleasant. Pittsburgh, Roy Lubove has noted, has been compared to hell more frequently than any other American city, and it was the heat and the arduous, dangerous work of the steel industry which earned it this unsavoury reputation. British steel workers were amazed when they learned in 1907 that their American counterparts were frequently driven to work by their wives in buggies, but American steelworkers were well aware of the enormous profits earned by companies like Carnegie's, and can hardly have believed that high wages were anything less than their due. When John Fitch studied the skilled steelworkers of the Pittsburgh region in 1907-1908, he found them 'resentful and bitter toward their employers'. No comparable study exists for the 1880s or 1890s but it is difficult to believe that the decline of the A.A. was rooted in a deep sense of contentment among the steelworkers.[9]

More difficult to measure and evaluate is the impact of social and geographic mobility on British and American manual workers generally, and on steelworkers in particular. Recently Stephan Thernstrom and other American scholars have begun to provide us with a clear picture of just how fast and in what ways American workers accumulated property, rose or fell on the occupational ladder, and moved from place to place.[10] Obviously these matters have a direct bearing on the question of class consciousness and group solidarity. Unfortunately, census returns, the most important source of data for the American studies, do not provide the same wealth of information about property holdings, earnings and occupations for Britain as America, and in any case are only available to scholars for England and Wales to 1871.

If some statistical method exists for isolating steelworkers from the rest of the population in Britain and tracing their geographic and social progress in this period, I have failed to discover it. It seems probable that faster rates of economic growth in the United States provided greater opportunities for social advancement and the *embourgeoisement* of workers there. On the question of geographic mobility, however, we know that rates of rural exodus, urbanization, and migration abroad were very high in 19th century Britain, and that British steelmaking centers were rapidly growing, highly mobile communities. Middlesbrough, for example, the Pittsburgh of Northeast England had a population of 154 in 1831, 18,892 in 1861, 55,788 in 1881, and 91,302 in 1901. In the early 20th century Lady Bell described the population of Middlesbrough as 'recruited by the incessant influx of fresh workers into the town of which a great part is forever changing and shifting, restlessly moving from one house to another, or going away altogether in the constant hope that the mere fact of change must be an improvement'. In general, the social and geographic mobility of steelworkers in Britain and America remains a murky subject and whether American steelworkers were a more volatile group, socially and geographically, than British ones remains unknown and possibly unknowable.[11]

For one vital class of British steelworkers, the open hearth melters who formed the hard core of the Steel Smelters' union, geographic mobility was certainly impeded by the system of promotion which developed in that branch of the industry. Promotion from chargewheeler to third hand melter to second hand melter to first hand melter was by seniority *within the firm*. A first hand melter who left his job to take up a position elsewhere started at the bottom again. Since, in 1892, a first hand earned about £5–£10 per week, a second hand two-thirds of this, a third hand one-half of the first hand's wage, and a chargewheeler about four shillings and sixpence per day, the incentive to stay in one place was obviously strong. Evidence bearing on promotion practices in the U.S. steel industry is hard to find but it would have been entirely out of character for American employers to accept this kind of restriction on their ability to hire and promote workers at will. It may be that skilled men in the U.S. steel industry moved about more than British open hearth melters and that the stability of A.A. lodges suffered as a result. However we are faced with a chicken and egg problem here. Promotion by seniority was something which the Steel Smelters imposed on the employers and their ability to do this may have reflected other sources of strength.

Even more elusive are questions relating to the spirit of labor/management and class relationships generally in Britain and the United States. According to Louis Hartz the failure of socialism in the United States owes less to the 'objective movement of economic forces' than to the absence of a feudal tradition in America. If there is anything in the view that Americans were peculiarly lacking in a 'sense of class' for reasons unconnected to the economic situation, then this could help explain the relative weakness of trade unionism in the United States. Whatever value one places on Hartz's theory, it is true that European visitors frequently commented on the relative openness and ease with which American workingmen approached and were approached by their employers and managers. Men like Superintendent Jones of the Edgar Thompson prided themselves on the good personal relationships they maintained with their men. Could it be that trade union development was hindered by the fact that workingmen sensed less social distance between themselves and their bosses than British workers?[12]

It is difficult to be sure but the answer is probably not. However easy relationships between employer and employee were on a day to day basis, the fundamental conflict of interest between capital and labor was too obvious to be ignored. When industrial disputes did break out in American steel plants as for example at Homestead in 1881 and 1892, Bethlehem in 1883, and Duquesne in 1889, the employers commonly refused to recognize the union, sacked union leaders, evicted strikers from company houses, called in non-union labor from far afield, and generally used every weapon at their disposal in order to defeat the men. Violence was far more common in U.S. labor relations generally and in the U.S. steel industry in particular than it was in Britain. Though the relationship between manager and men might be 'somewhat freer' a visiting British unionist wrote of the U.S. steel industry in 1903, 'it is not better than in this country. . .'. Managers might be more approachable personally but wage disputes were settled 'in the jingo spirit'.

All of the points under discussion so far, ethno-cultural and other divisive forces within the workforce, wages and working conditions, rates of social and geographic mobility, and the spirit of worker/management relations are related to the question of trade union strength and weakness in a similar fashion; all have a bearing on class consciousness and group solidarity. Yet there is good reason to doubt whether the collapse of the A.A. in the U.S. was caused by a comparative lack of class or group consciousness on the part of American steelworkers. The greatest single blow to the fortunes of the A.A. occurred at Homestead in 1892 where not only the A.A. lodges but the entire workforce demonstrated a high degree of group consciousness and solidarity. Though there are cases recorded of A.A. lodges simply folding up, usually during periods when mills lay idle for long periods, another common pattern was a head-on clash between the employers and the A.A. over the right to organize, followed by a lengthy and bitter stoppage, ending in a victory for the employers and the open shop.

Of course some of the A.A.'s defeats may have come about in whole or in part because the workers lacked sufficient solidarity, or because there were large numbers of non-union men willing to take the place of strikers in any dispute. One reason for the A.A.'s failure to organize the Duquesne plant was undoubtedly the fiercely anti-union policies adopted by the management, but the union's leaders also complained that the men there lacked the necessary spirit to maintain a successful strike. The record of industrial disputes in the U.S. steel industry during the 1880s makes nonsense of the notion that the workforce was so utterly divided or intrinsically contented that it lacked any will for collective action at all, but it is conceivable that, for one reason or another, group consciousness was comparatively weaker among American than British steelworkers.

It should be noted, however, that apathy and lack of militancy were not unknown among British steelworkers. The complaints of A.A. leaders that the men at Duquesne lacked solidarity and union discipline are little different in kind from dozens of items in the Monthly Reports of the British Steel Smelters about the same time. In Britain, as in America, steelworkers had often to be prodded into paying union dues, maintaining branches, and staying loyal in difficult strike situations. Whole steel-making regions remained almost untouched by unionism in Britain until well into the 20th century, Sheffield being a notable case in point. In summary, it remains uncertain whether American steelworkers possessed less of a sense of group solidarity than British steelworkers or not, and this is surely not the most obvious explanation for the total collapse of the steelworkers' unions in the United States.

Whether or not it was more difficult to persuade American than British steelworkers to join or support a trade union, the very structure of U.S. trade unionism may have inhibited efforts to recruit union members in the American steel industry. In both countries the first unions to enter the field were ironworkers' organizations, dominated by the puddlers and rollers of wrought iron. In Britain, as we have seen, the Ironworkers' union recruited some steelworkers in some regions but never threw itself into a vigorous recruitment campaign throughout the industry. Other organizations, notably the Steel Smelters sprang up to take on these tasks, and although the existence of several different unions within the British steel industry produced jurisdictional confusion and inter-union squabbles, it also ensured that efforts to expand union membership did not lapse. Rivalry may even have encouraged vigorous efforts at recruitment.

In America, on the other hand, the concept of one union per trade was fiercely defended by the national unions and formed the very cornerstone of the American Federation of Labor's policies after its formation. 'Dual unionism' was perceived as an unmitigated evil by union leaders in the United States and any effort to establish a rival organization within the jurisdiction of an existing union was bitterly resisted with the full backing of the AFL. The challenge of the Knights of Labor to the national unions in the 1880s may account in part for the American unions' obsession with jurisdictional purity, and other more general explanations have been put forward by labor historians. Whatever the reasons, the impact was significant and in some ways unhelpful to the cause of unionism in the American iron and steel industry. The A.A. claimed the sole right to organize skilled steelworkers in the United States and after 1886 could back up its claim with an AFL charter. Yet throughout the 1880s and 1890s it remained primarily an ironworkers' union and a Pittsburgh-centered organization. Since the main sources available to the historian for the study of the A.A.'s activities are the union's own *Proceedings*, and its official organ, the *National Labor Tribune*, it is difficult to be sure whether the A.A. neglected the interests of steelworkers, especially those outside the Pittsburgh area, or not. Obviously, union spokesmen did not advertise their leaders' failings. It is clear from these official publications, however, that the wrought iron industry was overwhelmingly the center of the union's concern in the late 19th century.

There were also cases where steelworkers expressed or demonstrated dissatisfaction with the A.A. as for example in Chicago during the mid-1880s, when several lodges seceded and joined the Knights of Labor. The Chicago steel mills were later re-organized by the A.A. but in the interval Carnegie had driven first the A.A. and then the Knights from the Edgar Thompson plant, arguing that lower wage rates in Chicago forced him to cut costs in Pittsburgh and reject the men's demands. The *National Labor Tribune* blamed the Knights for allowing this situation to develop, but it was the failure of the A.A. to maintain the loyalty of the Chicago steelworkers that had allowed the Knights to move in there in the first place. It seems possible, then, that the unionization of American steelworkers was hindered by the Pittsburgh ironworkers' dominating role in the national union's affairs.

So far attention has been concentrated on what might be termed 'internal' factors affecting trade union growth: characteristics of the unions themselves, their members, and their potential membership. It is also necessary to consider 'external' factors: i.e., aspects of the economic, social, and political setting within which the men labored and the unions organized. Obviously enough these were not identical in Britain and America.

Every British steelman, whether employer or employee, who inspected the steel mills of the United States from the 1880s onwards, and every American observer of the British steel industry was struck by the rapid pace of technical change in the American industry and the increasing obsolescence of British manufacturing techniques. Technical developments in some cases rendered traditional skills, such as iron puddling, completely obsolete. In other cases the degree of skill required by a workman to perform a particular manufacturing operation was severely reduced. Since semi-skilled workmen were easier to replace than highly skilled tradesmen, such changes weakened the bargaining power of the trade unions concerned. Could it be that the collapse of the A.A. came about in whole or in part because technical change had undermined the importance of its members' skills; skills which remained critical in the technically less advanced steel mills of Britain?

It should be noted first of all, that the impact of technical developments on the skills of steel workers was not uniform in all branches of the industry. In some, the main impact of technical innovation was to reduce the amount of physical labor required rather than the skills. This was true of the blastfurnaces, for example, and also of the open hearth furnaces, where the major innovation in this period was the introduction of mechanical methods for charging furnaces. How much skill was required of an open hearth steel worker at this time is difficult to determine, since employers and employees differed on the question. In 1902 Charles Schwab of U.S. Steel claimed he could train a 'fairly intelligent agricultural laborer' to be a steel melter in six to eight weeks. Ten years earlier James Riley of the Steel Company of Scotland had made much the same claim in strikingly similar language. A man 'off the fields' he said, could be turned into a melter 'within three months'. Union men, on the other hand claimed that operating open hearth furnaces required a great deal of skill and long experience, and when strikes were in progress, they almost invariably claimed that substitute labor was producing 'messes' and ruining the furnaces. Whatever the truth, the major change in the period involved the replacement of manual by mechanical labor and the degree of skill required cannot have varied significantly between Britain and American.

In the American rolling mills too the amount of physical labor required was greatly reduced by mechanization but in this case it is also true that the introduction of automatic mechanical devices reduced the importance of the roll hands' skills. Even union officials admitted as much. It was in

140

rolling mill practices that the British lagged farthest behind their U.S. compeititors, and it is probable that the impact of technical change on the position of the American rolling mill hands made the A.A. comparatively easier to defeat and destroy than the British unions. American employers certainly did use the threat of technical innovation to force the workforce into submission. In December, 1884, for example, the Carnegie Company shut down the Edgar Thompson plant for an indefinite period and paid off all hands. Shortly afterwards, Pittsburgh newspapers reported that when the mill reopened using new automatic rolling equipment it would require 1600 fewer men. Faced with this situation and news that the company's agents were recruiting non-union labor outside the district, some A.A. men deserted the union and signed new contracts on the employers' terms. Subsequently the A.A.'s two lodges at the Edgar Thompson disbanded.

Another feature which distinguished the British from the U.S. steel industry was the much larger scale of corporate organization in America. As early as 1878 the ten active U.S. Bessemer steel plants were producing, on average, one and a half times as much steel as their British counterparts. Faster growth within individual plants and horizontal mergers, such as that which produced the Illinois Steel Company in 1889, increased the disparity between the sizes of the largest British and American firms. By 1899 the Carnegie and the Illinois Steel Companies had annual capacities of over one million tons of steel. As late as 1905 the ingot capacity of the largest British firm was somewhat less than half of this figure.

For trade unions, large firms have their advantages, but they are more difficult to organize initially if they are determined to resist, as many of the American companies were. Multiplant operations, such as Carnegie's, after 1883, and the Illinois, after 1889, were particularly difficult opponents for the unions since these companies could maintain full production and profitable operations in non-union plants while strikes were in progress elsewhere. Carnegie used this tactic successfully during the Homestead struggle of 1892 and the gigantic U.S. Steel Corporation was able to squeeze what life remained out of the A.A. with similar methods in 1901. At the conclusion of the Homestead strike, the *National Labor Tribune* editorialized on this point: 'If, on July First, it had appeared reasonably possible that the [Carnegie] company would stick to the contest, regardless of cost in cash,' the editors wrote, 'then the issue would have been solved without a contest, for there was no workman of the A.A. but who knows that no labor organization under the sun could contend successfully against such immense resources as were at the disposition of the Carnegie company on July 1.' Certainly the resources controlled by the Carnegie company dwarfed those of any British steel firm at that date and the contrast was even more marked after the formation of U.S. Steel in 1901.

Perhaps more important than the enormous size of the great American companies was the sheer determination with which so many of them resisted efforts to unionize their mills, or in the case of the Carnegie company, drove unions out of divisions that were already organized. Whereas bitter struggles over union recognition were commonplace in the U.S. steel industry during the 1880s and 1890s, the principle of unionism was rarely an issue in the British industry during this period. There were employers who refused to deal with unions, John Hodge remarked, in a tone more of sorrow than anger, but clearly for Hodge the determined anti-union management represented more of an irritant than a serious threat to the growth and survival of his union. On the whole, according to Hodge, 'the employers are entitled to credit for always having played cricket'.[13]

Why was it that British employers were more willing to tolerate the existence of unions in their mills than their American counterparts? Surely not because they felt any positive enthusiasm for the unions. When Sidney Webb interviewed James Riley, manager of Scotland's largest steel-producing firm in 1892, Riley spoke bitterly about the obstructive tactics of both the Smelters and the Millmen and down-graded the value of the skill of their members. Yet Riley played a leading role in the establishment of conciliation and arbitration machinery for the Scottish iron and steel industry and his public stance towards the unions was invariably conciliatory. In this respect he typified the attitudes of British steelmasters towards the trade unions in the years when Carnegie's men were driving the unions out of their Pittsburgh mills.

Perhaps American employers were emboldened by the knowledge that they controlled vast resources and that rapid technical change was undermining the scarcity value of skilled workmen. If there is anything in the notion that American workmen lacked the solidarity and capacity for organization of the British, then this too could have encouraged U.S. employers to resist the emergence of trade unions. In other words, the attitudes of employers may not have been an independent variable in this situation but a function of other factors already discussed. Yet is seems unlikely that British employers were dissuaded from adopting more strongly anti-union policies by fear of the intrinsic fighting strength of the unions they dealt with or lack of confidence in their own resources, since the occasional anti-union employer in Britain demonstrated from time to time that determination and strong arm tactics could work as well in Glasgow as in Pittsburgh. Two examples will illustrate this point.

In 1889 the Millmen's union, which was recognized by most of the steel companies in Scotland, established a branch with about 30 members at a plant called Clyde Bridge. The management refused to recognize the union and dismissed the union men. A strike ensued, supported, according to the union, by most of the workforce. But the owner, one James Neilson, recruited enough non-union labor to keep the mill operating and boarded them inside the mill gates. After 19 weeks the strike was called off by the Millmen and Clyde Bridge remained a non-union mill until about 1904.

Just ten years after the Millmen's defeat at Clyde Bridge, the Steel Smelters, by this stage a well-established union which was recognized by most of the major employers in Britain also ran up against the Neilsons, this time at the Mossend works in Scotland. In August, 1889, the Smelters established a branch at Mossend which had been non-union until that time. Management responded by dismissing the branch secretary and about 20 other union members. Attempts to negotiate a settlement failed and a strike was called for October 21. The company hired non-union labor to keep their plant running and evicted strikers from company-owned houses, but the union fought back with picketing, 'meetings, games, concerts, dances, football matches, etc.' Over 400 men were supported with strike pay and the assistant secretary of the union, John T. McPherson, spent several months almost constantly at Mossend directing the struggle and addressing meetings. Throughout 1900 the Smelters' *Monthly Report* carried encouraging stories from Mossend assuring members that morale remained high among the strikers despite police harassment and the management's blandishments. Blackleg labor was alleged to be so inefficient that the firm would soon be driven into bankruptcy. Yet after 18 months of solid effort and the expenditure of over £13,000 (the union's total assets in Jan. 1901 were valued at £25,000) the Smelters admitted defeat and called off the strike.

Why did other more important British steel-producing firms not emulate the Neilsons of Clyde Bridge and Mossend and throw their much greater resources into the fight against unionism? This is a critical question but one that is extremely difficult to answer given the paucity of surviving evidence. Since the British steel industry never suffered a major confrontation between unions and employers, there was no great incentive to discuss problems of labor relations in public. Strikes and lockouts such as those at Mossend and Clyde Bridge were small scale affairs receiving little or no attention in the general press, and trade publications such as the *Iron and Coal Trades Review* discussed labor relations in only the most general terms. Some company records survive but these consist mainly of minutes from meetings of Boards of Directors and they contain little or nothing about managerial attitudes towards unions. Thus the records of the Steel Company of Scotland tell us that Mr. Riley, the manager, reported on the meeting between employers and unionists at Newcastle in 1889, but they do not tell us *what* he reported, how the meeting was arranged, or what deliberations, if any, went on among employers before this crucial meeting occurred.

All that can be done is to suggest some possible explanations for the attitudes of the British steelmasters. First of all, a general survey of British labor history reveals that British trade unions had to fight stubbornly, on both the industrial and political fronts, for the right to exist, before they were generally accepted as legitimate institutions. By the last quarter of the

19th century, however, many of the critical battles had been fought and won. In the United States, industrialism, the industrial proletariat, and the industrial union appeared much later. The violent resistance of many American employers to unionism in the late 19th century may simply have reflected the relative novelty of the 'labour problem' in the United States and perhaps should be compared with the activities of British employers in the era of the Combination Acts or the great lockouts of the 1850s. In 1892 the British economist, W. J. Ashley, thought it '. . . very apparent that the feeling of the comfortable classes in America is still in the same stage as that reached by the like classes in England a quarter of a century ago'.[14]

One remark of James Riley to Sidney Webb may provide another clue to the differing attitudes of British and American employers towards unions. He had been accused by other employers, Riley said, of being unduly kind to the unions, in order to protect the political career of his company chairman, Sir Charles Tennant who at one time represented a Glasgow constituency in Parliament as a Liberal. Though a direct link between the political aspirations and labor policies of individual employers was no doubt unusual, the influence of political pressures on labor relations is always critical, and the fact that manual workers formed a much larger proportion of the total population in Britain than in the United States meant that, even though partially disfranchised, the British working class was politically more potent. The frequent recourse of American state governments to the use of the National Guard in labour disputes, nominally to maintain law and order but usually in practice to protect non-union labor, President Cleveland's employment of federal troops to crush the American Railway Union in 1894, and the politicians-be-damned attitude of the Carnegie company during the Homestead contest, are all indications of the vulnerability of American trade unions to a hostile political environment in the late 19th century.

It has not proved possible to provide easy or conclusive answers to all of the questions raised in this study. On several significant aspects of the subject the evidence is scanty and conclusions can be no more than tentative. Neverthless, at least one salient point does emerge. Though the conditions and aspirations of steel workers, and the structure and leadership of their organizations may have had something to do with the contrasting fortunes of the steelworkers' unions in Britain and America, the most striking difference between the two situations concerns the behavior of employers rather than employees. In both countries, the impulse to organize was present among steelworkers but in one, most employers offered little resistance to union growth while in the other they generally fought back vigorously.

It may be that the truculent attitude adopted by so many American employers was encouraged by the attitudes of their employees and the tactics of the unions. If evidence suggesting that American steelworkers lacked the solidarity of British ones is less than compelling, it must be conceded that there could be an element of truth in the proposition. The dominating position of ironworkers in the one union with AFL jurisdiction in the U.S. steel industry is also a factor which must be taken into account when considering the disintegration of trade unionism there. But if union morale and group solidarity are to be stressed we must consider the odds against which the A.A. struggled, surely enough to dampen the spirits of the most ardent union man. When the Carnegie company closed down the Edgar Thompson plant for an indefinite period and let it be known new machinery would cost hundreds of jobs in the mill, it is not surprising that many unionists lost heart and signed on for work on the company's terms. When neither the united resistance of the workforce nor protest of press and politicians could dissuade the management at Homestead to settle for anything less than the complete eradication of the union from the mill, who can wonder that the A.A. lost members rapidly? The determination to resist the growth of trade unions by employers who possessed vast financial resources, who controlled a rapidly changing technology, and who were uninhibited by political constraints, may not have been the only reason for the collapse of unionism in the American steel industry, but it is surely the most important one.

A comparative study of some other industry common to Britain and the United States, or unionization among American and German steelworkers would undoubtedly produce a different emphasis. Still, many of the points made here about the U.S. steel industry do have a broader application. Rapid rates of technological change were characteristic of American industry in this period. Domination of national markets by a small number of very large firms was also much more typical of the United States than Britain. Though the standard work on British trade unions talks of an 'employers' counter-attack' on the unions in the 1890s, the goals of the British employers were limited and their tactics generally timid when compared to those of many American employers at that time. The victories of British employers over the boot and shoe workers' unions in 1895 and the engineers in 1897, for example, led not to the institution of the open shop in those industries but merely to restrictions on the unions' powers to impose restrictive practices.[15] The impact of an unsympathetic political environment on the outcome of labor disputes, so evident during the Homestead struggle, affected unions generally.

The weakness and political conservatism of the American labor movement in the late 19th and early 20th centuries have often been seen primarily as the product of a lack of class consciousness among American workingmen. In the United States, it is suggested, class lines were more fluid and opportunities for advancement more rapid than in European countries like Britain, where, according to Perlman, 'the hierarchy of classes keeps labor together by pressure from the top'. Perhaps so, yet as Perlman also acknowledges, in some ways the American workingman was more rather than less oppressed than his British counterpart. The retreat of so many American union leaders from a youthful socialism to a cautious and conservative 'business unionism' may have reflected less a growing enthusiasm for the economic and political status quo, than a resigned acknowledgement that in a land where the propertied middle classes dominated politically and the big corporations ruled supreme in industry, accommodation was more appropriate than confrontation.[16]

NOTES

[1] Clegg, Fox and Thompson, *British Trade Unions*, 204
[2] Except where stated otherwise, figures for British trade union membership have been taken from the Board of Trade, Labour Department, *Report on Trade Unions in 1889*, Cd. 442, and *Report on Trade Unions in 1903–1904*, Cd. 2838.
[3] Selig Perlman, *A Theory of the Labor Movement* (New York 1928), 162.
[4] Jones quoted in Bridge, J. H., *The Inside History of the Carneigie Company* (New York, 1903), 81.
[5] Victor R. Greene, *The Slavic Community on Strike: Immigrant Labor in Pennsylvania Anthracite* (Notre Dame, Indiana, 1968); 42–43, Brody, *Steelworkers*, 260–261.
[6] John Hodge. *From Workman's Cottage to Windsor Castle* (London, 1931) 118, 282–83; P. F. Clarke. *Lancashire and the New Liberalism* (Cambridge, 1971). 37; Patrick McGeown, *Heat the Furnace Seven Times More* (London, 1967), 15.
[7] McGeown, *Heat the Furnace*, 23, 94.
[8] Pelling, *American Labor*, 221; Perlman, *Labor Movement*, 154.
[9] Roy Lubove, *Twentieth Century Pittsburgh: Government, Business, and Environmental Change* (New York, 1969).
[10] See Stephan Thernstrom, *The Other Bostonians: Poverty and Progress in the American Metropolis, 1880–1970* (Cambridge, Mass., 1973), for an outstanding example of this work and a discussion of other literature in the field.
[11] Lady Hugh Bell, *At the Works*, (London, 1907), 9, 11.
[12] Louis Hartz, *The Liberal Tradition in America*, (New York, 1955), 6 and *passim*
[13] Hodge, *Country Cottage*, 91, 284.
[14] W. J. Ashley. 'Methods of industrial peace'. *Economic Review*, II (1892), 311.
[15] Clegg, Fox, and Thompson, *British Trade Unions*, 161–168, 201–205.
[16] Perlman, *Labor Movement*, 155–62, 164.

PART III

Economic Development

(a) *The Economic Effects of Labour Scarcity*

H. J. HABAKKUK

THE SUPPLY OF LABOUR IN THE U.S.A. AND ENGLAND

Industry started to develop in the United States at a time when industrial money wages were substantially higher than they were in England, according to some estimates for the early nineteenth century perhaps a third to a half higher. This was fundamentally because the remuneration of American industrial labour was measured by the rewards and advantages of independent agriculture. [. . .]

Land was abundant and, except possibly in Virginia before the abolition of entails, it was accessible to purchase by men of small means. In the 1820s it could be purchased from the Federal Government at $1.25 per acre, which was well within the reach of a skilled labourer, who might at this time earn between $1.25 and $2.0 per day. 'The men earn here (in the cotton textile factories at Lowell) from 10 to 20 dollars a week,' wrote an English observer in 1842, 'and can therefore lay by from 5 to 10 dollars, after providing for every want, so that in two or three years they accumulate enough to go off to the west and buy an estate at 1¼ dollars an acre or set up in some small way of business at home.' In England, by contrast, land was scarce in relation to labour, and the supply of land on the market, particularly of small properties, was restricted by the existence of large estates supported by legal restraints on alienation; the return on the cultivation of land in England up to 1815 was high since new techniques were available, and food prices were rising; but to set up as a tenant-farmer required considerable capital, and, even if an English artisan had been able to acquire the capital, the supply of farms to be let was limited, and absorbed by the demand of the sons of existing tenants. In England, therefore, a man could, generally speaking, enter agriculture only as a labourer commanding low wages.

H. J. Habakkuk, *American and British Technology in the Nineteenth Century*, Cambridge University Press, 1962; pp. 23–76. Abridged.

149

The abundance and accessibility of land plus the fact that much of it was fertile meant that output per man in American agriculture was high. Moreover, since the cultivator was often also the owner, and his family supplied the labour, the advantage of the high output accrued to the cultivator. His income included: (1) an element of rent, which would in England have been a heavy charge on output and payable to the landowner, (2) agricultural profits, which in England accrued to the tenant-farmer, as well as (3) the wages, which in England went to the agricultural labourer. Furthermore the new land was brought into use in such a way that the returns to settlement on the frontier sometimes included elements of exceptional gain. Many American farmers had heavy debt charges; but there were no tithes, and taxes were low. Finally since the total earnings of the family in American agriculture tended to be divided among its members, there was less disparity between average and marginal earnings. In order to attract labour, therefore, industry had to assure the workers in industry a real wage comparable to average earnings in agriculture. English industry, by contrast, could acquire labour from agriculture at a wage equal to the very low product of the marginal agricultural labourer plus an addition to cover the costs of transport and of overcoming inertia. Thus, while in England industrial wages equalled the marginal product, in the U.S.A. the reward of the marginal labourer in industry was above his product, unless the manufacturer took steps to increase the product.

Moreover the course of agricultural technology in the early decades of the nineteenth century may well have accentuated the disparity between the terms on which labour was available to industry in the U.S.A. and England. In America improvements in agriculture took the form primarily of increasing output per head and the increase initially was probably more rapid than in industry; in England on the other hand, agricultural improvement was devoted primarily to increasing yields per acre and, even where there was an increase in output per head, the abundance of labour made it difficult for the labourer to enjoy the increase. In America agricultural improvements raised, and in England prevented, a rise in the terms on which labour was available to industry.

Comparison of industrial wage-rates does not of course measure precisely the difference in labour-cost, in terms of output, in the two countries. For, on the one side, the hours of work in America were generally longer, and conceivably effort was more concentrated. It may also be, as some contemporaries said, that better nutrition and more spacious working and living conditions, made the American a more efficient worker. On the other hand it might be supposed from the alternatives open to labour in America that the workers recruited into American industry were inferior, in relation to agricultural labour, when compared with the English; it is possible that is, that the pull of agriculture showed itself in the quality as well as the price of industrial labour in America. Then again,

American employers had to incur higher costs than the English on housing and working-facilities of a kind which made the worker more agreeable but added little, if anything, to labour productivity. Probably also the rate of turnover of workers was higher in America, and therefore the likelihood smaller that they would acquire industrial discipline. Finally, England at the start was technically superior and this must have reflected itself in higher labour productivity. Since we cannot measure these conflicting influences, it is impossible to be precise about the differences in labour-costs in the two countries, but there is no reason to doubt the opinion of contemporaries that American industrial labour was substantially dearer than the English.

But American industrial labour was not dearer than the English; its supply was less elastic. It was more difficult to obtain additional labour for the industrial sector as a whole. This was partly owing to the abundance of land and the difficulties of internal transport, which required technical solutions and heavy capital outlays before they could be overcome. It was also partly owing to America's geographical remoteness from the areas of abundant population. [. . .]

Dearness and inelasticity are logically distinct; the consequences of a high level of wages prevailing over time are not the same at all points as those of a wage-level which rises when demand for labour increases. There have been situations where the floor set to industrial wages by *per capita* productivity in agriculture was low but the supply of labour was inelastic, for example in England for much of the eighteenth century. There have also been situations where the floor set to industrial wages was high but where abundant labour was forthcoming at this wage—in some respects this was the case in the U.S.A. in the second half of the nineteenth century when there was a large amount of immigration. But in the first half of the nineteenth century, with which we are here mainly concerned, there was a contrast on both points, and a more marked contrast than existed either before or since; industrial labour was dear, and its total supply inelastic in the U.S.A., and it was cheap and elastic in England. Since the general level of labour-costs was so closely connected with the elasticity of the supply of labour, it is difficult to discuss their effects separately except at the cost of repetition. In most of the following discussion, therefore, they are treated together.

THE INDUCEMENT TO MECHANIZE

It seems obvious—it certainly seemed so to contemporaries—that the dearness and inelasticity of American, compared with British labour, gave the American entrepreneur with a given capital a greater inducement than his British counterpart to replace labour by machines. The real problem is to determine how the substitution took place. Where the more mechanized method saved *both* labour and capital per unit of output it would be the preferred technique in both countries. It was where the more mechanized method saved labour but at the expense of an increase in capital that the American had the greater inducement than the English manufacturer to adopt it. (The term capital-intensive will henceforward be used to describe such a method). [. . .]

There is little readily available information about the labour requirements of various techniques or about the price of different types of labour, and the following discussion is therefore conjectural. But a plausible case can be made for supposing that in the early nineteenth century in the U.S.A. an increased demand for labour raised the wages of skilled labour *less* than the wages of unskilled labour, and that, in many cases, the capital-intensive technique required, for its construction plus operation, more skilled labour per unit of output than the labour-intensive technique. [. . .]

The distinction between skilled and unskilled labour is, of course, constantly shifting; technical progress creates new categories of employment and calls for continual redefinition of skill. Skilled labour at the beginning of the nineteenth century was very different from skilled labour at the end. At the end of the century there was a whole spectrum of degrees of skill. At the beginning of the century there were three broad categories of labour. First there was the undifferentiated mass of unskilled adult labour. The money wage of such labour was a third or a half higher in America than in England. Secondly there were workers who performed tasks which required dexterity and aptitude but which, granted these qualities, could be performed after a short period of training and experience, for example some of the tasks performed by women in the textile industry. For such labour the American wage was rarely more than 20 per cent higher than the English. Finally there were the craft skills which were so technically complicated that they could be acquired only after a long term of training. Craft operations were so diverse that, more than in other types of labour, it is extremely difficult to make direct comparison, especially as rates varied widely according to season and from place to place, and we have no independent tests of the degree of skill being priced. Only a very detailed analysis of labour capabilities and of the relative values placed upon them in the two countries would establish the differences in this respect between America and England. But the random selection of rates given by Clark[1] suggests that the premium on artisan skills was generally lower in America than in England in the early nineteenth century.

How far differences in the premium on skill between the two countries represent difference in supply and how far differences in demand it is impossible to say, but there are some general reasons why we should expect the supply of skill, in relation to common labour, to have been more abundant in America than in England:

(1) As has been evident since 1939, a general shortage of labour is most acutely felt in the unskilled grades, in a shortage of recruits for heavy tedious work; workers in low-paid activities are more prepared to leave their jobs and seek better ones when labour is scarce, in relation to demand, than when it is abundant. A general shortage of labour raises the labour-costs of instrument-users more than those of instrument-makers. Where there is a persistent surplus of labour, it is those who are without skill, particularly the newcomers to the labour market, who have most difficulty in finding work; it is on the wages of the unskilled that the surplus has most effect.

(2) The pulling or retaining power of American agricultural expansion was felt most on unskilled labour. It was, of course, easier for the skilled worker to accumulate the capital necessary for settlement; but at the opening of the nineteenth century the costs of settlement were probably sufficiently low in relation to industrial earnings not to restrict the possibility to the highest-paid workers, and it was the worker without special industrial skills who stood to make the largest relative gain from agriculture. Furthermore, investment in social overhead capital, particularly transport-systems, made heavy demands on general labour, that is labour not trained for particular operations, and the construction of canals, roads, and railways seems to have been more attractive to such labour than the factories. This type of investment was a more rapidly increasing proportion of total investment than in England.

(3) Literacy was more widely diffused in America and popular education developed earlier. [. . .] Thus a higher proportion of the population than in England was capable of being trained to skilled operations.

(4) There was much more international mobility of skill than of general labour, and a high proportion of English migrants to the U.S.A. before the start of mass migration were skilled workers. In the early decades of the century therefore, immigration did more to alleviate the shortages of artisan skills than of unskilled labour.

(5) Mechanical abilities of a rudimentary sort were widely spread in the U.S.A. at the opening of the century. [. . .]

(6) The up-grading of unskilled to skilled labour was less impeded in the U.S.A. because, though skilled workers were in fact organized earlier in the U.S.A., trade union restrictions, conventions, apprenticeship rules, were less effective than in England.

We may reasonably conclude, therefore, that in America an increase in the demand for labour raised the cost of the methods which required a great deal of unskilled labour more than it raised the cost of the methods which required a great deal of skilled labour.

It is not always the case that the capital-intensive methods require more skilled labour per unit of output than the labour-intensive. But in the technology of the early nineteenth century there are likely to have been several cases where it did so. The *manufacture* of power-looms required more skill than the manufacture of hand-looms; and the same was probably true of the 'superior' as compared with the 'simpler' machines of all kinds. In the U.S.A. when demand for labour rose, the labour-costs of the machine-makers rose less than the labour-costs of the machine-users, and the costs of the machines which were expensive in terms of output rose less than the cost of the cheaper machines. At the very start, of course, 'power-looms' may have been more expensive in terms of 'hand-looms' in America than in Britain, because American deficiencies in engineering skill, compared with the British, were more marked in the making of complicated than of simple machines. The point is that, with the increase in industrial capacity, the ratio between the costs of manufacturing the equipment fell more rapidly in America than in Britain, quite apart from any possibility that the Americans were catching up on the English in engineering skills.

The position of the *operating costs* of capital-intensive and labour-intensive techniques is not so clear. There may have been industries in which the operation of the capital-intensive machine required a *lower* ratio of skilled to unskilled labour, which, to a greater or lesser degree, offset the higher ratio in the costs of its manufacture. But the probability is that, in a significant number of cases, the manufacture plus use of the more capital-intensive techniques required more skilled to unskilled labour than the labour-intensive. Where this was so, the fact that unskilled labour, in relation to skilled labour, was dearer in America than in England gave the American an inducement to make a more capital-intensive choice of technique. There is also the additional point that the type of labour which was relatively dearest performed the simple, unskilled operations which were, from a technical point of view, most easily mechanized.

Thus there were at least four circumstances in which a rise in the cost of American labour provided the American manufacturer with an incentive to adopt the more capital-intensive of known techniques, in order partly to check the rise in wages and partly to compensate for it. As, from experience, it became evident that labour was the scarcity most likely to emerge during a general attempt to expand capacity, we should expect an increasing number of American manufacturers to have this in mind when choosing equipment and to become conditioned to adopting the method which did most to alleviate this particular scarcity. It is not, however, strictly necessary to assume that all, or indeed any, manufacturers consciously reflected in this way on the resource-saving characteristics of different techniques. Investment may have adapted itself to relative factor-scarcities by a process of natural as well as of conscious selection. If some manufacturers, for whatever reason, adopted improvements which were more appropriate to the factor-endowment of the economy, these men fared better than those which made a contrary choice. They competed more successfully in product- and factor-markets and by expanding their operations came in time to constitute a larger share of their industry. Moreover they brought influence to bear not only via the market but by force of example. Their success inspired imitators, and shaped entrepreneurial attitudes toward the most likely lines of development.

In England, where the supply of labour to industry as a whole was elastic, there was no reason, so far as labour-supplies were concerned, why accumulation should not proceed by the multiplication of machines of the existing type. Thus even if the general level of labour-costs had not been higher in America, the difficulty of attracting additional labour might have pushed the American entrepreneur over a gap in the range of techniques and induced him to adopt one which was not only more capital-intensive than he had previously employed, but was also more capital-intensive than those currently adopted by his English counterpart. But the fact that American labour was also dearer than the English provided the American entrepreneur with an incentive to adopt more capital-intensive techniques than the English, even had the supply of labour been equally forthcoming.

For this argument it does not seem essential that the cost of finance in industry should have been lower, in relation to labour-costs, in the U.S.A. than in Britain. It is enough if machines were cheaper in America in relation to labour, either because they could be imported or because they were made with the type of labour which was relatively most abundant. But the bias towards capital-intensity would obviously have been greater if in fact finance was cheaper in relation to labour in America.

The cost of finance to a manufacturer who reinvested his profits is more ambiguous than the cost of labour, because we do not know what, if any, imputed rate of interest was used. It follows from the assumptions of the simplified version of events to which we have previously referred that the country with the higher wages in terms of output has the lower rate of profit on capital, and this can be regarded as, in some sense, the relevant rate of interest. But this is not a very helpful guide to what actually happened. For although there are many quotations of profits for particular firms in particular years, it is rarely clear what definition has been employed and it is difficult to derive any general rate of profit. In any case accounting methods in early nineteenth-century manufacturing were extremely rudimentary, and it is wildly unlikely that, in comparing alternative techniques, anyone ever applied a notional rate of interest equal to the anticipated rate of profit.

For many of the simple techniques of the period it probably did not matter much if the entrepreneur neglected to impute a rate of interest on his locked-up capital. When the capital per unit of output was substantial, as it may have been in the construction of cotton mills, the need to impute some rate of interest would have been more evident, and probably rule-of-thumb methods were devised which corresponded well enough in general effect with more rigorous accounting principles. It is possible that manufacturers reckoned the cost of their capital by the alternative uses to which they could put their savings. Over a country so large and diverse it is impossible to say much in general terms about the consequences of proceeding in this way. The opportunity-costs of industrial finance in America were clearly higher in the U.S.A. as a whole than in Britain. But the extremely high rates of interest which are sometimes quoted, for example on business paper, reflect a considerable degree of risk and other market imperfections, and therefore greatly exaggerate the disparity between the two countries. While finance as well as labour was dear in America, the scarcity of finance attracted English funds more readily and earlier than the scarcity of labour drew out migrants. There were so few impediments to the import of British capital into America that the yields on long-term obligations in the two countries cannot have differed by very much more than the risk premium. An American textile manufacturer, asked by the Select Committee on Manufactures of 1833 to describe his methods of calculating capital-costs, said that he reckoned his interest upon the purchase price of the machinery and for this purpose took a rate of 6 per cent in America, and of 5 per cent in England. The choice of these rates would have biased the American choice of technique towards the more capital-intensive methods.

In many cases, however, early manufacturers neglected to take account of interest except when they had to borrow from outsiders; each year they withdrew from the business enough to live on and ploughed back the rest irrespective of the yield on alternative methods of employing their funds. In effect, they behaved as if their capital cost them nothing. If entrepreneurs in both countries behaved in this way finance would certainly have appeared to be cheaper, in relation to labour, in America, than in England.

THE NATURE OF THE SPECTRUM OF TECHNIQUES

The practical importance of the inducements in the U.S.A. to adopt capital-intensive methods depended on the nature of the techniques available, and the possibilities they afforded for substitution between labour and capital. There clearly were several occasions on which one technique was manifestly superior for any likely range of factor-prices, and would therefore have been the most appropriate choice in England as well as America. The new techniques for spinning which were invented in the later eighteenth century were so much more productive for all factors than the old spindle that they were the best choice at any conceivable level of wages. But there were other situations in which the possible methods of production were sufficiently competitive, one with the other, for the manufacturers' choice to have been influenced by relative factor-prices. It is difficult to say how far the various new methods of spinning were substitutes for each other—Hargreaves's jenny, Arkwright's water-frame, and Crompton's mule—and how far the suitability of each type of machine for the production of particular types of yarn specialized their uses; but, at some stages of development, some manufacturers may possibly have been influenced, in choosing between them, less by the market for particular grades of yarn than by the relative costs of the methods in the production of similar grades. In the years immediately after its invention the power-loom was not so decisively superior to the hand-loom that its adoption was uninfluenced by relative factor-prices; and even as late as 1819 it was not clear that in England the saving of labour was sufficient to outweigh the increase in capital-costs of the power-loom: '. . . one person cannot attend upon more than two power-looms, and it is still problematical whether this saving of labour counter-balances the expense of power and machinery, and the disadvantage of being obliged to keep an establishment of power-looms constantly at work'. On balance it seems reasonable to suppose that in the textile industry in the first half of the nineteenth century, the range of possible methods of production was sufficiently wide and continuous in respect of the proportions in which they used capital and labour for the choice of techniques to be responsive to relative factor-prices. And though the point could be settled only by detailed investigation, there is a general reason for expecting that similar conditions prevailed in other industries often enough to make labour-scarcity worth considering.

In the first place technical progress was still more empirical than scientific, that is it depended more on the response to particular and immediate problems of industrial practice than on the autonomous development of scientific knowledge. Technical development was therefore likely to take the form of slow modifications of detail, as opposed to spectacular leaps to a new technique decisively superior from the start to its predecessors; most even of the 'great inventions' of the period resolve themselves on close inspection into 'a perpetual accretion of little details probably having neither beginning, completion nor definable limits'. (For the same reason the process of improvement was more likely to be sensitive to the factory-needs of the economy in which they were made.) In the second place a large sector of industry was organized on the domestic system. Under this system circulating capital was more important than fixed, and the commercial capitalist was always facing the question in what proportions to distribute his investment between fixed and circulating capital, that is, how much of his funds to lay out in raw materials to be worked up by domestic workers and how much on machines of his own. This choice was very sensitive to the cost of labour; and so long at least as the costs rose and indicated a shift *into* fixed capital; the commercial capitalist was in a better position to respond to the stimuli than his successors with a high proportion of their funds locked up in fixed capital. [. . .]

Moreover, even when the range of basic techniques likely to interest a manufacturer was very narrow or when one process was distinctly superior over a very wide range of relative factor-prices, it was possible to use them in a more capital-saving or a more labour-saving way, for example by varying the number of machines per worker, by running the machines for shorter or longer hours (by arranging workers in shifts) or at more or less rapid rates, and by variations in the amount of space per worker or per machine.

The existence of methods of varying the factor-intensity of the basic techniques meant that there was usually a fairly continuous range of methods and that the method which used a little more capital saved a little more labour. But relative factor-prices would still be influential even if there were discontinuities such that, at some point, the alternative technique saved a great deal of labour but required a great deal more capital. Indeed the most striking disparities between English and American technology were probably established in just such cases. The gap between the hand-loom and the power-loom, and again, towards the end of the nineteenth century between the ordinary power-loom and the automatic loom, was wide. The capital-intensity of the 'superior' machine could be modified by running it longer, which some Americans did, but the need to make this modification is probably itself evidence that the new technique was much more capital-intensive than the old. The conditions of their labour-supply gave the Americans a much stronger incentive than the English had, to leap such a gap in the spectrum of techniques, with effects on subsequent technical progress which will be discussed later.

We have so far considered only the consequence for the choice of technique of the fact that labour was scarcer in America than in England, and have referred to natural resources only in so far as the abundance of agricultural land was a condition of the scarcity of labour. We must now take natural resources more explicitly into account.

The price of natural resources had an effect on the choice of techniques ranked by reference to the proportions in which they employed capital and labour. If natural resources were employed in the same proportions in the capital- as in the labour-intensive techniques, the price of natural resources would not affect the tendency of a rise in wages to shift the manufacturers' choice towards greater capital-intensity. If the supply of natural resources were inelastic, so that attempts to widen capital met rising costs for natural resources as well as for labour, the bias towards capital-intensity would be *strengthened* if the capital-intensive technique saved natural resources as well as labour, and *weakened* if it was more expensive in natural resources.

But this does not exhaust the possible effects of natural resources. For there may have been some alternative techniques, the principal difference between which was in their possibilities of substituting between natural resources and either capital or labour or both. Some techniques were important principally because of the proportions in which they used capital and natural resources: large blast-furnaces may have allowed a substitution of capital for raw materials, and the application of steam to water-transport may have involved the reverse sort of substitution—of power for capital; it is also possible that methods of building factories differed in respect of the proportions in which they used land and capital. There were also techniques in which there was substitution between natural resources and labour; in particular there were possibilities of using power from water and steam instead of man-power.

Because of the unhomogeneity of natural resources and variations in their price within regions it is impossible to make any general statement about their cost, in relation to labour and capital, in the two countries. Land was certainly more abundant in the U.S.A. in relation to both other factors, and this fact dictated the choice of American agricultural techniques, which substituted land for labour. The abundance of land, and the nature of the American climate also enabled some substitution of natural resources for capital. There was less need than in England for investment in farm-buildings—the maize-stalks were left standing in the fields and they provided winter shelter for the cattle who were sometimes not brought in at all; and because of natural pasturage there was less need for winter feed. In some regions the type of agriculture was influenced by the ability to substitute natural resources for captial and/or labour: maize growing, for example, was a labour- and capital-saving, land-intensive form of agriculture. American agricultural methods which 'mined' the soil in effect substituted natural resources for labour and capital and so did the use of wooden frame houses. In industry too the lower rents for sites enabled New Englanders to economize in labour and capital in the construction of cotton-textile mills and also to build mills which enabled more effective use to be made of the textile workers and textile machines by allowing them more space. Similarly the American railways were built in ways which, in effect, substituted land for capital, as contrasted with the English railways which were built with a disregard for natural obstacles, a disregard which increased their engineering cost.

Almost certainly also, power was cheaper, in relation to capital and labour, along the Fall Line and its supply more elastic than that available to some areas in England, and it may be that the mechanization of the

Massachusetts cotton-textile industry was a substitution not so much of capital for labour as of cheap water-power for labour. If, in order to use cheap power, it was necessary to use more capital per unit of output, the high cost of labour gave an additional inducement to the substitution, but if the power was very cheap the substitution might have been profitable even had American wages been at the English level; and in support of the argument it might be pointed out that mechanization was much slower in sectors of the American cotton-textile industry, for example in Rhode Island, where labour was no less dear but where power was expensive. Moreover, water-power was, in effect, substituted for capital as well as labour. The Americans ran certain types of textile machinery faster than the English, and this practice represented, to some extent, a substitution of natural resources for capital. 'Driving machinery at high speed', wrote Montgomery, 'does not always meet with the most favourable regard of practical men in Great Britain; because in that country where power costs so much, whatever tends to exhaust that power is a matter of some consideration; but in this country (that is, the U.S.A.), where water-power is so extensively employed, it is of much less consequence.'[2] The American cotton-textile manufacturers also obtained their raw cotton on somewhat better terms than did the English, and this enabled them to economize in labour by using a better grade of cotton; in Lancashire manufacturers economized cotton at the expense of wages, using a great deal of short-stapled cotton. In the construction of ships, cheap timber enabled American ship-builders to economize in labour and capital.

This general line of argument is tantamount to the familiar view that the high productivity of American industrial labour was due principally to the fact that it was combined with richer natural resources rather than with more capital, though sometimes more capital per head may have been technically necessary to combine the labour with the resources.

But whatever force this argument may have for the later nineteenth century, in the period we are discussing it is not evident that, with the possible exception of cotton and wood, the natural resources relevant to industrial manufacturing were cheaper in relation to capital and labour in America than in Britain. [. . .] We feel justified therefore in proceeding on the assumption that the dearness of American labour is the most fruitful point on which to concentrate in an examination of the economic influences on American technology.

LABOUR-SCARCITY AND THE RATE OF INVESTMENT

In the immediately preceding subsection we have explained how the dearness and inelasticity of supply of American industrial labour gave American manufacturers an inducement to adopt methods which were labour-productive even though they were capital-intensive. But these characteristics which explain the *composition* of investment would impose a restraint on the *rate* of investment. The shift to the more capital-intensive techniques partly offset the effect of rising labor-costs on the rate of profit, to an extent which depended on the adequacy of the existing range of techniques for the purpose. But the offset—in principle at least—could not be complete since, if the more capital-intensive method was as superior in productivity as this, it would already have been adopted in the U.S.A. before the rise in wages and in England at the lower wage-level. Once labour-costs had risen, the rate of profit would be higher with the more capital-intensive method than with the less, but it would nevertheless be lower than it was before the rise in the cost of labour, and, on reasonable assumptions, lower than in England; that is, other things being equal, the inducement to expand capacity would now be less than formerly and less than in England. Moreover, unless we assume (as was obviously not the case) that wage-earners were prepared to save the full increase in their earnings, the amount of new capacity that could be financed was reduced. So long as the volume of investment depended on the profit-rate, investment in the U.S.A. must have grown more slowly than previously for, since the machines in the more mechanized methods were more expensive, in terms of output, than the simpler machines, it must now have taken longer for the American manufacturers to accumulate the capital to produce a given output; and on these assumptions investment would also have grown more slowly than in England. In so far as the more capital-intensive equipment employed in the U.S.A. was produced in the U.S.A. the move to the capital-intensive end of the spectrum lowered the rate at which capacity was expanded to an even greater degree, because the capital-goods industry had to devote itself to producing equipment which was expensive in terms of output. To this extent labour-scarcity was a disadvantage which might partially be offset by substituting machinery, so far as this was technically possible within the range of existing methods, but which was none the less a disadvantage.

To put the matter in slightly different terms, the desire to widen capital was more likely in the U.S.A. than in England to run up against rising labour-costs. Hence the desire to widen capital was more likely to lead to its deepening in the U.S.A. than in England, deepening being the method of partially offsetting the fall in marginal profit rates. But since, within the range of known techniques, the fall could not be completely offset, it imposed upon the desire of American manufacturers to widen capital a restraint to which English manufacturers were not subject.

This is the sort of situation envisaged by Marx. According to him, labour-scarcity—the exhaustion of the reserve army of labour—would lead the capitalist to substitute machinery for labour, that is constant for variable capital; this would lead to a decline in the rate of profit, a fall in accumulation and in the demand for labour and a consequent replenishing of the supply of labour. The size of the reserve army was maintained by variations in the total of accumulation and in the proportion between fixed and circulating capital. With a smaller reserve army of labour, the tendency to substitute machinery for labour was stronger in America; but by the same token, the rate of investment was subject to a more severe restraint.

In some industrial activities the dearness and inelasticity of labour did in fact exercise a powerful restraint on the rate of investment. This happened even in an industry like the manufacture of small arms where techniques were · available which, at first sight, might be supposed adequate to compensate for the high cost of labour. 'High wages,' wrote the Chief of Ordnance in a report to the Secretary of War in 1817, 'makes the business unprofitable to the contractors, and ultimately in many cases has occasioned their ruin.' The true rate of profit on the manufacture of arms, when the capital-costs were accurately accounted, was low; and many concerns remained in business only because their primitive accounting concealed the fact that they were, in effect, treating capital as income and failing to provide for depreciation. [. . .] For these, among other reasons, a very high proportion of the early small-arms manufacturers went into liquidation.

Nevertheless in a number of industries investment was rapid and in the industrial sector as a whole it is at least not evident that investment was slower in America in the first half of the nineteenth century than in England, despite the restraints of dear labour. It may be that the assumption which creates a problem out of this—the dependence of investment on the rate of profit on capital—is not valid; but for the moment we shall retain it, and try to consider what circumstances in America might have exerted a favourable influence on the rate of profit.

One possibility is that natural resources were cheaper and their supply more elastic in the U.S.A. than in England to an extent which offset the effects of its dearer labour. In this case the restraint which labour imposed upon accumulation in America would have been matched by a natural-resource restraint in England. But, as has already been argued, it is not evident that the natural resources most relevant to manufacturing industries were in fact cheaper in the U.S.A. and they would have had to have been considerably cheaper to offset the dear labour, since in most industrial products labour was a higher proportion of total costs than natural resources. We must therefore inquire in what ways dearness and scarcity of American labour might have favourably influenced the *rate* of investment. We shall consider three main ways.

In the first place, the American manufacturers had a greater inducement to organize their labour efficiently. The dearness of American labour gave manufacturers an inducement to increase its marginal productivity in all possible ways, and not merely in ways which involved the adoption of more capital-intensive techniques. The shortage of labour in America from colonial times encouraged prudence and economy in its use—Washington, for example, calculated with care the proper output of various types of labour on his plantation. Americans from early times were often faced with a situation where a job had to be done—a house built or a river bridged—with the labour available on the spot, because the place was isolated and it was impossible to attract more labour. This gave them an enormous incentive to use their labour to most advantage, to make use of mechanical aids where this was possible, but in any case to organize the labour most effectively. Possibly lack of domestic servants led to an early rationalization of domestic duties and a corresponding increase in family efficiency; certainly the shortage of labour led generally to longer hours of work, to a general emphasis on the saving of time and a sense or urgency about getting the job done. In his account of his visit to America in 1818 Cobbett observed that 'the expense of labour . . . is not nearly so great as in England in proportion to the amount of the produce of a farm'. The greater productivity of America, compared with British agricultural labour was partly the result of the fertility of the land; since labour was scarce, land which yielded a low return per unit of labour was just left uncultivated. It may also have been due to the avoidance of the more labour-intensive crops (for example dairy produce) as well as to the avoidance of labour-intensive soils. The superior physique and education of the Americans may partly have been responsible. Probably also, even in 1818, the American cultivator not only co-operated with superior natural resources, but had superior equipment. But Cobbett seems to suggest that the high productivity of American agricultural labour was in some measure due to the fact that its operations were more efficiently organized. The use of labour in English agriculture was much more wasteful than in English industry, partly from inertia and habit, partly because farm labour was so easy to get.

This labour- and time-saving pattern of behaviour was established on the farm from the early days of settlement—it was an ingrained attitude and not simply an economic calculation—and it was carried over into other activities. 'In England,' observed an English visitor to America in 1851, 'we cover our (railway) lines over with superintendents, police, guards, porters and a host of other officials; and relieve the passenger of many of those troubles which, in America, he contends with himself.' 'The American omnibus,' wrote the same author, 'cannot afford the surplus labour of a conductor. The driver has entire charge of the machine; he drives; opens and shuts, or "fixes" the door; takes the money; exhorts the passengers to be "smart", all by himself—yet he never quits his box.'[3] This attitude to labour was also carried over into industry and led to the more efficient organization of operations. [. . .] The most conspicuous example of efficient use of labour is the training that the American manufacturers gave their workers so that each was able to handle more looms. Whereas, in England, the weaver spent some of his time doing unskilled ancillary jobs, the American weaver did nothing but weave. The American arrangement probably involved a somewhat lower output per loom, that is, an increase in capital per unit of output, but there is little doubt that the English manufacturer would have found it profitable to adopt the same method of economizing labour. The point was that his need to do so was less; abundant labour, like the salt on the edge of the plate, tends to be wasted. [. . .] In the manufacture of small arms, also, specialization of labour was carried much further in England than America, even before there were significant differences in technical processes; in England a workman specialized on one part of the weapons, but carried out all the operations on that part—in the U.S.A. several workmen each performed only one or two operations on the part.

Even, therefore, where there were no differences in technology or at least only such as involved the different disposition of identical machines, differences in the organization of operations may have ensured that the intensity or effectiveness of an hours' labour was greater in the U.S.A. than in England, and this tended to make up for the fact that the price of an hour's labour was higher in the U.S.A. It is not an accident that scientific systems of labour management originated in America. [. . .]

Secondly, dear labour not only provided an incentive to organize it more efficiently. It compelled American manufacturers to make a more careful and systematic investigation of the possibilities of the more capital-intensive of existing techniques. Thus labour-scarcity could have had a favourable effect on the rate of investment by inducing the Americans to adopt, earlier and more extensively than the British, mechanical methods which would have been the most profitable choice even at the lower wages prevailing in England.

Labour-scarcity might, in the third place, have stimulated technical progress. Technical progress, that is movements of the technical spectrum as opposed to movements along it, would, by increasing manufacturing productivity, raise or at least keep up profit-rates, whether the progress was manna from heaven or induced by rising labour-costs. But manna from heaven one would expect to drop more readily in England, since England initially had much larger supplies of technical knowledge. The point about labour-scarcity is that it constitutes a favourable influence on technical progress which was exerted more strongly in the U.S.A. than in England. Any manufacturer had an inducement to adopt new methods which made a substantial reduction of cost for all factors. But in their early stages, many of the methods devised in the nineteenth century could not be confidently assumed to effect such a reduction: before they had been tried out in practice for some time, estimates of their costs were highly conjectural. Where the best guess that could be made of a new method was that it promised a reduction of labour but some increase of capital, the Americans had a sharper incentive than the English to explore its possibilities. This is to say that labour-scarcity encouraged not only a careful and systematic investigation of the costs of the more capital-intensive of existing techniques, but the early adoption of any additions at the capital-intensive end which resulted from inventions of purely autonomous origin, even when they were made outside the U.S.A. [. . .]

In the early decades of the century the principal effect of labour-scarcity in America was probably to induce American manufacturers to adopt labour-saving methods invented in other countries earlier and more extensively than they were adopted in their country of origin. The number of autonomous inventions was greater in the older industrial countries. But where their principal advantage was that they were labour-saving, they were more quickly adopted in the U.S.A. and labour-scarcity then induced further improvements, each additional improvement being perhaps small in relation to the original invention. And already in the early nineteenth century there were a number of important American inventions induced directly by the search for labour-saving methods and these became increasingly common as time went on.

Moreover, it was probably also easier for the Americans to adopt such methods. In England, where labour was abundant, labour-saving was likely to involve replacing, by a machine, labour that was already employed; in the U.S.A. it involved making a physically limited labour-force more effective by giving it machinery, but without displacing anyone, and with some increase in wages. There was, therefore, less opposition in America to the introduction of labour-saving practices and machines and of administrative methods for economizing labour: the fear of unemployment was less and the likelihood greater of gaining in higher wages from the increased productivity. In England, where there was a superabundant supply of hands and therefore 'a proportionate difficulty in obtaining remunerative employment, the working classes have less sympathy with the progress of invention'.

For the same reasons, more changes in production methods came spontaneously from the workers in America than in England; particularly when the worker had been self-employed earlier in life, and most of all when he had been a farmer, for he carried over into industry the inclination to seek his own methods of doing his job better. Thus in American canal-digging, the English methods were modified by the American farmers who devised a sort of primitive, horse-drawn bulldozer, similar to a device some of them had improvised on their farms. No improvement originated among the Irish navvies who dug the English canals.

If the methods adopted or developed by the Americans did no more than offset the initial disadvantage of high labour-costs, American entre-preneurs would have been on an equality with the English. In most cases, the methods must have done less than this. But in some cases they may well have done more. In exploring the borderland of blueprints, designs and embryonic ideas and hunches which lay beyond the end of the spectrum of existing techniques, it would not be surprising if the Americans hit upon some new methods which were so productive that they more than offset the high cost of labour, methods which reduced labour and capital per unit of ouput so greatly that they would have been the most profitable techniques even in the case of abundant labour. Very often the substantial reductions in cost came from ancillary developments and modifications made after the new technique had been operating for some time, and these benefits accrued most fully to those who had adopted the method earliest; and the process tended to be cumulative, since the successful application of machinery to one field of activity stimulated its application to another, and the accumulation of knowledge and skill made it easier to solve technical problems and sense out the points where the potentialities of further technical progress were brightest.

Furthermore, quite apart from the effect of labour-scarcity on the incentive and ability to develop superior methods, the shift of American industry towards the more capital-intensive techniques provided the American machine-making industry with an active market which stimulated inventive ability among the manufacturers of machines and machine tools and perhaps also afforded it some advantages of scale. Ability to produce a labour-saving machine in one field also made it easier to develop machines in other fields. Thus the United States developed the typewriter, not simply because in America 'copying clerks could not be bought for a pittance' but also because in Remingtons, the Illinois gunmakers, there were manufacturers available who could put ideas into practical effect. Standardization could be applied not only to final products but to the machines which produced them. [. . .] For these reasons there were cost-reducing improvements in the production of machines. Certainly by the middle decades of the nineteenth century there were some fields where the cost of the superior machines, relative to that of simpler machines, was lower in the U.S.A. than in Britain, and this was an independent stimulus to the adoption of more mechanized techniques in the U.S.A. There were also fields in which a superior machine was available for some operations in the U.S.A. but not in England.

Once a number of industries had been established in the U.S.A., a rise in real wages in any one of them due to technical progress exerted a similar effect on choice of methods as the initial high earnings in American agriculture. Where labour is scarce, any increase in productivity and real wages in one sector threatens to attract labour from other industries which have either to contract their operations or install new equipment which will raise their productivity sufficiently to enable them to retain their labour-supply.

In England where labour-supplies were abundant the technical progress in a single industry was not likely to stimulate technical progress in other industries by threatening their labour-supplies. It might, of course, stimulate technical progress in other industries by threatening their markets and in some cases their supplies of raw material; but not by threatening to draw off their labour. Any tendency for wage-earners within the technically progressive industry to establish a claim upon the fruits of their increased productivity was inhibited by the existence of a reserve army of labour, and the benefits of technical progress were likely to be diffused by means of lower prices over consumers as a whole, as in the case of the English cotton-textile industry.

In these ways the scarcity of labour gave Americans a keener incentive than the English had, to make inventions which saved labour. But it also gave them some reasons for being concerned with capital-saving. Throughout the previous argument the assumption has been made that the scarcity of labour biased the American entrepreneur's search for new methods towards those which specially saved labour; since this is what contemporaries seem to assert. But scarcity of labour, by exerting pressure on profits, did also provide some incentive to search for ways of economizing other factors as well. Contemporaries only rarely suggested that dear labour was a reason for saving capital, but Montgomery seems to have been arguing in this way when he wrote: 'the expense of labour being much greater in this country (the U.S.A.) than in Great Britain, the American manufacturers can only compete successfully with the British by producing a greater quantity of goods in a given time; hence any machine that admits of being driven at a higher speed, even though it should exhaust the power, if it does not injure the work, will meet with a more favourable reception in this country than in Great Britain.'

There is another link between labour-scarcity and attempts to save capital. When, from a given range of techniques, the American choice was more capital-intensive than the British, this in itself provided the American entrepreneur with an incentive to reduce capital-costs, in order to modify the large amount of machinery per operative; particularly where there were indivisibilities in the equipment, he needed to get more out of his machines in a given period of time in order to bridge gaps in the spectrum of techniques. He could do this, without any significant change in the technical characteristics of the machine, by running it longer and faster. Both these were methods of paying for the machine in a shorter period of time, that is of diminishing the interest bill on the cost of the machine and increasing the speed at which the amortization fund was built up. Because of the capital-intensity of their output, the Americans saved more on interest charges per unit of output than the English would have. (Thus, though running machines faster and longer is in effect substituting labour for machinery, it is usually a sign of a capital-intensive technique.)

Montgomery observed in the 1830s that the Americans ran their cotton-textile factories longer hours than the English and drove their machinery at a higher speed 'from which they produce a much greater quantity of work'. At the end of the century it was said of the American ironmaster that he 'wears out his furnaces much faster than the English ironmaster—in America furnaces require lining about every five years—and argues that the saving of interest on his fixed capital account justifies him in so doing'.

But running machines faster and longer was only one of the ways of reducing capital-costs per unit of output. When the capital-intensive labour-saving machines had been installed, there usually proved to be possibilities of technical improvement in their construction and use. For the economy as a whole, one important form of capital-saving consisted of labour-saving improvements in the manufacture of machines, and to such improvements we can apply the previous argument about labour-saving improvements in general. The cost of machines in terms of output could also be reduced by improvements which increased their performance. Many of the inventions which were capital-saving in this sense were made as a result of attempts to improve machines whose principal advantage when they were first introduced was that they were labour-saving. In the textile industries there were few specifically capital-saving inventions. The initial effect of most of the great inventions was to save labour per unit of output at the expense of some increase in capital or at least without much saving. The saving of capital came later from such improvements as the increase in the number of spindles on each mule and the increase in the speed of the spindle. It was the manufacturers who installed the more complicated capital-intensive techniques who were in the most favourable position to make the subsequent improvements of this type. [. . .]

American manufacturers were readier than the English to scrap existing equipment and replace it by new, and they therefore had more opportunities of taking advantage of technical progress and acquiring know-how. This is a convenient place to consider the relationship of labour-scarcity to this American habit. In its extreme form the readiness to scrap is represented by Henry Ford who is reputed to have said that he scrapped existing machines whenever a new one was invented. But to judge from scattered instances and contemporary comment, this readiness was a characteristic of American industry very much earlier than Ford. The Secretary of the Treasury reported in 1832 that the garrets and outhouses of most textile mills were crowded with discarded machinery. One Rhode Island mill built in 1813 had by 1827 scrapped and replaced every original machine. It would be difficult to parallel this from Lancashire. The English inclination was to repair rather than to scrap, and to introduce improvements gradually by modifications to the existing machines. John Marshall the Leeds flax manufacturer said in 1833 that his concern had 'reconstructed' its machinery twice in the forty-five years or so that he had been in business. In the English textile industry as a whole it is doubtful whether equipment was often scrapped except when a firm went bankrupt. The American readiness to scrap was noticed in other industries. One of the first English handbooks on woodworking-machines observed that 'there are throughout American factories but few wood-machines that have been running for ten years, and if any such exist there is a good and sufficient reason for abandoning them. The life of most machines used in joinery is not on an average more than six years . . .' Contemporaries seem agreed on the general pattern of American behaviour: the American got something going, obtained his profits as quickly as possible, improved upon his original plant, and then scrapped it for something better. The problem is to explain his behaviour.

Scrapping is justified on strict economic grounds when the total costs of a new technique are lower than the prime costs of the old. The effect of high wages on decisions to scrap depended on the type of equipment being used and its age. The more mechanized and the newer American equipment was in relation to the English, the smaller incentive the Americans had to scrap in favour of a given new technique. This however does not exhaust the effects of dear labour on the incentive to scrap.

In the first place for a variety of reasons which we have already mentioned, the Americans tended to run machines faster and longer hours than the English; they also built them in a more makeshift fashion. In these circumstances, though capital per unit of output would still be higher in the U.S.A. than in England (otherwise it would have paid the English to adopt the same methods), the capital would be physically used up in a shorter period of time, and the American manufacturer would be in a better position to buy a new machine embodying the latest technique.

In the second place, American manufacturers seem to have expected a higher rate of technical obsolescence than the English. An American friend of de Tocqueville told him in 1832: 'there is a feeling among us about everything which prevents us aiming at permanence; there reigns in America a popular and universal belief in the progress of the human spirit. We are always expecting an improvement to be found in everything'. While a rapid rate of achieved technical progress is favourable to scrapping, expectations about technical progress have a more complicated effect. If the entrepreneur expects technical progress to be rapid, especially if he expects it to be more rapid than it has been in the past, if, that is, he assumes that the latest available technique will have a very short economic lifetime, its high average costs may prevent its adoption. In these circumstances the entrepreneur will put off the decision to scrap until a major technical advance appears, unless he believes that, in order to acquire the experience to take advantage of such a major advance, he must keep up with all the intermediate stages.

But the expectation of rapid technical progress had other influences which were more favourable to scrapping. The entrepreneur who expected new equipment to become obsolete, not so soon as to deter him from installing it, but sufficiently soon for him to want to ensure against the possibility, would not pay for durability. This is another reason for the flimsiness of much of American equipment. [. . .] The less optimistic expectations about technical progress among the English is one reason for the durability and heaviness of English machinery; no doubt the professional pride of machine-makers was mainly responsible, but if their customers had calculated on a rapid rate of technical obsolescence they would surely have been able to modify the prejudices of the engineers. There is another point. Because the Americans made their arrangements on the assumption that better methods would soon be available, they were more concerned to get their money on new equipment as soon as possible. At the end of the century a French delegation to the Chicago Exhibition reported that American manufacturers invariably seemed to amortize their capital with the settled intention of replacing their machines by new and improved patterns. And this was probably the reason why earlier in the century Americans had the reputation of wanting their profits quickly. Thus technical, economic, and physical obsolescence were more likely to coincide in the U.S.A. than in England at least in those branches of activity in which American expectations about the rate of technical progress were most closely realized.

In the third place, in so far as technical progress took the form of inventing machines which saved labour, but with some increase (or at least no demonstrable saving) in capital-costs it might pay the Americans to scrap when it did not pay the English. The same considerations which warranted the American manufacturer shifting towards the capital-intensive end of the spectrum of existing techniques when he was adding to his equipment, might also warrant his replacing existing equipment when new methods were invented at the capital-intensive end. Where labour was abundant, and widening of capital could proceed at a constant wage, there was no inducement to replace existing equipment unless the new equipment yielded a higher rate of profit on the value of the old and new machines together. Where labour was scarce the preoccupation of the industrialist was with retaining or expanding his labour-force. His primary interest was with methods which would increase the productivity of labour and this was a more urgent concern than the return on capital, at least in the short run and so long as the return was enough to service any external finance and provide a conventional minimum return to the manufacturer. Accounting methods in the early nineteenth century were primitive—it was easier to calculate the likely labour-saving of a new process than its capital-costs. Manufacturers had to make their choice of technique on very rough-and-ready calculations on extremely inadequate data. The bias imported into the calculations by the nature of the labour-supply could therefore be a decisive factor. The American manufacturer was averse to retaining old equipment when more labour-productive equipment was available because the old equipment made poor use of his scarce labour. So long as the saving of labour was vouched for, the capital-costs were less important, at least within a fairly wide range, and in the absence of clear ideas and relevant data about the proper components of capital-costs, manufacturers were probably disposed to underestimate rather than overestimate them. But where, as in England, labour was abundant, and there was no pressing *need* to scrap, the calculations *had* to show, in order to warrant scrapping, a *higher* rate of profit on both machines than on the old equipment, and the results of calculations in these terms was almost inevitably biased against scrapping. The crucial difference is where the onus of proof rested: in America the presumption was in favour of any equipment which raised labour productivity; in England the presumption was in favour of existing equipment—the onus of proof was on new equipment, it had to be demonstrated that it would yield a higher rate of profit.

The fact that maintenance-costs were mainly labour-costs, and that they tended to increase rapidly with the age of equipment, reinforced the American inducement to scrap; the costs of keeping a given piece of equipment intact were greater than in England.

Given the high costs of labour, and the inadequacy of existing accounting concepts and data, the readiness of Americans to give new labour-saving methods the benefit of any doubt about their capital-costs was a rational one. Even so, in particular cases, it may have led to scrapping in circumstances when it was not justified; the scrapping of old machines and the installation of new ones must sometimes have involved wastes which only capitalists who enjoyed superiority in respect of some other factor could afford to bear. [. . .]

But American readiness to scrap was partly unrational from an economic point of view. The expectation of more rapid technical progress was to some extent the result of the general optimism of the American character, and was initially independent of economic facts, rigorously defined. The Americans were, as Cobden said, a 'novelty-loving people'. In so far as the decision to scrap was taken from mere love of the latest method, it was even more likely to let down those who acted on it. Even in such cases, however, the decision, though 'unrational', may have turned out to be warranted by the eventual course of technical progress. Ford's readiness to scrap whenever a new machine was available might be reconciled with the orthodox criteria by assuming that, though it could not be reliably predicted of the new machines *before* their introduction that they would reduce costs to the requisite to justify scrapping, in more cases than not they proved to do so in practice. [. . .] Possibly also—a variant of the same explanation—the constant pursuit of the latest invention may have led to the adoption of machines which, though not themselves economic, ultimately put those who adopted them in a position to take advantage of later inventions which made spectacular reductions in cost. If the more capital-intensive of the existing range of techniques had the greatest possibilities of technical progress, a persistently optimistic view of the costs of new labour-saving methods led in the long run to the accumulation of experience and to further technical progress which outweighed the waste of capital into which it sometimes led American entrepreneurs.

This technical progress was not without its costs. The pursuit of the latest method must sometimes have dissipated a firm's resources without yielding a commensurate increase in experience. Possibly there was too much imitation of the successful leaders, and capital-intensive methods were adopted by some concerns which would have been better advised to close down. Expectations about technical progress were not always realized, and equipment which could have been made more durable at modest expense when first installed had to be renewed at greater expense because it had fallen to bits well before new methods became available. Sometimes equipment was so makeshift that it quickly deteriorated, worked very inefficiently, and was costly in repairs. But it seems reasonably clear that on balance and over the economy as a whole, the American habit of not building the equipment to last and the closely-associated readiness to scrap were favourable to growth. For they meant that the American capital stock tended to be younger than the English and to embody more technical knowledge. Once achieved technical progress in any line became more rapid in America than in England, this in itself weighed strongly in favour of earlier scrapping; the point we have now been making is that the American propensity to scrap developed *before* technical progress was more rapid in America, and is therefore to be included among the independent sources of such progress. In this field, if not in others, what entrepreneurs expected came to pass because they expected it.

The scarcity of labour may therefore have exerted favourable influences on the rate of investment by inducing (i) a more efficient organization of labour, (ii) a more rapid adoption of autonomous inventions, (iii) a higher rate of technical progress and (iv) greater readiness to scrap existing equipment in order to take advantage of technical progress. There is also another way in which the composition of American investment might have exerted a favourable effect on its rate. The propensity to save out of profits may have been a function of the degree of capital-intensity. A plausible case can be made out for this view. A man who runs a machine is more likely to be interested in the possibilities of mechanization than the man who runs a sweat shop. The industrial capitalist whose capital was tied up in his factory and its equipment was more concerned with technical development than the commercial capitalist under the domestic system—and indeed the gain, in the early days, from any shift from the domestic system to the factory may have arisen principally from the increasing role it assigned to the type of capitalist who was interested in technical possibilities. [· · ·]

We can now summarize the argument to this stage. The dearness of American labour and the inelasticity of its supply provide an adequate explanation of why, from a given range of techniques, the choice of the American manufacturer should have been biased towards those which were more productive per unit of labour because they were more expensive in capital per unit of output. The same circumstances might also have exerted favourable influences on the rate of investment by providing an incentive to devise new labour-saving methods, and because capital-intensity of investment increased the ability to devise such methods and also increased the propensity to save out of profits. The main point is the favourable effect of labour-scarcity on technical progress. This might resolve the sort of dilemma emphasized by Marx. It is often said that this dilemma was resolved by autonomous technical progress which sustained the rate of profit. The implication of the argument which we have been pursuing is that technological progress might itself have been the result of the exhaustion of the reserve army and not something introduced from outside the system.

The difficulty about this theory, as of any theory which regards 'restraints' as a net favourable influence on growth, is that it does not, in itself, explain why American manufacturers should have been able and prepared to continue investing in capital-intensive methods to the point where this investment yielded rapid and substantial gains in technical knowledge. Shortages frustrate as well as stimulate.

EXPANSION OF THE MARKET

In most of the preceding discussion we have assumed that the rate of industrial investment was limited by the supply of factors and depended on the rate of profit. We have assumed that, via the rate of profit, the level of investment in both the U.S.A. and in England was adjusted to the rate of increase of supply of all factors, and we have considered the consequence of the fact that, when investment increased at these rates, shortages of one particular factor, labour, appeared earlier in the U.S.A. than in England. But the rate of investment also depended on the expansion of the market. We must now consider the possibility that, in relation to the total supply of factors to industry, the demand for American manufactures in the first half of the nineteenth century was expanding more rapidly than the English.

This is prima facie probable. The major part of the demand for American manufactures came from the rise in agricultural incomes as cotton-exports from the southern states rose and as the country was opened up and population increased. In contrast, though a substantial part of the demand for English manufactures also came from an increase in consumers' incomes in primary producing-areas, a considerable part came from a switch of demand from domestic-type industry to English factory industry, and depended on a fall in the cost of the English products. Thus the long-term growth in the demand for American industrial goods probably warranted a rate of investment, in relation to the supply of factors as a whole, which was more rapid than that in England.

Moreover, it is probable that any given increase in demand was likely to lead to a larger increase in investment in America than in England. In England an increase in demand was met from the existing centres of production where there were generally some possibilities of increasing output with small changes in existing equipment. In the U.S.A., because of the imperfections in the product-market which we have already discussed, an increase in demand in a new area of settlement was likely to be met by the creation of new capacity and new concerns within the area, even though there may have existed some slack in the older area, and without corresponding disinvestment in the older areas.

The rate of investment in relation to total factor-supplies is relevant to our argument in two ways. It is relevant, first, to the effect of factor-supplies on the invention and adoption of new methods. To the extent that investment was pressing more closely on total factor-supply in America than in England, the advance of technology would have been more sensitive to factor-endowment in America. Technology may be expected to edge along, adjusting itself to relative resource-scarcities, only when there is, to begin with, rough balance between resources and investment—when the increase in capacity is constantly pressing on the available supplies of labour, natural resources and finance. It is in these circumstances that manufacturers are most likely to get clear indications of relative resource-scarcities, that those who adopt methods which are inappropriate to the relative resource-scarcities of the economy are penalized and that a new technique—whatever resource it saves—is likely, when introduced into one firm or industry, to have repercussions on other firms or industries and force them either to contract or innovate. Thus the firms in the U.S.A. which in the 1820s and '30s adopted labour-intensive techniques would have been placed in a disadvantageous position in competition with firms in the same or competing industries which had made a more appropriate choice and had adopted capital-intensive techniques. But this was not true to the same extent of firms which adopted capital-intensive techniques in England, the main effect of which would simply have been to depress wages. For the same reason new techniques which increased the productivity of all inputs had a more general effect in the U.S.A. than in England. If, in the early decades of the century, the actual rate of growth was higher in the U.S.A. compared with the possible rate of growth, this fact must be counted as a circumstance favourable to technical improvement, quite apart from the relative scarcity of labour *vis-a-vis* other factors.

The fact that investment in America was rapid in relation to the supply of all factors except agricultural land gave an incentive to improvements which were capital-saving as well as to those which saved labour. Where the existing techniques afforded no possibilities of alleviating the dearness of labour but the entrepreneur still persisted in the attempt to widen, the difficulty of getting capital would induce him to concentrate on making the most of his machinery in all ways which did not involve the use of additional labour per unit of output. Where the range of existing methods *did* allow the entrepreneur to compensate for dear labour by substituting capital, the adoption of more capital-intensive techniques would provoke the problem of finance even more acutely, especially if the techniques were very effective in saving labour. When investment is pressing against resources as a whole, the temporary resolution of the most severe scarcity is likely to be followed by the emergence of scarcity in some other factor.

A 'scarcity' of capital not only provided the user of machines with an inducement to get the most out of them: it gave the manufacturer of equipment an inducement to provide them as cheaply as possible. Many of the goods, the manufacture of which was most highly mechanized, were not single-use consumer goods but equipment designed to increase labour productivity or at least to meet a production problem (like the steel ploughs which were necessary to open up prairie soils). Where the cost of the minimum feasible piece of such equipment was large in relation to the funds available to the typical user, the demand was very sensitive to its price. This was said to be the case with woodworking-machinery and it was probably also true of some types of agricultural machinery, of such goods as sewing-machines and of such activities as ship-building. This was one reason for the flimsiness of much American equipment. According to the American friend of de Tocqueville, whom we have already quoted, 'one reason why our ships do not last long is that our merchants often have little capital at their disposal to begin with. It is a matter of calculation on their part. Provided that the ship lasts long enough to bring them in a certain sum beyond their expenses, their aim is attained'.

Almost every observer pointed to this contrast between the durable English and flimsy short-lived American equipment. [. . .] For this general contrast there are many reasons. The flimsiness of American construction may have been partly the result of the technical inability of American engineers to make high-quality durable machines, and to the high cost of iron and the low cost of wood. It was partly the result of the fact that American engineers were not so long-established a profession, applied less rigorous technical standards and so allowed more weight to be given to economic considerations, in contrast to English engineers who were apt to subordinate economic considerations and who sometimes boasted of the fact. [. . .] If British purchasers of machines had consulted exclusively economic interests, unconfined by the technical prejudices of engineers, they might have preferred cheaper and less durable machines. But in addition there were quite rational economic reasons why Americans should have attached more importance than the English to building cheap machines of the sort which would bring quick returns. There was the need discussed earlier to modify the burden of the large amount of capital involved in the choice of capital-intensive techniques; though the American chose the more capital-intensive of existing techniques, any given technique was apt to be embodied in a less durable form in America than in England. This need made the American purchaser of machines readier to accept standard products, and less inclined to force upon machine-makers minor, but expensive, modifications. Then there was the expectation of more rapid technical obsolescence. But all these reasons had greater force in so far as investment in America was pressing closely on capital as well as on labour.

In building transport-systems, too, the Americans attempted to economize capital more resolutely than did the English. Edward Watkin, a leading English railway-builder, put the contrast between the methods of the two countries at the middle of the century in the following terms:

> The cost of American lines has been brought down by the necessity of making a little capital go a long way, and by the sacrifice of many of the elements of permanent endurance which attach to our railways. We have deemed the inventions of railways a final improvement in the means of locomotion, and we have, therefore, constructed our works to last 'for ever' of bricks and mortar. We have made our rails strong enough for any possible weight of engine; our drainage capacious enough to remove any conceivable flood . . . our bridges firm enough for many times the weight that can ever come upon them.

The Americans believed that the English desire for permanence was 'a bar to future improvement; while their [the American] plan for putting up with "what will do" leaves the door open for invention'. These were typical of the views held by most people who had experience of the two countries. 'In making railways in the United States,' said an American witness before the Committee on the Export of Machinery, 'we aim to economize capital, and we therefore are not so particular about reducing the gradients as you are.'

> In the construction of railways [said another observer], economy and speedy completion are the points which have been specially considered. It is the general opinion that it is better to extend the system of railways as far as possible at once, and be satisfied in the first instance with that quality of construction which present circumstances admit of, rather than to postpone the execution of work so immediately beneficial to the country . . . .

[. . .] The American canals seem also to have been built quickly and cheaply. 'They have built the longest canal in the world in the least time for the least money' wrote one observer about the Erie canal.

At least in the case of railroads, however, there are some explanations of flimsy and rapid American construction which are independent of desire to economize on capital. Thus, over its entire lifetime, an American railway was likely to be less intensively used than an English railway and therefore did not need to be so well built. There was also in America a much greater disparity between intensity of usage in the immediate future and in the longer run. In America a system big enough to carry the load expected when the new region was fully opened up would be much too big for the traffic in the years immediately after building; and therefore the railways were built in ways which allowed them to be modified most easily when the increased demand came. The English, who could expect the load soon after building to be not dramatically below its maximum, had no reason not to build to last from the start. Rapid building was also prompted by the desire to obtain strategic advantage in relation to other competitors, which involved covering as much territory as possible despite limited resources; and by the wish to qualify for land-grants, which were a function of miles built. In these ways some of the differences between American and British railway-engineering can be explained without supposing that the Americans were more interested in saving capital per unit of output. But it is probable that an additional reason was that a higher rate of return on capital was expected of public utilities in the U.S.A. than in Britain, and this would result in lower capital-intensity. British canal- and railway-builders tended to project on the basis of 5 or 6 per cent rather than the industrial rate of profit. The Americans required more, and even 1 or 2 per cent more could make a substantial difference in projects in which capital is important in any case.

In a number of instances, therefore, the rapid rate of American investment, in relation to factor-supplies as a whole, was a reason for American interest in methods of economizing capital, over and above the reasons previously discussed.

The long-term growth of the market as a result of rising incomes in agriculture and the filling-up of the country is relevant to the argument in a second way: it sustained the incentive to widen capital. According to the argument in an earlier section the level of real wages in American industry was set by the absolute level of investment in relation to labour-supplies, subject to the minimum below which real wages in manufacturing could not go, a minimum determined by earnings in agriculture. The desire to widen capital—because of the protection of tariffs and high transport-costs and the filling-up of the country—which determined the level of investment, came up against rising marginal labour-costs, and therefore led to capital-deepening, in order partially to offset the fall in marginal profit-rates. But, within these assumptions, the fall in marginal profit-rates could not be completely offset and would therefore reduce the desire to widen capital which was the impulse which set the whole process in motion. If one introduces technical progress, whether autonomous or induced by the fall in profit-rates, this would help to keep up profit-rates and might raise them, thus maintaining the desire to widen. The relevance of the long-term growth in demand is that it would help to sustain the level of accumulation for normal widening-purposes even in periods when technical progress was sluggish. The growth in demand, that is, contributes to resolving the problem of reconciling the rate of accumulation with the bias towards capital-intensity. This explanation would not be inconsistent with those offered at an earlier stage in the argument but it might render some of them otiose.

NOTES

[1] V. S. Clark, *History of Manufactures in the United States* (Washington, 1929).
[2] James Montgomery, *A Practical Detail of the Cotton Manufacturer of the United States . . . Compared with that of Great Britain* (Glasgow, 1840) p.71.
[3] E. W. Wakin, *A Trip to the United States* (1852), pp. 130, 139.

(b) The American Impact on British Industry, 1895–1914

S. B. SAUL

It has long been customary to discuss the condition of British industry immediately before the First World War in gloomy tones, to stress the weaknesses and shortcomings and to indicate how rapidly its rivals were moving ahead. In this paper I want to suggest that the situation was more complicated than is sometimes made out; that there is much evidence of an awakening in certain vital sectors during these years and that this recovery owed not a little to the spread of American ideas in the engineering industry in particular. Amongst other things such a view is a matter of considerable moment to any analysis of the debate over tariff policy which began to rage at the turn of the century. That campaign had military and imperialistic connotations of course, but from a purely economic point of view it is important to discover exactly where the advantages of free trade lay and how serious were the encroachments of other countries. I propose therefore, to discuss the American impact upon British industry with this more general theme constantly in mind and in the final section to try to draw the two strands together.

I

There is no space here to trace in detail the successes of American goods in overseas markets before 1914; largely they were due to a new technology in which the major elements were standardisation and mechanisation, the use of interchangeable parts and the development of the art of management to plan and co-ordinate these processes of mass production. Firearms, sewing machines, typewriters, agricultural machinery and watches were some of the products of this new approach. During the last few years of the nineteenth century more and more American goods began to appear on the

Business History, Vol. 3, 1967 (2933 71000), pp. 19–38.

British market; 'machinery of all kinds down to patent hair curlers; fresh meats to liver pills; oil stoves to mouse traps; cotton seed oil to shaving soup.' Financiers moved into Atlantic shipping and London transport, the meat trust into Smithfield. Some alarm and despondency was generated by the heavy imports of neat, beautifully finished American shoes which came to challenge an industry that had fallen way behind technically and commercially. Yet it is significant that British firms reacted with remarkable speed; shoe makers went to the United States and came back to introduce new methods, stylings, and fittings, Changes in manufacturing techniques were encouraged by the American United Shoe Machinery Company establishing a subsidiary to import and, after the Patent Act of 1907, to make the latest machinery. 'There can be no doubt that the boot and shoe industry is now in process of a more sudden and complete revolution from a hand to a machine industry than any other great English industry' noted an American report in 1904.

Another surprising feature of the American 'invasion', as it was called, was the unprecedented import of locomotives. Though it was only short-lived, this episode aroused a most searching enquiry in the technical press over the relative merits of British and American engines and manufacturing methods generally. Here was an industry in which Britain considered herself supreme, but so fast were American engines making their way in overseas markets that many wondered if there were not certain fundamental weaknesses in British practice. The answer seemed to be that each country manufactured to suit its own needs. The British was a beautifully built, expensive engine, very rigid and requiring good track and ballasting. The American, though less perfect technically, was cheaper, more flexible and rode better on a poor track which the British engine had a tendency to jump. The crucial fact from the point of view of exports was that most overseas tracks were mediocre at best and American engines gave greater satisfaction, holding the line better, taking sharper curves and causing less wear. The Americans also had the advantage in that their locomotives were less complex, parts were made interchangeable and the design standardised so that it was possible to build for stock. The difference was one of technical versus commercial perfection which British engineers too often ignored. For this the locomotive builders sought to blame the consulting engineer who was the keystone in the organisation of their trade.

The practice of employing an intermediary, unconnected with buyer or seller, was common in Britain whereas in the United States such an outside designer was rare. If used at all he simply issued general specifications to bidders who then offered such of their stock designs as were suitable. The British consultant, his detractors urged, ignored commercial factors because he had no stake in the matter beyond his fee; 'he was more concerned in maintaining a reputation for infallibility (or for being different) than in endeavouring to execute the work in the most economical manner. In short, money—other people's money—was no object'. Locomotive builders complained bitterly of the engines designed for the Indian and Colonial railways which they said were too perfect technically, were subjected to unnecessarily strict testing procedures and were made yet more expensive to build since no attempt was made at standardisation. Consequently colonial governments had to pay dearly for unsuitable engines and the makers had no firm basis from which to build up an export trade with non-colonial countries.

At this time too, several contracts for bridges in the colonies were awarded to American firms. The most famous of these was the Atbara bridge in the Sudan which was urgently required for military purposes. The Pencoyd works at Philadelphia actually delivered for shipping in six weeks—much earlier than any British offer—and though price was a secondary factor, the best British offer was half as much again as the Pencoyd. Again the consultants were blamed for designing entirely new bridges for each occasion and rendering impossible the degree of standardisation achieved at Pencoyd. In the United States many bridges were constructed to pattern as multiples of a given span, the builder being responsible for his own design. On the other hand, as the journal *Engineering* commented, 'In this country it has been the custom since iron bridges were first constructed for each engineer to design his own bridge with the main object of making them somewhat different to every other engineer's design.' Possibly some of these designs were more pleasing aesthetically, but they were certainly expensive and provided no good production base for an export trade. These practices were deeply rooted and would take long to change but at least the American successes brought their methods vividly to the fore and, behind all the cries of woe, there was much informed discussion which helped to initiate slow but definite progress towards greater standardisation.

II

Possibly the sector of the engineering industry to come most powerfully under American influence was the machine tool trade. During the first half of the nineteenth century men such as Maudslay, Nasmyth and Whitworth had led the world with their lathes, planers, slotting and shearing machines. But after 1850 it was American builders who took the initiative with the machine tools and precision gauges which alone made interchangeability possible. None of these machines had more influence on productivity than the turret lathe. Probably first developed in England, the idea was taken across the Atlantic by emigrant craftsmen; such lathes were used for some time in the shops of tool builders and first sold commercially in the 1850's. The turret was a round or hexagonal block which rotated about its axis with a hole in the middle of each side into which tools were inserted and brought successively into contact with the work. In its automatic form it was often called a screw machine but in fact it was ideally suited to the production of many kinds of duplicated small parts, since drilling, boring, turning and facing could all be done on the same machine. Another radical change came through the milling machine in which the ordinary cutting tool of the planer or shaper, for example, was replaced by a rotating disc or drum with teeth cut in the rim. With its continuous motion the machine was technically more perfect than the reciprocating tools which wasted power on the return stroke, it had a broader working edge than the traditional tools and, above all, unlike them could cut to any geometrical shape. Milling machines were used for many operations which had previously been carried out laboriously by hand but one vital development was their adaptation for the cutting instead of casting of gears. It was most important to obtain accurate gears as the speeds of mechanisms began to increase so markedly and when the automatic machine appeared in 1877 it became possible to produce them cheaply and in quantity. The grinding machine largely displaced the more costly scraping and became indispensable in any shop working to fine limits. There was too the micro-caliper for machinists which played a major part in raising standards of accuracy. Pre-eminence in design and manufacture passed over the Atlantic; it was a serious matter, for the machine tool trade was a vital education for many others and by losing it Britain was falling behind in other directions as well.

These machine tools found their way only slowly in England outside the government arms factories, which gave a large order to Robbins and Lawrence of Windsor, Vermont during the Crimean War. In 1865 Charles Churchill, son of a New England engineer, became the first distributor in London to deal exclusively in American tools. His business began to prosper in the 'seventies when the Brown and Sharpe milling machines first came to Britain and one of the first complete plants tooled by him was the Gatling Gun works, opened in Birmingham in 1889 under an American manager. Many saw and were convinced and for the next six years orders rose by 15 to 20 per cent. a year. The real turning point, however, came with the bicycle boom.

During the 1890's a craze for the new safety bicycle swept the country and for the next few years the industry expanded rapidly. Considerable numbers of American machines were sold in Britain but most of them were so poor that they did little more than engender widespread distrust of the quality of all American goods. On the other hand, the boom itself had a varied and vitally important impact upon British manufacturing methods. One writer thought that its great contribution to mechanical engineering came in the machinery for making ball bearings, first introduced in Coventry in 1893. Another was the development of steel stampings by American manufacturers to replace the old heavy machined castings, but pride of place must go to the consequences of the bicycle boom for the machine tool trade. Here, almost for the first time in Britain, was an industry requiring numerous standardised parts in large quantities and many firms were starting business with no antiquated appliances or traditional ideas to hamper them. Hundreds of American machine tools were imported. Charles Churchills were flooded with orders and were forced to increase their capital in 1897. Exports to Britain from four leading American machine tool makers rose from £86,165 in 1895 to £337,528 in 1897. The upshot was to give a great boost to the manufacture of these tools in Britain and also to make industrialists throughout the whole engineering trade deeply aware of the significance of the new American methods.

British machine tool makers certainly had plenty of leeway to make good. Firms in the north had long dominated the trade and some continued to do so in the heavier class of tools. But it is clear that many had long been resting on their laurels and were utterly indifferent to new ideas. The view of a *Times* correspondent was:

> It must be admitted that the machine tool shops of Lancashire and Yorkshire have not maintained their early supremacy. They have remained at the head of certain classes of manufacture but in regard to others in which innovation has been most active the inspiration has nearly all come from America and has been caught on this side in the Midlands rather than the North.

In addition, whereas most American firms built one or two machines and could therefore employ mass production methods in their manufacture—moulding machines, for example, which were little used in Britain—and could better afford the initial outlay on jigs, cradles, etc., nearly every British firm attempted to produce the whole range of tools and many other things as well. Worse still, many British makers had come to regard themselves as professional men, above the hurly burly of commerce, and accustomed to instruct their customers as to what was good for them. Engineering firms were almost clients of particular makers, and made little attempt to bargain and compare one tool with another. With but few exceptions the machine tool industry in Britain had degenerated into the most unscientific of the mechanical engineering trades; rule of thumb methods and the minimum of calculation were the rule, catalogues were full of useless generalities and design was at a standstill. American machines were not accepted without criticism of course, even among their most enthusiastic supporters. Their convenience for the worker, accessibility and numerous ingenious devices were all widely applauded, but many argued that they were too light, and certainly the poorer makes were often frail and unstable. The British tradition was for heavier and more durable tools—a doubtful advantage in a period of rapid innovation. Both sometimes went to extremes, but in the best American models the amount of metal required had been carefully calculated, whereas the British method was said to be to give about enough metal and add 50 per cent. to make sure!

Certain firms led the way in the revival, and of these probably the most notable was Alfred Herberts of Coventry, now the largest machine tool firm in Europe. Alfred Herbert began business on his own by taking over a small engineering concern in Coventry with the help of capital from his father, a Leicestershire farmer. Soon he turned to making simple tools and components for the expanding cycle trade. Luck then played a part for, through his brother, Alfred acquired the sole selling agency in Britain for the weldless tubing made by a French firm. With this windfall as the financial basis he committed himself more deeply to machine tool making. In 1890 the first turret lathe was made, and seven years later the firm acquired the services of an American engineer, Oscar Harmer, who immediately reorganised the works and greatly extended the turret lathe output. At this time they also secured the agency for several American machine tool makers. Herberts employed only 12 men in 1887; a decade later there were 500, and by the middle of 1903 the number had risen to 930. The machines were widely praised in the technical press and stood out at the cycle shows of the late 'nineties which were otherwise dominated by American tools. In 1905 an office was opened in Paris and four years later another in Berlin to deal with enquiries for their machines, and an American report of that year noted that more of their machines were to be found on the Continent than any other British make. Their plant was described as one of the finest in Europe *'with methods that are essentially American'* and of their hexagon lathe it was noted, 'it would seem that the best American features, coupled with a British sense of stability have been united in this design'. It is significant that in 1912 when an important American firm, the Fellows Gear Shaper Company of Springfield, Vermont, needed a new shop superintendent, they brought in a man who had been trained by Alfred Herberts.

Progress in the industry was most marked in the Midlands but the revival was in fact very widespread. *The Times* was soon writing of 'stagnation having given way to many-sided developments'. More important is the testimony of overseas experts; the *American Machinist* observed in 1907 that the Olympia Exhibition of that year had shown that if American builders decided to inaugurate another campaign for trade with Britain, 'they will find a different condition of things from that which prevailed ten years ago'. Two years later it was reported that machines formerly almost wholly of American origin—universal grinders, special turret lathes, light and medium drilling machines—were now built regularly for stock by British makers, and in 1911 a correspondent referred to the rapidly narrowing gap between European and American methods. A French business-man told another American journal that though the French automobile industry had been built up on American machine tools, so great had been recent progress that French car builders could get all the tools they wanted from Britain, Germany and to some extent from France. One of the most penetrating observers of the trade, Joseph Horner, wrote of its vitality; 'existing conditions are such that no manufacturer, however eminent, can feel sure any one type of machine or machine tool . . . may not be superseded if not rendered obsolete at no distant period'. The remodelling of lathe design he described as 'absolute, astonishing and amazing'. Many firms found it necessary to extend their shops; in 1901 Charles Churchill had bought a small works in Salford for 'tooling up' imported machines; five years later he opened a works at Pendleton and developed there a manufacture of precision grinding machines which did much to encourage their use in Britain. The older manufacturers of reciprocating machinery, now faced with the rivalry of milling machines, set about remodelling their planers and shapers for higher speeds and seeking ways to offset the loss of power on the return stroke. For them the electric motor was especially valuable and indeed there was an all round increase in the use of individual electric drive for machine tools. Undoubtedly the revival was much helped by the discovery of high speed steel by the Americans, Taylor and White, in 1898. Various Sheffield firms took up the new steel with great energy and soon achieved world pre-eminence in its manufacture. Enormous stresses were now carried at the point of the tool and demanded not merely that the drive be powerful but also that the carriage and indeed the whole machine be heavy. What had been a debateable fault in British machine tools now became an essential virtue. It was a great stroke of fortune, and firms such as Tangyes and Armstrong Whitworth were soon producing huge high speed lathes and dominating the market, causing the *American Machinist* to comment on the 'tremendous strides (that) have been made in the last three years'.

Of course all the deficiencies were not made good by any means. Exports from both Germany and the U.S. were much greater than those from Britain. American statistics show that exports of 'metal working machinery' to Britain were well maintained, averaging £342,000 per annum from 1897/98 to 1901/02 and £368,000 from 1907/08 to 1911/12, though more than anything these figures indicate how eagerly British industry was modernising its equipment. Some highly specialised tools were not made in Britain because the market was too small—precision lathes and multiple spindle drilling machines for example. Chucks for holding the work in the lathe were still largely imported and there was room for considerable improvement in the use of gear cutting machines. Moulding machines were only making their way against great prejudice and were almost all imported. Nevertheless, the American impact had done its work and with the growing pressure of demand from the motor car and electrical industries, the years from 1900 to 1914 saw rapid if belated strides made by this vital sector of Britain's economy.

III

The rejuvenation of the machine tool trade was accompanied by a parallel awakening in many other trades. It was not before time for, with certain exceptions such as shipbuilding, the engineering industry was certainly desperately backward in its use and understanding of machine tools. This scathing comment was made by *The Engineer* in 1898:

> It is impossible to go through most shops in this country without finding a more or less large proportion of tools which are only fit for the scrap heap. Curiously enough there is nothing which an engineer grudges so much as money spent on machine tools, which are, so to speak, the very life blood of his establishment.

Years before the same journal had warned that British machine shops were too slapdash, spending huge sums on machines that were not kept up: 'surfaces meant to be flat are not flat, things that should be round are oval, that which should be straight is crooked . . . Our duty is to warn our readers in good time and urge upon them more and more the imperative necessity of maintaining their reputation against the world.' Many overseas visitors were impressed by the poor relationship between masters and men which did so much to inhibit the development of more modern manufacturing methods.

> Nothing is more frequent than the remark that the workingman does not need more than so many shillings a week . . . This view among employers has prevailed for so long and is so nearly universal that their every effort is to obtain more work for a traditional wage rather than to decrease the cost of production by means which will justify a higher wage . . . Workingmen have come to accept the view widely too and it is the acceptance of this theory of status which is at the bottom of the deadlock in British industry.

In these circumstances workmen, unlike their American counterparts, rarely offered new ideas and when they did were likely to be rebuked for 'cheek'. As for machine tools, managers often knew little and cared less what their men thought of them. 'We give a man a tool suitable for the work he has to do and if he don't like it there are others that will' was the attitude found by an American observer, and a Manchester journal wrote of the 'stinging reproof that rings through every shop in England—"you are paid for working, not for thinking".' Yet it was the view of a high official in a major American machine tool firm that their superiority derived above all from improvements suggested in the shops.

All this obviously could not be changed overnight by the American example but nevertheless there is much evidence of a widespread improvement in engineering practice even outside those industries in the Midlands and the South which had less trouble from these traditional shortcomings. In 1900 the *American Machinist* was remarking upon the changed atmosphere. Sneers and disgust at American ideas in the technical and daily papers had turned to open-mouthed admiration; 'only those who are acquainted with the facts know what a paralysis was taking hold of the engineering trades of this country as a result of unreasonable methods' but now had come recognition of the need for change 'and men who were foremost in opposing improved methods and tools have even been found abusing the English shops for lacking such things'. Some years later an American consul made this comment:

No one who has not lived in England during the last seven or eight years can realise how great has been the awakening here nor how changed the British mental attitude is regarding new ways of doing things. There has been much wise and clever adaptation to British cheaper labour of American machinery ideas.

Other reports spoke of automatic machinery which had hitherto been unknown outside arms factories and a few cycle works finding its way rapidly into the leading engineering establishments. Electrical engineering, steam turbine, and gas and oil engine builders were particularly affected and hosts of machines were sold to produce castings and forgings, for cutting off, grinding, and sharpening in all manner of works.

One of the most important features of American establishments was the tool room where tools of special sizes were kept for stock and constantly checked for accuracy. All kinds of machine tools were employed there for making and sharpening tools—work of great precision which was carried out by skilled mechanics, less skilled labour now being required for repetition work in the machine shops themselves. In itself the tool room was not a new idea but in Britain the practice had generally been for the machinist to sharpen and reset his own tools in the shop. There each machine soon became the centre for the accumulation of tools, many of which were eventually lost, and in any case many workers were not competent to carry out such skilled operations accurately. Even where a tool room had existed, it normally consisted of no more than a forge and a grindstone but with precision tools these were utterly inadequate for the task. With the new machines, tools could be set and kept up only by first class craftsmen and the advantages of a tool room of the American type were so obvious that the method was widely adopted in progressive British works in the two decades before 1914. The development of interchangeable manufacture in the United States also encouraged the use there of new wage systems of which the Halsey Premium Bonus plan was probably the most famous. In a modified form it made its way rapidly in British engineering works from about 1898 onwards and in turn helped to bring about important modifications in machine tools themselves. Such payment systems made it more important than ever to ensure absolutely correct speed for each operation and new kinds of variable speed mechanisms were introduced for this purpose.

Naturally the pace of change varied between one branch of engineering and another and between different areas. In the Midlands one reads of wide developments in the use of drop forgings, of cut gears being substituted for cast on a growing scale and 'in this industrial awakening more and more firms were seeing the value of an official whose sole job was to ensure a continuous flow of work to each tool'. On the other hand in 1912 *The Times,* though praising what had been done, castigated the engineering centres of the north for continuing to grudge every penny spent on improvement and for renewing nothing until absolutely obliged to do so. This malaise was to take longer to dissipate but clearly the lessons were being learned most thoroughly in the places which were to be the key centres of engineering in the future.

IV

By the mid 1890's the electrical engineering industry in Britain was lagging way behind its competitors in Germany and the United States. Undoubtedly this was partly due to faulty legislation which paralysed for a time the development of both supply stations and electric traction, but certainly too it derived from a general suspicion of the industry which followed the wild speculative boom and subsequent losses of the early days. Because of the slow growth of public supply, for some years the only field for heavy electrical engineering was for private supply to shops, hotels, large houses etc.; every installation was different, standardisation impossible and as a consequence business tended to be ruled by the technician and not by the business-man. Electrical engineering took on a tinkering character; many of its leaders were telegraph and telephone men, inventors, wiring contractors, good enough in their fields but rarely engineers in the broad sense. The supply industry came to be organised as a collection of small stations with quite grotesque differences in practice and in equipment. Most of the machinery for these early stations was supplied by British firms, for it was plant of a simple nature, requiring no great engineering skill for its production, but the industry remained ill prepared to meet the challenge when much larger power stations and electric traction came along with far more complex demands. The industry had its bright spots of course. Mather and Platt, a Manchester general engineering firm, had obtained from Edison the first British rights to his dynamos and did considerable pioneer work for electric railways and industrial electrification. A Wolverhampton firm, the Electric Construction Corporation, makers of the Elwell-Parker motor and possibly the biggest works solely devoted to electrical engineering in Britain at the time, attracted the attention of an American manufacturer of dock machinery. In 1893 the Elwell-Parker Electric Company of Cleveland, Ohio was incorporated and began making motors to the British design, the E.C.C. taking 7½ per cent. of the initial stock issue. The firm of Willans and Robinson had some 2,000 of their central valve engines installed in power stations in the decade after the first was built in 1885 and drew world-wide attention on account of their works organisation and extreme use of interchangeability.

But even the best in Britain could not approach the growing technical and financial strength of foreign firms and by the mid 1890's their competition was being fiercely felt. American influences had been strong from the first. As early as 1880 the Anglo-American Brush Electric Light Corporation had been formed to acquire for £200,000 the Charles Brush arc lighting patents. American engineers and formemen were brought to the works at Lambeth and a nephew of Brush was made chief engineer. The Babcock and Wilcox Safety Water-Tube boilers which were widely used in power stations were also of American origin. Boilers were manufactured in Britain in part of the Singer Company's works at Glasgow from 1881 onwards but not until 1891 was a British company formed to take over all Babcock and Wilcox's foreign business and even so American share-holders still retained a substantial interest in the new company. In 1889 a Westinghouse subsidiary began to distribute their products in Britain; the Thompson Houston Company three years previously had formed the firm of Laing, Warton and Down for the same purpose. They began to supply more and more equipment for ordinary generating purposes and when tramway construction belatedly got under way in the mid 'nineties these two firms used their already wide experience to dominate that market both as regards the power stations and the cars themselves. The car bodies were usually, though by no means always, built in Britain but apart from the need to import motors and controllers, the difficulty lay in producing a suitable truck. In a horse tram this was a simple mechanism but in electric trams it formed an integral part with the motor, transmitted the driving power, and needed to carry greater weights at faster speeds. To 1900 every truck was imported from the American Brill or Peckham companies. The peak of this competition came with the building of the Central London Underground Railway. The electrical equipment was obtained from the American G.E.C. for approximately $450,000 and the 49 electric elevators were supplied by the Sprague Company at a similar cost. In the generating stations six engines of 1300 H.P. each were purchased from the Allis Company of Milwaukee which had already taken many orders in Britain for its powerful slow speed engines. It was estimated that of the 300,000 H.P. of steam engines used in generating plants for lighting and traction purposes at this time 73,000 was American and of the 200,000 kw. capacity of generators in use 71,000 came from American machines.

The recovery of British industry was certainly helped by one stroke of fortune. No sooner had the design of massive reciprocator-driven engines been brought to practical perfection by the Allis firm and others, than Charles Parsons transformed the situation with his steam turbine. The first turbine was used in a power station at Newcastle in 1888 but it was only in 1900 when the city of Elberfeld boldly ordered from Parsons two 1,000 kw. units, that the capabilities of the turbine were demonstrated on a large scale. All this coincided with and much encouraged the campaign in parliament for larger electric supply areas. Reciprocating sets, though magnificent feats of engineering, had almost reached the limit in size, and power station development as we know it could not have taken place but for the smaller dimensions and higher efficiency of the turbine. Soon after Parsons' patents expired in 1904, ten British firms were making Parsons type turbines and several sold rights to American firms. The Parsons monopoly had already been broken when the American GEC began to build the Curtis impulse turbine and by 1914 most of the turbines made in Britain were of the impulse type. Even so, Parsons had made his great contribution towards recovering ground lost to American engine makers and still in 1914 supplied a turbine to a Chicago power station with four times the capacity of any built to that time.

In the electrical engineering industry proper there emerged around 1900 several new works fully capable of meeting this overseas competition. Using American techniques, managers, engineers, capital and research to varying degrees, operating on a considerable scale with the most up to date machinery, they dominated the industry which had so recently been a pitiful collection of inefficient, unprogressive, small firms. The two American companies which had previously only traded in Britain opened large new factories. The British Thomson Houston Company began manufacturing at Rugby in 1902 and by 1911 could claim that they had supplied a third of the tramcar equipments then in use and three-quarters of the motors for Britain's electric railways (including London Underground lines). Even more spectacular was the huge Westinghouse factory erected at Trafford Park, Manchester. Despite strong promotional activities and many orders for power stations and tramways at home and abroad, however, the firm was never able to obtain sufficient orders to justify the size of the initial investment. One adverse factor was their strict adherence to American designs, which they tried with little success to force upon the customer—a mistake that machine tool makers avoided. British Westinghouse were never popular and their financial difficulties caused some jubilation in other sections of the industry for they were widely accused of responsibility for the bitter price cutting which plagued the industry after 1900 as they sought business for the vast plant at almost any price.

A third firm, though of British parentage, followed American ideas and methods closely from the first. Late in 1899, under the leadership of the Kilmarnock engineering firm, Dick Kerr and Co., the English Electric Manufacturing Company was formed and began manufacture at Preston with an American engineer, Sidney Howe Short, as technical director. Short had pioneered the conduit system of electric traction and several new types of electric motor and when the Walker Company with which he was associated, amalgamated with Westinghouse, he was free to cross to England. Under his direction the works were laid out and equipped with the most modern American machinery and soon work was begun on generators for the London surface tramways, the largest machines made in Britain to that time. An American journal commented that 'it speaks volumes for the progressive policy of English Electric that they are enabled to do such work shortly after their reorganisation'. In 1902 the new company was absorbed by Dick Kerr; shortly afterwards an electric car building works, also controlled by them, was amalgamated with two others and by 1905 the group was capable of turning out 1,000 complete cars a year. With its electrical engineering, general contracting and steam turbine manufacture as well, Dick Kerr became one of the most important and progressive firms in the industry.

Possibly the largest firm at this time was the General Electric Company, which had begun business in 1887 and moved into heavy electrical engineering on a large scale at a new works in Birmingham just before 1900. Here the influence came from Europe rather than the U.S.A., and they manufactured in several vital fields under Continental licences— particularly the new polyphase motors and metal filament lamps. G.E.C. fought a bitter and successful struggle to break the Continental monopoly of the supply of carbons to this country and undertook the manufacture of telephone equipment which to that time had also been largely imported. Other developments included the building of a large new works at Stafford by the Siemens Company which was then leased to the parent German firm. Rapid if unprofitable progress was made in the production of heavy equipment there, more especially electric locomotives for export and machinery for industrial electrification. The Brush Company had moved into an existing works at Loughborough in 1889 and much extended them, placing the shops, significantly enough, under an American engineer. In the supply of tramway equipment they were pioneers in many ways, being the first British firm to make their own trucks and the first to build all steel cars.

The overall effect of these changes is hard to measure. For tramways and for local supply station equipment foreign competition was largely eliminated. In the contracting field gains were made too. In 1900 the well-known New York firm, J. G. White and Co., established a subsidiary in London to handle all their extra-North American business; by 1906 they had completed tramway contracts worth over £3m. and had others in hand worth £2m. The Sprague elevators which had won the large contract for the London Underground in 1899, developed serious faults in practice and disappeared from the market; later elevators for the underground were provided mostly by British firms.

Huge strides had been made though this is not to deny that the industry faced serious problems. Internal competition was acute, for home capacity had expanded rapidly, foreign firms still had open access to the market and demand was not growing as had been hoped. By 1906 the basic tramway network was complete and the invention of the metal filament lamp effected such an economy in the use of current as to leave the supply undertakings temporarily with excess capacity. British railways, in many cases poorly managed and heavily overcapitalised, took advantage of the technical dispute over third rail or overhead transmission to delay plans for electrification. Great hopes were placed upon electric drive in textile mills but very little was done. The electrical industry was at fault for not studying more closely the special problems involved, but steam drive in many mills had been brought to such perfection that electric drive was normally only worth while in new mills, and the great boom in building had come in Lancashire between 1905 and 1907 before the necessary electrical equipment had been fully developed in Britain. Nearly every electrical engineering firm was in financial difficulties between 1906 and 1910, and many were forced to cut down already meagre research staffs and fall farther behind in new techniques and ideas. Yet while British firms struggled for the highly competitive work for public bodies, overseas firms concentrated on the less competitive contracts for industrial electrification where they had greater experience and a long lead in the manufacture of A.C. motors. In many shipyards, collieries and steel mills their machinery was paramount.

These difficulties of British industry were heightened by a disastrous lack of standardisation and by the small degree of combination and co-operation which was achieved, almost insuperable obstacles in an industry where the economics of large scale production were so great. The weakness in financial power was serious too. Foreign firms often had strong support from financial institutions and on several occasions were able to secure large contracts for schemes financed by their backers. Nor could British firms help to finance electrical engineering projects at home. Whereas textile machinery and steam engine makers, for example, were often prepared to accept payment in mill shares, few electrical engineering firms, in their parlous financial condition, could afford to emulate them. They were forced to form connections with tramway and contracting concerns but with many of these financially embarrassed too, the gains were distinctly limited.

In 1913 output in Britain remained well below that in Germany and the U.S.A. British exports of electrical goods, apart from cables, did not compare with those of Germany, but all this should not be allowed to conceal the very real progress that was made. The table below shows that exports of electrical machinery, for example, were growing much more quickly than imports.

British Trade in Electrical Machinery
(Annual Averages. £000)

	1904–07	1908–10	1911–13
Exports	688	1,463	2,010
Imports	515	524	1,107
Imports from Germany	164	322	749
Imports from U.S.A.	417	159	285

(Note total imports are imports less re-exports, but imports from Germany and the U.S.A. are gross imports. Re-exports were something like 7% of total gross imports).

The establishment of American branch plants obviously helped to reduce imports of American machinery and the table indicates how successfully British industry pushed for overseas markets during the depressed years from 1906 onwards when internal competition was so acute. Certainly the pre-war boom brought a considerable rise in imports from Germany but with home output of electrical equipment rising quickly in those years too, there is no doubt that from 1910 to 1914 industrial electrification was at last going forward very rapidly. The point reinforces our evidence of a renaissance in engineering generally at this time and indeed the electrical industry itself argued that it was after rather than before the war that British industry began to lag most seriously in its use of electricity.

V

This brings us back to our point of departure—the implications of American industrial competition for British tariff policy in the early years of this century, and the general interpretation of British industrial progress at that time. Certainly there were no grounds for complacency but we have argued that it would be equally incorrect to exaggerate the shortcomings. Much progress had been made in following and adapting the American example but the latest advances in all too many industries continued to be made abroad, and for many products manufactured by mass production techniques Britain still depended on imports from the U.S.A. or upon assembling parts manufactured there. Precisely why Britain was lagging is difficult to say. Differences in size of internal markets alone will not suffice, though perhaps the argument gathers more weight when one includes the concept of 'social depth' of demand which made the U.S. a paradise for the sale of standardised products. Without further detailed information it is difficult to know how far differences in factor prices played a part. Capital was probably cheaper in Britain though it was not always readily available for new ventures. It is true that there was a relative abundance of skilled labour in Britain but this did not prevent the more forward looking British firms from quickly adopting American techniques once they were well known, even though they had not pioneered the way. There is certainly much evidence to show how seriously the weight of tradition hindered industrial progress—in methods of working, in industrial relations and particularly in the form of a wanton disregard for the commercial aspects of business life.

Yet it would have been a serious mistake to have attempted to cure all this by restricting foreign competition. In all the industries we have discussed imports from overseas helped to create new demands and to stimulate British industry to action. It was the absence of enterprise during the 70's, 80's and early 90's in the engineering industry above all which set Britain behind, but when American and German exporters began to exploit this weakness, the response, especially in the newer trades, was immediate. As we have shown, their example began to bring changes in the more traditionally inclined industries too. Even had the reaction been slower, it would have been disastrous policy to deny British industry the opportunity of learning about and using the new tools and factory methods. It has been argued that imports made it difficult for British firms to reach a scale of production large enough to become viable, but in the electrical engineering industry at least this was a minor matter compared with their inability to organise into less numerous units. As it was, it still remained convenient to import machinery such as precision lathes and moulding machines where demand was not yet sufficiently great to justify laying down special plants to their manufacture in Britain.

There are serious pitfalls facing those who generalise too freely over the shortcomings of British industry at this time. Certain sectors obviously were more vigorous than others but it is extremely difficult to measure these divergencies, especially when they exist between different geographical areas of the same industry. The difficulty is heightened by the fact that in the absence of such figures, progress is often analysed through foreign trade statistics which are more readily available. These are at best ambiguous. As our analysis shows, imports may continue to rise, not necessarily because the producing industry at home is inefficient, but simply because industry in general is becoming more aware of the potentialities of the product. This happened with machine tools and electrical machinery just prior to 1914. One must remember too the growing importance at this time of licensing arrangements and the establishment of branch plants overseas, which could both much affect the pattern of trade. Parsons, for example, sold few turbines in Europe or the United States, though thousands of that type were soon in use there; on the other hand, almost every diesel engine and electric lamp made in Britain before 1914 was manufactured under foreign licence. Some economists have based their arguments on figures for imports of 'manufactures' into Britain but here even more confusion arises. At the height of the 'invasion' over 40% of American exports to Britain under this category consisted of refined oils, copper, leather and wood manufactures, none of which competed seriously with any major British industry. True competition was largely confined to those industries using interchangeable methods—machine tools, sewing machines, typewriters, agricultural and electrical machinery. In 1913/14 these provided about a half of Britain's imports of American machinery.

These difficulties of measurement therefore make it all the more important to study complex industries such as engineering with the greatest care, sector by sector. Here we have concentrated upon machine tools which were basic to the whole industry and electrical engineeiing which was to be so crucial for all future developments. The automobile industry would repay similar attention and older trades such as locomotive engineering obviously had problems of their own. It is clear that both the sectors we have studied and others such as the footwear industry gained immensely from the American 'invasion'—from the stir to action, from new tools and factory methods, from direct investment, from the experience of American engineers who came to work for so many British firms. And as these industries belatedly matured so their influence permeated back through the whole engineering trade and began a rejuvenation of old fossilised trades. Industrial change is always a complicated process with growth and stagnation side by side between and within industries. It would be difficult to think of a period when this was so more than in those two decades before 1914.

PART IV

The City

(a) The English and American Industrial City of the Nineteenth Century

LEON S. MARSHALL

Cities throughout history have been the focal points of civilization; and the association of such cities as Babylon with the ancient Oriental empires, Athens with Greece, Rome with the Mediterranean empire of the Caesars and with medieval Christianity, and Venice and Florence with the Renaissance are commonplaces in history and literature. Although trite from frequent repetition, true and significant is the observation that, with all that cities have been, in no previous age has urban society had so complete domination over the life of mankind as at the present. To the student of English or American history, therefore, the rise of the industrial city of the nineteenth century is particularly important, for in that history may be found the origins of many of the critical problems troubling our own disjointed and embittered society.

The supremacy of earlier towns over their neighboring countrysides was due to the domination of commerce over industry: that is, the facilities of the city for the distribution of productions beyond the means and requirements of household and simple agrarian economy stimulated the productive energies of the surrounding population and, in consequence, the economic needs of the city set up the pattern of economic life existing around it. In the present day, however, the economic system created by the industrial city has approached the solution of the problem of production, but has created a new set of problems arising out of that of distributing the wealth produced by this modern industrial system.

In an economic sense, an industrial city is one whose resources are almost wholly devoted or subordinated to the producing of *form* utility—the shaping of raw materials into goods for human use. London, Liverpool,

Western Pennsylvania Historical Magazine, Vol. 20, September 1937, The Historical Society of Western Pennsylvania, pp. 169-80. Reprinted in Alexander B. Callow Jr (ed.), *American Urban History. An Interpretive Reader with Commentaries*, (3rd edition), Oxford University Press, 1982.

and New York, where manufacturing plants are only incidental to the principal business of the city, are commercial rather than industrial cities since exchange (wholesale, retail, or financial) together with transporation is their chief activity. On the other hand, Manchester, Birmingham, and Pittsburgh, even though they are not now so predominantly characterized by factories and mills, are industrial cities because their wealth, population, and economic activities are largely devoted to the supplying of their factories and those of the surrounding communities with the essentials of industrial life, and their prosperity is dependent upon that of their leading industries.

In the first half of the nineteenth century, Manchester, Birmingham, and other towns in England developed into industrial cities according to a pattern which recurred in Cincinnati, Pittsburgh, and other American cities whose leading businesses were transformed by the industrial revolution. The adoption of a series of labor-saving inventions and of improved processes of manufacture led to the concentration in factories of the cotton industry around Manchester, the iron industry around Birmingham and woollen manufacture around Leeds, where facilities for labor, power, and capital were abundant. The increased prosperity and the demand for labor accompanying this concentration of industry brought in a flood of immigrants to these towns. The earlier balance in a town society composed of gentlemen, merchants, and artisans was shaken to its roots by this influx of what soon became an urban proletariat badly housed, subject to extremes of temporary affluence and poverty, and not easily adapted to the discipline of town and factory life. On the other hand, self-made capitalists accumulated fortunes by amazing combinations of luck, foresight, determination, and energy. Recognizing their importance in the community and in the nation, these frequently uncultured and ruthless factory owners seized political leadership from the older dominant interests, and ultimately forced government to protect and foster the system that had enriched them. At the same time, green spaces and quaint old buildings disappeared as land was needed for offices and warehouses, and beyond the new 'business districts' grimy factories pushed rows of jerry-built dwellings past the original limits of the town. Disease, poverty, crime, industrial conflict, and social animosities broke down the traditional institutions that had controlled smaller and more orderly populations, while the bewildered and alarmed inhabitants strove to erect new political and social machinery to control and refine the social revolution that was going on around them.

Wherever this pattern of development recurred, its most striking effects appeared in the growth of urban population. By 1860 more than half the people of England lived in cities and factory towns, and by 1920 more than half the population of the United States lived in urban centers. In the first fifty years of the industrial revolution, the American, as had the English cities previously, received the greatest impact of the population movement. Paterson, New Jersey, grew from 7,500 in 1840 to 68,000 in 1890; Philadelphia from less than a hundred thousand to over a million in the same period; and Pittsburgh and Allegheny from 31,000 to a third of a million fifty years later. Chicago, Cincinnati, Milwaukee, Kansas City, and scores of other cities rivaled this growth, and the rise of the automobile industry produced a recurrence of this phenomenon in the twentieth century.

The influx of population was much more rapid than the expansion of housing facilities. Congestion affected all classes, driving first the wealthy and later the middle classes to the suburbs; but for the incoming workers, too poor to afford better, the only accommodations were cheap lodging houses, and run-down tenement buildings from which absentee landlords derived as much rent with as little expense as possible while awaiting the profits of rising real-estate values. Five families living abroad and contributing little to the community in the form of taxes or improvements of their property drew most of the rentals from Pittsburgh's slums, a fact that accounts for much of the great following of Henry George's single-tax program in Pittsburgh.

Until epidemics of cholera, typhoid fever, and smallpox terrified the middle classes of townspeople into attempting sanitary reforms, the disease and death lurking in the dark squalor of the slums was hardly known to the general public. Whether in England or America the discoveries made by sanitary reformers reveal a depressing similarity. Manchester with two hundred thousand inhabitants had scarcely a sewer, irregular scavengers' carts hardly touched the filth that rotted in dumps to make it more marketable as fertilizer, and until the middle of the century the town's water supply was not sufficient for more than one-third its population. Such facts as these explain why in 1841 the average expectation of life at birth in Manchester was only a few months over twenty-four years. In America, a little later, few cities possessed half as many miles of sewers as of streets, and half the latter were unpaved. Fully one-third of the houses in the eighties relied upon private vaults and household utensils for the disposal of human waste. A large part of Philadelphia's million inhabitants drank water from the Delaware River into which had been emptied daily thirteen million gallons of sewage. Typhus, typhoid, and scarlet fever were the natural concomitants of such sanitary inadequacies, and Pittsburgh's share in this ghastly record consisted of the highest mortality rate for typhoid in the world between 1899 and 1907, or 1.30 per thousand.

Public philanthropy tried first to stem this invasion of disease and death by erecting hospitals, of which Pittsburgh added eight between 1882 and 1895. Street improvements because of the demands of traffic proceeded more rapidly than improvement in sewage, which also involved scientific knowledge as well as expense to property. Although building societies for the erection of model cottages were common in the English towns as the result of experience with congestion, only a few such attempts were made in the United States, and only where industrial corporations erected model 'company houses' in the new industrial areas were these successful. Except in the new cities of the West, such as Salt Lake City, the United States lagged far behind England in city planning.

A report on a survey of Pittsburgh in 1908 pointed out another feature of industrialism 'an altogether incredible amount of overwork by everybody, reaching its extreme in the twelve-hour shift for seven days in the week in the steel mills and the railway switchyards'. Although the report considered the proportion of women in local industries as 'menacing'. Pittsburgh's mills were not so adaptable to the labor of women and children as were canning and textile factories, where light though fatiguing routine made possible their employment because of their cheapness and amenableness to discipline. In the single decade of the eighties, the number of children employed increased from 1,000,000 to 1,750,000. In spite of ten-hour laws the usual working day in many industries even where women and children were employed was twelve hours. Although the labor of women and children was not new, the factory and the industrial city created new problems of family disintegration, fatigue, delinquency, and industrial superannuation, and impressed the criticalness of these problems by the vividness of the industrial scene. The public reaction to these conditions were the factory and public-health movements in England in the thirties and forties, and state agitations in America for ten-hour laws and legislation for sanitary improvements.

Legislative protection for women and children in industry in response to the demands of public opinion was achieved more rapidly in England than in America. Using as an accepted principle Sir Robert Peel's Act of 1819, which attempted to remedy abuses in the employment of children in cotton mills, societies of English humanitarians and factory workers forced Parliament to pass the Factory Act of 1834, the Mines Act of 1842, and the Ten Hours Act of 1847 in spite of the millowners' appeal to the currently accepted theory of laissez-faire in the relations between the state and industry. In America the manufacturing interests entrenched themselves in the state legislatures behind the argument that regulatory legislation would enable industries in those states not having such regulations to ruin the manufacturers of the states where the employment of women and children was limited. In spite of this opposition the National Eight-Hour League succeeded in obtaining such laws in six states. Although the effect of these laws was greatly vitiated by lax enforcement, the enlightened opinion aroused by the agitation, the example of a few states, and the constant pressure of shorter-hours advocates brought a gradual reduction of the hours of labor and an improvement in health conditions in American factories.

The increase in leisure afforded by the shorter-hours movement and the belief that the open air of the country made the agricultural population healthier than the urban produced considerable activity in the founding of parks, and in the census of 1880 the acreage and description of such places received a prominent place in the report for each town. A Boston society in 1880 provided sand gardens for children, and by 1898 thirteen other cities in the East had established children's playgrounds. Philanthropic organizations such as the Women's Christian Temperance Union, the Society for the Prevention of Cruelty to Animals, the Society for the Prevention of Cruelty to Children, the State Charities Aid Association, and the Red Cross were established to deal with other problems of industrial life.

The human animal appeared to be changing his habitat and his manner of living with all the effects known to biology of such changes in animal life. The entire effect upon human physiology of the transition in dwelling place and even in diet (particularly because of the widespread use of factory-made foods) has not even yet been determined, for historians of this period have given their attention principally to the alterations of the industrial environment by which the inhabitants of the city tried to make it a more suitable place for living. That improvements were possible was due in large part to the greater productivity of the new system of manufacture and distribution.

Startling as was the growth of population in the towns of the nineteenth century, it was far exceeded by the increase in productions. In the last half of the century American textile production increased sevenfold, agricultural implements twenty five, packing fourteen, and iron and steel, ten. In this increased productivity, laborers as well as capitalists shared. If Professor Clapham is correct, industrial wages in England advanced forty per cent and the cost of living decreased seventeen per cent in the sixty years after 1790; Miss Coman has estimated that in the United States wages increased twelve and a half per cent and prices decreased forty between 1867 and 1900;[1] thus there were approximate net gains of seventy and eighty-six per cent for the English and American workingmen, respectively, in the margin between earnings and subsistence as compared with the initial years. While capital gains from this improved position appear in the increase of savings-bank deposits and in insurance, the mass of wage earners did not invest in either of these but spent the difference upon a higher standard of living which the greater variety of manufactures made possible.

From the point of view of the city the significant fact was that this increased economic productivity and the improved economic position of the mass of its inhabitants with respect to subsistence did not bring economic security. The replacement of skilled laborers by machinery produced a series of crises in various trades. This and the constant lowering of the limit of industrial superannuation added constantly to the number of unemployed. The competition of women and children and of immigrants of low standards of living augmented suffering and discontent. Finally, incapacitation from industrial accidents and disease completed the demoralization of a large section of labor and made poverty a norm of existence even in prosperous times. Commenting on these conditions, a French visitor to Manchester in 1844 thus compared the poverty in the old with that in the new cities, 'At Paris, half the population go to the hospitals and almshouses to die. At Manchester, half the births take place in the public charities.'[2]

Cyclical depression, which appeared in both England and the United States almost regularly every decade after 1815, demonstrated the failure of the new system to provide economic security to the laboring population. During the depression of 1837 a charitable society in Manchester found forty thousand pawn tickets representing an indebtedness of $27,500 at sixteen per cent in four thousand working-class homes. In the United States nearly half a million were thrown out of work on the railways alone by the panic of 1873, only 400 out of 666 furnaces were in operation in the following spring, bread lines were common in every large city, and wages fell on an average of ten per cent and did not reach their former level until 1890. During the panic of 1907 the surveyors of Pittsburgh reported: 'Low wages for the great majority of the laborers employed by the mills, not lower than in other large cities, but low compared with prices,—so low as to be inadequate to the maintenance of a normal American standard of living; wages adjusted to the single man in the lodging house, not to the responsible head of a family.' To Englishmen and Americans who remembered that under the domestic system the wage earner had owned a plot of ground to supply him with food in bad times and that in earlier days the West had offered homesteads to oppressed craftsmen, the pre-industrial era appeared as the golden age now replaced by suffering and chaos.

Of Manchester in 1844 Léon Faucher said: 'At the very moment when the engines are stopped . . . moral order . . . disappears in an instant. The rich man spreads his couch amidst the beauties of the surrounding country, and abandons the town to the operatives, publicans, thieves, and prostitutes, merely taking the precaution of leaving behind him a police force whose duty it is to preserve some material order in this pell-mell of society.' A visitor described Pittsburgh in the eighties as 'hell with the lid off'. Pittsburgh, Chicago, Detroit, and Cincinnati were centers of organized crime, and in the nation the homicide rate quadrupled while the population doubled. The failure of the police to cope with this growing disorder was accompanied by a series of embittered industrial disputes which appeared to be the first skirmishes of a social revolt.

Between 1816 and 1850 scarcely a year passed without a great strike in either the cotton industry or the building trades in Manchester, while these conflicts were increasingly supported by unions in other cities. The panic of 1873 produced a long strike in the New England textile mills. A ten per cent cut in wages in 1877 precipitated the first nationwide railway strike marked by battles between soldiers and workmen in Baltimore, Reading, and Pittsburgh. The workers of Baltimore foreshadowed the contemporary sit-down strike when they seized the railway yards and prevented the moving of trains, and in Pittsburgh the defeat of the militia gave control of the town to a lawless mob for two days. The bloody Homestead strike of steel workers in 1892 inaugurated an almost continuous series of strikes and lockouts lasting during the remainder of the century.

To restore order to a society that appeared near self-destruction, the philanthropically-inclined wealthy and other community leaders attempted to strengthen the church, the schools, charitable institutions, and the local government. In England, the distress uncovered during the cholera epidemic led six wealthy Manchester philanthropists to found the first statistical society in the world in 1833 'to assist in promoting the social improvement of the manufacturing population' by 'collecting facts concerning the inhabitants'. Clergymen, merchants, and manufacturers supported monitorial schools under rival organizations in the twenties; temperance societies, mechanics' institutions, and savings banks in the thirties; and associations to promote public health, factory reform, public parks, and national education in the forties. The leaders of the new British manufacturing communities neglected few opportunities to inculcate what they believed to be the virtues of urban citizenship: knowledge of the 'useful arts', temperance, industry, and thrift.

So closely parallel were the problems of the cities within the industrial pattern that the counterpart of each of the foregoing activities might be found in the history of almost any American manufacturing city. Local and national scientific associations took up the task of fact-finding. Washington Gladden of Columbus, Ohio, and other clergymen supported the rights of labor in its battle with capital and reorganized their congregations into 'institutional churches' with charitable and educational agencies. American advocates of broader educational opportunities were more successful than the English in obtaining the assistance of the state to education, and illiteracy dropped from seventeen to eleven per cent in the last twenty years of the century. In adult education the business genius of Redpath and Horner combined with philanthropy and local patriotism in an attempt to raise the general level of culture through the lyceum and the Chautauqua movement.

As philanthropy and mutual assistance proved at best only ameliorative, the pressure of these problems and of the interests affected by them was greatest upon government. In the 1760's the residents of Manchester had congratulated themselves on their lack of a municipal corporation, but in 1790 they began to create a series of new governmental agencies to perform tasks too complex for the traditional institutions. Beginning with watching and poor relief, the local government added before 1850 the regulation of hackney coaches (the traffic and transport problem of the day), street improvement, water supply, gas lighting, fire protection, sewage disposal, and market and public park administration. As in American municipal growth, this progress was accomplished by struggle with vested interests and against corruption: Manchester had a 'boss Nadin' sixty years before New York experienced 'boss Tweed'.

There is not sufficient space within the limits of this article to present details illustrating the expansion of American municipal government, but the facts are sufficiently well known and depart but little from the Manchester pattern. Whether contemporary municipal government has restored the order and security demanded by its citizens is still an open question but not a new one, for the issue has been raised in each town as it has developed into an industrial city and is inherent in its life, as, indeed, are each of the problems that have been suggested as elements in the history of English and American industrial cities in the nineteenth century.

While the conception of a pattern of development is of invaluable assistance in the study of the rise of contemporary society, the student of this history must realize that four points of differentiation between the English and American industrial revolutions make parallels and analogies not only hazardous but if not carefully done very misleading. Briefly these differences are: first, the priority of the industrial revolution in England; second, the existence in England of privileged classes strongly intrenched in government and in social influence; third, the powerful influence of the agricultural West and South in America; and fourth, the enormous proportion of foreign-born population in the United States due to immigration. In these differences, however, lie additional reasons why the American social scientist should be intimately acquainted with the evolution of the English industrial city.

The first great advantage in the study of the English pattern in the nineteenth century is that in the earliest phases the basic processes of a society undergoing industrialization appear in relative simplicity, since the historian has but to consider the impact of a relatively few new developments upon a traditional background. With the passing of the West and the industrialization of the South, those purely American differentiations will be of less importance in analyzing the continuation of the processes at the present time. Finally, the influence of foreign immigration upon the United States may not have exerted so differentiating an effect as might be supposed, and because of the present immigration policy and the rapid Americanization of the descendants of the foreign-born the greater part of this difference in conditions is bound to disappear.

The industrial revolution, it has been said, has been succeeded by a scientific revolution, industrial capitalism by finance capitalism, urbanization by metropolitanization, but the process is not yet complete, and as long as remain the problems created by the industrial revolution—the control of disease, poverty, and crime by urban communities, the raising of cultural standards necessary to urban citizenship, and the removal of economic insecurity—social scientists and historians will be interested in the American and English industrial city of the nineteenth century.

NOTES

[1] John H. Clapham, *The Early Railway Age, 1820–1850*, 561, 601, 602 (*An Economic History of Modern Britain*, second edition, vol. 1—Cambridge, 1930); Katharine Coman, *The Industrial History of the United States*, 306 (revised edition, New York, 1925).

[2] Léon Faucher, *Manchester in 1844: Its Present Condition and Future Prospects*, 145 (London, 1844).

(b) Police Authority in London and New York City 1830-1870

WILBUR R. MILLER

Policemen are a familiar feature of modern urban life, the most conspicuous representatives of the political and social order. However, until American society seemed to be falling apart in the mid-1960s, social historians on this side of the Atlantic gave only a passing nod to the cop on the beat. Like other institutions which people have taken for granted, the police are products of distinct historical circumstances, the complex process of social discipline and resistance fostered by the industrial revolution. As Allan Silver points out, the police represented an unprecedented extension of the government into the lives of ordinary citizens.[1] Some people welcomed and others resented this extension, while at the same time its nature and degree varied in different societies. A comparison of the mid-nineteenth-century London police—the first modern full-time patrol force, created in 1829—and the New York City police—the second such force outside of the British Empire, created in 1845—reveals how different political and social developments influenced the principles and practices of police authority.

I

The statutes which established London and New York's police forces provided only a skeleton around which a definition of authority and a public image of the police could develop. Consequently London's Metropolitan Police owed much to Charles Rowan and Richard Mayne, the army officer and lawyer whom Sir Robert Peel appointed to head his new force, while the New York police were formed and reformed by a succession of elected and appointed officials throughout the mid-nineteenth century. However much individuals may be credited or blamed

Journal of Social History, Winter 1975; pp. 81-95.

for various aspects of the police, they worked within a social context which encouraged some responses and discouraged others. To understand the nature of police authority one must examine the societies which produced the forces.

Although the British metropolis was a much larger city than the 'metropolis of the New World,' both were heterogeneous cities marked by gulfs between wealth and poverty and recurrent social conflict. Michael Banton, to whom I am indebted for much of the conceptualization later in this article, argues that police authority reflects the degree of heterogeneity in modern societies. He finds that the stability of Scottish police authority reflects a culturally homogeneous society with widely shared expectations, while the instability of American police authority reflects a culturally heterogeneous society with few shared expectations.[2] However, it is difficult to maintain that nineteenth-century London was more homogeneous than contemporary New York. Disraeli spoke of England's 'two nations, the rich and the poor,' despite their ethnic homogeneity, and social conflict in London had more serious political implications than ethnic squabbles in New York. An examination of the *quality* of conflict in the two cities seems more promising for understanding the nature of police authority than an effort to measure their relative degrees of heterogeneity.

Formed in response to political violence and ordinary crimes against property, the London force took to the streets amidst England's constitutional crisis over parliamentary representation for disenfranchised middle-class citizens. The politically dominant landed aristocracy met the challenge from the industrial and commercial middle classes, backed by a reserve of working-class anger and violent protest, by tying them to the existing order through the electoral reform of 1832. The next challenge, fended off rather than co-opted, arose from various working-class groups dissatisfied with selecting 'one or two wealthy men to carry out the schemes of one or two wealthy associations,' the political parties under the new system of representation. Culminating in Chartism, which included demands for universal suffrage, annually elected Parliaments and abolition of the property qualifications for M.P.s among its demands, working-class protest was defeated largely by the middle-class commitment to the social order. After a lull during the prosperous fifties and early sixties, working-class groups again demanded the franchise. Reflecting the increased economic power of workers organized into trade unions, the reform of 1867, another co-optive measure, gave urban workers the vote without altering the balance of social and economic power.

Recurrent political crises were of profound importance to the police force charged with upholding the social order and controlling a turbulent population in the national capital, to which people looked with hope or apprehension in difficult times. Since disenfranchised protestors could have impact on Parliament only 'out of doors'—demonstrations in the streets—policemen inevitably collided with them. Would these confrontations feed the fire of social conflict? Would the police be identified as the cutting edge of the ruling minority's oppression? Since their role was fundamentally political amidst challenges to the legitimacy of the government, the commanders of the force had to devise a strategy for containing conflict if they expected the new police to survive the Tory government which created them.

The New York police worked within a different context than their London brethren. New York was not a metropolis in the European sense, the seat of national government as well as center of culture and commerce. Except in the spectacular draft riots of 1863, Americans did not look to New York for the nation's political fate as Englishmen looked to London.

New York did have its own local disorder, the ethnic conflicts which punctuated the era. While not as portentious as London's political disturbances, they did have consequences for the nature of police authority. The presence of large groups of immigrants in American cities gave a distinct tone to class conflict. Antagonism between skilled and unskilled urban workers increased with the filling of the unskilled ranks by immigrants, especially Irish, in the mid-nineteenth century. Native-born workers, concerned about the degredation of their trades by industrialization, regarded the unskilled Irishman, willing to work for longer hours and lower wages, as an economic and social threat. This rivalry between elements of the working class undercut their sense of common interest against the employers. In fact, the nativeborn skilled workers who dominated American trade unions accepted the existing political system of representative democracy, believing that it gave all men an equal chance to rise in the world. The rowdy Irishman threatened to disrupt cherished institutions. Organized labor joined the propertied classes in denouncing the Irish draft rioters. While George T. Strong 'would like to see war made on Irish scum as in 1688,' the leading labor newspaper pictured them as 'thieving rascals . . . who have never done a day's work in their lives.' The paper remarked, 'The people have too much at stake to tolerate any action beyond the pale of the law . . . No improvement can be made by popular outbursts upon the great superstructure created by the wisdom of our fathers.'[3] In England such rhetoric was rarely embraced by workingmen; America's propertied and working classes alike saw a political order they valued threatened by irresponsible foreigners who did not appreciate democracy.

Since the New York police upheld the political institutions of representative democracy which most Americans valued, there was little pressure for them to transcend social conflict to ensure their own survival. Instead of supporting the rule of a small elite which was challenged by the majority of London's population, the police supported a political order threatened by an alien minority. Thus to a great extent the police were free to treat a large group of the community as outsiders with little fear for the consequences as long as their actions coincided with most people's expectations.

What sort of police authority emerged from the different social circumstances of London and New York? In both cities pure repression was unacceptable, in London because of past failures and tendency to promote more violence, and in New York because it was unacceptable to American democracy. In societies with representative governments, whether aristocratic like England or democratic like America, the police ultimately depend on the voluntary compliance of most citizens with their authority. As Edwin Chadwick said, 'A police force . . . must owe its real efficiency to the sympathies and concurrent action of the great body of the people.'[4] The commanders of the two forces had to define the institution to win this public support.

London's Police Commissioners. Rowan and Mayne, had an especially difficult task: they had to develop a force sufficiently strong to maintain order but also restrained enough to soothe widespread fears of police oppression. The combination of strength and restraint became the foundation of the London Bobby's public image. To achieve acceptance the Commissioners sought to identify the police force with the legal system, which embodied the strength of national sovereignty and the restraint of procedural regularity and guarantees of civil liberties. While the laws of England were hardly a pure realm of justice above contemporary social inequality, they were the broadest available source of external legitimation for the police.

Definition of the force as agents of the legal system made their authority *impersonal*, derived from legal powers and restraints instead of from the local community's informal expectations or the directives of the dominant political party. Amid social conflict the Commissioners, in their own words, 'endeavoured to prevent the slightest practical feeling or bias, being shewn or felt by the police.' With varying levels of success during their long terms of office Rowan and Mayne determined that 'the force should not only be, in fact, but be believed to be impartial in action, and should act on principle.'

Behind this commitment to impersonal authority was the strength the police gained from being an independent agency of the national government. The Metropolitan Police, created by Act of Parliament, had no links with London's local government, and the Commissioners, appointed for life, were responsible to the Home Secretary who exercised only a broad authority over them. As a national institution the police could draw upon a reservoir of symbolic as well as physical power. 'Power derived from Parliament,' said a contemporary observer, '. . . carries with it a weight and energy than can never be infused by parish legislation; and in respect of an establishment for general security, it is doubly advantageous, by striking terror into the depredator, and arming the officer with augmented confidence and authority.'Similarly, 'the mob quails before the simple baton of the police officer, and flies before it, well knowing the moral as well as physical force of the Nation, whose will, as embodied in law, it represents' Although both the strength and moral authority of the police required several years to develop, impersonal authority proved to be a secure foundation of police legitimacy.

Rowan and Mayne's notion of impersonality extended into many aspects of their force's structure and practice. They made the police into a tightly-disciplined body of professionals divorced from the localities they served. The men were kept out of partisan politics (Bobbies could not vote until 1885) and were often recruited from outside of London. They wore a blue uniform which further separated them from ordinary citizens. The Commissioners inculcated loyalty and obedience, enforced by quick dismissal for infractions, expecting the men to be models of good conduct by subordinating their impulses to the requirements of discipline and the legal system they represented. An observer of the 1850s vividly captured the police image: 'P.C. X 59 stalks along, an *institution* rather than a man. We seem to have no more hold of his personality than we could possibly get of his coat buttoned up to the throttling point.'

The New York policeman was less thoroughly molded than his London brother, but he did embody a distinct image which reflected conscious efforts as well as circumstantial results. His authority was *personal*, resting on closeness to the citizens and their informal expectations of his power instead of formal bureaucratic or legal standards. Instead of having to rise above social conflict by indentification with the legal system. New York officials created a force which conformed to pre-existing, widely accepted patterns of democratic government. Survival of the new police depended originally on its ability to incorporate ideals of democracy in which authority was not only supposed to serve the people but also be the people. Until 1857, when the state government took over the force, it was directly controlled by popularly-elected local officials and policemen were recruited from the population of the district they patrolled. They did not wear a distinguishing blue uniform until 1853. As representatives of municipal instead of national government, the New York policeman did not have the symbolic authority his London colleague could invoke. Nor did he have the same reserve of physical force to back up his power: he was much more alone on the streets than his London colleague (New York always had fewer patrolmen in proportion to the citizens than London) and his effectiveness depended more on his personal strength than on broader institutional authority.[5]

New Yorkers rejected many important features of the London police as too authoritarian for democratic America. In the late fifties, the *Times* and Mayor Fernando Wood agreed that New York policemen were not as disciplined and efficient as their London brethren, but this was a necessary price of America's healthy social mobility and its citizens' independent spirit. The New York patrolman was more a man than an institution because democracy suspected formal institutional power and professional public officials. Paradoxically, lack of institutional power also meant lack of institutional restraints, and the personal New York policeman often ended up with more awesome power than his impersonal London counterpart.

II

The most important element of the distinction between the impersonal and personal approach is the amount of discretionary authority the patrolman exercised. Every policeman has to exercise personal discretion in his duties—decisions about when and how to act, whom to suspect and whom to arrest. Such choices are the most important part of his work, distinguishing the policeman from the soldier who does not act without direct orders. Nevertheless, the commanders of the force and the judiciary set wide or narrow boundaries to discretion, and various public reactions to the police often center around the degree of discretion people think patrolmen should exercise. Consistent with his image of impersonal authority derived from the powers and restraints of the legal system, the London Bobby's personal discretion was more regulated than that of his New York colleague. Not as closely bound by the legal system, the New York patrolman often acted in the context of official and public toleration of unchecked discretionary power. The London policeman upholding an aristocratic, hierarchical society had more limits on his personal power than the democratic New York policeman.

The patrolman's most formidable discretionary power is his ability to use force to maintain his authority. The commanders of both the London and New York police warned their men to use lethal violence only for self-defence and prescribed punishments for violators of this essential principle. In practice, however, the New York policeman's use of force was much less carefully monitored than in London.

As is well known, the London Commissioners carefully supervised Bobbies' use of force. They inculcated coolness and restraint, restricting the police arsenal to the truncheon. Except in unusually dangerous circumstances, London patrolmen never carried firearms. The Peelers could rely on muscle and blunt weapons partly because their antagonists were not usually more formidably armed, although revolvers seemed to be spreading in the underworld in the late sixties. There was some excalation of weaponry and incidents of unwarranted police violence did occur, but the Commissioners punished men who flouted their rule that restraint was

214

the best way to win public acceptance of the force.

New York's locally-controlled Municipal Police carried only clubs, but when the state government took over the force in 1857—prompted by a mixture of reform and partisan motives—many New Yorkers violently expressed their hostility to the new Metropolitan force and the police replied in kind. Individual Captains encouraged their men to carry revolvers for self-protection against a heavily-armed underworld. By the end of the 1860s, revolvers were standard equipment, although they were never formally authorized. Guns seemed to be popping throughout the city, the civilians uncontrolled by effective legislation and the police unchecked by their superiors. The New York *Times* complained that shooting was becoming a substitute for arrest and described the patrolman as 'an absolute monarch, within his beat, with complete power of life and death over all within his range ... without the forms of trial or legal inquiry of any kind.' Amidst a vicious cycle of criminal and police violence, the patrolman was free to exercise much greater physical force than his London colleague.

Whether he made his arrest violently or quietly the New York patrolman consistently exercised broader personal discretion than the London Bobby. In both cities policemen had wide power to arrest people on suspicion of criminal intent, from stopping and searching people in the street to taking them to a magistrate for examination. Such arrests were more carefully scrutinized by police and judicial officials in London than in New York.

The London Commissioners reduced (although they did not eliminate) complaints of arbitrary arrest by warning their men to be extremely careful about whom they detained, directing that they pay attention to external indicators of social class as a guide to their suspicions. These guidelines did not lift police scrutiny from workers in middle- and upper-class neighborhoods and Parliament endorsed this use of police authority and later expanded stop-and-search and arrest powers. However, the judiciary contributed to control of police discretion by carefully checking patrolmen's grounds for arrest, and higher courts directed that people could be detained without formal trial and charges for only five days in normal circumstances or a maximum of two weeks in unusual cases. Generally magistrates' committals of suspects for jury trial did not keep pace with London's population growth during the 1830-70 period, possibly reflecting declining crime or the shift of many petty offenses to Justice of the Peace's summary jurisdiction from 1847 to 1861. However, since the conviction rate in higher courts in proportion to magistrates' committals *increased* during the period, and higher court convictions in proportion to policemens' arrests also increased, it is quite likely that policemen were arresting and magistrates committing people on grounds that were increasingly firm over the years.

Contemporary American observers testified to London's cautious use of arrest on suspicion when they mistakenly reported that Bobbies could arrest only for overt acts. George W. Walling, who joined the New York force in 1848, said that 'A New York police officer knows he has been sworn in to "keep the peace," and he keeps it. There's no "shilly-shallying" with him; he doesn't consider himself half-patrolman and half Supreme Court judge.' He did not hesitate to arrest on suspicion even if it were 'often a case of "giving a dog a bad name and then hanging him."'—men being arrested merely because they are known to have been lawbreakers or persons of bad character.' Moreover, the Police Justices (elected Justices of the Peace) did not check this aggressiveness. Judges in over-crowded courts did not take time to investigate police charges, tacitly encouraging hasty or arbitrary arrests on suspicion by accepting police testimony without oath or corroboration, refusing prisoners the opportunity of defending themselves, and failing to inform them of their rights or frightening them into confessions. People arrested on suspicion were usually held in the Tombs, but the magistrates also allowed the police to confine them in the station house while they 'worked up a case' against them. There was no time limi⁺ for detention on suspicion until a reforming judge instituted the English practice in the early 1850s. This seems to have satisfied the New York Prison Association, which had led a public outcry against abuses of detention on suspicion, but it did not attempt to change other practices.

Discretion played an important part in arrests for overt acts as well as on suspicion. Checks could help prevent arbitrary arrests because sometimes both London and New York patrolmen charged people with disorderly conduct when their offence was merely unruliness or disrespect for the officer's authority.

Rowan and Mayne warned Bobbies 'No Constable is justified in depriving any one of his liberty for words only and language however violent towards the P.C. himself is not to be noticed . . . ; a Constable who allows himself to be irritated by any language whatsoever shows that he has not a command of his temper which is absolutely necessary in an officer invested with such extensive powers by the law.' They put teeth into the warning by forbidding desk officers to discharge people arrested for disorderly conduct who promised to behave in the future. Thus they prevented policemen from using the disorderly conduct charge to scare people into respecting them without having to bring a weak case before the magistrate. The only grounds for station house discharge was false arrest, which had to be reported immediately to Scotland Yard. Although they never eliminated arbitrary disorderly conduct arrests (an epidemic of them broke out in the sixties), the Commissioners kept them in check.

The commanders of the New York force also expected their men to be calm under provocation, and a high official said that disorderly conduct arrests were covered by 'a good many rules.' However, there is little to suggest that such arrests were limited in practice. A journalist contended that they usually depended 'exclusively upon the fancy of the policeman,' who had 'a discretionary power that few use discreetly.' New York patrolmen made many more disorderly conduct arrests than their London brethren. In 1851 they made one for each 109 people: London officers made one for each 380 people. In 1868-69, New York's absolute number of disorderly conduct arrests was greater than London's: 14,935 compared to only 2,616 in the much larger British metropolis. Although there is plenty of evidence that New York was more rowdy than London, the great discrepancy probably reflects London's discouragement of disorderly conduct charges. The heads of the New York force left disposition of patrolmen's charges, without any special checks on disorderly conduct arrests, up to station-house desk officers.

New York patrolmen's free hand for disorderly conduct arrest may illustrate the use of personal action to compensate for lack of institutional authority. Patrolmen could not arrest for assault without a warrant unless they had seen the attack or the victim was visibly wounded. London policemen labored under a similar restriction until they were granted full powers in 1839. In New York, arrests for disorderly conduct may have compensated for limitations of arrest for assault.

After arrest and lock-up came police interrogation and evidence-gathering. Earlier discussion of arrest on suspicion revealed that in New York there was little regulation of these practices. Judges readily accepted police evidence with little concern about how they obtained it. Moreover, the police had no scruples about obtaining confessions by entrapment or 'strategem.'

In London all levels of the criminal justice system scrutinized interrogation and evidence-collection. With judges and high officials looking over their shoulders, the Commissioners reiterated warnings against false incrimination or distortion of evidence in the courtroom. Repetition of such warnings suggests that policemen engaged in improper practices, but the men at the top were determined to keep them in line.

Until the 1850s. English courts were extremely sensitive about police interrogation, especially inducement of prisoners' confessions by promises or threats. Their concern may have been a carry-over from the days of a harsh penal code when confession of even minor crimes brought death or transportation for life. The Commissioners' directives to their men reflected this sensitivity. Sometimes Bobbies took such cautiousness too much to heart, preventing voluntary confessions because they feared criticism from judges and defense counsel. Following a Court of Queens' Bench decision in 1852, judges began to relax their restrictions on confessions, increasingly accepting prisoners' statements as evidence against them. Nevertheless the Attorney General of England and the Police Commissioners were concerned that patrolmen not carry this too far by presenting all incriminating statements as confessions. The courts seem to have returned to earlier strict interpretations in a case of 1865, and the police fell into line.

Official concern was important because of the power of the police within the criminal justice system of England—they served as public prosecutors, taking charge of serious cases in the higher courts with jury trial as well as petty cases before magistrates. In New York, serious cases left police hands after arrest and became the popularly elected District Attorney's responsibility. He decided whom to prosecute and how to conduct the case. Critics charged that he was lenient towards his constituents and abused 'plea bargaining,' which allowed criminals to escape deserved punishment by pleading guilty to lesser offenses. New York policemen, with greater leeway in arrest and interrogation practices than their London brethren, had less power over the outcome of serious cases. Because of the police role in the courtroom, the London Commissioners realized that suspicion of deceit or prosecutorial bias would undermine public acceptance of the force. Watchfulness at all levels of the criminal justice system satisfied a Parliamentary inquiry that England did not need a public prosecutor like the American District Attorney.

The trial is the last stage of police participation in the administration of criminal justice. Police-judicial relations are important for understanding patrolmen's attitudes toward discretionary power and procedural regularity. From their viewpoint, their most significant relationship with judges is how many arrests are rewarded with convictions. A vital element of the policeman's psychology, convictions make the officer feel that his job is worthwhile, giving meaning to his work by validating his judgment to arrest a person. Having made a quick decision, he finds it hard to admit error. Low convictions in proportion to arrests can make policemen into frustrated antagonists of the judiciary, ready to substitute street-corner justice for procedural regularity. London Bobbies often criticized judicial decisions, but the Commissioners insisted that they keep their comments to themselves and required strict decorum and impartiality in the courtroom. Perhaps more significant, convictions for all crimes in the higher and lower courts increased relative to arrests during the mid-nineteenth century. Averaging about 45 percent of arrests during the 1830s and 1840s, convictions rose to around 55 percent of arrests during the 1860s. Bad in the early years of the force, police-judicial relations improved after 1839, with settlement of a jurisdictional dispute between the Commissioners and magistrates. Increasing convictions suggest that police and judicial standards of proper procedure were moving toward each other.

Although judges in New York made few procedural demands on policemen, from the early days of the force and increasingly after state takeover of the police in 1857, police officials complained of bad relations with the judiciary and charged judges with leniency toward major and minor offenders alike. Lacking statistics comparable to those of London, it is difficult to evaluate these accusations. Available information indicates high conviction rates for drunkenness and vagrancy, slightly fewer convictions for petty larceny compared to arrests than in London, very few assault and battery convictions and in more serious crimes during the 1860s about one conviction for every three arrests. Judges seem to have been more lenient toward serious than petty offenders, whereas in London conviction rates were generally higher for serious crimes. Paradoxically, judges seemed to have overlooked arbitrary arrest practices but let many offenders off. This may have been a last-minute effort to regulate the police—Police Justice Michael Connolly was a crusader against brutality—but the absence of clear guidelines for the police made patrolmen and judges into adversaries. They never moved toward a single standard of conduct.

III

Looking back over the survey of police practices, we have seen the London patrolman's impersonal authority resting on control of discretionary power through the legal system and the directives of the judiciary and heads of the force. In contrast, the New York policeman's personal authority rested on unregulated discretion and less concern for working within legal restraints. The two forces did not develop their images in isolation. As part of the societies which created them public perceptions of crime and the role of the police were important underpinnings of their authority.

Recognizing that various classes or groups would react differentially to the police, the London Commissioners hoped that the new force had 'conciliated the populace and obtained the goodwill of all respectable persons.' On the whole they achieved this goal, although antagonism to the force remained in 1870.

'Respectable persons' were not always middle-class, but the Victorian middle classes did see themselves as custodians of respectability. Although hardly united in interest and outlook, the groups composing the middle classes would have shared suspicion of a police too closely linked to the landed aristocracy. They accepted aristocratic domination of politics as long as it was not oppressive. They were always ready to criticise arbitrary policemen, but as their own political influence consolidated over the years, they came to see Bobbies mainly as useful servants for coping with the various unpleasantries of urban life. Rowan and Mayne noticed that predominantly middle-class complaints against the police shifted from oppressiveness to inefficiency during the 1830s. They had to remind complainants that policemen lacked legal power to do many of the things that were expected of them.

The middle classes came to depend for protection and peace and quiet upon an institution which fostered social stability by the restrained exercise of power. Karl Polanyi's argument that the fragility of the industrial and commercial economy tied to the stock market made riotous disorder intolerable in the nineteenth century applies to repressive violence as well. 'A shooting affray in the streets of the metropolis might destroy a substantial part of the nominal national capital . . . stocks collapsed and there was not bottom in prices.'[6] In England the military, not the mob, had done the shooting in the past. A police force which contained disorder with a minimum of violence increased people's sense of security and contributed to economic stability. Generally, London's propertied classes believed that public order was steadily improving in the metropolis. Commentators recognized that police restraint as well as power contributed to this orderliness. In the Sunday trading riots of 1855 in Hyde Park, when policemen got out of hand and brutalized innocent spectators as well as participants, the London *Times* joined radical working-class papers in condemning police excesses. The lesson was clear: respectable citizens as well as the populace expected restraint. The middle classes, seeing themselves as the repository of such virtues, usually took pride in a police force with a reputation for respectability and 'habitual discretion and moderation of conduct.'

During the sixties, a period of economic uncertainty and working-class unrest, 'respectable' fear of crime and disorder mounted. The garotting or mugging scare of 1862, the reform riot of 1866 and increasingly violent robberies along with hunger riots in the winters of the late sixties made Londoners question police efficiency. Significantly complaints focused on lack of manpower and the declining quality of recruits, poor administrative methods and excessive bureaucratization and militarization, instead of demands for arming the police or allowing them broader discretion than the law defined. Parliament's response was tougher laws for the police to enforce rather than a redefinition of the force's impersonal authority. Alan Harding is right in calling some of the harsher provisions of the Habitual Criminals Act of 1869 (aimed at the paroled convicts whom most people blamed for the crime wave) 'positively medieval,' but the act was a precise administrative control which judges interpreted strictly, continuing to monitor police discretionary power. The new law expanded authority but also defined its limits. The police themselves recruited more men, reformed administrative procedures and after Mayne's death in 1868, expanded the detective division which he had always distrusted. They did not resort to violence or unregulated discretionary power. Although strained by a crime wave, impersonal authority was still viable.

Having obtained and retained the 'good will' of at least most 'respectable persons,' could the police achieve the more formidable goal of conciliating 'the populace?' Although working-class reaction to the police was as varied as the often conflicting and competing groups which made up the proletariat, generally a working man or woman was more likely to see the police (whom they preferred to call 'crushers' instead of 'Bobbies') as masters instead of servants. Subordination of the force to the legal system simply meant that it was part of the apparatus which upheld 'one law for the rich, another law for the poor.' This view that the scales of justice were weighted in favor of the rich and powerful, and only slightly less so toward the middle classes, was the most common theme of working-class social criticism. The Commissioners' concern for the rights of 'respectable' Londoners meant that social class was often the basis of police treatment of citizens. Although the Bobby was expected to be polite to 'all people of every rank and class,' a writer friendly to the police could say, 'although well-dressed people always meet with civility . . . it is possible that the ragged and the outcaste may occasionally meet with the hasty word or unnecessary force from the constable, who is for them the despot of the streets.' The other side of the coin is that some workers felt that the police were ignoring their neighborhoods, allowing disorder they would not tolerate in 'respectable' areas. This partly reflected the dangerousness of some rookeries and dockland slums, but also the Commissioners' policy of 'watching St. James's while watching St. Giles's'—patrolling slum areas not to protect the inhabitants from each other, but to keep them from infiltrating nearby prosperous neighborhoods. Workers could complain of both too much and too little police power. Their feelings came out in the popular music-hall songs of the sixties, such as 'The Model Peeler,' an off-color account of police oppression and dereliction. 'Oh, I'm the chap to make a hit. No matter where I goes it,' runs the chorus; 'I'm quite a credit to the force,/And jolly well they knows it./I take folks up, knock others down./None do the thing genteeler,/I'm number 14, double X,/and called the Model Peeler.' Impersonal authority, like so much else in Victorian England, seemed reserved for 'respectable' people.

Nevertheless, the force does seem to have worked toward conciliating 'the populace.' Except among persistently antagonistic groups like the costermongers, the police did achieve at least a grumbling working-class acquiescence to their authority. By the 1860s, there was more violence against them in the music halls than in the streets. Partly this acquiescence reflected the clearly-established power of the force—'People feel that resistance is useless.' Mayne declared. However, the police also made some effort to reduce working-class antagonism. Their concern for restraint in handling political demonstrations was one (imperfectly achieved) aspect. They also deliberately stayed as much as possible away from the enforcement of Sunday blue laws, which working-class Londoners bitterly resented as middle-class dictation of their life style. This was not a case of failure to enforce existing laws, for that would undermine police subordination to the legal system, but of successfully lobbying in Parliament against new measures which evangelical Sabbatarians sought in the Victorian era. Upholding a hierarchical social order, the police never won the 'good will' of the working classes, but because they rejected pure repression the Commissioners achieved at least acquiescence to police authority. The force had authority, not mere power.

Across the Atlantic the reactions of both middle- and working-class New Yorkers to the police were more ambivalent than in London. By limiting the force's institutional power but tolerating broad personal discretion, New York's officials revealed a distrust of institutions but great trust in men. Alexis de Tocqueville argued that democratic Americans impowered their officials with broad discretion because they elected them, being able to remove them if they were dissatisfied. In aristocracies like England, on the other hand, appointed officials independent of both rulers and ruled had to have more formal checks on their discretion to prevent oppression. Although New York policemen were never themselves elected, they were at first directly and after 1853 indirectly accountable to elected officials and the broad directives of public opinion remained their guidelines instead of formal limitations of their personal power.

Turning from theory to public reactions to the police. Tocqueville's notion is complicated by the institutional rivalry of the police and judiciary. 'Respectable' New Yorkers, although they criticized democracy's immersion of the force in partisan politics and sought to move it closer to London's independent professionalism, usually sided with the police in their controversy with the judiciary, which often owed its position to local, in many cases working-class Irish, constituencies. This taking of sides was most pronounced after state (Republican) take-over of the police in 1857, while the Police Justices remained in the unclean (Democratic) hands of local politicians who courted the votes of ignorant and impoverished immigrants. Thus, to a great extent, the propertied classes formed the constituency of the police force, while the propertyless made up the support of the lower levels of the judiciary, the Police Justices. Recurrent quarrels between police officials and judges were contests, to some extent before but especially after 1857, between representatives of different class and ethnic constituencies. Such battle lines had been occasionally drawn in the early years of the London force, but rarely later on.

Since respectable citizens did not expect justice from the courts, they turned to policemen, tolerating their broad personal authority in the war against crime. Although one's view of the police often depended on one's politics, this toleration frequently transcended partisanship. If to put down crime, said the Democratic *Herald* in 1856. 'it were necessary for us to have a Turk as Chief of Police, we, for our own parts, would go for the Turk, turban, Koran and all.'

A later journalist remarked of John A. Kennedy, the tough Republican General Superintendent of the Metropolitan Police, that although called 'king Kennedy' among 'the masses,' respectable citizens regarded him more

WILBUR R. MILLER

highly. 'He has often exceeded his power, and has committed acts that
smack strongly of petty tyranny; but there can be no doubt of the fact that he
has earnestly and faithfully labored for the cause of law and order.' A little
petty tyranny was acceptable in the interests of law and order, especially in
light of 'a general, and perfectly natural feeling in the community, that it is
a positive godsend to get rid of one of the many scoundrels who infest our
streets, by any means and through any agency possible' when people lacked
faith in 'the capacity or common honesty of our legal tribunals.' New York
was a violent city, whose disorder seemed to be steadily outstripping a
police force plagued with manpower shortages and disciplinary problems.
Citizens worried about the well-armed politically influential lumpen-
proletarian 'volcano under the city.' Violence and distrust of the courts
placed a premium on physical force and personal authority instead of
London's restrained impersonal authority. Democratic ideology and
disorder combined to create a policeman who often seemed more
authoritarian than aristocratic England's London policeman.

How did New York's largely Irish immigrant 'masses' view the police?
James Richardson suggests that they had fewer grievances against the
locally controlled Municipal Police than the state-controlled Metropolitan
Police. Nevertheless, the large number of Irish patrolmen in Irish wards,
because of the Municipal force's local residency requirement, did not
guarantee smooth relations with the working-class Irish public. Irish
officers often arrested their countrymen for petty offenses, and complaints
of violence or improper arrest, averaging some 29 a year between 1846 and
1854, were not much fewer when Irish officers confronted their countrymen
than when WASP policemen dealt with Irish citizens. Common ethnicity
may not have been sufficient to overcome class antagonism—policemen
seem to have been recruited from skilled workers while the people they
arrested were predominantly unskilled laborers. Relations worsened under
the state-controlled Metropolitan Police, despite a proportion of Irish
patrolmen similar to the levels of the old force. Hatred of the new force,
often politically motivated, underlay much of the draft rioters' ferocity, to
which Irish policemen replied, in kind, earning the gratitude of respectable
New Yorkers. Irish Democrats' antagonism to the Republican state force,
roused by judicial and journalistic champions, resembled London radicals'
hatred of the police in the 1830s. The anger was as much against whom the
police represented as what they did.

The Metropolitan Police do not seem to have made efforts to reduce Irish
working-class hostility. Their enforcement of Sunday laws, as bitterly
resented by immigrants in New York as by London workers, increased
hostility to the force. The old Municipal Police had ignored blue laws
except under sporadic Sabbatarian pressures; the Metropolitans,
responding to sustained Sabbatarian influence, enforced strict new
measures which roused the opposition and evasion of normally peaceful

Germans as well as the volatile Irish. The police could not claim impartiality when they enforced laws passed by one group against another's customs and amusements. Eventually enforcement of the blue laws broke down, becoming a convenient tool for Boss Tweed to keep saloon keepers in line and a lucrative source of pay-offs for all levels of the police force. Such corruption seems only to have increased "respectable" criticism without significantly improving relations with the working classes.

IV

Although she wrote before the creation of New York's force, Harriet Martineau captured the difference between London and New York's police. She identified the English police as "agents of a representative government, appointed by responsible rulers for the public good," and the American police as "servants of a self-governing people, chosen by those among whom their work lies."[7] The London policeman represented the "public good" as defined by the governing classes' concern to maintain an unequal social order with a minimum of violence and oppression. The result was impersonal authority. The New York policeman represented "a self-governing people" as a product of that self-government's conceptions of power and the ethnic conflicts which divided that people. The result was personal authority.

ACKNOWLEDGEMENT

This article is a revised and enlarged version of a paper presented at the American Historical Association convention in New York, December 1971.

NOTES

[1] Allan Silver, 'The demand for order in civil society: a review of some themes in the history of urban crime, police and riot,' in David J. Bordua, (ed.), *The Police: Six Sociological Essays* (New York, c. 1967), 12–14.

[2] Michael Banton, *The Policeman in the Community* (New York, 1964), esp. ch. 8.

[3] *Fincher's Trades Review*, July 25, 1863.

[4] Edwin Chadwick, 'On the consolidation of the Police Force, and the prevention of crime,' *Fraser's Magazine* 67 (Jan., 1868), 16.

[5] In 1856, New York had one policeman per 812 citizens, London one per 351.

[6] Karl Polanyi, *The Great Transformation* (New York, 1944), 186–87, phrase order rearranged.

[7] Harriet Martineau, *Morals and Manners* (Philadelphia, 1838), 192. Here 'police' refers to the old constabulary and night watch system which preceded modern forces in America.

(c) Boss Cox's Cincinnati: A Study in Urbanization and Politics, 1880-1914

ZANE L. MILLER

Many observers of the turn-of-the-century urban scene have depicted bossism as one of the great unmitigated evils of the American city, as a tyrannical, authoritarian, relentlessly efficient and virtually invulnerable political system. Between 1904 and 1912, for example, George B. Cox was castigated by writers in four national magazines. Gustav Karger called him the 'Proprietor of Cincinnati', Lincoln Steffens declared that 'Cox's System' was 'one great graft', 'the most perfect thing of the kind in this country'. Frank Parker Stockbridge claimed that 'The Biggest Boss of Them All' had an organization 'more compact and closely knit than any of the political machines which have dominated New York, Philadelphia, Chicago, St. Louis or San Francisco'. And George Kibbe Turner concluded that in the 1890s 'the man from Dead Man's Corner . . . seated himself over the city of Cincinnati. For twenty years he remained there–a figure like no other in the United States, or in the world.' Yet these knowledgeable and sensitive journalists obscured as much as they revealed about the nature of Queen City politics in the Progressive era. A new kind of city had developed, and 'the boss' comprised only a fraction of its novel political system.

Paradoxically, Cox and his machine were produced by, fed on, and ultimately helped dispel the spectacular disorder which engulfed Cincinnati in the late-nineteenth century and threatened the very survival of the democratic political process. In these years, increasing industrialization, technological innovations in communication and transportation–especially the coming of rapid transit–and continued foreign and domestic migration had reversed the physical pattern of the mid-century walking city and transformed Cincinnati into a physically enlarged, divided, and potentially explosive metropolis.

Old citizens were shocked as familiar landmarks and neighborhoods

Journal of American History, Vol. 54, March 1968; pp. 823-38

vanished. By 1900, railroads and warehouses had monopolized the Ohio River bottoms. The financial and retail districts had moved up into the Basin around Fountain Square, the focus of the street railway system; new club, theater, and tenderloin districts had developed; and industries had plunged up Mill Creek Valley, converting Mohawk-Brighton into 'the undisputed industrial bee-hive of the Great Queen City of the West', surrounding once fashionable Dayton Street, creating a new community called Ivorydale, and reaching out to the villages of Norwood and Oakley in search of cheap land, ready access to railroads, and less congested and more cheerful surroundings.

The Over-the-Rhine entertainment section along Vine Street became tawdry with commercialism. It now had, complained one habitué, 'all the tarnished tinsel of a Bohemianism with the trimmings of a gutter and the morals of a sewer'–a repulsive contrast, he felt, to 'the old-time concert and music halls . . . where one could take wife, sister, or sweetheart and feel secure . . . that no one obnoxious word would profane their ears'.

The fashionable residential districts which had flanked the center of the walking city began to disintegrate. One family after another fled the East End for the hills around the Basin, leaving only a small coterie led by the Charles P. Tafts to stave off the advance of factories and slums. The elite West End seemed to disappear overnight. It 'did not go down imperceptibly,' recalled one old resident. 'It went to ruin almost as if a bombshell sent it to destruction.'

The Hilltops, at mid-century the private preserve of cemeteries, colleges, and a handful of wealthy families, became the prime residential district in the new city. The crush to get in generated new tensions. In 1899 one observer acidly remarked: 'when rapid transit came the Hebrews . . . flocked to' Walnut Hills

> until it was known by the name of New Jerusalem. Avondale was then heralded as the suburb of deliverance, but again rapid transit brought the wealthy Hebrews . . . in numbers greater than the flock of crows that every morning and evening darkens her skies, until now it has been facetiously said that the congregation has assembled in force and . . . when Avondale is roofed over the synagogue will be complete.

The diffusion of wealthy families, the reduction in casual social and business contacts, and the construction of new communities made ardent joiners of the Hilltops elite. Each neighborhood had an improvement association, and between 1880 and 1905 five new businessmen's organizations devoted to boosting the city's lethargic economy had appeared. In the same period six social clubs opened downtown facilities, and three country clubs were started. By 1913, moreover, there were twenty-two exclusive clubs and patriotic societies and innumerable women's groups. These developments helped counteract the disruptive effects of the 'country movement', as one visitor labeled it, which was so general that church-going became an affair of some difficulty' and 'society itself . . . more or less disintegrated'.

But not all those moving out were affluent. Liberated by rapid transit, skilled and semiskilled workers and moderately prosperous professional and white-collar men with life savings, the courage to take out a mortgage, an equity in a building and loan association, or a willingness to rent a flat in a double or triple decker, also fled the Basin. They took refuge in a no-man's-land between the center of the city and the Hilltops frontier which was similar to an area dubbed the Zone of Emergence by Boston social workers.

Zone residents formed what the Cincinnati *Post* referred to as 'the so-called middle class . . . , the class that makes any city . . . what it is . . . [,] the class that takes in the great body of people between wealth and poverty' and builds up 'many organizations, societies, associations, fraternities and clubs that bring together people who are striving upward, trying to uplift themselves, and hence human society'.

They, too, found life in th new city a novel experience. A retired leather factory porter who moved into the Zone lamented:

> When I lived down on Richmond in a little house we cooked the corn beef and cabbage in the house and ate in there, and when we wanted to go to the toilet we went out into the yard, now I live in a fine house, I am made to eat . . . out in the yard, and when I want to go to the toilet I have to go into the house.

Graham R. Taylor had noted that since most Zone residents commuted they suffered a severe 'dislocation of the normal routine of factory and home': they had to adjust to 'the need for travel and its curtailment of leisure and income . . . ', to eating lunches away from home, to doing without 'customary city facilities', and to knowing the feeling of 'isolation from their fellows'. Price Hill—like the rest of the Zone a heavily Catholic area—felt itself conspicuously cut off. In the 1890s the editor of the *Catholic-Telegraph*, denouncing the traction company as the 'octopus', joined the Price Hill Improvement Association in begging both city and traction company officials to bring the area 'within range of the civilized world' and suggested secesssion as a means of dramatizing to the 'people east of Millcreek' that a new public school, 'granted by the unbounded munificence of the City of Cincinnati', did not amount to a redemption of the city's annexation pledges.

The exodus, however, did not depopulate the Basin. Instead, a great residential Circle formed around the central business district. It filled with newcomers and those who lacked the means to get out—rural whites and Negroes from the South, Germans, Irish, Greeks, Italians, and Jews from eastern Europe. Working at the poorest paying jobs available, they were jammed into the most congested quarters. The Circle led all other areas of the city in arrests, mortality, and disease.

Although the pressure to escape was enormous, the barriers were formidable. Ignorant of the ways of the city, as an Associated Charities report put it, Circle dwellers had to be 'shown how to buy, how to cook, how to make the home attractive, how to find employment'. Many, 'utterly friendless and discouraged', succumbed to 'the damnable absence of want or desire' and grew 'indifferent . . . to their own elevation'. Plagued by 'physical bankruptcy', they found it difficult to find and hold jobs, let alone form and maintain the kind of organizations which enabled Zone residents to shield themselves from economic disaster, legal pitfalls, social isolation, and apathy.

The immediate impact of the emergence of the new city pushed Cincinnati to the brink of anarchy. In March 1884, the *Enquirer* complained that the police had failed to choke off a crime wave although, in the last year alone, there had been twelve arrests for malicious shooting, twenty-nine for malicious cutting, forty-seven for cutting with intent to wound, 284 for shooting with intent to kill, ninety-two for murder and manslaughter, and 948 for carrying a concealed weapon. The total number of arrests came to 56,784. The city's population was 250,000. Later that same month, a lynch mob descended on the county jail. While police and militia fought off the mob, gangs looted stores and shops on the fringe of the downtown district. In three days of riot the courthouse was burned to the ground, fifty-four people were killed, and an estimated 200 people wounded.

During the fall elections, violence erupted in the lower wards; two policemen and one Negro were killed. Congressman Benjamin Butterworth remarked that he had 'never witnessed anywhere such coarse brutality and such riotous demonstrations. . . .' Cincinnati, he concluded, 'seems . . . doomed to perdition.'

Less than two years later the city faced another major crisis. On May 1, 1886, Cincinnati workers joined in nationwide demonstrations for the eight-hour day. These were followed by a series of strikes. The militia was called out, and for two weeks the city resembled an armed camp. Only the show of force and, perhaps, the memory of the courthouse catastrophe prevented another riot.

Yet labor remained restive, and a rash of strikes followed. By 1892, the paternalistic system, which had dominated the breweries was smashed. And in 1894, Judge William Howard Taft spent the hot days of June and July 'trying to say nothing to reporters' and 'issuing injunctions' in an effort to control and prevent the railroad strike from leading to mass violence.

The Sunday-closing question was another explosive issue. The *Post*, the *Catholic-Telegraph*, a Committee of Five Hundred, and many Protestant clergymen all leveled scathing attacks on the continental Sabbath. 'Sunday in Cincinnati,' asserted one Methodist minister, 'is a high carnival of drunkenness, base sensuality, reeking debauchery and bloody, often fatal crime.' Other spokesmen tied the open Sunday to anarchism, atheism, corrupt politicians, a decadent daily press, indifferent public officials, and the ruthless exploitation of labor. 'The modern Puritan,' insisted Charles P. Taft, 'intends to rise up and oppose to the uttermost this kind of Sunday'.

When, in 1889, the mayor announced his intention to enforce the Sunday-closing law for saloons, the city almost faced another riot. Some 1,000 saloonkeepers vowed to ignore the new policy. When a cadre of police and firemen marched over the Rhine to close Kissell's saloon, an unruly crowd gathered, epithets were hurled, but no violence occurred. Kissell's was closed; the 'era of the back door', with 'front doors locked and curtains up, but back doors widened', had opened.

These spectacular outbreaks plus other pressures overwhelmed city hall. Indeed, scarcely a residential area, economic interest, or social or occupational group was left unscathed by the multidimensional disorder. As the physical area of the city expanded, officials were beseiged by demands for the extension, improvement, and inauguration of public services of all kinds and for lower taxes. Simultaneously, the relative decline of the city heightened the urgency of the agitation. Municipal institutions and agencies, established to meet the needs of the walking city, became overburdened, outmoded, and dilapidated.

The new city, with old ways shattered, provided a fertile breeding ground for turmoil and discontent and, as it turned out, for innovation and creative reconstruction. Initially, however, this unprecedented change accompanied by unprecedented demands for government action produced only the hope of reform. In 1885, on the eve of the repudiation of a Democratic administration, William Howard Taft predicted that 'the clouds are beginning to break over this Sodom of ours and the sun of decency is beginning to dispel the moral miasma that has rested on us now for so many years. It's the beginning of an era of reform.'

Yet for almost a decade no party could put together a decisive ruling majority. The city's political processes seemed frozen by a paralyzing factionalism. The division of the city into residential districts which roughly coincided with socio-economic lines made it difficult for the wealthy and well-educated to keep in contact with and control ward politics. As a result, extreme factionalism developed which could, apparently, be surmounted only by appealing to a host of neighborhood leaders and by constructing alliances which crossed party lines.

According to close observers, the chief products of this system were the use of money in city conventions and the rise of what Charles P. Taft called the 'bummer', a 'queer creature' who 'evolves somehow from the slums. . . .' In youth 'a bootblack, a newsboy or a general loafer', he matured into 'an Arab' who needed only 'a good standing with a saloon that has a fine layout during the day'. A 'hustler at the polls and conventions', the bummer was in such demand that he could accept money from competing candidates, thus lengthening the convention and contributing to inter-factional dealing. After studying the influence of the 'bummer', Taft gloomily concluded that the 'day of pure politics can never be . . . until a riot, a plague or flood kills off all the ward bummers'.

By 1897, however, and without divine intervention, all this had changed. In January of that year, three months before the city election, the *Post* gravely announced its intention to describe 'impassionately and without bias the means employed' in Cincinnati's 'superior and unrecorded government'. It was controlled by 'the boss, whose power is absolute'— George B. Cox.

The *Post's* analysis closely paralleled those made after the turn of the century. It dissected the patronage system, outlined the sources of financial support, and noted the attempted appeasement of the city's various special groups—the soldiers, the Germans, the Republican clubs, the Reform Jews, the legal and medical professions, the socially prominent Hilltops businessmen, and certain cooperative Democrats. It excitedly reported the effectiveness of the organization' intelligence system, the way the 'plugger' and the 'knocker' wore 'beaten paths to the office of the boss to urge the appointment of this man, the discharge of that [,] or to report some feature of misconduct or expression. . . .' The paper noted that Cox was always available for consultation with any citizen regardless of station or status and that he had been little more than one of several important factional leaders until, in 1886, Governor Joseph B. Foraker selected him to serve as chief adviser on patronage and political affairs in Hamilton County.

Foraker made a shrewd choice; Cox had grown up with the new city and received a liberal education in its ways. The son of British immigrants, he was born in 1853 and reared in the Eighteenth Ward, a district which by the 1880s contained fashionable as well as slum housing, factories, and its share of saloons and brothels. His father died when Cox was eight. Successively, Cox worked as a bootblack, newsboy, lookout for a gambling joint, grocery deliveryman, bartender, and tobacco salesman. His school principal, who later became superintendent of schools, claimed that Cox was frequently in boyish trouble in classes, exhibited an 'undisguised love for his mother', and 'never lied . . . bore malice, sulked, whined or moped'. Cox had also been exposed to religion. Although not a churchgoer, as an adult he had, according to one journalist, 'dormant powerful sentiments, which rest on foundations of the firmest faith'.

In the mid-1870s Cox acquired a saloon in his home neighborhood. He entered politics and served on the city council from 1878 until 1885 when, after joining forces with the republican reform mayoralty candidate, he ran unsuccessfully for county clerk. He tried for the same post in 1888, failed, and never again stood for public office.

At the time, moving away politically from the Circle, Cox worked with

George Moerlein, perhaps the strongest of the GOP professionals in the Zone. In 1890, he and Moerlein quarreled over patronage; and in the city convention of 1891, Cox was able, with the support of the Blaine Club, a kind of political settlement house that he had helped to establish, to defeat Moerlein's candidate for police judge and nominate his own man. Moerlein men now became Cox men. So, too, did Charles P. Taft and the *Times-Star*, which had been one of the last, the most influential, and the most outspoken of Cox's critics in the Hilltops Republican ranks. It accepted Cox, the paper announced, to secure a 'New Order' for Cincinnati. And the president of the gas company, sensing the political drift, confided to his diary that he had 'concluded [an] arrangement with Geo. B. Cox for services at $3500 per year quarterly to last for three years'. In the spring election of 1894 the Republicans carried the city with a plurality of over 6,500 votes, the first decisive municipal election in a decade. In 1897, Cox was the honest broker in a coalition composed of Circle and Zone Negroes, Zone politicians, the gas and traction companies, and Hilltops the Republican reformers.

Election returns after 1885 disclose a clear pattern. The GOP won five successive contests by uniting powerful Hilltops support with enough strength in the Zone to overcome the Democratic grip on the Circle. Until 1894 the margins of victory were perilously thin. The substantial triumph of that year merely marked the completion of the alliance which pitted a united periphery against the center of the city.

The heart of the Republican 'New Order' coalition, and the critical factor in the election of 1894, was its appeal to voters in the Hilltops fringe who demanded order and reform. To satisfy the Hilltops, Cox and his associates eliminated the bummer, provided brief and decorous conventions, enfranchised Negroes by suppressing violence at the polls, reduced the rapid turnover in office, and cut down the incidence of petty graft and corporation raiding.

Moreover, the 'machine' heeded the advice of its reform allies from the Hilltops. Cox accepted the secret ballot, voter registration, and a series of state laws which, though retaining the mayor-council form of government with ward representation, were designed to give the city a stable and more centralized government. The administrations which he indorsed started to build a professional police force, expanded and reequipped the fire department, pushed through a $6,000,000 water-works program, renovated municipal institutions, supported the growth of the University of Cincinnati, launched extensive street-paving and sewer-constructing projects, and tried to reduce the smoke problem and expand the city's park acreage. They also opened the door to housing regulation, suppressed the Sunday saloon, flagrant public gambling, and disorderly brothels (the city was never really closed), began to bring order into the chaotic public-utilities field by favoring privately owned, publicly regulated monopolies under progressive management, and succeeded in keeping the tax rate low. The Republican regime, in short, brought positive government to Cincinnati.

While this program also won votes in the Zone, it was not the sole basis for the party's popularity there. Many of the lieutenants and captains closest to Cox were Zone residents. They composed a colorful group known variously as 'the gang', 'the sports', or the 'bonifaces'—a clique which met nightly Over-the-Rhine either at Schubert and Pels, where each had a special beer mug with his name gilded on it, or at the round table in Wielert's beer garden. Three of them owned or operated combination saloons, gambling joints, and dance halls; one was prominent in German charitable associations and the author of several textbooks used in the elementary schools; another served twenty consecutive terms as president of the Hamilton County League of Building Associations; and one was a former catcher for the Cincinnati Redlegs.

Their tastes, behavior, and attitudes were conveniently summarized in the biographical sketches of ward leaders and city officials in the 1901 *Police and Municipal Guide*. All were characterized as friendly, well-known, 'All Around Good-Fellows' who liked a story, belonged to several social and fraternal groups, gave generously to charity, and treated the poor and sick with special kindness. They were all among the most ardent supporters of any project to boost the city.

Cox is pictured in the *Guide* as an adherent to the code of the Zone who had risen to the top. He was a *bon vivant* who enjoyed good cigars and good jokes, a man of wealth whose recently completed Clifton mansion was luxuriously decorated and adorned with expensive works of art, a man of impressive but quiet and private charity. Above all, he was true to his word, loyal to his friends, yet quick to reprimand and replace those who betrayed his trust by misusing public office.

Cox and his top civil servants—surrounded by a motley crowd of newspaper reporters, former boxers and ball players, vaudeville and burlesque performers, and other Vine Street characters—provided an attractive model for men awed by the glamor, wealth, and power which was so visible yet so elusive in the new city. Cox's opponents in the Zone seldom attacked him or this inside group directly. Even in the heat of the 1897 campaign, the *Volksfreund*, the German Catholic Democratic daily, carefully described Cox as an 'amiable man' who had to be 'admired' for his 'success' and, either ignoring or unaware of the process of negotiation and mediation by which he ruled, criticized him only for his illiberality in imposing 'dictatorial methods' on the GOP. Indeed, most Zone residents, like those of the Hilltops, found it difficult to object to a government which seemed humane, efficient, and progressive.

Yet it would be a mistake to overestimate the strength of the 'New Order' Republican coalition. Its victories from 1885 to 1894 were won by perilously close pluralities. The organization, moreover, failed to carry a referendum for the sale of the city-owned Southern Railroad in 1896 and lost the municipal contest in 1897 to a reform fusion ticket, and the fall elections of 1897, 1898, and 1899 to the Democrats. In all these reversals, crucial defections occurred in both the Hilltops and the Zone. Skittish voters grew indignant over alleged corruption, outraged by inaction on the traction and gas questions, piqued by the rising cost of new city projects, annoyed by the slow expansion of the educational program, or uneasy over the partial sacrifice of democracy to efficiency within the Republican organization.

Thereafter, however, the Republicans rallied and won three of the next four city elections by unprecedented margins. The strategy and tactics remained essentially the same. Although not wholly averse to raising national issues, Cox's group gave local affairs the most emphasis. The organization was occasionally purged of its less savory elements. Cox and his Zone advisors continued to consult with their Hilltops allies on nominations. The party promised and, in fact, tried to deliver order and reform. Without abolishing ward representation in the city council, it strengthened the mayor and streamlined the administration. The party also broadened and deepened its program as civic associations, women's clubs, social workers, social gospellers, and spokesmen for the new unionism—all novel forces in urban politics—expanded and elaborated their demands.

But voting patterns underwent a fundamental and, for the GOP, an ultimately disastrous change. By 1903 the Republicans dominated the entire city, carrying not only the Zone and Hilltops but also the center. The Circle was now the invincible bulwark of Cox's power.

There were several factors involved in the conversion of Circle Democrats to Republicanism. First, Cox had extensive personal contacts with them which dated back to his unsuccessful races for county clerk in the 1880s. Second, the Democrats had been unable to put down factionalism. By the late 1890s there were two reform elements in the party, both of which belabored the regulars from the center of the city as tainted with corruption, too cozy with Cox, and perhaps worst of all, as a discredit and burden to the party because they wore the charred shirt of the courthouse riot.

In the wake of the fusionist victory of 1897, Mike Mullen, the leader of a riverfront Democratic ward explained why he would henceforth work with the Republican party.

> I have worked hard [for the Democratic party] have suffered much and have won for it many victories. Yet all the while there was a certain element . . . that looked on me with distrust. . . . [L]eaders of the Fusionist Party did not think enough of me to let me look after the voting in my own ward, but sent down a lot of people to watch the count. That decided me.

He was later joined by Colonel Bob O'Brien who, like Mullen, specialized in Christmas turkey, soupline, and family-service politics. These Democrats led their constituents into the Republican fold.

It was this alliance with the Circle which ultimately destroyed Cox. Anti-machine spokesmen were convinced that they had to educate the city before they could redeem it. They felt, too, that politics was a potent educational tool. But campaigns had to be spectacular in order to engage the voters' attention and participation. As A. Julius Freiberg notes, the 'psychology' of the electorate was such that years of 'speaking, writing, explaining, even begging and imploring' had been 'to no purpose'. The 'reformer and his fellow students may sit about the table and evolve high principles for action, but the people . . . will not be fed by those principles unless there is a dramatic setting, and the favorite dramatic setting is the killing of a dragon'. And all the people 'love the dramatic; not merely the poor, but the rich, and the middle class as well'. All that was needed was a situation which would enable the right man to 'bring to book the boss himself'.

Reformers hammered relentlessly at the theme that Cox was not a good boss; he was the head of a 'syndicate' which included the worst products of slum life. In 'that part of the city where vice and infamy hold high revel', went one version of the charge, 'the boss-made ticket finds its most numerous supporters. Every dive keeper, every creature who fattens upon the wages of sin . . . , all the elements at war with society have enlisted.' Men 'who claim to be respectable', the chief 'beneficiaries of this unholy alliance . . . , go down into the gutter and accept office from hands that are reeking with the filth of the slums'. Worse still, this 'alliance of the hosts of iniquity with the greed of special privilege and ambition for power and place' plays so successfully 'upon the prejudices and . . . superstition of the many that wrong is often espoused by those who in the end are the victims of the wrong'.

The reformers also inpugned Cox's personal integrity. Democratic County Prosecutor Henry T. Hunt secured evidence that Cox had perjured himself in 1906 when he said he had not received a cent of some $250,000 of interest on public funds which Republican county treasurers had been paid by bankers. In the spring of 1911, Hunt and the grand jury indicted Cox and 123 others during a broad investigation of politics, corruption, and vice.

Finally, Hunt, stressing the issue of moral indignation, ran for mayor in the fall of 1911 on a Democratic reform ticket. Using the moral rhetoric of the muckraker, Hunt and his associates tied bossism, the chaos, poverty, and vice of the slums, and the malefactors of great wealth together and pictured them as a threat to the welfare of the whole city. Once again the Hilltops and Zone voted for order and reform. Hunt's progressive coalition swept the periphery, lost only in the Circle wards, and won the election.

By that time, however, Cox was no longer boss. President Taft and Charles P. Taft had wanted Cox to step aside as early as 1905, but they found him indispensable. After the grand jury revelations, however, they were able to convince the 'bonifaces' that Cox was a liability. With the organization against him, Cox retired. For a time, he insisted that his two chief assistants, August Herrmann and Rudolph Hynicka, should also quit, apparently convinced that they, like himself, could no longer command the confidence of the periphery. Charles P. Taft's *Times-Star* agreed. The two men, backed by the Blaine Club, merely resigned their official party positions but refused to get out of politics entirely.

What then, was Cox's role in politics and government in the new city? He helped create and manage a voluntary political-action organization which bridged the racial and cultural chasms between the Circle, Zone, and Hilltops. He and his allies were able to bring positive and moderate reform government to Cincinnati and to mitigate the conflict and disorder which accompanied the emergence of the new city. With the crisis atmosphere muted, ardent reformers could develop more sophisticated programs and agitate, educate, and organize without arousing the kind of divisive, emotional, and hysterical response which had immobilized municipal statesmen in the 1880s. In the process, while battering at the boss, the slums, and the special-privilege syndicate, they shattered the bonds of confidence which linked the Zone 'bonifaces' and the moderate reformers of the Hilltops to Cox's organization. Cox, it seems, said more than he realized when, in 1892, he remarked that a boss was 'not necessarily a public enemy'.

(d) A Comparative Historical Geography of Streetcar Suburbs in Boston, Massachusetts and Leeds, England: 1850–1920

DAVID WARD

Some of the most striking contrasts in the appearance of British and American cities are inherited from regional differences in the type and scale of urban growth in the sixty years before the outbreak of World War I. This period was characterized by the construction of improved dwellings in new suburban locations which were linked to the industrial and business sections of the city, at first by horse-drawn and later by electrically powered streetcars. Today these streetcar suburbs are surrounded by the more extensive, and often morphologically quite distinct, residential developments associated with the period after World War I when the internal combustion engine provided more flexible means of local transportation.

Innovations in local transport, however, were introduced more rapidly in North America than they were in Britain, and the streetcar tracks and services were also much more extensive. Accordingly the streetcar exerted a much greater influence upon the growth and upon the social and economic life of American cities. In considerations of nineteenth-century urbanism, regional variations in the effects of local transportation upon the growth and characteristics of cities have received only limited attention and it is proposed in this paper to explore some of the contrasts exhibited by the streetcar suburbs of Boston and Leeds and, further, to relate these contrasts to the different developmental experiences of British and American cities between 1870 and 1914.

With the exception of London, the late Victorian additions to British towns were limited in their areal extent and often represented only a modest

Annals of the Association of American Geographers, Vol. 54, No. 4, December 1964; pp. 477–89.

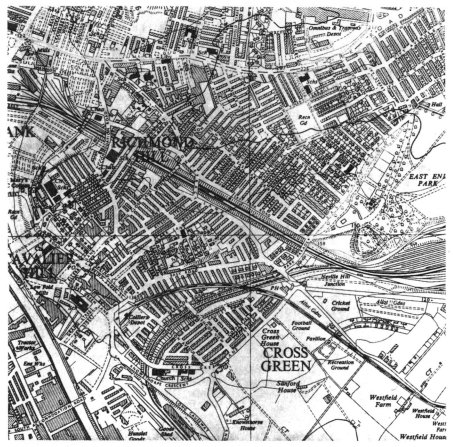

Fig. 1 Streetcar suburban development in Leeds. Scale: approximately 6 inches to 1 mile. (Reproduced from the Ordnance Survey Map with the sanction of the Controller of Her Majesty's Stationery Office. Crown Copyright Reserved.)

advance on former housing conditions. Throughout this period much building took the form of the filling in of vacant areas near to the city center. Terrace dwellings (Fig. 1) arranged in a rectilinear pattern in certain peripheral districts near to streetcar services did, however, provide improved homes for a restricted number of middle-class people. In contrast, the detached or semidetached house set in its own lot (Fig. 2) was the dominant type of suburban residential building at this time in the United States. These houses were not only laid out in a more spacious fashion but they also represented a greater advance on former living standards than did the British terraces. Electrified streetcar services were introduced only slowly in Britain and, indeed, many early routes were

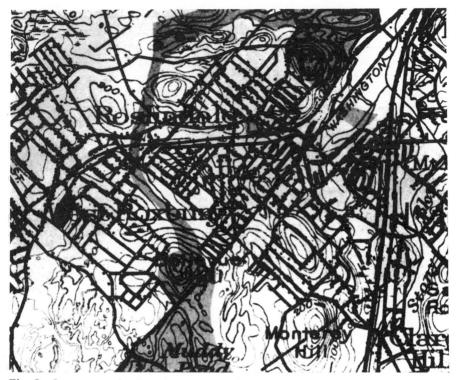

Fig. 2 Street car suburban development in Boston. Scale: 1 : 24,000.

specifically provided by municipalities to link isolation hospitals, parks, and cemeteries with the city proper. In the United States, at a much earlier date, street railway tracks were extended by private companies well beyond the continuous built-up areas and the electrification of much more extensive systems was almost complete before the first modest adventures in electrified services had commenced in most British provincial cities.

By the later decades of the nineteenth century the populations of American cities were increasing at their greatest rate whereas in Britain the rate of population growth in large cities was greatest in the earlier decades of the century. In the second half of the nineteenth century British cities grew more slowly partly because emigration depleted their populations in the eighties and again in the first decade of the twentieth century. A proportion of this emigration was, moreover, partly responsible for swelling the populations of American cities in the same decades. In 1870 Boston and Leeds each contained about a quarter of a million people; by 1920 Leeds had doubled its population whereas Boston had increased threefold.

Table 1 Peaks and troughs in the British and American building cycles 1860–1920

Great Britain		United States	
Peaks	Troughs	Peaks	Troughs
1863			1864
	1871	1871	
1877			1878
	1887	1890	
1899			1900
	1912	1909	
1920			1918

THE DIFFERENCE IN PHASE OF THE RESIDENTIAL BUILDING CYCLE IN BRITISH AND AMERICAN CITIES

The growth of the populations of American cities was greater than that of British cities whereas the periods of intensive residential building occurred in different decades on either side of the Atlantic. In general, building activity in British cities was most pronounced in the mid-seventies and at the turn of the century, whereas in American cities intensive building occurred in the late eighties and early nineties and also in the middle of the first decade of the twentieth century (Table 1). This difference in phase of British and American building cycles has been related to the migration of people and capital from Britain to the New World when economic conditions were attractive in the United States and a corresponding tendency for greater domestic investment and internal migration in Britain when economic conditions in America were less attractive. Residential building in the United States would thus reinforce the general boom in investment and immigration whereas in Britain residential building, as a major item of domestic investment, would occur when opportunities for foreign investment were restricted and, therefore, stand in an inverse relationship to the trade cycle.

This complementary relationship between migration, investment, and residential building in Britain and the United States has been regarded as a fundamental characteristic of the Atlantic economy in the two generations before the First World War. More recently, reservations concerned with the degree to which investment in, and migration to the New World could affect the secular trend of residential building in Britain, have been expressed and some observers have been inclined to attribute fluctuations in the British building cycle to local and domestic rather than to international conditions. Nevertheless, the difference in phase of residential building on either side of the Atlantic, whether it was created by local or by international conditions or indeed by both, reflected the different chronology of the growth rates of British and American cities. The timing of such spurts and lags in the amount of residential building may well have been affected by, or indeed, have had an effect upon the successful introduction of innovations in local transportation.

THE RESIDENTIAL BUILDING CYCLE IN LEEDS

Although residential building may respond to local conditions and exhibit marked regional variations, all the larger northern English industrial cities experienced a marked boom in residential building in the mid-seventies and in the late nineties whereas in the eighties and in the decade immediately preceding the First World War there were pronounced slumps. From gaining over 200,000 people by migration during the seventies, the northern English industrial towns lost nearly 60,000 by emigration in the following decade. Leeds, however, received a substantial influx of Jewish immigrants from Eastern Europe during the eighties and by 1890 there were as many as 8,000 Jews largely occupied in the growing ready-made clothing industry of the city.

Indeed, Leeds gained more people by migration in the eighties when foreign emigration was high than in the seventies and nineties when migration within Britain was more pronounced (Table 2). But over half of this gain by migration in the eighties represented the substantial influx of Eastern European Jews who were finding their way to American cities in even larger numbers at the same time. In Leeds, therefore, there was a counterpoise to the effects of native emigration and the prolonged period of

Table 2 Population growth in Leeds

	Total population	Net increase	Natural increase	Gain or loss by migration
1871	259,212			
1881	309,119	49,970	42,503	7,404
1891	367,505	58,386	41,012	17,374
1901	428,968	61,463	47,098	14,365
1911	445,568	16,582	47,979	-31,397
1921	458,232	4,077	26,001	-21,923

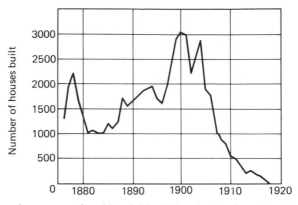

Fig. 3 Annual amount of residential building in Leeds, 1876–1920.

depression in the building trade. The local building cycle, therefore, shows a minor peak in the late eighties which punctuated the lengthy depression between the national peaks of the mid-seventies and late nineties (Fig. 3).

Although Leeds thus was somewhat insulated from the more severe effect of the building slump and emigration in the eighties, the city lost over 30,000 people by emigration between 1901 and 1911 which, in one decade, eliminated the gain by immigration of the two preceding decades (Table 2). In spite of this heavy emigration, the boom in residential building which started in the late nineties continued on into the early years of the twentieth century; between 1898 and 1903 the amount of building was greater than in any other preceding five-year period (Fig. 3). Since construction continued on into the period of emigration, the number of empty houses in the city rose rapidly and by 1904 amounted to over 5 per cent of the total number of dwellings.

This large number of empty houses, however, need not indicate a miscalculation of demand on the part of the building industry, for new tastes in the style and location of dwellings can also stimulate the removal of existing residents. The distribution and the rents of many of the empty houses in the city suggest that a large proportion represented the former homes of middle-class people who had taken advantage of the new streetcar facilities to move on to improved terrace houses. Over half the empty houses were situated in a zone between a half mile and a mile from the city center where the proportion of empty houses in 1905 amounted to 6.1 per cent. In the congested central districts and in the outer suburbs the proportion empty was about 4 per cent (Table 3); for the city as a whole it was 4.8 per cent. Some two-thirds of the empty houses were of intermediate rents (i.e., five shillings or more)[1] so that they would be beyond the means of most of the residents of the central slums.

Thus the boom in residential building at the turn of the century was

Table 3   The distribution and rents of empty houses in Leeds, 1905

Distance from city center	Total number of houses	Rents below five shillings	Rents above five shillings	Total number empty	Percentage empty
Within 0.5 mile	16,859	445	255	700	4.2
Beyond 0.5 mile } Within 1 mile	28,546	734	1,007	1,741	6.1
Beyond 1 mile	34,841	874	524	1,398	4.0
Total	80,246	2,053	1,786	3,839	4.8

Note: Most of the new suburban houses were beyond 1 mile from the city center. See Fig. 7.

associated with the movement of people, whose income had already enabled them to live at some distance from the city center, to better residences in suburban locations. The large number of empty houses, which were only slowly reoccupied as rents decreased and as building declined in the decade before the outbreak of World War I, indicated an internal redistribution of an existing population. Since it was only in the late nineties that the Leeds streetcar system was fully electrified and the track extended, the building boom which these developments sustained was hardly started before emigration began to drain the city of much of its natural increase in population. Under these circumstances the streetcar suburban developments must have been somewhat curtailed. In Leeds transportation innovations stimulated a pronounced boom in suburban residential building but both the dimensions of this boom and the scale of new local transport provisions must have been reduced by the coincidence of the application of the innovations with the beginnings of heavy emigration.

THE RESIDENTIAL BUILDING CYCLE IN BOSTON

Boston experienced fluctuations in the volume of residential building which were distinctly out of phase with those which occurred in Leeds. Boston experienced pronounced peaks in building activity in the early seventies and in the late eighties and early nineties whereas the slumps in residential building occurred in the late seventies and early eighties and again around the turn of the century (Fig. 4). The relationship between migration and building activity is, as in Leeds, somewhat obscured in the first decade of the twentieth century. In Leeds building continued at a high level in spite of heavy emigration but in Boston, although there was exceptionally heavy immigration between 1905 and 1915 (Table 4), the increase in building activity was relatively subdued (Fig. 4).

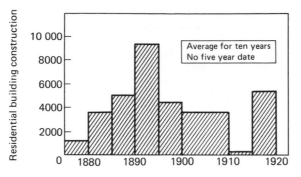

Fig. 4 Residential building in Boston by five-year periods, 1875–1920.

Most of the immigrants into Boston in the decade before World War I were from Italy, Russia, and the Eastern Mediterranean lands and they mainly occupied the central tenement districts by the further subdivision of existing structures.[2] In 1900 there were 8.44 people per dwelling in Boston but by 1915 this index of congestion had advanced to 10.05 people per dwelling. As in Leeds, empty houses were the abandoned homes of middle-income people who had moved on to better dwellings and for long the rents of these dwellings were beyond the means of the newly arrived immigrant in Boston. For a decade contemporary American observers had been impressed by the effect of the streetcar in facilitating the dispersal of people from central areas but after about 1900 their impressions were rapidly

Table 4 Population growth in Boston

	Total population	Net increase	Natural increase	Gain or loss by migration
1870	287,532*			
1875	341,919	54,387	34,954	19,433
1880	362,839	21,021	23,230	-2,209
1885	390,394	27,556	9,057	18,499
1890	448,477	58,082	33,205	24,877
1895	496,920	48,443	26,217	22,226
1900	560,892	63,972	49,417	14,555
1905	595,380	34,488	19,690	14,794
1910	670,585	75,205	44,230	30,975
1915	745,439	74,854	50,908	23,946
1920	748,060	2,621	24,670	-22,049

*Includes areas annexed in 1872.

revised as Boston was once again flooded with immigrants who had neither the income nor, in some instances, the desire to move to suburban locations.

The earlier confidence in the effect of street railroads in the improvement of the conditions of urban life had, however, been based upon the impressive scale and successful application of innovations in local transport in the late eighties and early nineties. Moreover, in Boston the electrification of the streetcar system occurred at a time when large numbers of immigrants from the Maritime Provinces of Canada were arriving in the city.[3] These Maritime Canadians, unused to urban congestion, had a predilection for the more open housing of the streetcar suburbs and, unlike later immigrants from Russia and Italy, the Maritimers had the economic means to take immediate advantage of suburban residences. Indeed, Maritime Canadians dominated the house building industry in Boston. Thus the residential building boom stimulated by the provision of improved means of local transport had the added impetus of heavy immigration of people of moderate means and with a preference for suburban living.

Innovations in local transport in Boston initiated a residential building boom but the dimensions of this boom must have been greatly enlarged by the contemporary arrival of large numbers of immigrants. This supplementary stimulus of population growth may well have encouraged the confident investment in local transport and residential building far beyond the proportions suggested by the tentative experiments in electrified streetcars in the eighties. British investors in local transport at the same time had not this insurance of the effects of immigration[4] quite apart from any differences in real wage levels in the two countries and, in spite of experimentation with steam as well as electricity, the application of electricity to local transport and more particularly the extension of track awaited municipal initiative in the nineties.

LOCAL TRANSPORTATION AND RESIDENTIAL BUILDING

The urban geographer is primarily concerned with the size, location, and characteristics of streetcar suburbs, for these properties represent the spatial consequences of the secular changes in the volume of residential building and of improvements in local transport. Accordingly, the different type and scale of suburban development in Britain and the United States between 1870 and 1914 can be related to the contrasts in the developmental experiences of cities on either side of the Atlantic. The chronology of transportation innovation affected the timing of the residential building booms whereas the circumstances of migration affected the dimensions of the boom. In the last analysis, however, the differences in the standard of living and in the size of the British and American middle classes may have exerted the strongest influences of all on the development of streetcar suburbs.

Discussions of the different fluctuations of the residential building cycles in Britain and the United States only rarely have considered the relationship of these cyclical contrasts to the different chronology and scale of innovations in local transportation in the two countries. Certainly Walter Isard has endeavored to relate not only the booms in residential building, but also those in immigration and general economic conditions in the United States, to the critical innovations in transportation which took place during the nineteenth century. Isard, however, does not elaborate upon the different chronology of building booms in Britain where the residential building associated with the introduction of electrified streetcars occurred several years later. It would appear that the earlier introduction of more comprehensive and extensive transit systems in American cities can be related to the demographic conditions in cities on the western side of the Atlantic at the critical period of innovation. It is, therefore, to the contrasts in the timing of transportation innovations and their effects on the type and scale of urban growth in Boston and Leeds that the analysis now turns.

THE DEVELOPMENT OF LOCAL TRANSPORT IN BOSTON

Local transport facilities in Boston had been well developed long before the introduction of the electric streetcar in 1887. The steam railroads had provided commuter services in the forties for wealthy merchants who lived in neighboring towns but conducted their businesses in Boston. During the fifties the introduction of the horse-drawn streetcar opened up land adjacent to the contemporary built-up area. It was the horsecar that facilitated the residential development of the South End in the fifties and sixties and of the inner parts of Dorchester and Roxbury during the seventies and eighties when costs were falling and streetcar tracks were extended into a sparsely settled countryside (Fig. 5.)

Throughout this period the fare was five cents within the immediate Boston area so that the journey to work was restricted by time rather than by cost. During the seventies and eighties the density of crosstown services and routes increased whereas the limit of such facilities expanded outwards so that people whose places of work were neither central nor fixed had adequate facilities. The extension of track opened up considerable areas of land so that residential development was relatively sparse and, as the area of possible residence was enlarged once more by the electrification of the streetcar services, the intervening areas within the horsecar suburbs were filled with less ostentatious buildings.

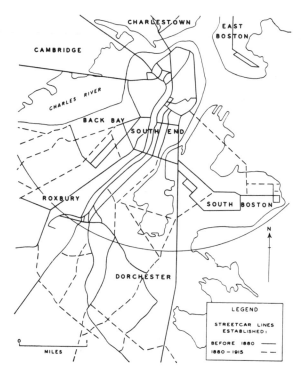

Fig. 5 The growth of Boston's public transport system, 1880–1915. The arc is 2.5 miles from the city center.

The slow pace of the horsecar placed definite limits on the distance from which people could commute each day. In 1880 it was reported that:

> . . . between two and a half and five miles from the city center, there was abundant undeveloped land, since it was as quick and as convenient to travel by steam railroad from five miles or more as by horse railroad for three or four miles.

Seven years later the problem was alleviated by the rapid electrification and amalgamation of almost all the private horsecar services in the Boston area under the single management of a new company known as the West End Street Railway Company. The success of experiments in the use of electric power for streetcar services conducted by the original West End Company prompted the owners to purchase, coordinate, and electrify most of the then existing streetcar services in and around Boston. In 1894 the Boston Elevated Company was formed to provide rapid transit facilities in the form of elevated tracks and subways and in 1897 this company obtained a

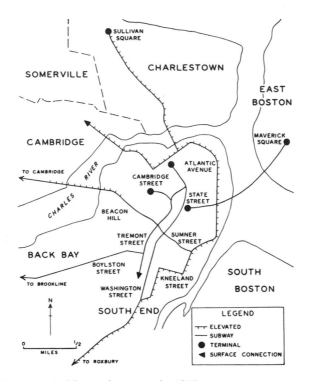

Fig. 6   Boston's rapid transit system in 1915.

lease of the West End Company so that the future developments of elevated and subway services would be integrated with the surface system (Fig. 6).

In 1887 the West End Company had acquired 91.8 miles of track and a system which catered for over ninety million passengers each year (Table 5). In 1897 the Boston Elevated Company acquired 316.05 miles of track of which over 300 miles were already electrified and a system which catered to about 180 million passengers each year (Table 5). By the outbreak of World War I the Boston Elevated Company operated over 500 miles of surface track and over thirty miles of rapid transit track (Figs 5 and 6) but passenger traffic especially after 1905 increased at a rate faster than that of the population of the city as a whole and faster than the company could install more adequate facilities. By 1914 the company was handling almost 350 million passengers each year (Table 5).

At the turn of the century, just as the electrified streetcars appeared to be creating the possibilities of universal suburban living and thereby fulfilling the hopes of so many optimistic observers of the nineties, the financing and management of American street railroads became one of that

Table 5 The expansion of public transport facilities in Leeds and Boston, 1870–1920

	Boston*		Leeds	
	Number of passengers (in millions)	Total track (in miles)	Number of passengers (in millions)	Total track (in miles)
1871	34			
1881	68			
1887	92	212		
1895	155	275	1894	27.5
1899	191	338		
1904	242	445	1902	48	71
1909	281	484		
1914	343	515	1916	94	114
1919	325	535		

*The Boston system also served several adjacent towns which together with Boston contained a total population of about one million people in 1900 and about 1.2 million people in 1920.

group of urban problems which to many reformers expressed the generic condition of city life. The heavy capital investments in elevated track and subways came at a time when labor and material costs were rising and it became increasingly difficult for the already overcapitalized company to attract further capital or to yield an operational profit at the uniform five-cent fare to which it was committed by its charter. Certainly construction works were often designed to milk the operating company but in Boston the municipality actively participated in the construction of some of the subways and allowed the company merely to lease them.

Regardless of these later difficulties which were to force the Boston Elevated Company into the hands of receivers by 1919,[5] the facilities provided and the volume of traffic which they handled was on a scale unprecedented in any English city except London. Equally impressive was the reduction in the time of the journey to work made possible by both the electrified and rapid transit services, and between 1885 and 1895 the boom in residential building was heavily concentrated in areas beyond two and a half miles from the city center (Fig. 5). It was during this period that the positive effects of the street railroad in improving the conditions of urban living were extolled. Much of the achievement of the early electrified streetcars was obscured by the preoccupation on the part of later reformers with the abuses and problems of railroad management in the decade before World War I.

The commissioners appointed by the Massachusetts Legislature in 1898 to investigate the street railway conditions in Europe found that European experience in local transportation was surprisingly limited and suggested that:

> ... to institute a comparison ... between the street railway transportation of Boston as at present developed and that of Birmingham or Glasgow, is so absurd as to suggest ignorance. The appliances in use in the European cities so named may, and probably do answer the demands made upon them, but they pertain to conditions of urban life and of urban movement wholly different from those which now prevail in Massachusetts.

In England in 1898, 618 miles of track served the seven and a half million people who lived in the largest cities and the annual number of passengers carried amounted to 474 million people. In the Boston district alone there were 316 miles of track serving the needs of only a million people and handling 181 million passengers a year (Table 5).

THE DEVELOPMENT OF LOCAL TRANSPORT IN LEEDS

In the early nineties observers in Boston were still optimistic about the benefits to urban living which would be derived from the streetcar, but a Sanitary Congress held in Leeds could suggest only the sober procedure of the compulsory purchase of peripheral estates, the construction of public housing, and the provision of municipal transport. Apparently there were not enough middle-income people to encourage the private builder and consequently little encouragement for the streetcar company to expand its services beyond the existing built-up area. Indeed, in the nineties the horse omnibus, which had been forced off the streets of Boston in the fifties by the horsecar, still remained the most flexible and extensive form of public transport in Leeds.

It was in 1870, some twenty years later than in Boston, that a street railway company had been formed in Leeds. This new Leeds Tramway Company was granted a twenty-one year lease by the City of Leeds to lay tracks and to operate horsecar services on condition that cheap fares were provided for artisans, mechanics, and laboring classes. The horsecar services were neither extensive enough nor speedy enough to encourage commuting by working men. The first improvements in speed came with the introduction of steam power in the eighties but this form of power proved inappropriate to congested city streets. In 1891 experiments in the use of electric power proved successful, and in 1894 the Corporation of Leeds took over the system and proceeded to implement the conversion of the whole system to electricity. In spite of these changes the system was still confined to the main roads out of the city, and the crosstown routes were still dominated by the horse-omnibus companies. Even when the city decided to operate and electrify the street railways, it inherited only 27.5 miles of track (Table 5).

Thus, in 1884 a witness reported that in Leeds:

> . . . there was no tendency, active or passive, for sections of the population to move from the center to the outskirts. There was no difficulty in obtaining good houses at a short distance from the city center . . .

Five years after the municipality began to operate and electrify the system, however, a contemporary observer commented that:

> . . . there were wide excellent roads and along them for about three and a half miles from the center of the city, tramways with horse, steam and electric traction offered ready and cheap locomotion; giving to many householders the opportunity of residing away from their shops, offices and factories and rendering building land more valuable than it otherwise would be.

By the turn of the century the municipality had doubled the length of track and electrified most of the system (Table 5). Although the demand for

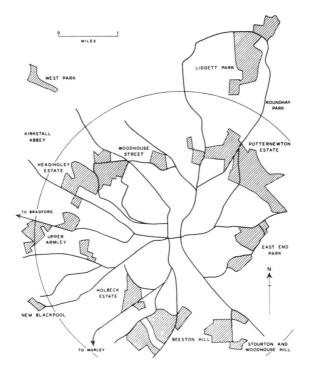

Fig. 7 Local transport and building developments in Leeds, 1890–1919. Circle is 2.5 miles from the city center.

suburban and improved housing was growing in the late nineties and the town was making substantial gains to its population by immigration, most of the extensions to the streetcar system were designed to serve such amenities or services as parks, isolation hospitals, and cemeteries located on the edge of the town (Fig. 7). In this way the public streetcar system moved into areas in which the private company had feared to operate in view of the sluggish demand for suburban houses in the late eighties and early nineties.

Thus the application of innovations in local transport was sustained in the mid-nineties by the provision of services to public institutions on the edge of the city, and only later in the nineties and in the early years of the present century were suburban residences, related to the new streetcar services, built in large numbers. The boom in suburban residential building, however, occurred at a time when Leeds was beginning to feel the effects of emigration in retarding the growth of the city's population. Many of the new routes provided by the municipal transport system were designed to replace the horse omnibus on cross-city services or to link the Leeds system with that of neighboring towns (Fig. 7); and the demand for suburban housing was not large enough to affect the development of the large areas of land brought within daily commuting distance of the city by the electrified streetcar. Unlike Boston, only limited areas beyond two and a half miles from the city center were developed by suburban builders (Fig. 7).

In Leeds the suburban residential development associated with the new streetcar services was, in fact, confined to certain well defined districts. These suburban developments had a more spacious and regular layout than terrace rows in more central locations and consequently, in a city dominated by small landholdings, were located in those areas where large estates could be purchased for building purposes (Fig. 7). Land suitable for suburban building thus had not only to be accessible to the business district by means of streetcar services but also to be of suitable dimensions to accommodate the larger scale of building. In Leeds the demand for improved dwellings, whether dependent upon the level of real wages or upon taste, was so limited that only some of the restricted number of estate lands available were actually utilized for building purposes before the First World War.

The expansion of the built-up area of Leeds under the stimulus of improved local transport facilities was then decidedly modest before the First World War. By 1916 Leeds was served by 114 miles of track which handled 94 million passengers each year or less than one-third of the capacity of the Boston system (Table 5). The limitations of demand in a city which was losing population by emigration, at the very time that the electrified services began to stimulate suburban residential development, must have affected the dimensions of the streetcar suburbs. Similarly, demographic factors had been unfavourable during the late eighties when the critical innovations in local transport were made; whereas, in Boston, heavy immigration provided a stimulus to the more confident application of electric power.

MUNICIPAL CONTROL AND THE RESIDENTIAL BUILDING PROCESS

Differences in the scale of suburban growth in Leeds and Boston were also conditioned by the contrasting methods devised by the local authorities to direct and control building in the new suburbs. In Boston the scale of individual building operations was quite small and the constant changes in the alignment and orientation of the grid arrangement of streets are a result of a great number of developers who contributed to the construction of streetcar suburbs. The impression of great uniformity and monotony within the streetcar suburbs was a consequence of the lack of originality in house design and street layout on the part of developers and suburbanites.

In the process of buying farms and building homes, restrictions were at a minimum but since developers often stressed the material superiority of their new subdivisions, a necessary minimum of utilities and paving was often provided to attract the middle-class clientele. Inadequate utilities in a subdivision usually reflected the intention of the developer to cater to low-income groups. Although Boston introduced a rigorous code governing the construction of tenements, the control of subdivisions was always limited and designed to facilitate the process of suburban growth. Some suburbs were indeed destined to become shantytowns because of lack of adequate municipal direction in the provision of utilities and layout; most of the streetcar suburbs, however, suffered little contemporary disadvantage from the limited degree of municipal control.

In Leeds the control of new building was quite comprehensive in the second half of the nineteenth century. As early as 1866 local laws dictated the arrangement of houses, minimum street widths, maximum continuous house frontage, structural dimensions, and, above all, the approval of the plans of all new building by a special committee. This legislation was later codified and applied to most large British towns with the approval of the Public Health Act of 1875. An underlying assumption of this legislation was that further building would take the form of terrace rows and, therefore, the problem of congestion could be controlled by geometry. In Leeds the more regular and better spaced terraces which, at first, filled in vacant spaces in central parts of the city and, later, characterized the streetcar suburbs represent the consequences of this legislation. In Leeds, however, most of the improved terrace houses were still built back to back[6] and it was 1901 before the problem of cul-de-sacs was encompassed by the legislation.

Clearly the adoption of the detached or semidetached house by the American middle class removed many of the imperative needs to control building which exist when dwellings are arranged in the form of terraces. The single house set in its own lot represented a nostalgia for the farmhouse or the single houses of the main streets of small towns and also indicated the close relationship between improved living conditions and owner occupancy. Although the number of middle-class Bostonians who lived on lots of any size and who were able to pay off their mortgages was quite small, the intention and the achievement of this aim was well represented by the detached house and its small-town architecture. Ownership of a segment of a terrace has not quite the symbolic and actual quality of separateness possessed by a detached or even a semidetached house. Even when multifamily structures began to appear on the inner margins of the streetcar suburbs, they took the form of 'three-deckers' in which three families on three separate floors would enjoy the separateness of a small lot.

CONCLUSION

The different conditions of urban growth in Leeds and Boston between 1870 and 1914 greatly affected the application of innovations in local transport, the degree and type of control over building exercised by local governments, the physical extent and appearance of the improved dwellings of the streetcar suburbs, and the popular confidence in and imagery of the possibilities of suburban life. In the late nineteenth century innovations in local transport and the rising incomes and changing tastes of middle-class people sustained the growth of streetcar suburbs. But the decisions to build improved dwellings in new locations were made under somewhat different conditions of urban growth.

In the United States the confidence in the possibilities of suburban living and the rapid population growth of the period around 1890 sustained the rapid application of innovations to, and the rapid expansion of, the street railway systems and thereby insured the rapid growth of streetcar suburbs within the framework of extremely limited control of building by local authorities. In Britain urban growth was somewhat sluggish at this time and innovations were applied only later in the nineties when population growth was more sustained. This belated application of improvements in local transport, however, was largely accomplished by municipal enterprise and in scale was infinitesimal in comparison with developments in American cities. Improved dwellings were the result of the modification of the old terrace form of housing and conceptions of improved living were rather based on the more idealistic and comprehensive solution of new 'Garden Cities'.

DAVID WARD

Notwithstanding the current controversy concerning the cause of the differences in phase of residential building cycles in Britain and the United States, these differences do, however, express the important distinctions in the chronology of population growth and of the introduction of improved local transportation. The secular and quantitative differences in residential building cycles in Leeds and Boston are clearly recorded in the contrasting characteristics of their respective streetcar suburbs. Even today the late nineteenth-century streetcar suburbs survive as part of the contemporary urban scene and their different appearances and dimensions in Britain and the United States are the result of regional contrasts in the conditions of urban growth some fifty years ago.

The effect of technical innovations and especially of transportation upon the spatial structure of cities and economies is a recurrent theme of economic geography but the spatial consequences of the same innovation may well be quite distinct because of the conditions and rates of urban or economic growth in a particular place at a particular time. Local transportation did not refashion the internal spatial structure of cities in precisely the same way or for precisely the same reasons even within the Western world. Indeed, if the cultural geographer is to analyze the distributional aspects of industrial capitalism and, in particular, one of its most enduring memorials, the industrial city, there will need to be a more systematic investigation of the regional variations in the chronology and rate of economic growth, and also investigation into the aspirations and organization of social groups which are affected by and which at the same time also stimulated the process of social change. As Meinig has recently suggested, the necessary and exhilarating task of the geographer is to reconstruct the 'geographical context' of that constellation of situations, objectives, and possibilities with which decision makers are faced. Certainly to understand those parts of our cities created by nineteenth-century growth requires not only an understanding of the temporal setting but also the varying conditions of regional growth.

NOTES

[1] Contemporary observers regarded a rent of five shillings per week or more as beyond the means of working-class wage earners.

[2] In fact, at this time efforts were made to check the overcrowding in tenements by legislation. The result, however, was that no further tenements were built and the existing tenements provided the only large supply of low-rent housing.

[3] From 1890 to 1900 Canadians formed 50 per cent of the total number of immigrants arriving in the port.

[4] The Jewish immigrants into Leeds in the eighties were concentrated in the Leylands district near to the city center and consequently had only a small effect on the demand for suburban houses.

Streetcar suburbs in Boston and Leeds

[5] In 1919 the state of Massachusetts organized the street railways of the Boston District as a Metropolitan Agency.

[6] A back-to-back terrace was one in which dwellings extended only halfway through the terrace and consequently different dwellings fronted onto the two streets enclosing the row of houses.

PART V

Citizenship and Welfare

(a) Woman Suffrage in Britain and America in the Early Twentieth Century

DAVID MORGAN

> We who have come down from the last generation are reformers, but reformers are poor politicians
> (Carrie Chapman Catt, December 1916)

> What a ridiculous tragedy it would be if this strong Government and Party . . . was to go down on Petticoat Politics
> (Winston Churchill, December 1911)

Women first voted in a British parliamentary election in December 1918. By ensuring in America a Republican-led 66th Congress the mid-term elections a month earlier had made it almost certain that women would vote in the presidential election in 1920. Elsewhere women were enfranchized at this period only in revolutionary conditions in Soviet Russia and defeated, newly republican Germany. Victorious France and Italy did not participate in this flood of the feminist tide; both were free of the Marxist necessities of Russia and the German desire to emulate the victors: neither had had strong suffrage movements. Only in Britain and America had there been a long political campaign and large scale organizations, the leaders of which were the acknowledged pace setters of world wide political feminism.'

The general outline of the rise of feminism in these two leading countries has been the object of several studies. The final, climactic years when the question was before Congress and Parliament are now more clearly understood. It may, therefore, be possible to attempt a more systematic comparison of elements of the final campaign than has hitherto been possible. It is acknowledged, of course, that such comparison between significantly different societies, economies and policies is fraught with difficulties. The patterns of mass and elite expectation contrasted considerably in the nineteenth century and, indeed, continued to do so after

---

H. C. Allen and R. Thompson (eds.), *Contrast and Connection: Bicentennial Essays in Anglo-American History*, London, Bell, 1976; pp. 272–95.

1900. Yet it was in the early twentieth century that Britain converged more quickly with America in the granting of political rights at the same time as both countries took important steps in the direction of ameliorating gross inequalities in the distribution of political, social and economic resources. In terms of Louis Hartz's analysis.[1] Woman Suffrage was granted in both countries precisely at the time when the 'fragment' society returned to 'confront' the parent society and culture. It was granted at a time, moreover, when the political preoccupations of both societies were becoming more similar. Most particularly, it was granted when both countries were deeply involved in a war which forced them, formally at least, to deepen and clarify their attachment to participatory and egalitarian norms. Despite their differences both societies showed similarities in the range and speed of their responses to feminist demands. Suffragists, in both countries, could not fail to notice the similarities in the values lying behind the different political façades. Comparison, then, may be a more valid exercise in this period than in the nineteenth century.

It is already possible to regard the woman suffrage campaigns as the first *feminist* revolution. Revolution in the sense that a significant, if not fundamental, redistribution of power between the sexes took place; first in that we are now in the middle of a second feminist revolutionary impulse which might well be more thoroughgoing in its effects than the first. The second revolution like the first will need, eventually, further legislation and regulation, that is, its outcome will be political actions directly involving the state. Thus, while the Suffrage campaign may be intrinsically interesting to study, it may also be of some interest to examine how such legislation in the past impacted on the political system and how it was moulded by it. In the first revolution the lead was clearly taken by feminists in the United States and Britain and, thus far, the second revolution seems likely to be similarly characterized. In neither country has the political system changed in most critical respects. There may, then, be clues from the Suffrage campaign as to the interaction of Women's Liberation and the political systems in the two countries. More of that later, however.

Feminism came out of eighteenth-century philosophical radicalism, was embodied in nineteenth-century liberalism, and carried to its first major victory by early twentieth-century 'Progressivism'. Britain provided the leading spokeswomen in the first phase, and the most 'militant' activists in the third phase.[2] America had the first real national organization, could show the most widespread and sustained political activity in the second phase, and closely paralleled the British campaign in the third phase.

Feminist ideas spread most widely when feminism and feminists were seen as part of larger causes. Thus, despite the powerful intellectual case made by Mary Wollstonecraft in the 1790s, feminism had to wait a further half century before an organization was created among American women who had come to see feminism as significant, if not vital, to their other causes. Similarly, in England an organization for women's rights came out of the mobilization of radicals and liberals for, *inter alia*, the Reform Act of 1867. In both countries the movements split in the 1870s as the reformist tide ebbed, and reformers, women included, had to establish their priorities. In America, the ostensible cause was the refusal of Radical Republicans to include women in the *post bellum* settlement. The movement there split, and the dabbling of some Eastern feminists in more general revolutionary ideas tailed off. Feminism, thereafter, took on a more Western, homogeneously American, conservative hue. Hence in the 1890s many Populists were sceptical of feminism and refused to endorse it. Not until the movement began to attract women who were 'Progressive' did it advance steadily in the West and then, later, in the East. In general, feminism came to be attractive to the 'clean government' school of thought, the Americanizers of immigrants, the declared enemies of corrupt boss-ridden city politics. Women Suffrage, like Prohibition, *could* be portrayed as part of a backlash, a last attempt of native Americans to retain their control over American politics and life. But, along with measures allowing voters the Initiative, the Referendum, Primaries, the Recall and the Short Ballot, Woman Suffrage could, by Suffragists and 'Progressives', be set in the context of attempts to refurbish American democracy. For this growing school, only by breaking the grip of party organization could the allegedly flagging faith of voters in their political competence be restored. Thus, while the 1890s gave the feminist cause only two states, Colorado 1893 and Idaho 1896, to add to their former territories Wyoming and Utah, the short period from 1910 to 1912 saw the cause triumph in Washington in 1910, California 1911, Arizona, Kansas and Oregon in 1912. Together, this meant that the women of nine states and a territory (Alaska) voted by the time Woodrow Wilson took office, a significant number in the very section where the party battle was at its keenest precisely because it was becoming the area whose choice was decisive in national elections.

The subsequent campaign may, briefly, be outlined. Wilson's inauguration marked a resurgence of Suffragist interest in pressing for a Constitutional amendment prohibiting state sex discrimination in setting franchise qualifications. This in turn helped split the National American Woman Suffrage Association (N.A.W.S.A.) leading in 1913 to the expulsion of the Pankhurst disciple Alice Paul and her followers and the creation of the Southern States Woman Suffrage Conference which was hostile to the proposed amendment. In 1914, after the Democrats in caucus had declared Woman Suffrage to be a state matter, and only two out of seven state referenda—Montana and Nevada—had succeeded, the N.A.W.S.A. embraced a state-orientated policy symbolized by the proposed Shafroth—Palmer Constitutional amendment. This overcame the problem of securing Suffrage referenda in the states by allowing referenda upon petition of only 8 per cent of the votes cast at the last presidential election. This position was, in effect, endorsed by both parties right up to August 1916 when the Republican presidential candidate, Charles E. Hughes, came out for the original Susan B. Anthony amendment which positively prohibited state discrimination and gave Congress power to enforce the prohibition. One month later the N.A.W.S.A. changed both its officers and its policy and, until 1920, conducted an enormous campaign aimed at securing state victories for the express purpose of enacting the Susan B. Anthony amendment.

Until 1916 Woodrow Wilson had refused to involve himself in the campaign. From his re-election onward, nevertheless, he became steadily entangled. Not, however, until the United States was at war could he be persuaded to press Congress to allow a vote on the amendment, only to find that his own party was principally to blame for the failure to secure the two-thirds vote in the Senate of the Sixty-fifth Congress. In the November 1918 elections the Republicans became the majority party and hence the amendment passed Congress quickly in the summer of 1919. The ratification campaign was successful in just over a year and Tenessee, the thirty-sixth state, ratified in time to allow both presidential candidates to appeal to the new women voters in time for the November 1920 presidential election. In both the Congressional and ratification campaigns the sectional characteristics of Southern hostility and Western enthusiasm were very clear.

In Britain the nineteenth century saw the franchise extended to men on an instalment basis and, after 1867, to women for local elections if they were qualified, but unmarried or widowed. By 1904 this process of enfranchisement was complete for local government and marriage had long ceased to be a bar. But anomalies and inequities abounded and Liberals, particularly, gave vent to considerable concern. Suffragists, chiefly organized in the National Union of Women's Suffrage Societies (N.U.W.S.S.) had strong reason to hope that the next government would be Liberal and would have to face up to franchise reform quickly. In that process they could hope to persuade or coerce a Liberal government into granting Woman Suffrage. The appearance after 1906 of a *Labour* wing of the Liberal party merely increased these expectations.

The Liberal party at large, however, had other priorities and the clash between the two opposed sets of expectations was the stuff of the violent campaign that followed the Liberals taking office. The party was moving steadily away from the old Gladstonian mould—a half of those elected in the huge majority of 1906 were in Parliament for the first time. Neither the old guard nor the new men put Woman Suffrage anywhere but low on their list of priorities and to this the Liberal—Labour members assented. Campbell-Bannerman, the Prime Minister, though generally sympathetic—as seven-eighths of Liberal M.P.s were—knew that the party was preoccupied with other questions and would not agree easily on a bill. In 1908 on his retirement he was replaced by H. H. Asquith whose strong opposition was intensified by the kind of campaign waged against his government. By 1909 the government had authorized the forcible feeding in prison of Pankhurst 'Suffragettes'—organized in the Women's Social and Political Union (W.S.P.U.).

Only after the Parliament Act of 1911 was on the statute book was there any possibility of Woman Suffrage, and then only a slight one. The government's proposed Franchise Bill—which supposedly could take a Suffrage amendment—added to the growing stress being felt inside the government. The debacle of January 1913 when the Speaker forced the withdrawal of the bill, the subsequent 'Suffragette' fury, the 'Cat and Mouse Act' and a general stalemate on the question were the results. Not until the war broke up this impasse was any advance possible. The question of votes for soldiers brought up general franchise reform and, in turn, Woman Suffrage. The replacement of Asquith by Lloyd George at the head of a broad coalition government created the bipartisan situation in which, *inter alia*, a Suffrage solution was possible. In the event the actual bill went through its stages speedily and women over thirty years of age were enfranchised before the Armistice gave them the chance to vote in their first parliamentary election.

So much for the familiar outlines of the campaigns. What now may be said by way of comparison both of the operations of the political systems, and of the Suffragists? First, it is clear that reactions of political leaders to the issue in both countries were more conditioned by constitutional and party political considerations than they were by considerations of justice, or even the needs of women. More will be said later of Wilson and Asquith personally on this question, but it is idle to see the reactions of either out of the context of, for example, the ramifications of the question of the Lords for Asquith, or the South for Wilson. These and other inhibitions were direct products of the constitutional situations and need elucidating.

In Britain the unitary constitution meant that women must be given the parliamentary vote all over the Kingdom, or not at all. In America, under a federal system, Western states might grant full Suffrage but, at first, this meant little in the East or South. In Britain where, after 1906, the Liberals controlled the Commons and the Unionists the Lords, any government Suffrage Bill stood to be rejected by the Lords, given the political context. In America the actions of the federal government were conditioned, constitutionally, by state control of franchise qualifications and, politically, by the special tie between that and the racial question in the South. The eleven former Confederate States, if they opposed solidly, would need only two allies to prevent the ratification of an amendment to the Constitution. The task of securing two-thirds majorities in Congress, and thirty-six ratifications was a huge test of political organization and pressure even without any concerted sectional opposition.

In Britain, the failure to settle the Irish question before 1906 meant that there was something of a British equivalent of the American sectional vote. After 1910 this was of great significance since it fostered the myth among Unionists that the absence of an *English* majority behind the Liberals plus the 1911 curb of the Lords, put the constitution in abeyance and left them free to oppose government measures by virtually—as the Curragh seemed to prove—all means. Again, the American Constitution fixed the timing of elections and this contributed directly to the frustrating of some of Wilson's legislative intentions after 1916. Thus Woman Suffrage may be regarded as a failure for Wilson in the last days of the Sixty-fifth Congress. On the other hand, in Britain, while the constitution gave the government the choice of election dates and issues—within limits—the Parliament Act of 1911 at once narrowed these limits from seven to five years and—via the Lords' two year delaying power—made a legislative log jam inevitable after 1912. The Suffrage position was worsened by this.

Conversely, however, the constitutional and political situations provided compensations. In America, if it was sectional fear that inhibited federal action, it was also sectional pressure in the West that kept the issue before the dominant party and ultimately secured the Nineteenth Amendment. When both parties were bidding for the control of the West, both would have to pay—eventually—part of the West's price of support. In Britain a sectional vote existed—the Irish—and this was largely hostile to Suffrage in the key period from 1911 to 1913, principally to prevent a Cabinet split and preserve the Home Rule Bill. The Cabinet system, however, provided something of a sectional equivalent to the American situation in Congress. While in America the President's cabinet was secondary, in Britain the decisive struggle lay in the Liberal Cabinet where Asquith opposed most of his principal colleagues. By 1912 the fact that Grey, Lloyd George and Haldane were ready to press Asquith very hard on the question meant that Suffrage was 'in the swim', would be before Liberals and the country at the next election, and could not be ignored by Asquith thereafter. The pressure of powerful friends in the Cabinet made up—to an extent—for the fact that, lacking a federal system, British women voted nowhere in parliamentary elections and lacked the leverage of *voters*.

The power of a Prime Minister was great, especially when rivals and not he were hurt by scandal, but it was not overwhelming and Asquith could not have stood indefinitely against a majority of his Cabinet and party. It is interesting to note that, assuming there had been no war, an Irish settlement, and a Liberal victory in 1914 or 1915, Asquith would have had to be 'converted' to Suffrage by 1916, anyway, in order to ensure that— under the Parliament Act— the issue would be ready for an election in 1918 or 1919.

Suffrage could not be made a party issue in either country. A large majority of the Liberals were for it, but until 1911 the Lords would have certainly rejected a Liberal measure. Thereafter, parliamentary time and the sheer weight of legislation told heavily against Suffrage when added to the fears of a Cabinet split held among Irish Nationalists and the Liberals. In America the Democrats controlled the Presidency throughout, and Congress until 1919, but they alone could not provide the two-thirds vote required for an amendment. Both parties had large programmes and resented the forcing of Suffrage on them by a militant direct action policy. Mrs Pankhurst first appeared to Liberals as something of a Labor ginger group and then, later as a Unionist Trojan Horse. Democrats from South and North could rightly regard Suffragists as more a Republican than a Democratic phenomenon. For both parties the issue became a danger when re-election had to be considered. For Liberals this period was around 1912–13 when—because of the Parliament Act—the 1914 or 1915 manifesto had to be envisaged. For Democrats it was during 1916 when Wilson realized that the price of Western support in November entailed some gesture towards Suffrage. The declarations of Roosevelt and Charles Evans Hughes only made the point more explicit. In 1912 Asquith's government could plead the problem of time, while in 1916 Wilson could plead the South. Neither plea had indefinite validity.

For parties and politicians the war was the catalyst forcing conversions to Suffrage, and giving both a way to save face. In Britain, with the Irish question in abeyance, the war issue of 'votes for soldiers' carried Suffrage explosively back into the political swim and, by helping, cost Asquith his position, put an active Suffragist in office as Prime Minister of a coalition government; producing, in short, the conditions most likely to produce a successful conclusion to the campaign.

In America the impact of the war strengthened the President's hand in relation to Congress in general, and his own party in particular. It also weakened the capacity of Anti-Suffragists of all shades and, as in Britain, highlighted the role and status of women war workers. In both countries the extension of political, social and economic democracy became part of the rhetoric of politicians concerned to boost morale and prepare for post-war reconstruction. It is well to note, nevertheless, that in both countries the war would not have been the catalyst it was had there not been the large-scale campaigns of pre-war days. Suffrage was at the edge of the pre-war spectrum of practical politics—the war hastened its move towards the centre. In that process both Irish and Southern objections were disregarded, the Irish having an immediate political price to pay in the destruction of the Nationalists. An irony of the 1918 election in Britain in consequence was that the only woman elected—the Countess Markievicz—could not take her seat, not because she was a woman, but because she was a Sinn Feiner.

On Suffrage the constitutional and party political systems pivoted importantly around the President and Prime Minister, certainly after 1916. The attitudes of both were of great importance. Asquith made no secret of his hostility, while Wilson only very slowly moved to further Suffrage and was never an ardent champion. Asquith was converted too late to be in charge of the Suffrage Bill, but did include the issue in the Speaker's Conference after he had declared for it. Wilson bowed to the South in 1916, but not thereafter and paid the price in his own failure and that of his party in the Sixty-fifth Congress. Subsequently he did his best to repair the damage both in Congress and during the ratification process. In Britain, after the departure of Asquith, Lloyd George had no real difficulty in securing Suffrage via the speedy passage of the Representation of the People Act. Both Asquith and Wilson had fond memories of essentially non-political first wives and lived with second wives who enjoyed their voteless state when it went along with power and influence. Both resented militancy—Asquith with his 'want of imagination' concluding militants to be criminal and unbalanced, while Wilson saw their activities as a direct slur upon his good intentions. Had Asquith swung over in 1912—and insisted on Irish support—it is likely that the Reform Bill could have gone under the Parliament Act and have been ready for implementation in 1914—unless the Lords passed it in an attempt to force an earlier election.[3] Likewise had Wilson been more vigorous in 1916 he might have prevented the solidifying of the Southern position. By being so fearful he allowed racists and 'Wets' to make the running and thus hurt the Democrats in 1918, and even in 1920. Fear and lack of vision in 1916 forced him to work very hard thereafter merely to avoid further damage.

The two cases were not really contemporary. The Americans had before them the example of what could happen should frustration among women boil over into Pankhurst militancy and by 1917 this was beginning to happen. Neither Wilson nor the run of politicians in Congress and the states were ready to accept this—and refused to believe that what had occurred in pre-war Britain simply could not happen in America. In addition to fear, emulation and rivalry had a place. The success of the movement during 1917 was a precedent that Americans might follow. There was a traditional rivalry with monarchical Britain and the fact that the constitutional monarchy stood to look more 'democratic' was an incentive to action in wartime America both among Suffragists and politicians who were unimpressed by Australasian, Scandinavian and even their own Western precedents. This was especially true when, in November 1917, the New York state referendum on Suffrage was carried by the Suffragists—just as the Commons was sending the Representation of the People Bill to the Lords. The New York victory was a turning point for Wilson who swung his influence immediately in favour of a successful House vote. America could hardly lag behind when Britain was preparing to admit that votes for women was necessary for victory and reconstruction.

The British victory was, then, of some importance coming when it did. The militancy of the Pankhursts and Alice Paul had shaken American politicians and Suffragists alike—the success of the British movement reassured the politicians and strengthened the Suffrage cause in America.

A noticeable difference between the campaigns was, of course, the overt political machinations of certain business interests in America. Both the liquor and textile industries opposed Suffrage because each felt directly threatened by a female vote which was presumed to be 'moral' in its outlook. It seems clear, nevertheless, that in Congress when the two industries were counter-attacked in force, they were only successful where their cause coalesced with a more strictly political opposition, namely Southern fears of the Negro. British Suffragists were less joined in the public mind with the image of a specifically moral, crusading temperance vote. Mrs Pankhurst, especially, drove home the notion that Suffragists were, overwhelmingly, people who sought the vote as a right. In America corrupt politics and business saw its enemy in the vengeful native American matron, certainly in 1916 when there was less likelihood of a successful Socialist party. The parties there were more vulnerable to dedicated groups of strategically placed voters. In Britain a Labour party existed and was growing. It, rather than militant women, was cast in the role of nemesis.

Finally, among the political factors, it is worth noting the similarities between the two dominant parties which faced the demand for Suffrage. Both had become more sectionally based and both were at the time facing a backlog of demands for measures of adjustment and compensation for sectional inequalities. They shared a distaste for big business, war and overseas commitments, though both had wings favouring the latter. Within their areas of strength they were 'town and country' parties—outside them they were seeking to be the parties of the lower classes of the growing cities. They were more loosely organized than their opponents and this meant that a question like Suffrage which at first lacked a powerful sectional thrust, or faced a sectional veto, stood little chance of becoming party policy. Both parties had staunch Protestants and Catholics in their ranks—both groups cool or hostile to female emancipation. Both had to face the violent opposition of opponents who had come to see governing as their prerogative and who were not favourably inclined to Suffrage. Both had strong factions who had seized the ground of 'reformism' and resented the fact that their party's treatment of the Suffrage question seemed to make them less 'reformers' than sectional, social, economic 'outs on the make'. It is only fair, then, to add that this was more apparent than real. The two parties were coerced and cajoled into overcoming their sectional prejudices, and it is very doubtful if either opposing party would have acted more quickly or easily in power. Democrats and Liberals alike were much preoccupied with other questions and it is of great importance to realize that Suffrage impinged unfavourably on two very important sources of preoccupation, namely the Irish question for Liberals, and the race question for Southerners.

The Suffragists themselves have been written up more than the politicians they sought to influence. Even so, there are still comparisons and contrasts which can be usefully made in face of the changing political situations the Suffragists dealt with. Again, the connections between the British and American movements after 1905 are worth some clarification.

There are some immediately obvious similarities in the movements. By 1905 both had a history of more than fifty years, both had survived major splits, and both had seen the first generation of leaders give way to younger, more organizationally minded leaders. Both movements were weak in popular support but both entertained high expectations, the British especially. In Britain the rise of the Labour party encouraged some of the older leaders to believe that future gain lay in working for its success, and using its rise to force the other parties to act. Likewise, in America the faith of many Suffragists was put in the Progressive movements of the West and the urban reformers of the Eastern cities.

The time lag in the incidence of militancy is, equally, an obvious contrast. Almost twelve years separated the beginning of American from British militancy—and even then it was initiated by conscious disciples of the Pankhursts. This contrast is somewhat lessened, however, by the fact that militancy *did* occur in 'America at that moment when, to Suffragists at least, the political context was as promising for them as it had been in England in 1906. Both groups seized their main chance—the Americans twelve years after the British.

The appearance of militant, competing organizations had somewhat comparable effects on both parent movements. In America, after 1913, Alice Paul speeded up the process by which the old movement abandoned its Southern incubus, and proclaimed itself ready to use Western women voters to coerce Northern and Border Democrats and Republicans alike. Likewise, in the same year that Alice Paul appeared on the national scene in America, the older British movement opened negotiations with the Labour party thus signalling its disillusionment with the Liberal party. One movement abandoned a section, the other embraced a party—or so it seemed.

Two features of this change of political alliances may be compared. First, the change for both was largely a matter of legislative tactics and not of ideology. Accepting new allies in the campaign for the vote did not involve any commitment to the political programme of those allies. Thus, when the position in the legislature changed, there was nothing to prevent a return to former allies. Therefore, the American movement by 1919 was ready to gain any Southern support it could get by ignoring Southern women if they were black. Equally, the British movement was quite prepared to ignore the Labour party—as a party—once Lloyd George was Prime Minister and ready to enact its demands in 1917.

Secondly, both leaderships worked very hard to resist the logic inherent in the militant position. The Conciliation Bills of 1910–12 in England and the Shafroth—Palmer amendment of 1914 in the United States were both efforts to obtain Suffrage via a consensus of parties unable, and unwilling, to make the issue a party one. Both moves traded on the influence and power possessed by the older movements within high political circles. In America Mark Hanna's daughter, the Republican Mrs Medill McCormick, and the Tory Lord Lytton in Britain—the respective agents—were both the victims and proponents of the delusion that there must and could only be a bipartisan solution. Formally, at least, they appeared to have been proved correct—both measures were enacted in bipartisan votes. In Britain, however, the old party lines had been transformed into those for and against the Lloyd George government while, in America, the Republicans took care not to provide the necessary votes in the Senate and during Ratification until Democrats had been seen resisting their leader and President in the Sixty-fifth Congress. Woman Suffrage was put through by those in the Executive in Britain and out of it in America. In neither case was its intrinsic factors and qualities of greater importance than the political gain seen in it by its chief sponsors. Women were being recruited by parties rather than accorded 'justice' as such. The component of expediency can be overstressed but, seen from the perspective of party leaderships, it appears to have been the dominant motif.

So much for the movements in general in the final period of their history. Some valid comparisons may also be made of the leaders produced after 1905. First, the two non-militant leaders—Mrs Millicent Fawcett of the N.U.W.S.S. and Mrs Carrie Catt of the N.A.W.S.A. Both were widows and both, by the standards of their societies, were upper-middle class and of independent means. Both had served long apprenticeships in the movement and appeared at its head at about the same time. Both were internationally minded and both retained this outlook through and after the war. As leaders, both were single-minded in the pursuit of the vote and refused to allow other gestures to entangle their campaigns. Hence both resisted their pacifist wings after 1914, and urged war service as a duty which properly used could provide the desired reward. Both, nevertheless, saw the vote as more than a symbol of status, and neither had much of the bitterness towards men apparent among many of their militant co-Suffragists.

Both leaders resisted militancy though conceding that it made political sense at least in the early period from 1906 to 1908 in Britain and early 1917 in America. Both acted decisively when it was clear—by 1912 in Britain and 1915 in America—that persuasion of politicians must give way to party coercion. Both cultivated those who had access to leading politicians—for example Mrs Helen Gardener in America, a friend of Wilson's and the influential and well connected Ladies Frances and Betty Balfour in Britain—and, while retaining their independence, tried hard to accommodate politicians who were genuinely trying to promote Suffrage.

Mrs Catt and Mrs Fawcett may be justly accused of not giving enough attention to the conversion of male voters who stood behind the male politicians they worked so hard to convert. Yet Mrs Catt in her distance from immigrant males and Mrs Fawcett in hers from working-class men were hardly alone among their social kind. The American middle classes were in this period reacting sharply against the immigrant vote, while their British counterparts could still view Labour M.P.s as a wing of the Liberal party. Formally, at least, so far as the working classes were concerned their chief organizations were in favour of Suffrage. If Suffragists seemed to concentrate too much on the middle-class voters this was surely because they realized that these needed converting and were—because of their education—accessible to the printed and spoken word. To expect that Suffragists should have foreseen the power of organized labour is to ignore the fact that this was not obvious before 1905 when the basic Suffrage strategies were laid down in both countries. Moreover, it is to ignore the fact that, as ardent feminists, both women saw the political advent of voting women as of greater importance than any conceivable Labour faction or political party.

Mrs Catt, unlike Mrs Fawcett, set up in the League of Women Voters, an organization designed specifically to press for feminist objectives using the newly enfranchised voters. That it largely failed, as did both leaders' pleas for women to become active in political parties, may hardly be said to be entirely the fault of the two Suffragist leaders. Both, until their deaths, strove to lead their erstwhile followers in the cause of sex equality and opportunity and also to urge them to participate in the quest for international harmony.

In their dealings with both governments and legislatures both women were sanely realistic. Wilson, Mrs Catt understood, had to overcome the hesitation of the very Southerners he needed for the rest of his programme. Asquith, as Mrs Fawcett saw, had some cause for asserting that after 1911 the Liberal burden was heavy enough until the Home Rule and Welsh Church Bills were safely out of the way. Both women realized that party leaders were busy men who were personally affronted by militant unlady-like behaviour and politically affronted by tactics which smacked of outright blackmail. More importantly they realized that such men had legitimate party concerns. Might there not be a higher Republican than Democrat turnout among women voters? Likewise in England would not Tory women be more likely to vote, and could a Liberal government really believe that a limited property-based extension of the franchise would not favour Tories? In disowning militancy, Mrs Fawcett after 1909 and Mrs

Catt after 1917 performed the negative function of pressing their cause and the positive one of offering inducements to politicians who would join it.

The militants by comparison performed a complementary function, namely that, however much detested by politicians, their activities made too spectacular a subject for both hostile and friendly newspapers to ignore and thus kept the movement in daily contact with the public. Non-militants made friends, militants made news—both were needed. Woman Suffrage was an issue which, since they could not adopt, parties would prefer to ignore. It had to have the means of gaining publicity, and that frequently. Soothing ruffled politicians became a routine task which non-militants were well placed to carry out. This task, anyway, was easier for them than the one which would have faced them had there been no militancy, namely that of preventing Suffrage from being ignored through the fears, uncertainties and sheer preoccupations of politicians.

Newsworthiness, however, had its limitations. The militants in both countries found themselves misreported and misrepresented. More, they found themselves tempted constantly to change their tactics in order to keep their publicity. They had, again, the parallel task of controlling the increasingly desperate element recruited by the chance of personal publicity and possible martyrdom. Hence picketing and heckling gave way to attacks on property and this, in turn, to assaults on politicians and threats of worse. In Britain the cycle of militancy—repression—more militancy was fully developed by 1912. The separation of Mr and Mrs Pethick-Lawrence from the Pankhursts meant that there was no check on where Christabel Pankhurst was leading, or not leading, the movement. In America victory came before the pattern included major assaults on property and persons. It is almost certain that there would have been a similar development—Christabel could after all be distracted by the war; Alice Paul was not so distracted in April 1917 and the fury and exasperation engendered in wartime America was as great as anything seen in pre-war Britain.

On balance, however, no accusation that militancy retarded Suffrage will stand. As was noted, the only real chance in Britain of success before 1914 was marred more by Asquith's personal opposition, Lloyd George's political weakness, and the action of the Speaker than by Mrs Pankhurst. Likewise the Negro problem and the Prohibition campaign slowed Suffrage more than did Alice Paul and her activities. Politicians who claimed to be alienated by both would have overlooked much had political considerations allowed or forced them to do so, Southern gentlemen notwithstanding.

The formal leader of the Women's Social and Political Union was Mrs Pankhurst, but the real moving spirit became her daughter Christabel, and it is she who must be compared with Alice Paul. While Christabel was a fluent, forceful platform speaker, the charisma of both was seen more in committee than on the platform. Both acquired an impressive personal following and were quite ready to use this to overawe any opposition in their organizations. Christabel Pankhurst, the more overtly autocratic, felt sure enough of her position virtually to expel both the Pethick-Lawrences and her own sister Sylvia, all the while running the organization from Paris. Both women shared the conviction that the weakness of the Suffrage movement, and the hostility of politicans alike, testified to the need for new tactics. The readiness of the press to report their activities was, they realized, of far greater significance than condemnatory editorials and biased reporting.

Militant tactics in 1906 may have stemmed directly from the personal frustrations of the Pankhursts, but they were continued and later used in America because they were seen as the only way of securing publicity and forcing action on the Suffrage question. Both women realized that militancy had a certain boomerang effect, but they judged this to be less politically important than continuous publicity, and might be allowed for when the reasons for opposition to Suffrage had been exposed and neutralized. The superpatriotism of the Pankhursts during the war, and the absence of militancy during the American Ratification campaign were in part such allowances. Both may be seen as gestures towards politicians then in process of conversion or actively bent on helping Suffrage.

The career of Alice Paul is the most significant example of the interaction between the British and American movements. Arriving in Britain in 1908 as a student at the Quaker Woodbrooke Settlement School in Birmingham, she departed two years later as a fully-blown Pankhurst militant with imprisonments and forcible feedings to her credit. Arriving as a young American Quaker and social worker convinced of the need for Suffrage as a right and a social necessity, she left having been fully exposed to the charisma of the Pankhursts and their non-Quaker methods of political agitation. Arriving a believer that men as voters and politicians were indifferent, she left having seen how a dedicated group, ready to accept imprisonment and personal indignities, might seize national publicity and convert male amazement and hostility into passive or even active support.

The Pankhurst policy of continuous opposition to the party in power, to Alice Paul, made political sense in England since that party, if converted, could put the issue through the legislature. The policy was modelled on the Irish Nationalist tactics which Mrs Pankhurst believed her husband had been an electoral victim of in the 1886 election. The British system of *party* government encouraged groups and small parties to believe that within a party in power the way to coerce factions—even leaderships—hostile to their aims, was to set against such groups their own party colleagues whose policy proposals—related or not—were actually or potentially in jeopardy because of external or internal opposition or instability. The Irish had used this 'across the board' opposition successfully. The Pankhursts, in short, set out after 1906 to push Liberal ministers into conflict with their backbenchers.

After 1912 Alice Paul was accused of blindly trying to follow this tactic in the different constitutional setting of America where there was a separation of powers, and where no one party had ever secured two-thirds of the seats of both Houses; where in fact a bipartisan policy seemed the *sine qua non* of success. Politically, however, the policy had some justification. So long as both American parties competed for the allegiance of the West, so would they have to be sensitive to the demands of that section. This necessary sensitivity was their Achilles heel to Alice Paul for, after 1912, in the West many women voted. In Britain, opposing the party in power after 1906 meant asking Liberal *husbands* and *brothers* to abstain or vote Conservative. In America, the policy meant asking Western *women* to vote Republican in 1916 and 1918—and this at a time when Wilson was a minority President needing the West for re-election. The possession of the vote by women of the section which decided elections was the crucial element making for success once it was exploited.

As states granted the presidential vote after 1913, Mrs Catt herself was quite ready to use this increasing weight in Washington. She did not, however, go among Western voters and ask them to coerce Democrats. It was left to the Pankhurst-trained Alice Paul to show her that politicians had to be as sensitive to hostility as to co-operation. Western Democratic politicians were grateful to Mrs Catt, but they feared Alice Paul and their fear was as potent a political force as their gratitude.

Much of Alice Paul's success stemmed from the fact that she was well backed from the beginning of her rebellion against the National American Woman Suffrage Association. Prominent among her backers was the imperious Mrs O. H. P. Belmont. She provides an example of an American contribution to British success, since it was she who had helped support Christabel Pankhurst during her exile in Paris in 1912. In Alice Paul she clearly saw an American version of Christabel and backed her forcibly despite her own close connections with the parent organization. Mrs Belmont thus played the American equivalent of the Pethick-Lawrence role in the Pankhurst organization, namely that of the wealthy, well-connected, zealous backer. She was familiar with the Pankhurst organization and not merely via press reports—a familiarity which may be put down as a further British contribution to success in America. For this to be understood it is necessary to turn to the background of the Suffrage victory in New York State in 1917, to the work of Elizabeth Cady Stanton's daughter, Harriet Stanton Blatch.

Mrs Blatch lived in England from 1882 to 1902, met Mrs Pankhurst in the circle of Jacob and Ursula Bright, and participated in the work of the Equal Franchise Committee after it split off from the parent organization in 1889. In addition, she was active in the Women's Liberal Federation, became a

Fabian, and was a friend of the Peases and the Webbs. On her return she immediately moved into women's trade union circles in New York, and by February 1907 was appearing at Albany as a labour spokeswoman. In December 1907 she sponsored a visit from the militant daughter of Richard Cobden, Mrs Cobden-Sanderson, and in October 1909, from Mrs Pankhurst herself. Eight months later she organized the first Suffrage parade and, helped by Mrs O. H. P. Belmont and Mrs Mary Beard, she launched the Women's Political Union. Unlike the Pankhursts, seven years earlier, she did not insert 'Social' into the title in order to attract those fearful of its trade union overtones.

Mrs Blatch continued to organize Suffrage parades and, in 1912, took agitation a step further when she set up silent pickets outside the New York State legislature when it debated a Suffrage proposal. In this same year Mrs Blatch introduced Alice Paul to Jane Addams and helped Miss Paul to gain the Chairmanship of the Congressional Committee of the National American Woman Suffrage Association.

From this position Miss Paul went on to an independent and larger status—and a policy of attacking Democrats. This may have been second nature to a Philadelphian, but Mrs Blatch had made Democrats her allies against upstate Republicans and had secured, in 1912, a promise from 'Commissioner' Murphy of Tammany to allow a Woman Suffrage amendment to the state constitution to come to a referendum. National political necessity, as seen by Miss Paul, dictated threatening Democrats. Murphy, happily, resolved the dilemma by ordering the defeat of all amendments including Suffrage in the referendum of 1914. Mrs Blatch merged her organization with that of Alice Paul in January 1916, though she kept up her personal contact with Tammany. By 1917, when New York State again voted on Suffrage, Tammany saw fit to stay neutral and this allowed a New York majority to swing the whole state, crack open the reluctant East and lead directly to the successful January 1918 vote in the House of Representatives.

Mrs Blatch was a minor figure in the national Suffrage picture but, in several respects, she was important. She had pioneered both the Suffrage parade and Suffrage picket—both used heavily by Alice Paul. In 1912, when she still had influence in the National Association, she helped Alice Paul to become its Congressional Chairman and stimulated Mrs Belmont to take an interest in the new beginning being made in Washington by a disciple of Mrs Pankhurst. Being the daughter of Elizabeth Cady Stanton gave her a certain standing with the press and she capitalized on all of this, when, on 5 October 1916 after Hughes had been 'converted', she revealed Wilson's reasons for refusing to follow as being concerned essentially with the Negro question in the South.

Mrs Blatch can hardly be described as a Pankhurst disciple. Rather, both had shared in the same educational experience at the hands of the Brights, the Fabians and later in the women's trade unions. Mrs Blatch herself, however, remained more as she had begun—the war did not make her bellicose and the peace found her still a socialist. In her role in the Suffrage movement she bore a close resemblance to her old friend and former colleague, Mrs Pankhurst. Both were politically sophisticated widows who, from a sense of frustration in Suffrage organizations, formed separate groups, pioneered new methods of agitation and then saw their movements pass into younger hands. Though Mrs Blatch, unlike Mrs Pankhurst, did not gain a national or international reputation, she yet deserves a mention as a significant figure in the Anglo-American aspects of the Suffrage movement.

The Woman Suffrage campaign lasted seventy-two years in America and fifty-one years in Britain. On the face of it, this was a long campaign. In fact, the time lapse after the issue had come before Congress and Parliament as a serious question was relatively short—less than ten years in both cases. Partly this was because the Suffrage movement had helped create and sustain an élite and engendered some favourable sentiment in educated, middle-class circles. Much more so this was owed to the fact that the rate of economic and social change had created for this élite a mass of potential followers who might be mobilized not for Woman Suffrage or notions of justice for women but for what might be done with the support of women voters. Inevitably the prior political commitments of such people could give rise to disputes over both the principle and priority of Woman Suffrage. The Irish in England and the Southern Democrats in the United States were very visible in their opposition but there were others, too, who questioned the priority of Woman Suffrage, even among those supposed to be friendly. The delay caused by such factors outweighed any due to the opposition of Asquith, the vacillation of Wilson or the folly of some Suffragists. Woman Suffrage, then, was delayed by potential political issues. In both countries it required the political consequences of war to break the log jam of party inhibition. Yet broken it was. Legislation deemed to be of considerable social consequence was enacted notwithstanding supposedly potent objections on divine, family, industrial and short-run party political and special interest grounds.

In that process much light was cast on the two political systems. The decentralized nature of American politics, the interaction between levels and the constraints on Presidency and Congress alike were all too visible. Visible also, however, were the forces making for a degree of 'unitariness' and cohesion so that a carefully orchestrated and timed campaign at local, state and federal levels produced a fairly rapid result as opposition within parties was outflanked or eroded. The deadlock resulting in Britain with its unitary system when the leadership of the governing party was split, and the Prime Minister in particular was opposed, is in obvious contrast. Less obvious, however, was the *inability* of Asquith to prevent the erosion of his position of strength so that by 1914 he was forced to hint at change.

In this must lie grounds for hope for feminists. The political systems of both countries, which have not changed in critical respects, showed themselves responsive to sustained pressure by feminists if these could find allies in society. Grounds, too, for some concern. The price of allies was a public muzzling of questions which had been deemed vital in nineteenth-century feminism, e.g. the place of women in the family and society. To win the vote required hierarchic organizations which worked best when directed towards a simple goal—the vote—and which were not friendly environments for feminists who questioned the fundamentals of society. 'Organization women' could win the right to vote but seemed less able to infuse women with enthusiasm for making feminist use of the vote.

In retrospect it may be possible to assert that political rights, anyway, may be easier to extract than social or economic rights. The assertion of the 'emptiness' of political rights is still not, thankfully, beyond argument and would certainly have struck early twentieth-century Americans and Britons as simply not true. Suffragists, then, were certainly women of their time in their over-estimation of the impact of narrowly defined political rights and privileges but they can hardly be faulted for that. What they did do was to lay the foundations for their feminist successors, and what they did demonstrate was that their political systems were responsive to changes which, at the time, were seen as far reaching.

The Suffrage campaign must give pause to those who assert the immutability of the Anglo-American *status quo*. The political consequences of voting women are nowadays seen by feminists as minimal. It may well be that this is so because those consequences are defined in terms of the *personnel* of politics, i.e. the failure of women to 'surface' politically. If [. . .] we see the consequences in terms of party political agendas, for example in the steadily increasing emphasis on social policies, then the impact of women might be said to be considerable. Whether, of course, this is the proletarianization or modernization of politics, rather than its feminization, is a question which cannot be answered here.

NOTES

1 Louis Hartz, *The Founding of New Societies* (New York, 1964).

2 The term militant connoted principally a follower of the Pankhursts in the Women's Social and Political Union in England after 1906 and those of Alice Paul in the National Woman's Party in America after 1916. The label came to connote those who picketed, went to prison, hunger struck, etc. In both cases, as will be seen, the differences between militant and non-militant were not merely over tactics, but also over strategies for gaining and using the vote.

3 By precedent enfranchising acts were followed by legislation redistributing seats and, more, by a general election as soon as the new register of voters was ready.

(b) Social Legislation in Britain and the United States in the Early Twentieth Century

C. L. MOWAT

At the beginning of the twentieth century Britain and the United States faced similar issues in social policy. Both were large industrial countries in which more and more people were concentrated in the big cities; in both poverty in the midst of plenty was a concern to the social conscience; in both there was exploitation of working people in many industries; in both (though more in the United States) there was alarm at the unbridled power of the great agglomerations of wealth in big corporations, trusts and monopolies. In both there was a broadly similar response: the enactment of social legislation in which the power of the state was applied in the interests of greater equality and social justice. Moreover, the period of reform was more or less the same. In the United States it began with the Populists in the early nineties and merged into the Progressive movement which in part manifested itself in Theodore Roosevelt's 'New Nationalism' and Woodrow Wilson's 'New Freedom'; much of its force was spent by 1914. In Great Britain the change came more dramatically with the victory of the Liberals in 1906, but the ground for advance by way of social legislation had been prepared over the previous twenty years or more; and here the main impetus was over by 1912.

In spite of these similarities, the history of the period, or rather of social reform in this period, has usually been written in very different terms in the two countries. In the United States it appears as part of the history of ideas: the historian's task has been to describe the climate of opinion in which new social policies were advanced or enacted and the causes which helped to produce it. In Britain, by contrast, there has been little attempt to write the history of this period in the terms of the history of ideas; reform is

Historical Studies, 1969; pp. 81–96.

thought of as empirical, its origins to be found in the work of individual politicians or philanthropists or societies. Whether this reflects a certain blindness on the part of British historians or the excessive enthusiasm of a school of historians in the United States is open to question: this paper seeks only to point to the contrast and to ask whether there is need for a new approach to the domestic history of Great Britain, at least in the early twentieth century.

A long-lived and deservedly popular college textbook, Morison and Commager' *Growth of the American Republic*,[1] can serve as a starting-point. One chapter, 'The Battle of the Standards, 1890–1897,' begins with the Populists and follows with a straightforward account of political history from the election of 1892 to Bryan's defeat in 1896. A second, 'The Progressive Movement, 1890–1917,' precedes the three chapters which describe the politics and reforms of the administrations of Theodore Roosevelt and Taft and Wilson's first term. The Progressive Movement' begins with a section called 'The Promise of American Life' in which at the start the achievements of Americans over the past three generations are eulogised: 'the nation had advanced, in Jefferson's prophetic words, to "destinies beyond the reach of mortal eye".' Yet, as Wilson said in his First Inaugural, 'The evil has come with the good, and much fine gold has been corroded'. The indictment which follows is familiar: the ruin of the farmer, child labour, inadequate provision for the aged, the unequal distribution of wealth, slums, disease, crime, the exploitation of the negro, illiteracy, political corruption, 'On all sides men feared that the nation which Lincoln had called "the last best hope of earth" would prove instead the world's illusion.' But, it continues significantly, 'Americans are not prone either to exaltation or to despair. Against the crowding evils of the time there arose a full-throated protest which was neither unrealistic nor ineffective. It is this protest which gives a peculiar character to American politics and thought from approximately 1890 to World War I.' The manifestations are noticed: agrarian revolt, demand for greater regulatory powers on the part of government, concern for the poor and under-privileged, the reform of political machinery, the rejection of *laissez-faire.*

Even more interesting is the section on 'Challenges to American Democracy'. Five problems are isolated: the 'confusion of ethics' resulting from applying the individualistic code of an agrarian society to an industrialised social order; the rise of big business and the 'exploitation of social wealth for private aggrandisement'; inequalities in wealth and the growth of class divisions; the rise of the city; the breakdown of 'political honesty and administrative system'. Henry Demarest Lloyd's *Wealth against Commonwealth,* is cited alongside other works of protest such as David Graham Phillip's *Treason of the Senate,* Henry George's *Progress and poverty,* Edward Bellamy's *Looking backward,* and the writings of Thorstein Veblen. The section on 'The era of the muckrakers' fills out the list with the familiar titles: Jackob Riis's *How the other half lives*, John Spargo's *Bitter cry of the children*, Ida Tarbell's *History of the Standard Oil Company*, Steffens's *Shame of the cities*, and many others. A long section on 'Humanitarianism' treats such topics as women's rights, child labour, the care of the feeble-minded, the movement for prohibition; and a final section on 'Progressivism in politics' discusses leaders and achievements in outline.

The specialist literature on which this chapter rests is extensive, as one can see from a glance at George Mowry's pamphlet, *The Progressive Movement 1900–1920: recent ideas and new literature*. One thinks, for instance, of Louis Filler's *Crusaders for American Liberalism: the story of the muckrakers*, Arthur Mann's *Yankee reformers in the urban age* (1954), and Russel B. Nye's *Midwestern Progressive politics: A historical study of its origins and development, 1879–1950* (1951), to name only three. It would be wrong, however, to concentrate on this literature, which would be to miss the real point.

American history has seldom been written, perhaps cannot be written, as 'straight history', setting out the facts 'as they really were'. The American historian is a committed man: committed to history as building and embodying the nation's traditions, indeed the American nation itself, and often committed also to assumptions and interpretations in this same history which will reflect and forward a particular school of thought or direction of policy. As a rule, the assumptions and interpretations are 'liberal' in the American sense; for liberals (as for those who are not liberals) America is 'the last, best hope of earth' but only if its imperfections are revealed and purged. History becomes an act of faith, faith in progress in spite of man's wilfulness: V. L. Parrington's *Main currents in American thought*, and Charles and Mary Beard's *Rise of American civilisation* stand in this tradition. Rather the same point has been made by implication in a recent article by J. R. Pole under the title 'The American past: is it still usable?'[2] Pole believes that present-day American historians are less affected by 'presentism' (could one call it the sense of commitment to the nation?), and more ready to study the American past on its own terms. Thus to him Daniel J. Boorstin's *The Americans: the colonial experience*, and the *National experience*—two exciting volumes in a still unfinished series which has not yet reached the Progressive Era—represent a return to the older tradition, rather in the school of Frederick J. Turner. Certainly Boorstin's highly individual and often original scrutiny of the American past tends to discount the influence of ideas in favour of the forces of the material environment; he is to some extent reading present-day America into its past.

Whether 'committed' or uncommitted, many American historians have certainly studied their national history as the history of ideas. It is no accident that the volume in the well-known and significantly named

'American Life' series devoted to the Progressive Era, that by H. U. Faulkner, is entitled *The quest for social justice.* Three fairly recent books of more general scope illustrate this concern with history as the history of ideas.

The first is Henry Steele Commager's *The American mind* (1950); can one imagine, parenthetically, a book on the British mind? No, but we do have works broadly similar under other names: *Early Victorian England, Ideas and beliefs of the Victorians,* both collaborative works, and Holbrook Jackson's *The eighteen nineties.* Commager has a useful chapter on 'The watershed of the nineties'. Among other things this includes an effective contrast between William Graham Sumner's *What social classes owe to each other* (a late vindication of *laissez-faire*) and Lester F. Ward's *Dynamic sociology,* which rejected Herbert Spencer's ideas, so popular in late nineteenth-century America, and insisted on the need for state intervention: 'competition is, in fact, not the law of life . . . but the law of death'. Richard Hofstadter's *The age of reform: from Bryan to F.D.R.* (1956) seeks to uncover the seeds of reform. Of some importance was the agrarian myth of a golden age, corrupted by the cities and the sinister power of Eastern financiers: this 'soft' side of the farmer produced the Populist revolt, though the future lay with the 'hard' side of agricultural improvements, business methods and the political pressures of the Farm Bloc. Moreover Populism had naive and sometimes reactionary nativist undertones. The real Progressive movement was middle class and urban, the product of the 'status revolution' which, by elevating the businessman, had undermined the position of the old families and the professional class, especially the ministers and lawyers. The university teacher, and especially the social scientist, was, however, on the up grade, and correspondingly resented the influence of businessmen trustees on the governing boards of the universities. These scholars, some of them products of the German seminar or its American adaptation, sought to apply their ideas to the problems of the day: economists like Veblen and Richard T. Ely and John R. Commons, sociologists like Ward and E. A. Ross, Beard the historian, J. Allen Smith the political scientist, John Dewey the educational philosopher. Other influences were the growth of the trusts and the rise in prices which hurt the consumer; and also the very growth of the cities which not only favoured political corruption but seemed to people of simple rural ideas to pose 'a strange threat to civilisation itself'. 'The muckrakers have their due place, and Hofstadter emphasises that S. S. McClure was ready to spend large sums in payment to his authors, such as Ida Tarbell, for the articles which exposed the evils of big business or municipal corruption, because the interest they aroused led to a high circulation for *McClure's magazine;* indeed it had many imitators, *Munsey's, Hampton's Pearson's,* the *Cosmopolitan, Everybody's.* Finally 'the Progressive movement was the complaint of the unorganised against the consequences of organisation', the reaction to the citizen's feeling of helplessness. The choice was between paternalism or socialism, but two men as different as Roosevelt and Wilson strove to head off the latter while curbing the former. It was Theodore Roosevelt's merit to be the first to 'understand this need of the public for faith in the complete neutrality of the powerful state'. Later, inspired by Herbert Croly's *Promise of American life* (1909) it led to his 'New Nationalism' in which a strong government was to supervise big business for the good of all.

Other currents in the Progressive groundswell are charted in Eric Goldman's *Rendezvous with destiny* (1952), an eloquent and avowed history of liberalism since the Civil War. He makes much of the impact of Darwinism, which could both buttress the *status quo* (the argument of 'the survival of the fittest') or by the stress on evolution and adaptation justify policies of reform. He cites theologians who condemned the involving of God in defence of an unjust economic system (Walter Rauschenbush and Father John Ryan); Richard T. Ely arguing that true economics should be concerned to establish right social relations; E. A. Ross pointing out in *Sin and society* (1907) that blackmail, embezzlement, speculation, tax-dodging are not less sins because not called what they really are—piracy, theft, gambling, larceny; and the anthropologist Franz Boas showing the relativity of all the values of civilisation. In particular, Goldman shows how the law and the constitution were removed from their pedestals, partly by the doubts raised by J. Allen Smith and Charles A. Beard about the motives of the 'founding fathers' and partly by the recognition of lawyers such as Holmes and Brandeis and Roscoe Pound that judges acted from subjective motives and social considerations.

Very little of such analysis of changing opinion can be found in the histories of England covering this period. Sir Robert Ensor's magisterial *England, 1870-1914* (1936) by its organisation into chapters dealing respectively with political history, 'economics and institutions', and 'mental and social aspects', is hampered in connecting politics and legislation with changes in society and opinion. Ensor finds the nineties 'a period of unsettlement'.

> The nation was out of health. It passed through a phase like an adolescence; its temper was explosive and quarrelsome; it boasted itself with the harshness of immaturity. Whole classes or strata were, in some degree, tasting power for the first time; and as they pushed their way out of the inarticulate and into the articulate part of the community, a kind of upstart arrogance became vocal with them . . . The former clear objectives were gone, and as yet nothing took their place.

This is interesting comment, though it neither illustrates nor explains the traits it observes. Similarly, in surveying the 'mental and social aspects' of the years 1901-14 Ensor remarks that the young men of the time 'felt themselves at the beginning, not at the end, of an age. It was to be an age of democracy, of social justice, of faith in the possibilities of the common man'. Elsewhere he ascribes Balfour's education act to Sir Robert Morant (the civil servant) and to Balfour's 'concept of national efficiency', the militancy of the suffragettes to Christabel Pankhurst, and the great strikes of 1910–11 in part to syndicalist ideas imported from France.

Even Halévy, the philosophic historian of early and late nineteenth-century Britain, does not make much more of the force of ideas in his last volume. The great Liberal victory of 1906 is ascribed 'first and foremost to the purely negative opposition to tariff reform' but also to the agricultural labourers' dislike of the landlords and farmers and the disgust of the electors generally 'with a government of aristocrats and dilettanti which had shown itself incompetent either to preserve peace or to make war . . .'. 'Anti-Irish panics, waves of imperialist enthusiasm, the failure of the old Gladstonian party to understand the aspirations of the working masses, had kept the Conservatives in office. Their power was now a thing of the past. . .'.[3] Later, Halévy notices the dilemma of liberalism: a term originally denoting hostility to the state, and to socialism and militarism, it now involved the championing of social democracy and, for the government, the increase of armaments. In the formulation and administration of new policies the importance of the civil servants is noted and the influence of the Webbs recognised. The ideas behind the shaping of policy are perhaps most clearly (though very briefly) brought out in connection with the budget of 1909, which for the first time used the budget as an instrument to remedy the inequality of wealth. Shaw's plays and Galsworthy's are referred to in passing, Leo Money's *Riches and poverty* (1905) is cited, and we are told that:

> We are witnessing the decay of that Puritan asceticism which made the proletariat ashamed of its poverty as of a crime for which it was responsible and the rich regard their own enrichment by work and saving as the fulfilment of a duty. The rich man now wanted to enjoy himself, to display his luxury, to make a splash, and the revolt of the intelligentsia and the workers was the reply to this ostentation.

Of course there are explanations for the difference in the treatment of the period in the two countries. In America the Progressive movement continued in strength well into the years of the First World War, and its extinction in 1917 (until revived in the glories of the New Deal in the 1930s) could be ascribed to a conspiracy which ensnared an innocent nation in a European war. In Britain social legislation failed to arrest the 'strange death of Liberal England', and the decline, narrated more than analysed, has diverted attention from the positive aspects of the period. The story concentrates on the 'constitutional crisis' over the power of the house of lords, the Ulster crisis, the strikes, the suffragettes, the coming of war. In this last is a more general difference: British history must always be concerned with foreign policy, relations with other European powers, the growth of a world-wide empire. American history until the 1940s is largely the history of a continent in isolation (which is *not* the same as the history of an isolationist continent), with the difference in scale which this involves. Within their continental boundaries the Americans constructed a nation out of diverse peoples, all of them emigrants from Europe or the descendants, recent or remote, of emigrants. The strength of ideas and the hope of bettering one's condition were the binding forces: freedom, democracy, equality (the most potent, as De Tocqueville saw) were the themes. But mixed up with this, and deriving from the continental scale, were the differences between the sections; and these in turn were enlarged by the 'peculiar institution' of the South and all that flowed from it in resentment at Southern predominance in the federal government and rivalry over control of the new territories in the West. The winning of the West, the history of the ever-shifting frontier, provided another theme; and this also gave the farmer a place in history and in politics quite different from that of the landed interest in Britain. Beside American sectionalism the differences between the parts of the United Kingdom seem small scale: the claims of the North, Wales, Scotland against southern England are not the stuff of nineteenth- and early twentieth-century British history (perhaps they should be); Ireland stands in some ways to Britain as the South to the Northern states, but its history has not been written in these terms.

Then there are constitutional differences. In Britain parliament is sovereign, and the largest part of the reformer's task is over when parliament has acted; or perhaps one should say when the government of the day has decided to back the reform and introduce it in parliament. In the United States reform legislation has to run the gauntlet between long lines of opponents. There is the separation of powers: if the administration sponsors a measure, congress may refuse to pass it; what congress enacts the administration may fail to enforce. There is the constitution; if it is a federal law (or a state law, for that matter) the courts, and ultimately the supreme court, may declare it unconstitutional. There is the division of powers between the states and the federal government: many matters come within the police powers of the states, and it may be necessary to campaign for parallel legislation in several states. At a lower level, the diffuse and slackly articulated system of local government permits of endless obstruction, not to speak of downright perversion of the law, by municipalities and county boards of supervisors. True, there are compensations. The advanced legislation and administration in Wisconsin early in the century showed what could be done at the state level by a vigorous government which was also ready to draw heavily on the state university not only for the ideas of the experts but for the men to carry them out. And the congressional committee at its best is probably superior to a royal commission in uncovering abuses and corruption and preparing the way for reform: witness the effects of the Pujo Committee and the Senate Commission on Industrial Relations in revealing the stranglehold of the bankers and trusts upon the nation in 1911–13.

Furthermore there are the differences in the party politics of the two countries. The two American parties are themselves vast federations. Party discipline is sketchy. Whether it be from congress or the state assembly that legislation is desired, the reformer's task is to win over scores of individual congressmen, senators and assemblymen; the support of the majority party as such is likely to be impossible to win or useless if won, since party regularity cannot be counted on. Hence the greater part played by lobbies in the American system. In Britain most reform legislation has been initiated by the government of the day. This is not to say that lobbying has no place in Britain, as has been shown in connection with the Conservative measures to denationalise road haulage and to inaugurate commercial television in the 1950s. But in another way the British system differed from the American sixty years ago, and to some extent still does. The trade unions were accepted and consulted much earlier, and in the Labour party they came to have their representatives in parliament. This, plus the smaller scale of industry and the simpler structure of banking, largely freed Britain from the problems of controlling big business and according to trade unions a recognised sphere of action—problems which bulked large to the American Progressives before 1914. Another difference was that 'tariff reform' meant entirely opposite things in the two countries, and in spite of Joseph Chamberlain wasted far less parliamentary time in Great Britain.

All this helps to explain why social reform in the United States needed a change in the national spirit which the Progressive movement signified and supplied: only this could provide a sufficient head of steam. It must be noted, however, that businessmen also came to play a major part in securing reform. Efficient government, and regulation which limited competition, were to their interest once the early cut-throat days were over. Some of the resultant legislation and policy was federal: anti-trust suits under the Sherman Act, the Clayton Act which gave some recognition of the rights of labour unions, the Hepburn Act which strengthened the Interstate Commerce Commission, the Federal Reserve Act of 1913 and the creation of the Federal Trade Commission. An exhaustive official enquiry led to the setting up of the Children's Bureau in the department of commerce. Other laws were state enactments, and in many cases legislation only succeeded at the second or third attempt after the courts had thrown out the original statutes as unconstitutional: anti-child labour laws, laws governing the employment of women and fixing the maximum hours of work in certain industries, and providing for workmen's compensation. Corruption was tackled by political devices: the initiative, referendum and recall in which Oregon, under W. S. U'Ren's leadership, was a pioneer, and the direct primary which was first introduced in Wisconsin. In the cities an aroused electorate would briefly install a reform administration, as in New York and San Francisco, or individuals like 'Golden Rule' Jones in Toledo and Tom Johnson in Cleveland would give honest and enlightened government for several years: elsewhere the 'city manager' system brought improvement.

In Britain the social legislation of the comparable period began with the Workmen's Compensation Act of 1897, and ended with the coalminers' minimum wage in 1912. In between came the Education Act of 1902, the Unemployed Workmen's Act of 1905, the introduction of the medical inspection service in schools and the authorisation of school meals, the trades union legislation of 1906 and 1913, old-age pensions, the Children Act (1908), labour exchanges, the trade boards, and the National Insurance Act of 1911. Each of these has its own history, though not all have been studied in equal detail. Several owed their introduction to a fruitful collaboration of minister and civil servant: Balfour and Morant in the Education Act, Churchill and Beveridge and Llewellyn Smith for labour exchanges and trade boards and unemployment insurance. Lloyd George was the originator of national health insurance, supported by a large team of ministers and civil servants. Legislation concerning trade unions and miners' hours and wages resulted from the pressure of these groups inside and outside parliament. A back-bencher, Dilke, had worked for years for something like the trade boards. Several measures owed much to the example of Germany, particularly the idea of contributory insurance schemes. The experiments in social legislation made by New Zealand and Australia seem to have made little impression on the mother-country. The measure with the longest history behind it was that providing for old-age pensions. Joseph Chamberlain had taken it up in the 1880s and Charles Booth had studied it in the nineties, writing three books on the subject. The Royal Commission on the Aged Poor (1893–5) had gone into the question exhaustively if inconclusively; other official committees had gone over the ground later. Oddly, the royal commission which has been the most fully studied, and which at the time apparently aroused the greatest interest, was the one which was quite barren of results for years to come: the Royal Commission on the Poor Laws and the Relief of Distress (1905–9).

Now, are we to regard this record of social legislation as the product of accident? Was it simply the result of a number of combinations of individuals—instigators, collaborators, expert advisers—responding to general conditions of long-standing or to particular and immediate pressures (for example, from the trade unions)? Was it largely the work of Lloyd George and Churchill, filling out the old radical sails of the Liberal party to catch the wind ahead of the nascent Labour party? Or was it, rather, the result of some change of mood, some broad national movement? To answer the question one must attempt a study of the movement of ideas in the late nineteenth century.

This has already been done, though unfortunately on a small scale, in a book which has hardly received the attention it deserves, (Lady) Gertrude Williams's *The state and the standard of living*, published in 1936. Lady Williams's opening chapter, 'Opinion in the nineties', introduces her detailed account of the growth of state provision to help people in old age and to protect them during their working lives from loss of income through sickness, accidents or unemployment. She distinguishes two main elements leavening opinion in the nineties. One was the discussion of state interference, which implied a modification of the ideas of *laissez-faire* and was led, significantly, by the economists. It owed much to the increasing awareness of the extent and depths of poverty which existed amid modern industry. The work of the charitable societies contributed to this, and particularly that of the Charity Organisation Society. The C.O.S. did, it is true, ascribe the cause of poverty to the failure and moral weakness of the individual, but in its appeals for help and in its pioneering social work it inevitably drew attention to the ills of society, whether one accepted its remedy or not. The social surveys of Charles Booth and Seebohm Rowntree in the nineties only reinforced this lesson. Thus as early as 1883 Goschen addressed the Philosophical Institution of Edinburgh with the words:

> I have chosen '*Laissez-faire* and Government Interference' as the subject of my address tonight because, amongst all the complicated social and economic phenomena of the present day, none appears more interesting or of deeper importance . . . than the changes which have occurred and are daily occurring in the relations between the state and individual liberty.

W. Stanley Jevons, in *The State in relation to labour* (1882) put the choice between *laissez-faire* and intervention as purely subjective: each case must be treated on its merits. Alfred Marshall's 'the destruction of the poor is their poverty' presented an entirely different point of view from the earlier economists; as he himself said: 'while the earlier economists argued as though man's character and efficiency were to be regarded as a fixed quantity, modern economists keep constantly in mind the fact that it is a product of the circumstances under which he has lived'. It was no wonder that Charles Booth's investigations of London poverty forced him to abandon his earlier individualist views:

> For the state to nurse the helpless and incompetent as we in our own families nurse the old, the young and the sick, and to provide for those who are not competent to provide for themselves, may seem an impossible undertaking, but nothing less than this will enable self-respecting labour to obtain its full remuneration and the nation its raised standard of life.

The second element which was stirring opinion was socialism. Hyndman's Social Democratic Federation and the Fabian Society with its tracts and lectures may have been small-scale affairs, but Henry George's very successful speaking tours in the eighties, the Trafalgar Square riots of 1886-7, the new unions of unskilled workers, and the London dock strike of 1889 insistently drew attention to the extent of suffering and discontent and demanded from society some remedy. Socialism was proposed as the solution, the more loudly in the nineties with the founding of the I.L.P. and the influence of Burgess's *Workmen's Times* and Blatchford's *Clarion* in bringing recruits to the Labour movement and challenging the older leaders of the T.U.C. Canon Barnett, who when he began his work in Whitechapel supported C.O.S. principles of the individual's responsibility for his condition, published his article, 'Practicable socialism', in 1883. He said that his life in the East End had made him a socialist. 'In the labourer's future there is only the grave and the workhouse. He hardly dares to think at all, for the thought suggests that tomorrow a change in trade or a master's whim may throw him out of work, and leave him unable to pay for rent or for food. The state must provide the means for a better life than this.' So far had the older ideas of individual responsibility and the limited functions of the state been undermined that in 1896 W. S. McKechnie could assert that there were 'many statesmen of even cabinet rank in both camps [Conservative and Liberal] whose policy involves principles essentially socialistic, if carried out to their legitimate and logical conclusions'.

This shift in the winds of opinion was certainly evident in the Liberal party, though it was far from certain in 1906 that it would lead it to advanced social policies. Campbell-Bannerman, during the election campaign, wrote to Asquith: 'I had excellent meetings in Glasgow. I found that much mischief was being done by the notion that we had little or nothing to say about the unemployed. So I risked one foot upon the ice, but was very guarded and spoke only of enquiry and experiment.' It has been argued that the Liberals' social legislation was their response to the idea of social justice. It is true that this idea (the term seems not to have been used at the time) provided a means of reconciling individualism and collectivism. As J. A. Hobson put it:

> Liberalism is now formally committed to a task which certainly involves a new conception of the state in its relation to the individual life and private enterprise. That conception is not socialism . . . though implying a considerable amount of increased public ownership and control of industry. From the standpoint which best presents its continuity with earlier Liberalism, it appears as a fuller appreciation and realisation of individual liberty contained in the provision of equal opportunities for self-development.[4]

Tracing the sources of this change in opinion is, of course, only part of what the historian of ideas is concerned with. To present a fair picture of opinion at the turn of the century he must take into consideration other currents of thought in the 1880s and nineties. There was Chamberlain's 'unauthorised programme' and his 'Jack Cade' speeches. There was the teaching of T. H. Green and Arnold Toynbee and William Morris. The evidence of royal commissions, on the housing of the working classes (1884-5) or labour (1892-4) or the aged poor, is a mine of information. There were journalists and clergymen writing such as G. R. Sims, who published a series on 'Horrible London' in the *Daily News,* and the Rev A. Mearns with his pamphlet, *The bitter cry of outcast London* of 1883. W. T. Stead, England's only muckraker, might deserve a chapter to himself. W. H. Mallock was a prolific writer in defence of conservatism and property. Blatchford's *Merrie England* was a counterpart to Bellamy's *Looking backward.* And not to be neglected were the changing sentiments about the empire from Gordon's death at Khartoum to the conclusion of the Boer War.

In the new century the student of opinion must turn to literary works: Shaw's plays and H. G. Wells' social novels. Contemporary polemical works of evident influence were Leo Chiozza Money's *Riches and poverty* and Philip Snowden's *Socialist's budget* (1907). An 'anatomy of Britain' at the time by a very shrewd observer is C. F. G. Masterman's *Condition of England* (1909). The standpoint of the three parties was given, unofficially it is true, in three little volumes in the Home University Library by Lord Hugh Cecil on Conservatism, L. T. Hobhouse on Liberalism and Ramsay MacDonald on Socialism. And the files of the influential reviews, the *Contemporary, Fortnightly, Nineteenth Century,* the *Edinburgh Review, The National Review,* would furnish more grist to the mill. From these materials we might hope to get a picture of what might be called, perhaps, 'The Liberal movement'; part of the analysis would have to distinguish between liberalism with a capital and with a small 'l'.

There is, of course, a small body of work along these lines in existence, some of it, characteristically, by Americans. Helen M. Lynd's *England in the eighteen-eighties* (New York, 1944) is outstanding and unfortunately unique. Bernard Semmel, *Imperialism and social reform: English social-imperial thought 1895-1914* (1960) carries on, in part, the same task, with valuable analyses of social Darwinism, the ideas of Benjamin Kidd (*Social evolution,* published in 1894) and Karl Pearson and the hopes of the 'Coefficients', the small dining club founded by the Webbs in 1902 to promote a party of 'national efficiency'. It is a pity that Semmel's choice of subject leads him, in his later chapters, to desert this fruitful study of ideas favouring social reform for an exposition of various schools of imperialist thought.

Semmel's study has now been carried very much further in Bentley B. Gilbert's *Evolution of national insurance in Great Britain: the origins of the Welfare State* (London, 1966), which not only traces the movement of ideas from the eighties to the Liberal era but describes in fascinating detail the processes by which the various measures of social reform were put up on the statute book. Gilbert brings out, for example, the concern over 'physical deterioration' caused by reports of the poor physique of recruits for the Boer War. Among other historians Halévy has, of course, many suggestive passages in which he sketches the background for several of the measures he describes, and there is much to be found in Ensor's *England 1870–1914* of the same sort, though it is nowhere pulled together. Asa Briggs's essay, 'The political scene' in *Edwardian England*[5] is partly a history of ideas, but inevitably on a limited scale. Two books concerned with the coming of the welfare state (beside Lady Williams's already cited) devote attention to the background, particularly that of the nineteenth century: Maurice Bruce's *Coming of the Welfare State* and the work of a distinguished American scholar in the field of social work, Karl de Schweinitz's *England's road to social security* (Philadelphia, 1943). The handicap to this approach—and it is no criticism of the books themselves—is that an interest in the nineteenth century leads to a perhaps excessive preoccupation with the poor law and with the sprawling framework of the charitable societies.

There is, of course, one famous English work which might have been the history of ideas for this period—indeed its title promises as much: Dicey's *Lectures on the relation between law and public opinion in England during the nineteenth century*. This gave a lead which was never followed up, perhaps because at the time it seemed to say all that needed to be said, and after a few years the First World War intervened to delay further work on what was still recent history. *Law and public opinion* was published in 1905, with a second edition in 1914. Unfortunately, there is much that is unsatisfactory about Dicey's treatment of the nineteenth century, apart from the fact that the book ends too soon, and was written too soon, to summarise the state of opinion in the early years of the twentieth century. Dicey's three periods of legislation cannot now be accepted as a satisfactory classification for the nineteenth century, though they remain useful as a stimulus to thinking, and have played this part in the recent controversy over the springs of reform and administrative progress. The periods Dicey discovered were: (1) Old Toryism or legislative quiescence, 1800–30; (2) Benthamism or individualism, 1825–70; (3) collectivism, 1865–1900. This is not the place to criticise them, but it is interesting that Dicey as a Tory put the beginning of collectivism as early as he did, defining it as 'faith in the benefit to be derived by the mass of the people from the action or intervention of the state, even in matters which might be, and often are, left to the uncontrolled management of the persons concerned'. This strain of thought was certainly influential, along with several others; but it itself needs fuller analysis.

Enough has been said, I hope, to suggest that we need a new Dicey, or that we need a Parrington or a Hofstadter, to examine the stir of ideas in Britain at the opening of the twentieth century—or, for that matter, over a much longer period, both before and after. It would be a work not so much of discovery as of rediscovery, seeing old books and articles, plays and novels, government reports and parliamentary debates in a new light, and focusing less on political battles than on the tides of opinion behind them. The task is laborious, but the reward might be large. It might even throw light on that deepest of mysteries, the 'strange death' of the Liberal party.

NOTES

[1] S. F. Morison and H. S. Commager, *Growth of the American Republic* (2 vols.: New York: Oxford University Press, 4th edn., 1936). The book was first published in 1930.

[2] *Journal of American Studies*, i (1967), 63–78.

[3] E. Halévy, *History of the English people in the nineteenth century*, vol. VI; *The rule of democracy 1905–1914*.

[4] J. A. Hobson, *The Crisis of Liberalism: new issues of democracy* (1909).

[5] S. Nowell-Smith (ed.), *Edwardian England 1901–1914* (Oxford, 1964).

(c) Welfare Policy and Industrialisation

G. V. RIMLINGER

ECONOMIC DEVELOPMENT, SOCIAL CHANGE, AND SOCIAL SECURITY

Since the end of the Middle Ages, the developing nation-states of Western Europe have been confronted with the problem of poverty. Previously, this had been a matter of only local concern. With the emergence of national states and national economies, the problem of what to do with the poor necessarily became a matter of national significance. The national governments enacted laws and issued ordinances on how those who had become dependent on society should be treated. As a rule, the execution of the laws on poor relief, vagrancy, and begging were left to the local authorities. Characteristically, the laws were much more specific on punishments to be inflicted than on relief to be granted. But, basically, they did define certain reciprocal social responsibilities, such as the individual's duty to work and the local community's duty to provide work for the able and relief for the disabled.

This manner of disposing of the problem of the poor was eventually overcome by two major sets of forces put into motion during the second half of the eighteenth century. One of these sets was the Industrial Revolution, along with the economic and social changes it engendered. The other set of forces revolved around the radical new conception of the rights of the individual that was thrust on the world by the American and French Revolutions. Approximately one hundred years after these events, the modern form of social protection from want—social insurance—was introduced in Imperial Germany. From an eighteenth century perspective, Germany was an unlikely candidate for this social innovation. Other countries followed with poor law reforms and with social insurance programs of their own. The old repressive poor laws gave way to more

---

G. V. Rimlinger, *Welfare Policy and Industrialisation in Europe, America and Russia*, Chichester, John Wiley, 1971; pp. 2–11, 62–86 and 334–43. Abridged.

humane public assistance and social service programs. Today these programs have become all but universal.

A recent worldwide survey by the United States Social Security Administration shows that 120 countries have one or more social security schemes in operation. The most extensive programs are in the more industrialized countries, but developing countries are eager to follow the same pattern. In many countries, social security rights have been incorporated into their constitutions.

A brief discussion of what is meant by 'social security' is appropriate at this point. The term came into usage in the United States in the 1930s and has gained very wide acceptance in other countries in literal translation *(Soziale Sicherheit, Sécurité Sociale, Seguridad Social)*. Almost inevitably, its meaning varies somewhat from one national context to the other. Its common components have been summarized by the Social Security Administration:

> The term 'social security program' is usually reserved, in the first place, for programs established by public law, although administration of such programs may or may not be wholly in public hands. In the second place, it is usually considered to include programs that provide some form of cash payments to individuals to make up a loss of or a deficiency in earnings occasioned by such 'long-term' risks as old-age retirement, permanent disablement (or invalidity) of nonoccupational or occupational origin, and death of the family bread-winner; and by such short-term risks as temporary incapacity of non-occupational or occupational origin, maternity, and unemployment. It is also regarded as including programs that provide regular cash payments to families with children. Finally, public programs providing curative medical services to individuals (other than ordinary public health services), or that are concerned with the financing of such services, are also usually regarded as a type of social security program in countries where they exist.

Social security thus includes what we usually call social insurance (compulsory programs that are usually job related and financed, at least, partly from contributions), public assistance, family allowances, and state health insurance. It does not include those aspects of modern social rights that are primarily concerned with education, training, housing, children's services, and social case-work.

The development of social security involves a number of important policy issues which each country seeks to resolve in its own fashion. Perhaps the first question is whether or not a country should adopt modern programs of social protection. In the historical context this meant whether a country should shift from a deterrent system that furnished relief based on need to a system that furnished benefits as a matter of right. The old relief system, the poor laws, applied mainly to those at the bottom of the socioeconomic ladder. It was never just relief; it started from the assumption that people were in need because of some character deficiency;

relief, therefore, was provided under conditions that were intended partly as retribution for past failings and partly as a check against future failures. Social security implies an entirely different conception of social protection. Social insurance, in particular, is designed primarily for wage and salary earners, who represent a cross section of society rather than its lower layers. Its benefits are normally unrelated to the needs of the recipient; he receives them whether he needs them or not, he has no choice in the matter as participation in the programs is almost always compulsory. This inevitably involves interference by the state with the individual's freedom to allocate his income as he sees fit. Generally, social security programs tend to redistribute income among individuals, which involves issues of equity and social justice. These matters are obviously controversial.

The adoption of a new policy of protection somehow has to be justified. The exercise of the state's power on behalf of some individuals, often at the expense of others, must have a basis of legitimacy. The question, therefore must be answered as to what legitimizes social protection. To what extent is it the individual's responsibility to look after himself and his family, and to what extent is this a social responsibility? Clearly, the more emphasis a society puts on individual responsibility, the less room there would seem to be for social action. This, however, implies that only the interests of the individual are involved. In reality, social protection, whether it is poor laws or social security, is concerned with the interests of society as a whole as well as the ones of the individual. Even a highly individualistic society, one that stresses individual responsibility, may legitimize social protection for the common interest in social and political stability or in economic productivity.

If society recognizes the individual's right to protection, especially non-deterrent protection, this right also must be legitimized. There are two different tendencies in this legitimation. One looks on the right to benefits as something that the beneficiary has personally earned, either through payment of contributions, or through performance of work. This is the contractual orientation of the right to benefits. The second kind of justification emphasizes status rather than contract. Some writers argue that the right to social security in modern society is inherent in the status of the wage or salary earner. It derives from the right to subsistence, and those who depend on their labor for subsistence have a social right to income if their working capacity fails or if no jobs are available. Others consider the right to income as a perquisite of citizenship. In this case all citizens are entitled to protection regardless of how they earn their living.

The manner in which social security rights are legitimized has important implications for social security policy. There are a number of crucial decisions that have to be made. The first is the decision as to who should be protected, which is another way of saying: Who has the right to protection, or who needs to be protected in the interest of the community?

The protected group may be open or closed. An open program, such as the poor laws or public assistance, does not have a designated group of beneficiaries. It usually applies to all resident citizens. Social insurance programs, on the other hand, apply to closed groups. The question then is how broad the covered group should be. Should it include only wage workers in certain industries, or wage and salary earners in all industries, or should it be extended to all citizens who work, including the self-employed, regardless of their level of earnings? The question must also take into account the extent to which the dependents of beneficiaries are to be entitled to support. Obviously, the broader the conception of the right to protection, the more universal should be the coverage. Even under those circumstances, however, economic and administrative considerations may force a more narrow coverage than the country may wish to adopt.

After the decision is made about who should be protected, consideration must be given to the questions of how and against what risks. The historical trend has been to make protection more universal insofar as the coverage of persons is concerned, as well as more comprehensive with respect to the inclusion of protected risks. Different risks imply different degrees of involvement of the state in the affairs of the individual. Usually, it is easier to introduce compensation for industrial injuries. Programs that are relatively easy to administer and require only cash payments, such as old-age pensions, also can be readily accommodated. Unemployment and health insurance present more administrative difficulties and are more likely to offend strong vested interests. Wherever the medical profession is privately organized, it tends to resist the introduction of state health insurance schemes. Family allowances also involve issues on which there is division of opinion in most countries.

The question of how protection should be provided covers the whole range of issues regarding conditions of benefit payment, the level and structure of benefits, and their financing. All of these issues have implications that affect material and ideological interests. No society can afford simply to give away cash benefits or to render unlimited services. Some system of control must be established. One form of control is to pay benefits only in case of need and in an amount sufficient to meet minimum requirements. There are several types of problems associated with this procedure. One relates to the manner in which an individual's need is established; does it require a humiliating investigation of his personal and family situation, or is his need assumed from the size of his family, his age, or his income level without further investigation? The level of benefit that may be considered a necessary minimum is always open to debate. Should it prevent only physical hardship, or should it prevent 'relative deprivation'? The latter takes into account what society can afford and what the poor may expect. Another form of control is to pay benefits on the basis of a specified length of previous work or contribution. In this case it is the individual's previous record tht establishes eligibility. The procedure may be liberal or restrictive, depending on prevailing attitudes towards social rights and the evaluation of economic and social or political consequences.

Whatever manner of controlling eligibility is adopted, the benefits structure may be egalitarian or differentiated. A system that pays the same benefit to all, according to an established national minimum, has great appeal to those who favor social and economic equality. A flat benefit is most consistent with the view that benefits are a social right to which all have the same claim. But if benefits are a flat amount, the level is almost necessarily low. To prevent abuse, it tends to be somewhat below what ordinarily can be earned through regular work. A low benefit level requires low taxes or contributions and, thus has the advantage of limiting the state's interference with the income allocation process. For this reason it may appeal to those who are concerned with the individual's freedom to allocate his earnings as he sees fit. Those who hold this ideological position, however, are normally also concerned with limited income redistribution; they, therefore, tend to favor differentiated benefits, which may conflict with the desire to keep state interference with income allocation at a minimum. If the lower range of the benefit scale is to be adequate, benefits in the upper range are necessarily higher than what minimal state interference would demand. Differentiated benefits tend to require a deeper intervention in personal income allocation, but it may be a more market-consistent form of intervention insofar as it involves less interpersonal income redistribution. If benefits are related to previous earnings or contributions, they have more of a contractual than a social rights character. Although the contractual character may be found to be more suitable to a given country, its chief shortcoming tends to be social inadequacy at the lower income levels. There is always the danger that those who need protection most are able to earn it least. Society has to find the benefit structure that optimizes welfare by combining the incentive effects of differentiation with the adequacy guarantees of a stated minimum.

The question of who should pay for the benefits involves many of the same considerations as the benefit structure. The practical problem is how much of the burden should be borne by the beneficiaries themselves, their employers, or the state. The contractual approach emphasizes payments by employees and employers; in either case, the contributions may be looked on as being earned by the employees. The higher the contributions, the higher the benefits will tend to be, although in social insurance (unlike in private insurance) the relationship is hardly ever proportional. The emphasis on social rights tends to favor financing from general state revenue, which is presumably raised according to prevailing standards of distributional equity. Since social insurance programs almost always redistribute income (not merely reallocate it through time), exclusive financing via pay-roll taxes tend to put an undue burden on the low income earners. The contractual ideology, by favoring commercial equity, thus exacts a price in terms of social equity. Opponents of contributions from the public treasury, however, stress the need to keep social insurance free from the dangers of government paternalism and of the politics of budget allocations.

A final problem area, which should be mentioned, is administration. The administrative issues which have relevance for this study are mainly the ones that relate to the use of social security institutions in the pursuit of ancillary social and economic goals. Since social security decisions affect the welfare of large numbers of people, the day-to-day administration of the programs may give opportunities to influence economic or political behavior. A country may choose a judicial type of bureaucratic administration; or it may democratically involve the insured beneficiaries in the decision-making process; or it may exploit the system in an authoritarian fashion for the benefit of those in power.

The preceding listing of problem areas is not intended to be a comprehensive enumeration of public policy issues. Its purpose is merely to indicate broadly the kind of social and economic questions that are involved in the development of social income protection. [...] An outline of the main themes that underlie this study is in order. One is the changing nature of the problem of want as we move from a pre-industrial society to mature industrialism. Widespread poverty is the rule in the traditional, preindustrial society. This is not looked on as a problem in itself; in fact, it may be looked on as a positive good. This was the view of the mercantilists. They spoke of the usefulness of poverty as a means of keeping the masses industrious. Poverty as such was a problem for them only to the extent that it endangered public peace. Poverty was something to be relieved but by no means to be abolished. During industrialization the problem of want changed—it had new causes and new victims. The traditional sources of hardship seemed to be God-given and immutable; people had always been poor; wars, pestilence, and bad harvests only made matters periodically worse. The industrializing society held out the promise of improved well-being but the fruits seemed unequally divided. Some quickly became rich but many more had to discover new sources of want. They had become dependent on the wage of the family breadwinner; any interruption of the ability to work or of the availability of a job spelled dire want. Having left the land, the family was no longer a production unit. The aged and the children became a greater burden. These hardships were no longer God-given: they all seemed to be man-made; they were social. The victims were no longer the traditional poor. They were now the industrial proletariat. As industrialism has matured, many of the basic hardships have been alleviated, but the tremendous wealth has created new conceptions of social rights and of freedom from want. The poor in a rich country like America suffer from 'relative deprivation' because they can compare what they have with what is common in their society.

Another theme of this study is an emphasis on class relations as a determinant factor in the development of social protection. In the pre-industrial Western European society the lower classes were held in what John Stuart Mill described as a position of dependence and protection. The practical meaning of this varied widely, but the sentiment that those in power should reason and decide for the common folk was rather general. Those below owed obedience and deferrence, while those above owed protection and guidance. With the rise of liberalism, this conception of social inequality came under attack. Liberty and equality demanded that all legal privileges be abolished. All citizens were to be treated equally, which meant that none had any special claim to protection on account of his (low) economic and social status. Full citizenship implied the ability to look after oneself; dependence on others was not consistent with freedom and equality. Where this liberal concept of society triumphed (in England, France, and America), social protection was slow to develop. In Germany, where liberalism and individualism struck only shallow roots, the chances for social protection were that much better. [. . .] In the twentieth century, social income protection has lost much of its class attributes. The concepts of freedom and equality have changed from ideological barriers to justifications.

Closely related to class relations, as a determinant of social protection, is the nature of the political system. In the countries studied, the more democratic governments were slower to introduce social protection than the authoritarian and totalitarian governments. In democratic countries, public action depends on how various interest groups are represented and how well they are organized. There is a tendency for each group to seek legislation in its favour. Employer interest groups generally oppose the introduction of social security but labor groups favor it. This generalization, however, is a crude oversimplification. Certain labor groups, such as the American trade unions, the British friendly societies, and the German Social Democrats, were originally opponents of social insurance. German and Russian big business before World War I were generally in favor of it. The American Association of Manufacturers was an early supporter of workmen's compensation. In authoritarian and totalitarian countries the interests of the state, as seen by those in power, tend to take precedence over particular group interest. [. . .]

This study stresses also the role of economic factors in the development of social security. Aside from being a means to enhance welfare, social security programs also are measures that affect the quantity and quality of a country's manpower resources. The poor law constituted a manpower policy that was fairly well suited for a time when labor was abundant and most unskilled. The main requirement then was the maintenance of work habits among the marginal elements of the work force. The administration of the poor laws was an attempt (not always successful) to instill discipline and industriousness. As industrialization progressed, labor became not only more scarce relative to capital, but it achieved a much higher level of skill; its spontaneous cooperation within large-scale organizations became very important. At this stage it became profitable, from the point of view of productivity, to develop and to maintain the capacity and the willingness to work. The workers' physical strength and good will had become important assets. Social insurance became one of the means of investing in human capital. In the Soviet economy, social insurance has been an important means for the maintenance of industrial discipline. In market economies its explicit work-incentive role is less important, but its role as an automatic stabilizer is much more significant. The study is particularly interested in how various countries have adapted social insurance programs to their economic systems and to their national objectives.

Throughout, special attention is paid to the role of ideas. The changing views regarding the reciprocal rights and duties of the individual and the state are clearly important. Of particular significance are the ideas concerning the consequences of social protection. It is in this regard that prevailing economic and social theories must be taken into account. The mercantilists typically assumed that the poor had a backward sloping supply curve of labor, which meant that an increase in income entailed less labor offered. Another mercantilist idea was that wages must be kept low for a favorable balance of trade. Both of these views militated against raising the level of welfare of the common man. At a later time, the Malthusian theory of population and Social Darwinism were important intellectual weapons against poor relief. The concept of investment in human capital and the theories of aggregate demand, on the other hand, were ideas favorable to social security. Another way in which ideas were important was through studies of the extent and causes of poverty. Especially in England, at the turn of the century, surveys of poverty helped to stir the social conscience of the middle and upper class. [. . .]

THE LIBERAL TRADITION

From the closing decades of the eighteenth to the end of the nineteenth century the ideals of liberalism dominated social policy in the West. At the core of these ideals were the individualistic principles of freedom, equality, and self-help. These principles, which pervaded economic, social, and political thought, incorporated the antithesis of the concept of dependence and protection represented by the preindustrial society. A conflict between the old protectionism and the forces of liberalism was thus inevitable. But while new needs for social protection were arising, the young industrial states were busy denouncing the old protectionist system and were confidently denying that protection was either wholesome for the individual or advantageous for the nation. With advancing industrialism and the democratization of political power, the liberal principles became eroded. By the end of the nineteenth century, the setting was prepared for the modern concepts of social protection. The liberal tradition had to make room for new interpretations of the social rights of the citizen. [. . .]

The struggle with the liberal legacy in the United States

In the United States the commitment to individualism—to individual achievement and self-help—was much stronger than either in England or in France. The survival of the liberal tradition, therefore, was found to be stronger and the resistance to social protection more tenacious. The vogue of Spencer and Sumner was an obstacle to an intellectual shift in favor of the poor man. By the end of the nineteenth century, the social workers gathering at the annual Conference of Charities and Corrections still generally shared the attitude that the able-bodied pauper should be offered relief only 'under strict rules inside an institution'. As far as public policy was concerned, the almshouse was still the 'fundamental institution in American poor relief'. In the area of voluntary efforts, the charity-organization-society approach had been imported from England, with the same objective of helping the 'worthy' poor and bringing the 'unworthy' to their deserved punishment. Although a few critical voices were heard on behalf of the rights of the poor, the accepted view was still that poverty was primarily a matter of character deficiency and had to be dealt with on a strictly individual basis. The social plague of the slums had been exposed, but it neither shocked the national conscience nor did it establish the role of the environment as a fundamental cause of pauperism.

By the turn of the century, the idea that the poor man had a claim to a share in the national income other than the market value of his labor was still utterly foreign. There was neither a strong socialist movement nor a tradition of Tory democracy to give stature to such an idea. If the American citizen was to gain the social rights that were being granted in Europe, a means had to found to legitimize these rights within the context of an individualistic society. Forces working in this direction were gathering, but success was slow to come.

The deep transformation of American society under the impact of rapid industrialization in the late nineteenth and early twentieth centuries created the necessity for major readjustments in the relationship between the individual and the state. The emergence of a national market, brought forth by a national system of transportation, the development of large-scale industry, and a technology of mass production, gave rise to concentrations of economic power and control that were singularly incongruous with the spirit of frontier individualism. Big business and financial manipulators became convenient but misleading targets for those who suffered from the strains of rapid economic change. Those at the bottom of the economic ladder remained voiceless for all practical purposes, but there were other, more vocal, groups who managed to create an atmosphere of reform.

It was in the presidential campaign of 1912 that the 'Quest for Social Justice,' to use Professor Faulkner's term,[1] reached a national climax, at least, in terms of alternative formulations of individual social rights. All political parties sensed the need for a reformulation of the relationship between the individual and the state. American socialists followed their European comrades in insisting on the duty of the state to guarantee the economic security of the individual at social expense, but they had similar mixed feelings about remedial legislation short of fundamental social change. Of greater significance was the 'New Nationalism' of Theodore Roosevelt and his Progressive party; their platform called not merely for workmen's compensation but for the 'protection of home life against the hazards of sickness, irregular employment and old age through adoption of a system of social insurance adapted to American use'. Inspired by the writings of Herbert Croly, Roosevelt formulated a nationalistic rationale for the protection of the individual that paralleled the one of Lloyd-George and Winston Churchill. As early as 1901, Roosevelt had written in McClure's Magazine: 'It is impossible to have a high standard of political life in a community sunk in sodden misery and ignorance.' This theme was prominent in his 1912 campaign. His 1912 platform echoed the conservation theme of the Progressive Movement by calling for 'the conservation of human resources through an enlightened measure of social and industrial justice'.

The country, in 1912, was not yet prepared to follow Roosevelt's lead. It preferred instead Woodrow Wilson's concept of the 'New Freedom', which was based on faith in the competitive system but not on laissez-faire. In his campaign speeches Wilson never failed to stress the difference between his and Roosevelt's conceptions of how to protect the economic welfare of the citizen. He attacked Roosevelt's social program as an attempt to 'set up guardians over the people in order to take care of them by a process of tutelage and supervision in which they play no active part'. This approach, he warned, would leave the individual at the mercy of government: 'The minute you are taken care of by the government you are wards, not independent men.' To this he added the strictly partisan argument that the very same people who wished to bestow this false benevolence upon the worker were also seeking to legalize monopolies instead of abolishing them. And 'once the government regulates monopoly, then monopoly will have to see that it regulates the government'. The worker would consequently be left dependent on those who had previously robbed him of his capacity for self-help. 'After all this is done, who is to guarantee to us that the government is to be pitiful, that the government is to be righteous, that the government is to be just?'

This line of reasoning left little room for alternative solutions to the problem of protection. 'I don't want a smug lot of experts to sit down behind closed doors in Washington and play Providence to me,' said Wilson. 'I am one of those who absolutely reject the trustee theory, the guardianship theory. I have never found a man who knew how to take care of me.' This kind of partisan distortion of the crucial question of social protection relied for its success on the deeply embedded values of self-help and individual achievement. Wilson, no doubt, was correct in his instinct that most Americans favored his 'program of liberty' over Roosevelt's program of regulation'.He told his audience that they wanted justice, not benevolence; that workers did not want any special privilege, except liberty, which knew no privilege. 'America stands for opportunity. America stands for a free field and no favor.' Opportunity is the wellspring of American prosperity, whereas 'benevolence never developed a man or a nation'.

The 1912 political campaign has been used here as a convenient benchmark for gauging the movement toward social protection in the United States. There is no question that by then the ideology of laissez-faire had lost out and some aspects of the welfare state were accepted by all political parties.[2] The victory of Wilson over Roosevelt, however, indicated that the country was not yet prepared to go beyond a compromise with the liberal tradition. The acceptable level of protection was still far from a guarantee of a basic minimum of existence, or even a systematic alleviation of economic hardship. Its principle aim was the restoration and maintenance of conditions that were compatible with individual self-help. The doctrine that every individual could look out for himself was only partly altered—to the extent that it was made contingent on the maintenance of the freedom and capacity to compete. In the long run this proved to be an important and elastic concession but, for the time being, it received a fairly narrow interpretation.

Although laissez-faire was on the defensive, the social insurance movement could not get ahead without an intellectualization of its means and ends. The connection between social insurance and the broader aims of society had to be worked out. It became necessary, in other words, to formulate a social insurance ideology relevant for American conditions. One of the early contributors to this intellectual reformulation was Professor Henry Seager of Columbia University.[3] Seager tried to show that the need for social insurance is inherent in industrial society, regardless of a country's political organization. He did not limit himself to noting the empirical facts about the workers' need for protection but developed a sociological argument to show that this need was a consequence of industrialization, and that reliance on individualistic self-help was no longer a realistic solution. His argument rested on the transformation of the habits of the thrift of the farmer and craftsman as they become permanent industrial wage-workers. Seager's conclusion was inescapable; the spirit of individualistic self-help was appropriate for an agrarian society, but an industrial society needed cooperative action 'impelled when necessary by the compulsory authority of the state'. He called for a 'program of social reform', the purpose of which was to 'raise the whole mass of wage earners to higher standards of efficiency and earnings and to more intelligent appreciation of all life's possibilities'. This statement embraced the central themes of the rising social insurance movement, which sought to combine the aspirations for social betterment of the Progressive era with the contemporary drives for conservation, efficiency, and cooperation. It should be recalled that during this era the idea of cooperation, instead of unrestricted competition, gained wide acceptance in American industry while, also, scientific management promised a new age of industrial efficiency.

It is only in recent years that the significance of investment in human capital during industrialization has been fully recognized. For the early advocates of social insurance in America, however, social insurance was a major step toward the conservation and increased efficiency of human resources. By stressing these aspects of social insurance, its advocates developed a justification for a social protection that appealed to American values and was free from the close association of protection with dependence.

Thus it is not surprising to find the efficiency theme and the appeal to enlightened employer self-interest to be major features of the emerging ideology of American social insurance. Nor is it surprising that social insurance made most rapid progress where employer gains were most readily demonstrated. This was in the area of workmen's compensation. John R. Commons, one of the leaders in the workmen's compensation movement, was a master in the appeal to employer self-interest for the sake of social causes. Referring to his Wisconsin experience, he explained that employers were shown that they could make more profit by coming under the state's industrial accidents law. 'It was shown that, by preventing accidents, nobody, not even the consumers by higher prices, would bear any burden in paying the benefits to workmen stipulated in the compensation laws. In other words, appeal was made to a new kind of "efficiency", efficiency in preventing accidents, by which costs of production could be reduced, with the result that prices need not be increased.'[4] The appeal was to self-interest, not to paternalism or social solidarity.

Behind the movement for industrial safety was the momentum of the conservation movement, which got under way after the turn of the century. This was an important indication of maturing industrialism in America, especially since conservation was extended to include human resources. The growing awareness of the significance of the conservation of human resources naturally worked in favor not only of workmen's compensation but social insurance generally and health insurance in particular. Although the economic significance of health has only recently attracted serious attention from economists, a keen student, Irving Fisher, was already concerned with the problem at the turn of the century. His findings became part of the Report of the National Conservation Commission.[5] In this report, Fisher linked the promotion of health, or what he called national vitality, to the productive efficiency of the country. In his view, the preventable economic waste due to premature death and preventable illness was enormous. He estimated that the annual preventable loss from death and illness was at least $1.5 billion, which represented approximately five percent of national income in 1910.

It was not long before it was realized that widespread health insurance could become an important means for the improvement of the nation's health, just as workmen's compensation laws became an inducement to improve industrial safety. The leadership of the social insurance movement was taken over by the American Association for Labor Legislation, an organization made up of academicians, prominent social workers, and labor and civic leaders. In 1913 the association organized the first American conference on social insurance. One of the basic themes of this conference was the conservation of human resources. The case for sickness insurance under social security was presented by I. M. Rubinow.

Rubinow made a strong case for compulsory health insurance on the basis of the economic waste of ill-health to the nation, the inability of workers to pay for adequate care or insurance on their own, and the lag of America behind Europe in this area of social action.[6] He reminded his listeners that a committee of experts had estimated that the annual loss to American producers through disease was 'equal to nearly eight hundred millions of dollars'. His own computations, using European rates of sickness incidence, showed that America lost annually 200 million man-days of productive work on account of illness. Rubinow discarded voluntary efforts and commercial insurance as being inadequate for the task and unsuitable for an objective of overriding national significance. For it was not merely the interest and welfare of the individual that was at stake but the collective interest and public welfare of the entire nation. This required a collective rather than an individualistic solution. Although the cost of the proposed insurance scheme was high, Rubinow, the chief statistician for an insurance company, informed his audience that 'it is an investment that will pay handsome dividends in the increase of national health, happiness and efficiency'.

Similar arguments were advanced by the Commission on Industrial Relations, which was created by Congress in August 1912 to investigate the rising tide of industrial unrest. In its final report the commission noted that investigations made on its behalf indicated that the wage loss due to sickness was equal to 500 million dollars a year, in addition to which wage earners spent at least another 180 million dollars on medical expenses. 'Much attention is now given to accident prevention,' the report continues, 'yet accidents cause only one-seventh as much destitution as does sickness, and one-fifteenth as much as does unemployment. A great deal of unemployment is directly due to sickness, and sickness in turn follows unemployment.' this last link of the causal interaction is explained in the report by the argument that 'sickness among wage earners is primarily the direct result of poverty, the commissioners highlighted the social nature of the problem of ill-health and, hence, the need for social action. American society, in the view of the commissioners, had left more responsibility to the individual than he could handle. 'The greatest share of responsibility rests upon the individual, and under present conditions he is unable to meet it. This inability exists by reason of the fact that the majority of the wage earners do not receive sufficient wages. . . .' Given this situation, the commissioners concluded 'that new methods of dealing with the existing evils must be adopted. . . . A system of sickness insurance is the most feasible single method.' They recommended a compulsory system which shared the cost among employees, employers, and the community, since all shared in the benefits of better health. Among the more important benefits expected was a strong inducement to the spreading of preventive health measures. This particular stress is not surprising, since John R. Commons was a member of the commission.

The social benefits of health insurance figures prominently also in the inaugural address of Irving Fisher, in 1916, when he became president of the American Association for Labor Legislation. Addressing an audience of the joint meeting of the national associations of economists, sociologists, and statisticians, as well as his own organization, Fisher declared that 'After some fifteen years' study of the preventability of sickness, I am convinced that the great virtue of health insurance, for decades, perhaps centuries to come, will lie in the prevention of illness.'[7] Because of this strong belief in the social advantages of health insurance, and his awareness that many workers could not afford it on their own, he came out strongly in favor of a universal and compulsory public scheme. 'Workmen's health insurance,' he argued, 'is like elementary education. In order that it shall function properly it must be universal, and in order to be universal, it must be obligatory. Aside from the benefits directly derived by the worker through better medical care, Fisher perceived additional gains. Among these he included the prolongation of the years of earning capacity, more complete and more prompt recovery from illness, a lessening of industrial discontent, a reduction of poverty caused by disease, and a slight raise in the general level of wages through increased labor productivity. The challenging conclusion from one of the country's most prominent economists was that 'there is no other measure now before the public which equals the power of health and insurance toward social regeneration'.

Although efficiency was the central theme of the emerging social insurance ideology, there were, of course, a number of subsidiary themes. The idea that social insurance was a consequence of industrialization and, hence, a necessary feature of any industrial society, regardless of its economic or political system, was taken for granted by the adherents of the social insurance movement. There were opponents who argued that social insurance was an invention of authoritarian and paternalistic Germany for the purpose of keeping the working class weak and submissive. In response to this argument it was easy to point out that the German working class had not become weak and submissive, and that social insurance also was greatly appreciated in a democratic country like England, the home of liberal economic thought. Similarly, it was necessary to demonstrate that in spite of the fact that America was the land of opportunity, and that on the average workers were much better off here than abroad, there was still an ugent need for social insurance. Those who were in the social insurance movement knew very well that it is not the average income but the deviations from the average that matter most with regard to income security. The need for social insurance both in terms of worker income and in terms of the failure of voluntary insurance efforts, was a recurring theme of the debate. There was some disagreement as to whether this need of a given class made social insurance laws class legislation but not too much attention was paid to this issue.

There was general, if often only implicit, agreement about the concept of social insurance as a necessary, corrective adjunct to the free market mechanism. In other words, it was not viewed as a tool of basic economic and social reform. A participant in the 1913 Social Insurance Conference stated bluntly: ' . . . regardless of how one may feel about the unfair distribution of wealth at present, a discussion of social insurance is not a place for airing such opinions and the problem of social insurance can be tackled in a thoroughly democratic American way so that class feelings are lessened, not strengthened. Social insurance was not to hinder economic incentives; it was to work through rather than to interfere with the market mechanism. Benefits were to be clearly differentiated from charity and relief; they were not to be a dole but an encouragement to thrift. As Devine explained to the 1913 conference, American social insurance was to be a mechanism by which the competitive market could distribute an industry's 'full cost of its produce in human lives and physical vigor'.[8] He argued that industry eventually and 'in accordance with the well-known principles of competition, will adjust the price of commodities and of labor in such a way as to fairly distribute the burden'. Speaking of the incentive effects of compulsory health insurance, Commons suggested that to the extent that disease is preventable 'the proper American way is to offer to our businessmen a chance to make a big profit by preventing it'.[9] He became an ardent advocate of the extension of the prevention principle to unemployment insurance. He explained later: 'I was trying to save Capitalism by making it good'. This sentiment was no doubt shared by the majority of the early social insurance advocates.

The American advocates of social insurance did not conceive it as a tool for political action. [. . .] Most of their arguments had an academic, analytical flavor. Their appeal was to intellectuals, enlightened employers, and government and civic leaders; they did not seek to mobilize mass support for their cause. Indeed, the lack of strong, organized political backing was the major weakness of the nascent American social security movement. Rubinow lamented the fact that the large majority of Americans, including professional economists, businessmen, and even wage-workers still believed that conditions in the United States were so different from Europe 'as to make the organization of social insurance both superfluous and impossible'. The promoters of American social insurance at this time were primarily college professors, social workers, and isolated government officials and civic leaders. Organizations such as the National Conference of Charities and Correction and the American Medical Association established committees on social insurance, and a number of states appointed social insurance commissions. However, the main organizational backing of the movement came from the American Association for Labor Legislation, which was more a professional than a political organization. Nevertheless, the association carried out excellent educational campaigns. It drafted model bills, provided a forum for the discussion of basic issues as well as detailed provisions, and offered expert assistance to interested legislative authorities. But without broad support from the major political parties, or from business and trade unions, the movement was doomed to a stunted growth.

An exploration of the attitude of the business community in this early struggle to establish new social rights for the American citizen, is instructive. Let us keep in mind that this was a period during which industry was confronted with the labor and managerial problems of a maturing industrial society. Although the prevailing business ideology continued to stress individualistic values and to glorify individual achievement and self-help, the realities of the industrial environment were increasingly at odds with the individualistic slogans. The rise of giant corporations and large-scale enterprises meant that, with mounting frequency, the man in authority in industry was a hired manager who had worked his way up in the industrial bureaucracy, instead of a self-made rugged capitalist. With the expanding scale of firms and mass production methods, managerial problems inevitably became more complex.

One of the important discoveries by management in the early part of the century was the complex nature of the so-called labor problem. The tremendous surge of trade unionism, from 447,000 members in 1897 to 2,140,500 in 1910, and 5,047,800 in 1920, presented an unprecedented challenge to managerial authority. But quite aside from this challenge and the disturbing growth of industrial unrest, the nature of modern production methods had outmoded labor management based on the notion that it was simply a matter of eliminating misfits and malcontents. The costs of hiring and firing had become a matter for serious consideration. Moreover, efficiency in large-scale and complex production units is highly sensitive to the spontaneous cooperation of the work force. The problem of labor management gradually was viewed in the light of the need to create an environment and conditions that would affect individual behaviour in a manner consistent with the promotion of efficiency. The safety, health, and security of the worker thus became necessarily a matter of concern to the manager. Neither could the employer remain indifferent to how the worker felt about his job.

These considerations of profit and loss, rather than a burst of philanthropy or a gnawing conscience over social rights, were the determining factor in the support the business community gave to the enactment of workmen's compensation laws in the years preceding World War I. This was the only form of social insurance that had widespread business support before the 1930s. It must be remembered that indemnification for industrial accidents was subject to social control before workmen's compensation. Business support of workmen's compensation must be regarded in the light of the combined effects of rapidly rising industrial accident rates and the spreading of employer liability laws, which increased the legal risks facing employers. Aware of these problems, and dreading that unions might push for unfavorable legislation, the National Association of Manufacturers undertook extensive investigations at home and abroad. At its annual convention in 1910, the NAM revealed that 90 percent of its members were dissatisfied with existing arrangements, which were described as costly to the employer, of little benefit to the worker, and a source of industrial unrest. On presentation of a report, based on 10,000 replies, the convention adopted the following resolutions:

> Whereas, the National Association of Manufacturers occupies a leading position in all constructive work for industrial betterment and particularly for harmonious relations between American employers and wage-workers, and

Whereas, the United States is less advanced than progressive European nations in respect to employers' liability and industrial accident indemnity to the detriment of the nation, its institutions and its people;

Be It Resolved, that the present system of determining employers' liability is unsatisfactory, wasteful, slow in operation, and antagonistic to harmonious relations between employers and wage-workers; that an equitable mutually contributory indemnity system, automatically providing relief for victims of industrial accidents and their dependents, is required to reduce waste, litigation and friction, and to meet the demands of an enlightened nation;

Be It Further Resolved, that prevention of accidents is of even greater importance than equitable compensation to injured workers.

The basic themes of industrial betterment, harmonious relations, and prevention of waste clearly are in evidence in the resolutions. Notice should be taken also of the fact that the NAM was expecting workers to contribute to the scheme.

Employer activity in favor of workmen's compensation was not restricted to the NAM. The National Founders' Association collaborated with the National Metal Trades Association in the preparation of proposals for a workmen's compensation act. The iron and steel industries had reason to be concerned with the problem, since they had some of the highest accident rates in the country. But what seems to have prodded them into action was an avowed desire to prevent union leaders from securing 'oppressive and unjust laws of far-reaching consequence'. Of course, employers in these industries also were genuinely concerned with accident prevention, for reasons of efficiency and industrial betterment, as well as for the purpose of removing the grounds of the agitator for an appeal to sympathy and support. Another employer association, the United Typothetae of America, supported workmen's compensation laws as early as 1909. The National Civic Federation, a unique organization that included among its members large employers and labor and civic leaders, also was strongly in favor of compensation legislation. Since its declared objectives were the 'prevention of industrial revolution threatened by extremists and the promotion of industrial peace', it was understandable, as Bonnett reported, that its greatest legislative efforts were 'exerted in studying and discussing workmen's compensation and accident prevention, in formulating model bills, and in attempting to secure their enactment by legislative bodies'. Another important organization, the National Industrial Conference Board, a body composed of national and state industrial associations, concluded that the 'compensation principle is in line with the best conceptions of equitable industrial relationships'. By the middle of the second decade of the century, the fundamental principle of workmen's compensation, namely, the substitution of definite and speedy compensation in the place of uncertain relief through litigation, was generally accepted by American industry.

Nevertheless, there were still many businessmen, especially small employers and those in less industrialized states, who remained in opposition. Some objected to any kind of safety or compensation legislation 'because they thought it was simply a step toward Socialism'. Others, like the Philadelphia Board of Trade, argued that workmen's compensation laws made employers responsible for the workers' 'reckless indifference to danger'. This is a reminder that denunciations of the worker's character had not disappeared with the growing concern with 'harmonious relations'. The manufacturer associations in the Southern states often disagreed with the NAM on the compensation issue. For instance, the Secretary of the Tennessee Manufacturers' Association reported with obvious satisfaction that 'it was largely due to the activities of the employer class that a Workmen's Compensation Law was not enacted in Tennessee during either the 1913, 1915 or 1917 sessions of the Legislature".

Although the idea of compensation was widely accepted, American individualism reasserted itself in an ideological struggle over the organization of workmen's compensation. The question was whether the system should be organized on the basis of state insurance plans or through private insurance companies. A vociferous campaign against state insurance funds was led by an alarmed insurance industry. Speeches, pamphlets, and bulletins warned of the contagious evils of this invasion of private enterprise. E. S. Lott, the president of the United States Casualty Company, was one of the outspoken prophets of doom: 'State-fund insurance in our country has made a little hole in the dyke—that great dyke which for long years has protected American individualism. If we permit the hole to grow larger, it will grow large enough to let through sufficient water to inundate *all* private enterprise.' He called for help to preserve the dyke, 'that dyke builded and preserved by the hands and lives of staunch Americans since the Declaration of Independence; that dyke which protects individual freedom, individual initiative and individual responsibility from the mad waters of socialism'. Although the self-serving nature of these comments is obvious, they are significant as an indication of the obstacles to social protection even when the idea of protection itself was not at issue.

The insurance interests were reportedly in favor of the compensation principle, but they saw the threat of bolshevism in state insurance funds. The Red Scare and attacks on state socialism, which were mingled with anti-German sentiments, were exploited especially after the war. Frederick L. Hoffman, a vice-president of the Prudential Insurance Company, told an insurance conference in 1918 that 'extreme vigilance is necessary if the interests of the people are to be safeguarded against the danger of paternalism and autocracy inherent in every theory of state socialism'. He was persuaded that the insurance industry was peculiarly sensitive to the inherent evils of socialism. 'Insurance, on account of its intimate relation to individual needs and personal welfare, is peculiarly one of the functions which should not be brought within the control of an always more or less autocratic and arbitrary bureaucracy'. Sample expressions of this kind could be multiplied many times. One of the agencies that conducted the campaign on behalf of the industry was the Workmen's Compensation Publicity Bureau. During the 1920s, it published the *Workmen's Compensation Bulletin,* which listed the following as one of its aims: 'to answer the active propaganda for monopolistic state-fund insurance carried on by a number of radical organizations'. The label of radical organization was used liberally. The very first number of the bulletin accused the American Association for Labor Legislation of having abandoned American principles of government and of advocating state socialism.

If workmen's compensation remained controversial, the prospects for businessmen's acceptance of other forms of social insurance were slim indeed. At its 1910 convention, where the NAM endorsed workmen's compensation, it denounced compulsory sickness and old-age insurance as 'a departure from accepted doctrines, contrary to American ideas and detrimental to thrift and economy'. Ten years later, at the 1920 convention, the NAM's Committee on Industrial Betterment, Health, and Safety referred to state insurance as 'one of the vicious German ideas yet existent in this country'. In 1922 the same committee issued a final report condemning public sickness and old-age insurance as 'unnecessary and unwise' and 'unsound economically, placing an unknown burden upon the healthy'.

The National Civic Federation also expressed strong disapproval of compulsory sickness insurance. A spokesman for the NCF linked the demand for this insurance to disloyalty to the country's institutions. 'Do we realize that the proponents of social insurance are the very persons who would undermine our institutions. Is it necessary to bring compulsion here, when we have fought for the freedom of American citizens?' In a grand show of unity of business and labor minds, the *National Civic Federation Review* published an article violently denouncing the 'trickery of the group of social reformers who are attempting to foist upon labor a pernicious system of compulsory health insurance'. The article contains a long list of dangers inherent in such insurance, including bureaucracy, communism, personal tyranny, and the weakening of individual and family responsibility, in addition to unreasonable cost and unfavorable medical consequences. Its author was not a businessman but a labor leader; he was Grand Chief of the International Brotherhood of Locomotive Engineers and Chairman of the NCF Social Insurance Department.

A more sober but nevertheless negative position was taken by the National Industrial Conference Board. The board accepted the contention that there was an unnecessary amount of sickness in the United States and that this, in turn, was one of the principal causes of poverty. But it categorically denied that compulsory health insurance was a suitable remedy. It concluded that a program of this kind would reduce neither sickness nor poverty, that it would be unjustifiably costly, and that better results could be achieved by developing existing agencies.

It is quite clear that in the minds of businessmen there was a radical distinction between workmen's compensation and other forms of social insurance. This distinction was spelled out by M. W. Alexander, a representative of the General Electric Company:

> Workmen's compensation is not social insurance. Morally and legally it is based, not upon the duty of society, but upon the duty of industry to the worker. Legally its foundation principle is found in the old common law rule that the employer must furnish his employee a safe place to work, including the selection of careful and competent fellow workmen.

The key to this position is the implicit rejection of the theory that in going from employer liability to workmen's compensation, a social right, derived from a social purpose, had been created where formerly there were only private rights and private interests. 'The employer', Alexander explained, 'has not discharged a social duty; he has merely done justice as between himself and his employees. By no logic can workmen's compensation be called social insurance, nor can our legislation on that subject in this country be considered an opening wedge demanding the general adoption of a scheme of social insurance'. The motivation behind this kind of argument is rather obvious. Alexander's main objection was against noncontributory pensions, which he thought would lead to 'reliance upon State guardianship' in a country 'founded to secure individual liberty of thought and action with opportunities for working out one's own salvation'.

With regard to unemployment insurance, business resistance was even stronger than with respect to the other forms of social insurance, in spite of the efforts of men like Commons who tried to show how such schemes would stabilize employment. A *Wall Street Journal* editorial echoed the ancient but still generally held view that assistance to the able-bodied unemployed is bad in itself. 'Payment for the unemployed is a remedy incalculably worse than the disease . . . It is in effect a premium upon malingering and idleness. It is like the English poor law system which created three irreclaimable paupers for one it regenerated'. The editorial, instead, advocated improved labor mobility, on the accepted classical assumption that the jobs were there for those who were genuinely willing to work. The low opinion of the unemployed worker's character implied in this assumption was still very much alive.

Unemployment insurance bills were introduced in a number of states but encountered everywhere stiff employer resistance. Massachusetts is one of the states that had shown historically the strongest interest in the problem of unemployment. An unemployment insurance bill was introduced as early as 1916, but the indifference of organized labor and the hostility of employers assured its demise. Another bill, introduced in 1922, was referred to a special commission, which advised against it. The reasoning of the commission is indicative of the attitude of the business community:

> Like other forms of so-called social insurance, compulsory indemnification during unemployment is not consistent with American principles . . . Just as health insurance has apparently encouraged malingering, unemployment insurance bids fair to encourage shiftlessness and improvidence . . . to the industrious and independent American worker unemployment insurance apparently makes little appeal.

A subtle praise of the worker's virtues, just as the condemnation of his weaknesses, mingled freely in the antisocial insurance ideology. Although this ideology, perhaps, was strongest among employers, it was shared by many workers.

In spite of this general attitude of opposition, there was a small number of progressive employers who established private unemployment compensation schemes and, in some cases, even favored public programs. These people had a different interpretation of worker motivation and behavior. They were concerned with the effects of unemployment on the worker's efficiency 'on account of the deterioration of his physique, the loss of regular habits of work, and most of all, through the "laying down" on the job caused by fear that by working efficiently he will be merely working himself out of a job'. Stewart found 13 companies with formal unemployment compensation plans by 1930, although there were many more with informal arrangements.[10] During the 1920s, the movement for unemployment compensation, at least, the voluntary type, received assistance from an unexpected quarter. The advocates of modern management believed that their techniques were suited for the regularization of business activities, and some of them looked to unemployment compensation legislation as the needed incentive to induce managers to adopt these techniques for the stabilization of employment. The American Management Association was the leading organization that promoted modern management methods. A study published under its auspices warned business of the rising tide of social and political pressures that demanded a solution to the problem of employment security. It emphasized that the only alternative to compulsory employment compensation was the widespread adoption of private voluntary plans. In 1928, a speaker at an AMA Production Executives Conference told his listeners: 'It is now time for the modern business man to give up thinking of it as a business problem which directly affects his company's net income . . . Unemployment . . . is not only harmful from a social point of view, it is wasteful from a business point of view'.

The opinion that business had a social responsibility toward the unemployed was still held by a minority of American industrial leaders during the 1920s. *Iron Age*, the influential trade journal of the iron and steel industry, commented: "The notion that the [the businessman] has any direct responsibility for unemployment which requires serious consideration on his part is still novel.' Businessmen, like economists, believed that booms and busts were inevitable. However, there was a growing recognition by management of its stake in the economic security of the worker, for economic as well as for political reasons. A consequence of this recognition was the rise of welfare capitalism, as a substitute for compulsory social protection schemes and a prophylactic against the welfare state.

Against those odds, the struggle for the establishment of modern social rights had no chance to succeed unless it had the full support of organized labor. Unfortunately, unlike British trade unions, which paid at least lip service to the idea of social security in the early days, American unions were mostly hostile.[. . .] The labor leaders showed more concern for the welfare of their organizations than for the welfare of the working class. To be sure, as organizers of mass movements anywhere, they completely identified the interests of the labor movement with those of the workers. [This] negative attitude of the labor leaders was the result of a fear that social insurance would weaken their control over the working masses. [. . .]

For the leadership of American trade unionism, it was much more difficult to become receptive to social insurance, even though social insurance in this country was hardly promoted for the purpose of undermining the unions. The American Federation of Labor, which emerged in the 1890s as the largest and most powerful labor organization in the country, adopted an ideological position that was inconsistent with the social (state) protection of the individual. The federation, as Professor Perlman pointed out in his *Theory of the Labor Movement,* arrayed itself on the side of private property and individual initiative. It opted for 'the political weapon only sparingly and with great circumspection'. Samuel Gompers argued that political pressure may be used to increase the union's freedom of action, for instance, by seeking laws against injunctions but that the political method was not suited for improving the economic security of the worker. That was the job of the unions. It was the job of the constituent unions of the AF of L to promote the interest of their members through their own efforts and through voluntary cooperation with each other, without assistance from the state.

The ideology of voluntarism was a product of practical experience and of a pragmatic approach to the problem of trade union organization in an individualistic and hostile environment. It was a way of turning the ideological position of dominant interests in the community to the advantage of organized labor. Although voluntarism thus became an effective means to legitimize trade unionism, the eyes of both friends and enemies, the very success of the formula, even though it was limited, led to a doctrinaire rigidity on the part of top labor leaders, particularly Gompers. In a perceptive article, Michael Robin has called attention to the fact that Gompers defended trade union activities in the very same Social Darwinist terms which he abhorred when they were used to justify business behavior.[11] Gompers declared that the desire to lean on the state for support was an indication of 'a sort of moral flabbiness'. He considered it is a 'repudiation of the characteristics that enable Americans to get results'. Americans, he argued, 'never feared the hard places but dared to wrestle with a primeval country. They were red-blooded men and women with ruggedness in their wills. . . . This is the spirit that has made the American labor movement the most aggressive labor organization in the world. . . .' This identification of labor aggressiveness with the 'American spirit' helped to justify trade union action, but at the price of condemning the political approach.

The American Federation of Labor was painfully slow to recognize the workers' need for social insurance. It did not fully endorse workmen's compensation laws until 1909, at a time when the urgent need for those laws had been almost universally recognized. In later years, especially during the years 1917 to 1923, the federation fought for the extension of workmen's compensation coverage to waterfront employees, seamen, and the District of Columbia, for the inclusion of occupational diseases, and for the improvement of benefits. The 1911 AF & L Convention endorsed mothers' pensions, partly with the expectation that assisted widows would stay home to take care of their children instead of bidding down wages in the labor market. Similar labor market considerations, aiming at the enhancement of union power, were relevant for old-age pensions, which may account for a somewhat flexible attitude in this area also. At the 1902 AF of L Convention resolutions were defeated that urged Congress to provide pensions for all citizens over 60 who earned less than $1000 per year. By 1909 the federation endorsed a bizarre pension scheme under the subterfuge of an Old Age Home Guard of the United States Army, and again in 1911, 1912, and 1913 it supported a national old-age pension program as well as pensions for federal employees. Of course, these programs were aimed at needy aged, not active workers.

The strongest federation objections were raised against sickness and unemployment benefits. It is mainly with regard to these forms of protection, which were for active employees, that the federation sensed a threat to its position. Speaking before a social insurance convention in 1916, Grant Hamilton, a member of the AF of L Legislative Committee, was quite explicit that labor's first concern was whether social insurance would interfere with the worker's freedom, especially freedom to organize. On numerous occasions labor leaders expressed the fear that social insurance institutions would hamper organization by 'chaining the workers to their jobs' and by increasing the control of employers and the state over the workers' lives. Hamilton, for instance, maintained that 'it is well known that able-bodied, skilled workmen have been dismissed from employment at the recommendation of the company physician who found in them the disease of unionism and diagnosed the cases under convenient professional terms.' The possibility of using social insurance agents as spies also made union leaders distrustful. [. . .]

Aside from these misgivings, labor leaders looked on social insurance as utopian schemes that would lead the labor movement astray by diverting its energies away from immediate and practical improvement of wages and working conditions. 'Social insurance,' Gompers argued, 'can not even undertake to remove or prevent poverty. It is not fundamental and does not get at the causes of social injustice. *The only agency that does get at the cause of poverty is the organized labor movement.*' This view implied that 'outsiders' (social workers, college professors, and other intellectuals) were at best misguided in trying to improve the workers' lot through social insurance. At worst, the trade unionists suspected, outsiders were trying to 'use' the labor movement for their own purposes. It must have been this fear of having to share power and influence that led Gompers to the rather startling declaration:

> . . . I would rather help in the inauguration of a revolution against compulsory insurance . . . than submit. As long as there is one spark of life in me . . . I will help in crystallizing the spirit and sentiment of our workers against the attempt to enslave them by the well-meaning siren songs of philosophers, statisticians and politicians.

It is interesting to observe that in Gompers' mind social insurance increased rather than decreased social inequality. He deplored that:

> . . . the first step in establishing social insurance is to divide people into groups, those eligible for benefits and those considered capable of caring for themselves. . . . This governmental regulation must tend to fix citizens of the country into classes, and a long-established insurance system would tend to make those classes rigid.

This prospect was considered particularly damaging to a labor movement that had turned individualism and egalitarianism into ideological weapons. This may not have been true, but Gompers' concern touched on one of the fundamental problems of the drive toward greater equality through expanded social rights—the fact that, often, while one dimension of inequality was reduced another one was increased. The choice that Gompers made rested on his own evaluation of which of these dimensions was the more important.

The individualistic trade unionist argument against social insurance was expressed most sharply by Andrew Furuseth of the combative Sailors'

Union of the Pacific. Furuseth was convinced that social insurance would have a debilitating effect on labor. For him, a trade union was a fighting organization whose members had to be tough and courageous. In a crude social Darwinist way he suggested, at the 1926 AF of L Convention, that social insurance is a sentimental gesture that kills independence and courage:

> Sometimes it is better to let the wounded die, sometimes it is better to let the old die than sacrifice the fire of fighting and the ability to win battles . . . . This appeal for old-age pensions . . . for sickness insurance . . . for unemployment insurance—what is it? . . . it is nothing more than sentiment that stands in the way of real fighting.

These expressions, perhaps, were more indicative of a mood than of literal convictions, but they did reflect a sense of self-reliant social egalitarianism that spurned protection from above.

Of course, there were exceptions to the rule, that is, leaders and unions who looked favorably on social insurance and on other forms of economic improvement through legislation. At the annual conventions of the AF of L there were always minority voices objecting to the position taken by the federation, but they had a negligible impact. At the Chicago Social Insurance Conference of 1913, G. W. Perkins, the President of the Cigar Makers' International Union, Gompers' own union, declared himself in favor of social insurance, including unemployment insurance. However, he believed that unions should administer the programs and should be subsidized for this purpose by the state, an idea that could hardly appeal to Gompers. As Secretary-Treasurer of the United Mine Workers, William Green was able to envisage an insurance system, financed jointly by workers, employers, and the state, that might actually encourage the 'spirit of independence and freedom'. Even though Green was aware of the values of social insurance, his convictions were not deeply rooted. He did not hasten to promote social insurance after he became president of the AF of L. As late as 1932, he had doubts about its political desirability.

At the state level a number of AF of L conventions had approved social insurance measures by 1920, but many of the state organizations were 'open-minded', in other words, indifferent. Within the Executive Council of the AF of L there were differences of opinion. After declining to support federal bills for unemployment and health insurance during World War I, the council recommended a special committee in 1918 to study accident compensation and health insurance. The committee was approved by the convention of that year, which voted down a resolution demanding the establishment of a comprehensive social insurance program. After a couple of years' debate and discussion, the committee rejected the idea of compulsory health insurance. In 1921 and 1923 the federation reaffirmed its earlier endorsement of old-age pensions, but the labor leaders were still thinking primarily of pensions for the poor and needy, not for workers in general. The American labor movement did not change its attitude toward social insurance until the 1930s. Instead of leading public opinion with regard to social protection, it barely managed to keep up with the common consensus.

We have dwelt at some length on the American case, because it was in this country that liberal ideals and policies were most persistent in the face of the needs and demands generated by industrial society. The result was a vivid demonstration of the conflict between the old liberalism and the new protectionism. [. . .] The main difference between industrialized Europe and the United States was that here the tension could be successfully managed, for the time being, without the granting of substantial social rights. This difference has been explored in terms of the strength of the liberal tradition, but this does not mean that this strength is unrelated to other factors, such as a country's social and political structure, its resource base, and the speed of its industrial development. One interesting consequence of the strength of the liberal tradition in America was the attempt to formulate an ideology of protection that was suitable for an individualistic environment. This was an interesting attempt to reconcile old values with new policies and, unfortunately, was only partially successful. Nevertheless, although it failed to overcome the vested material and ideal interests of business and labour, it set a pattern for American thinking that became very influential when substantial security rights were finally granted in the 1930s.

ALTERNATIVE PATHS TO SOCIAL SECURITY

[. . .] It is clear that the need for a highly organized form of income protection increases as society becomes industrialized and urbanized and that this need is independent of the nature of the socio-economic order. Social security is as essential under socialism as it is under capitalism. Most of the countries that spend more than five percent of GNP on social security are highly developed countries. [. . .]

This study analyzes the manner in which the major industrial countries handled these problems in the course of their development. It shows how the problems of want and the means of handling them changed as the countries moved from a traditional agrarian setting to industrialization and then to a mature industrial society. Each stage has a configuration of economic conditions and social forces that has relevance for the development of social protection. The countries analyzed represent three different socioeconomic settings of industrialization. The first is industrialization by private entrepreneurs, under the aegis of the liberal state, with the entrepreneurial class achieving a dominant power position. This situation was achieved in the United States and approximated in

England and France. The second context is that of an authoritarian political and social structure; industrialization is still primarily the work of private entrepreneurs, but their interests and ideas do not become dominant; the class interests of the industrialists remain subordinate or must compromise with the interests of the monarchy, the state bureaucracy, and the landed classes (Imperial Germany and Tsarist Russia). The third setting is the one of socialized industrialization directed by a ruling totalitarian party (Soviet Russia).

Social protection in the traditional agrarian society was very limited for economic as well as for social reasons. In the traditional peasant economy the family was the economic unit that employed its members. In terms of the basic essentials of life, such as food, clothing, and shelter, the family achieved a certain degree of self-sufficiency. For the most part, employment was not determined through the labor market. The family took care of its aged and incapacitated members, often by assigning light jobs to them. Although protection from want was thus overwhelmingly an individual and family responsibility, one of the chief characteristics of the traditional setting was the subordinate position of the 'lower classes'. They did not share in the affairs of government, nor were they expected to have opinions about them. In theory, the reciprocity of traditional society consisted of the duty of work and obedience from those below and the duty of protection and guidance from those above. In this setting, there was very little social conflict over the question of social protection, no doubt because want was both general and customary and because the 'lower classes' accepted their subordinate position. Although there was a humane concern about destitution, public relief measures were shaped by the interests of the state in a numerous and industrious work force. Poor laws were intended to relieve destitution, not to eliminate poverty. Relief was to be sufficient to facilitate the maintenance of public order and to be administered in a manner that encouraged regular work habits. The problem of relief in the preindustrial society, therefore, was primarily a police and sanitation problem. It was not a question of social rights.

During industrialization the whole nature of the problem of social protection changes, in part, because of the great social and economic dislocations, that accompany the creation of an industrial work force. Bendix writes:

> These dislocations terminate the traditional subordination of the 'lower classes' in the preindustrial society. Though this development varies considerably with the relative speed and with the social setting of industrialization, its result is that the 'lower classes' are deprived of their recognized, if subordinate, place in society. A major problem facing all societies undergoing industrialization is the civic reintegration of the newly created industrial force.

The development of social rights inevitably plays a crucial role in the handling of the problem of civic reintegration. The establishment of socially guaranteed rights to protection from want is one of the major means by which a new status can be secured for the industrial masses. By helping to define a new reciprocity among the members of the industrial society, it helps to establish a new place for the common man—a place that is consistent with a new conception of his rights.

Several alternatives are open to the industrializing society with regard to the question of social protection. It may deny the claim to protection as being inconsistent with the new economic and social order. Or it may accept the claim to protection as a means of reinforcing the traditional authority relationships between the 'ruling' and the 'lower' classes. Or it may energetically promote the right to protection as a means of strengthening the authority relationships of a new social and economic order. Nevertheless, in any society in which social forces are free to express themselves, there are always conflicting tendencies.

The countries that denied the right to social protection during the period of industrialization were the ones with the strongest liberal and individualistic traditions—the United States, England, and France. Therefore, we must consider how these countries dealt with the problem of civic reintegration. England and the United States differ somewhat from France, insofar as in the latter country industrialization was much slower and, consequently, social dislocation was less acute. Both England and the United States succeeded in overcoming the alienation of the lower classes during industrialization without substantial social guarantees of protection from want. To a large extent, this success can be attributed to the high degree of acceptance by the industrial working classes of the liberal ideologies of the entrepreneurial classes. These ideologies identified the ability to be self-dependent with a readiness for individual freedom. By the same token the claim to protection was associated with an acceptance of the traditional tutelage of the lower classes. Within this ideological context, freedom and protection became mutually exclusive. These views were consistent with the interests of the entrepreneurial class in an unfettered labor market. The ideological emphasis, of course, was not on these private interests but on the national interest. In England the Malthusian theory of population provided the chief economic rationale for demonstrating the harmful consequences of social protection. It absolved, in effect, the new 'ruling class' from responsibility for the poor. In the United States a similar function was performed by Social Darwinism. Both of these theories embodied the more general proposition of classical liberalism that achievement of the highest national interest was conditional on the unhindered pursuit of individual interest. Within this framework, protection harmed not only the nation but the protected classes more than anyone else.

These views, of course, were not always fully articulated and were never completely accepted by all members of either the 'ruling' or the 'ruled' classes. In England and in the United States the workers were more successful than in France in turning the liberal ideologies to their advantage. If the liberal arguments for freedom, equality, and self-help were inconsistent with social protection, they nevertheless could be turned into weapons for self-protection. The trade unions arose in this manner as the workers' means of collective self-protection. They helped to define the place of the worker in the industrial society and to secure substantial rights for him through private instead of public action. The more successful the unions were in fulfilling this function, the more they were opposed to economic protection through governmental action. In retrospect, this opposition was based on mistaken conceptions of trade-union self-interest and of the need for broader social protection.

When modern social security did emerge in the countries that were the home of classical liberalism, economic development was well past the industrialization phase. The basis concepts of liberalism—freedom and equality—had undergone profound changes. In their new context, these concepts were no longer inconsistent with social protection; on the contrary, they required it. At this stage of industrial development, the growing scarcity of labor relative to capital and the higher requirements of skill and cooperation suggested a labor policy aiming at the conservation and improvement of the capacity and willingness to work. Protection of the worker from want and worry thus became an economically rational (profitoriented) activity even in a free market economy. In addition to concern with the economic aspects of productivity, there arose a broader concern with national efficiency that demanded a policy of protection. This need must be viewed in the perspective of the social changes wrought by industrialization. It was perceived clearly by writers like Croly and by statesmen like Theodore Roosevelt, Lloyd-George, and Winston Churchill. They realized that the loyalties that had bound society together in the past had become eroded in the conflict between the economic inequalities of capitalist civilization and the ideologies of freedom and equality which this civilization had nurtured. To be efficient, and in the long-run survive, the industrial state required the solid allegiance of its citizens. 'Citizenship,' T. H. Marshall has pointed out, 'requires a bond of a different kind [from that which existed in the past], a direct sense of community membership based on loyalty to a civilization which is a common possession.'[12] But there could be no common possession of a civilization in a society in which wealth accumulated while large segments of the population lived in or near destitution. The bond required by citizenship was further endangered as the deprived segments of the population gained organizational strength and political power. They would no longer tolerate the fact that in dire need they could obtain relief only under conditions that were humiliating and degrading.

By the beginning of the twentieth century the concept of citizenship had evolved to the point where a sense of community participation could no longer survive on patriotic sentiment alone but required substantial participation in the fruits of industrialism. In Marshall's words: 'The diminution of inequality strengthened the demand for its abolition, at least with regard to the essentials of social welfare.' Social security thus emerged, in the countries mentioned, as part of the array of social rights associated with the status of citizenship in the industrial state. Its principal objective was to guarantee a specified minimum level of income below which no citizen was to be allowed to fall. Subsistence below the national minimum, in effect, was declared inconsistent with the status of citizenship. Of great significance also was the nature of the income guarantee: it had to be free from any stigma that might impair the individual's status of full membership in the national community. In England this guarantee had from the beginning a strong egalitarian flavor, which made it independent of the individual's economic merit. In the United States, where the tradition of individual achievement and reward had remained much stronger, the income guarantees were scaled as closely as possible to the individual's previous performance.

The social right aspect was left in the background in America, and the individually earned contractual element was brought to the forefront. In this manner, social protection could be formulated in the accustomed language of individual self-help. The main deviation from traditional individualism, which was not emphasized, was that now the decision of whether he would provide for himself was no longer left to the individual. The compulsory contributory social insurance system established simultaneously the right and the duty of income protection. This right and duty became an important aspect of the new reciprocity among the citizens of the industrial state. It had important implications for the relationship among classes. To the extent that those who might become poor were forced to protect themselves from want, society as a whole, but particularly the rich, was protected from the poor. In this sense, social insurance has become an important form of protection for the rich. [. . .]

We have tried to assess the role of social security in the course of the industrialization of several leading countries. At that stage of development the major task of social security in the Western countries was to wipe out the extremes of inequality and insecurity, in order to attenuate alienation and alleviate suffering. [. . .] As we move now to the stage of the mature industrial economy, we may wish to compare the role of social security then and now. In looking over the historical experience, we find that there are important elements of continuity as well as change. Social security is now, as it was then, a means of integrating the individual into the social whole, a means of enabling him to participate to a greater extent in the common possession of our industrial civilization. What has changed is the nature of the problem of social integration and the aspirations of the average citizen. Originally, social insurance was mainly workingmen's insurance; it was intended for those who were presumed to be 'economically weak'. Today, it is no longer aimed at the working class but has become a right of all citizens. In all countries there are strong pressures toward making social security universal and comprehensive. This trend is consistent with the changing objectives of social policy, allowing for variations between countries. The reconciliation of mutually hostile social classes is no longer a major concern. The central objective has shifted to a higher plane of social integration: from combating hostility and discontent to building constructive collaboration and productive efficiency.

The basic reason for this shift is, of course, the fact that the social wounds inflicted by industrialization have been healed. In the meantime, however, the growing affluence of industrialized countries is changing the standards of social protection. In societies with a demonstrated productive capacity, it becomes almost daily less tolerable to have anyone living below an adequate national minimum. There is ample evidence for the growing intolerance of poverty in the midst of wealth. It is considered unnecessary and unjust, as well as economically wasteful. Students of economic growth have emphasized the role of skills and training as primary factors in raising national productivity. To the extent that poverty may be due to the lack of these factors, or to poor health, it is evidence of a waste of the most valuable of all resources—human beings.

In the United States, where extremes of wealth and poverty are associated with racial discrimination, there has been a remarkable rediscovery of the problem of poverty and inequality. This is a special case of the belated extension of the rights of full citizenship to racial minorities, but it poses acutely one of the problems of social protection in an affluent society. This is the problem of how a democratic society can adequately protect the able-bodied who have not shared in the cultural advantages of the industrial civilization and have not acquired the work ethic and achievement drive of this civilization. The news media refer to this problem under the heading of 'welfare crisis'. The argument of the critics is that social security, specifically public assistance, is creating most of the problem it was intended to solve. Welfare payments made on the basis of need but without strong deterrent are said to perpetuate the problem of dependency. Often these payments are made to members of the groups with the lowest level of skills, the least education, and the smallest hope for social advancement and economic improvement. The extension of the social right to an adequate national minimum to these groups leaves them only a limited incentive to work. Some of them, especially mothers of dependent children, are better off on public assistance than on the low wages they may be able to earn and be deprived of assistance. In the long run, the only solution of this problem is to develop assistance schemes with built-in work incentives and, more generally, to raise the level of skills, broaden the opportunities, and to heighten the aspirations of the underprivileged groups.

Sweden, which traditionally had adhered to a basic egalitarian benefit, has adopted differentiated benefits related to previous earnings. German old-age pensions go as high as 75 percent of earnings; Soviet old-age pensions range from 50 to 100 percent of earnings. The objective of the benefit structure has been made most explicit in Germany: it is to maintain the standard of living achieved through work, instead of merely preventing poverty. There are strong reasons for believing that this will become the accepted standard for mature industrial societies. In fact, it is part of a double standard that consists of a basic minimum for all and a rate calculated to maintain an established level of living for those whose earnings from work has lifted them above the minimum.

This double standard inevitably perpetuates among those no longer at work most of the income inequalities inherent in the structure of earnings from work. We learned earlier that Soviet officials believe that eventually their country will adopt an egalitarian system of benefits. At present, however, the Soviet Union and most other countries believe that, above a minimum level of protection, differentiated benefits are justified for efficiency. This is a kind of inequality that appears necessary and legitimate. Indeed, an attempt to maintain equal benefits, which necessarily would have to be below the normal earnings of common laborers, might have strongly adverse effects. It would create a situation in which large numbers of people would have to face a substantial drop in their standard of living on withdrawal from the active labor force. Although they may not have to live in poverty, the drop in the standard of living would still tend to cause an acute sense of deprivation. It is only by helping the citizen to maintain the rather high standard of living to which he has become accustomed, that modern social security can prevent what Runciman calls 'relative deprivation' and the sense of social injustice it generates. In the mature industrial society, social security, therefore, has the dual task of eliminating unacceptable manifestations of economic and social inequality and of maintaining inequalities that are legitimate and purposeful.

NOTES

[1] Harold U. Faulkner, *The Quest for Social Justice 1898–1914* (New York: MacMillan, 1931).

[2] The Republican party platform called for public health legislation, the legal limitation of the labor of women and children, and 'generous and comprehensive workman's compensation laws'.

[3] Henry R. Seager, *Social Insurance* (New York: MacMillan, 1910).

[4] John R. Commons, *Institutional Economics* (Madison: University of Wisconsin Press, 1959), Vol. II, p. 857.

[5] Fisher's contribution was also published separately. See Irving Fisher, *National Vitality, Its Wastes and Conservation* (Washington, D.C.: Government Printing Office, 1910).

[6] I. R. Rubinow, 'Sickness insurance,' *American Labor Legislation Review*, Vol. III No. 2 (June 1913).

[7] Irving Fisher, 'The need for health insurance', *American Labor Legislation Review*, Vol. VII, No. 1 (March 1917).

[8] Edward T. Devine, 'Pensions for mothers', *American Labor-Legislation Review*, Vol. III, No. 2 (June 1913).

[9] John R. Commons, 'A reconstruction health program', *The Survey* (September 6, 1919), p. 798.

[10] Bryce M. Stewart, *Unemployment Benefits in the United States* (New York, 1930).

[11] Michael Robin, 'Voluntarism: the political functions of an antipolitical doctrine', *Industrial and Labor Relations Review*, Vol. XV, No. 4 (July 1962).

[12] T. H. Marshall, *Class, Citizenship, and Social Development* (Anchor Books edition, Garden City, N. Y.: Doubleday and Co., 1965).

Index